Addiction

BPS Textbooks in Psychology

BPS Wiley presents a comprehensive and authoritative series covering everything a student needs in order to complete an undergraduate degree in psychology. Refreshingly written to consider more than North American research, this series is the first to give a truly international perspective. Written by the very best names in the field, the series offers an extensive range of titles from introductory level through to final year optional modules, and every text fully complies with the BPS syllabus in the topic. No other series bears the BPS seal of approval!

Many of the books are supported by a companion website, featuring additional resource materials for both instructors and students, designed to encourage critical thinking, and providing for all your course lecturing and testing needs.

For other titles in this series, please go to **http://psychsource.bps.org.uk**.

Addiction: Psychology and Treatment

EDITED BY

PAUL DAVIS
ROBERT PATTON
SUE JACKSON

WILEY

Registered Offices
John Wiley & Sons, Inc., 111 River Street, Hoboken, NJ 07030, USA
John Wiley & Sons Ltd, The Atrium, Southern Gate, Chichester, West Sussex, PO19 8SQ, UK

Editorial Office
The Atrium, Southern Gate, Chichester, West Sussex, PO19 8SQ, UK

For details of our global editorial offices, customer services, and more information about Wiley products visit us at www.wiley.com.

Wiley also publishes its books in a variety of electronic formats and by print-on-demand. Some content that appears in standard print versions of this book may not be available in other formats.

Library of Congress Cataloging-in-Publication Data
hardback: 9781118489741
paperback: 9781118489758

Cover image: © Max Krasnov/Shutterstock
Cover design by Wiley
Set in 11/12.5pt Dante MT Std by Aptara Inc., New Delhi, India
Printed in Singapore by C.O.S. Printers Pte Ltd
10 9 8 7 6 5 4 3 2 1

Table of Contents

List of Contributors

EDITORS

Paul Davis, Department of Psychology, University of Surrey, Guildford, UK

Sue Jackson, Psychology Department, University of the West of England, Bristol, UK

Bob Patton, Department of Psychology, University of Surrey, Guildford, UK

FOREWORD

Jim Orford, School of Psychology, University of Birmingham, UK

CHAPTER AUTHORS

Jamie Brown, Cancer Research UK Health Behaviour Research Centre, University College London, UK

Alex Copello, School of Psychology, University of Birmingham, UK; and the Addiction Service, Birmingham and Solihull Mental Health NHS Foundation Trust, UK

David Curran, School of Psychology, Queens University, Belfast, Northern Ireland; and the NHSCT Addiction Service, Northern Ireland, UK

Rudi Dallos, Department of Psychology, Plymouth University, Plymouth, UK

Lisa Dutheil, Camden and Islington NHS Foundation Trust, London, UK

Rebecca Fisher, Camden and Islington NHS Foundation Trust, London, UK

Alina Galis, Camden and Islington NHS Foundation Trust, London, UK

Andre Geel, Addictions Service, Central and North West London NHS Foundation Trust, London, UK

Jennifer Harris, Addictions Clinical and Academic Group, South London and Maudsley NHS Foundation Trust, London, UK

Robert Hill, Addictions Clinical and Academic Group, South London and Maudsley NHS Foundation Trust, London, UK

Adam Huxley, Change Grow Live, London, UK

Edward J. Khantzian, Department of Psychiatry, Harvard Medical School, Cambridge, MA, USA

Aska Matsunaga, Central and North West London NHS Foundation Trust, London, UK

Liz McGrath, Camden and Islington NHS Foundation Trust, London, UK

Mani Mehdikhani, Specialist Services Network, Greater Manchester West Trust, Manchester, UK

Luke Mitcheson, Addictions Services, South London and Maudsley NHS Foundation Trust, London, UK; and Alcohol, Drugs & Tobacco Division, Public Health England, London, UK

Fraser Morrison, NHS Lanarkshire, Scotland, UK

Jo M. Nicholson, Sheffield Teaching Hospitals, Sheffield, UK

Dominic O'Ryan, Camden and Islington NHS Foundation Trust, London, UK

Tony Rao, Psychiatry Department, South London and Maudsley NHS Foundation Trust, London, UK

Jenny Svanberg, Substance Misuse Department, NHS Forth Valley, Falkirk, UK

Arlene Vetere, VID Specialized University, Oslo, Norway

Sarah Wadd, Substance Misuse and Ageing Research Team (SMART), University of Bedfordshire, Luton, UK

Kathryn Walsh, Psychology Department, University of Birmingham, Birmingham, UK

Martin Weegmann, NHS; and Independent Practice London, UK

Robert West, Cancer Research UK Health Behaviour Research Centre, University College London, UK

Christopher Whiteley, Psychology Department, South London and Maudsley NHS Foundation Trust, London, UK

Foreword

Addiction is highly prevalent. The World Health Organization (WHO) estimates that the number of people globally who suffer from an alcohol or drug use disorder annually is in the region of 100 million. Harmful and hazardous alcohol use, like tobacco, is considered by WHO to be a major preventable contributor to the global burden of disease and disability. There is no estimate, to my knowledge, of the worldwide prevalence of gambling disorder, but in Britain alone the adult annual prevalence is in the region of a third to a half million, which is very similar to the prevalence of disorders associated with illicit drug use. So prevalent is addiction that it can reasonably be thought of, along with anxiety and/or depression, as one of the two most common forms of psychological disorder. Yet in most relevant professions and disciplines, including psychology, it remains strangely marginalized. In Chapter 14 in this volume, on AA and 12 Step programmes, Martin Weegmann admits that when he first worked in the area of the addictions he had had virtually no experience of this client group, and minimal training in the area during his clinical psychology course. My experience was even worse. I led two clinical psychology training courses, in Exeter for 17 years in the 1970s and 1980s, and then in Birmingham for five years in the 1990s. Despite my passionate interest in the addictions, the British Psychological Society requirements for a training course, plus the lack of availability of supervised practice, plus I suspect a lot of prejudice about the topic, meant that my success in giving trainees a better grounding in the subject than Martin and I had had was only minimally successful. Perhaps everything has changed. I hope so, but suspect not. That is one of the main reasons why this book is so important.

Judging by the enthusiasm shown by all the authors of the chapters of this book, it seems their experience of finding themselves working in the addiction field – like me, often by accident, I suspect – was of entering a field that is endlessly rewarding and fascinating. Large numbers of people overcome their addictions, often with our help and sometimes even without it, and when they do, their recoveries are frequently impressive, given the depths to which their lives have been harmed. Addiction has more than its share of sadness and despair, but it is also replete with hope and inspiration.

For all that we have learned about addiction and its treatment – including so much that is included in these chapters – there remains a great deal that is mysterious about it, and about recovery from it. The scope for researching and theorizing about addiction, for developing and evaluating forms of treatment, for applying knowledge and methods for understanding and treating such complications of addiction as brain damage or Hepatitis C – both topics accorded chapters here – is endless. In fact, no one book can explore anything like all the intriguing issues that surround addiction. How do gender roles influence the prevalence of the different forms of addiction?

What insights does psychology offer about how we might prevent addiction? What has psychology to say about what our relationships should be, if any, with the suppliers of the products to which people can become addicted – the commercial suppliers of alcohol, tobacco and gambling products and the legal and illegal suppliers of other substances? These are among the questions that must wait for a second edition.

This book treads dangerous ground in a number of ways, departing often from dominant thinking in the field. The latter is under the sway of a bio-psychological model of addiction which privileges diagnosis (very little mention of *DSM* can be found in this book), a rather limited approach to evidence-based treatment, and a greater emphasis on aggregated statistics than on a detailed understanding of the experiences of people who suffer from addiction and those others who are affected by it. Certain vital issues are neglected because of that dominant model of addiction, but they get proper attention here. One, which is repeatedly mentioned, is the importance for addiction of emotions and emotional regulation. This receives some attention in the dominant paradigm – the idea of self-medication, for example – but is rarely explored in any detail. Cognition tends to rule and emotion sits in second place. Emotions and emotional regulation have the great strength of being something that unites sub-topic areas such as attachment, psychodynamic and systemic approaches, and relapse prevention and mindfulness, albeit dealt with differently under those various headings.

There are chapters in this book which reach other parts of the mystery and despair of addiction which the dominant paradigm does not reach. One feature of addiction, rarely addressed elsewhere, is its effect on a person's ability to relate to others, variously described in different chapters as the replacement of affectional bonds by 'addictional bonds', empathic blunting, and the way addiction can interfere with sensitivities and capacities (see Nussbaum, 2000, a favourite book of mine, for an explication of the capabilities approach). Family members affected by their relatives' addictions, who are equally as numerous as those who experience addiction at first hand, and probably more so, often talk of how their relatives have ceased to be the people they knew and loved and how addiction seems to have robbed their relatives of the capacity to care for the family. For family members, addiction is truly a mystery – how can this person they knew be investing so much in something that seems so pointless and so damaging, and relatively less in what really matters? It is good, therefore, to see families highlighted early on in the book, and in more than one token chapter, as is often the case.

Another central feature, infrequently given the attention it deserves but properly addressed here, is the ambivalence and fragmentation that come with addiction (Adams, 2008). This can be seen as a surface phenomenon, as in the instability of motivation to change (an idea that West derives from PRIME theory), or the ambivalence which is central to motivational interviewing theory, or the conflict which is central to my Excessive Appetites model (Orford, 2001). But it can also be seen, as it is in a number of chapters, as a deeper fragmentation of the self. Rarely dealt with in psychology, one otherwise needs to go to the philosopher Levy (2011) for an appreciation of fragmentation of self as being close to the essence of addiction. His key idea was that an addicted person's preferences are inconsistent: the ability to make judgements about action is not impaired, but judgements shift from time to time. What characterizes addiction, therefore, is the fragmentation of agency, an inability to consistently exert will across time, and the loss of full capacity to effectively make plans and put in place long-term projects. I see this as a form of disempowerment, and I found it extremely helpful in developing my attempt to use the concept of power to integrate otherwise disparate areas of addiction studies (Orford, 2013).

Yet another topic which it is good to see given attention is the importance for change and recovery of the relationship with helpers or therapists. As I put it in my article, 'Asking the right questions in the right way' (Orford, 2008):

> The prevailing model of psychological treatment for addiction can be described, aptly, as a technology model. It is likened to a technique which, supported by a manual and good training and supervision, can be delivered to a high standard so that 'therapist differences' cease to be important. The therapist is the medium through which a standard technique is applied at a high level of fidelity. Some have referred to this as the 'drug metaphor', implying that treatment is seen, like a medication, as a piece of technology that requires only therapist skill and efficiency and patient compliance in order to be delivered effectively.

Like the authors of some of the chapters in this book I have always been suspicious of that model, and our experiences in the UK Alcohol Treatment Trial (UKATT) confirmed my suspicions. When clients were asked at follow-up to what factors they attributed any positive changes they had made, the most popular attributions were characteristics of the therapist and of the client's relationship with the therapist, more so than social-type attributions for Social Behaviour and Network Therapy clients or motivational-type attributions for Motivational Enhancement Therapy clients (Orford et al., 2009).

I could go on listing the aspects of addiction which the conventional wisdom downplays or dismisses but which are not avoided in this highly thoughtful volume. The importance of narratives and story-telling, of personal and social identity, of one's life values, of the very meaning of life are among them. The experience of trauma and the high frequency of addiction problems combined with other mental health problems are recurring themes in the book.

However, clinical psychology faces a number of problems – although they are by no means confined to clinical psychology. One is the question of evidence. Like all professions, it is required to demonstrate that its treatments 'work'. That can be problematic, not just because showing that something works can be costly, time-consuming and fraught with methodological and interpretive difficulties – research evidence is often so complex that it is difficult to draw clear conclusions – but also because what constitutes main outcomes may be debatable. Is the main aim symptom relief or adjustment to symptoms; abstinence or harm minimization? It is also problematic if a treatment method is comparatively new and innovative. Acceptance and Commitment Therapy (ACT) is an example, as McGrath and O'Ryan's Chapter 6 makes clear. Is ACT an example of running ahead of the evidence, they ask, or is it even, as they say one client put it, just 'hocus-pocus'? Even if it can be demonstrated that a treatment works, there is the all-important question, addressed in the final chapter, of translating evidence into practice. This is a book about psychology being used to innovate, to push forward at the frontier of a subject that needs new thinking and fresh solutions. It therefore takes us well beyond the safe and secure domain of cognitive behaviour therapy (although the point is made a number of times in this volume that new treatments can complement rather than replace existing ones).

There is, finally, another problem for psychological applications to the addictions, and that is the need to develop methods that can be applied to large numbers. Psychology has often been criticized on this score in the past. If its methods remain specialized, requiring lengthy training or specialized institutional infrastructure, then good will be done for small numbers but the impact on the huge problem of addiction will be limited. I have always agreed with the principle that psychology must be 'given away' if it is to be effective. We must think of training others who can deliver psychosocial treatments in non-specialized settings, or working remotely using modern communication technology. We must aim to make contact with hard-to-reach groups in our own countries, and the large numbers who might benefit from psychological methods in other countries, where specialized services and trained professionals are much thinner on the ground.

REFERENCES

Adams, P. (2008). *Fragmented intimacy: Addiction in a social world.* Sydney, Australia: Springer.

Levy, N. (2011). Addiction, responsibility, and ego depletion. In J. Poland & G. Graham (Eds.), *Addiction and responsibility.* Cambridge, MA: MIT Press.

Nussbaum, M. C. (2000). *Women and human development: The capabilities approach.* Cambridge: Cambridge University Press.

Orford, J. (2001). *Excessive appetites: A psychological view of addictions* (2nd ed.). Chichester: John Wiley & Sons, Ltd.

Orford, J. (2008). Asking the right questions in the right way: The need for a shift in research on psychological treatments for addiction. *Addiction, 103,* 875–885. doi:10.1111/j.1360-0443.2007.02092.x

Orford, J. (2013). *Power, powerlessness and addiction.* Cambridge: Cambridge University Press.

Orford, J., Hodgson, R., Copello, A., Wilton, S., & Slegg, G. on behalf of the UKATT Research Team (2009). To what factors do clients attribute change? Content analysis of follow-up interviews with clients of the UK Alcohol Treatment Trial. *Journal of Substance Abuse Treatment, 36,* 49–58. doi:10.1016/j.jsat.2008.04.005

Preface

Like many other complex health problems, addictions are probably best viewed within a biopsychosocial model (see, e.g. Ogden, 2012). It is, however, possibly a truism to say that the treatment of addiction is about changing behaviours, beliefs and feelings; something that psychology is likely to contribute to in a significant way. Understanding these processes from a psychological perspective, including using psychological approaches to recovery, is something academics and practitioners from all disciplines, professions and training backgrounds can benefit from. This book is intended to provide such an understanding and present an overview of the applications of psychology to addictive behaviours. The book is not written solely for psychologists, but rather is intended for all clinicians, practitioners and academics working in the addictions field, as well as those outside specialist services who may encounter addiction in their generic work. It brings together contributions from leading practitioners and academics in the addictions specialty, and provides in one volume a synthesis of psychological models and approaches used in this complex area.

Part 1 gives an overview of theories and models used to understand the aetiology and development of addictions and includes consideration of the psychological models used in the intervention approaches. Part 2 contains chapters on specific applications of psychology across selected addictive behaviour problems with a variety of service user groups, as well as practical guides to the implementation of addiction psychology in health and community care settings.

Many internationally recognized scientists, practitioners and experienced clinicians have contributed to this book, and we would like to thank them all. Gratitude is also expressed to the numerous service users who have informed the individual chapters; thank you.

REFERENCE

Ogden, J. (2012). *Health psychology: A textbook*. Maidenhead: Open University Press.

Notes on Contributors

EDITORS

Paul Davis is a Teaching Fellow in Clinical Psychology at the University of Surrey, Guildford, UK. He worked as a Consultant Clinical Psychologist and Specialist Lead for many years in several NHS mental health services in London, providing treatments for addiction problems and continues to practise as an independent consultant. His publications, research and academic work have focused on the psychology of addictions, and he provides training courses both in the United Kingdom and abroad on treatment interventions. He has held a number of national advisory roles within health and criminal justice bodies working on policy and guidelines development.

Sue Jackson is a chartered psychologist specializing in the psychosocial impact and treatment of chronic health conditions. In addition to managing an extensive research portfolio, she is a visiting lecturer at a number of UK universities. Dr Jackson supports a number of patient support charities, and is the first psychologist to serve on the Medical Advisory Committee for the Pituitary Foundation.

Robert Patton is a lecturer in Clinical Psychology based at the University of Surrey and a Visiting Research Fellow in Addiction at King's College London. He has run a research consultancy since 1993. During the 1990s he worked as a consultant for the Home Office Drugs Prevention Initiative and as research associate in health promotion for the University of Northumbria. Now based in London, he has worked for Royal Holloway, LSHTM, Imperial College, the Institute of Psychiatry and the Maudsley Hospital.

FOREWORD

Jim Orford. In his time as a clinical, and later clinical-cum-community, psychologist working in NHS and university settings in London, Exeter and for the last 20 years in Birmingham, Jim Orford has researched and written extensively about substance and gambling problems and particularly about their impact on the family. His best-known work is *Excessive Appetites: A Psychological View of Addictions* (2nd ed., 2001) and his most recent book is *Power, Powerlessness and Addiction* (2013).

CHAPTER AUTHORS

Jamie Brown is a Principal Research Fellow of the Society for Study of Addiction at University College London. He co-leads a programme of research to evaluate digital behaviour change interventions and runs the Smoking and Alcohol Toolkit Studies. In over 80 publications on a variety of topics, his focus has been on tobacco control, including e-cigarettes, harm reduction and the real-world effectiveness of smoking cessation treatments. He has been invited to present his work on e-cigarettes at international conferences, to the UK regulatory authorities for medicines, and has co-authored a briefing to the UK all-party parliamentary pharmacy group. He is a co-author of *Theory of Addiction* (2nd ed.) and *ABC of Behaviour Change Theories*, and is an Assistant Editor of the journal *Addiction*.

Alex Copello is Professor of Addiction Research at the School of Psychology, University of Birmingham, and Consultant Clinical Psychologist with the Birmingham and Solihull Mental Health NHS Foundation Trust addiction services, where he leads the addictions research and innovation programme. His career has combined clinical, service management and academic work. Alex has researched extensively on the impact of addictions upon families and family-based interventions and publishes regularly in scientific journals.

David Curran is a consultant clinical psychologist working for an Addiction Service in Northern Ireland, and Assistant Course Director with the Doctorate in Clinical Psychology training programme at Queens University Belfast. Areas of clinical and research interest include early adversity, attachment, trauma and co-morbid presenting problems.

Rudi Dallos is Professor of Clinical Psychology at Plymouth University, UK. Rudi is a clinical psychologist and systemic family therapist. Professors Vetere and Dallos have co-authored many articles and three books: *Systemic Therapy and Attachment Narratives: Applications across a Range of Clinical Settings* (2009, Routledge), is most relevant to their chapter in this book.

Lisa Dutheil trained as a clinical psychologist at the Institute of Psychiatry, Psychology and Neuroscience (King's College London). She has a long-standing interest in addictions, and worked for several years pre-qualification as a practitioner and manager within third sector substance misuse services. Since 2011, she has practised as a clinical psychologist in the alcohol services at Camden and Islington NHS Foundation Trust. She works with individuals and groups, primarily using CBT, Mindfulness Based Approaches and Motivational Interviewing.

Rebecca Fisher is a clinical psychologist who has worked with the National Problem Gambling Clinic. She has worked with problem gamblers in individual and group formats, assessing and treating them as part of the therapeutic programme at the clinic. She is now working in offender care in a London NHS Trust.

Alina Galis is a clinical psychologist who has worked in substance misuse services since 2007; in NHS Fife, in Camden & Islington Foundation Trust and in the South Westminster Drug & Alcohol Service, in partnership with the third sector. She completed her training as a clinical psychologist at the University of Edinburgh and has previously worked a part of a research group within the Centre for Addiction Research & Education Scotland, University of Dundee. Clinically, she works with individual and group interventions for substance misuse and dual diagnosis.

André Geel is a consultant clinical psychologist in Addictions for Central and North West London NHS Foundation Trust. He has considerable experience working in the

NHS, specializing in community, general mental health and addictions. He has been a management and clinical lead for a number of services, as well as contributing to a variety of psychology training courses in London and the South-East of England. He has held Project Lead positions for Addictions for the British Psychological Society, has acted as Chair of Substance Misuse Management in General Practice and is on the Executive of the Skills Consortium. He was one of the psychology contributors to the NICE Guidelines on Substance Misuse Services.

Jennifer Harris is a clinical psychologist working in inpatient and community addictions services at South London and Maudsley NHS Foundation Trust. She has a particular interest in working with trauma and is also an EMDR Therapist. Prior to this, she worked as a researcher in the field of addictions and holds an MSc in Health Psychology.

Robert Hill is a consultant clinical psychologist. His area of speciality is addictive behaviours, along with co-morbid psychological difficulties and neuropsychological functioning. He has previously worked as a Senior Lecturer at Middlesex University, focusing on the reduction of stress and burnout among community and inpatient mental health staff. He has a particular interest in philosophy and holds an MA in Modern European Philosophy. His most recent publication is *Principles and Practice of Group Work in Addictions*, published by Routledge, with his colleague Dr Jennifer Harris.

Adam Huxley is a consultant clinical forensic psychologist. He is currently the national psychology lead for Crime Reduction Initiatives, a leading charity providing support to vulnerable people facing addiction, homelessness and domestic abuse. His research and clinical interests include the impact of substance misuse on marginalized groups.

Edward J. Khantzian is Clinical Professor of Psychiatry, Harvard Medical School, and a founding member of the Department of Psychiatry at The Cambridge Hospital, MA, USA. He has spent more than 40 years studying psychological factors associated with drug and alcohol abuse. Dr Khantzian is a practising psychiatrist and psychoanalyst, a participant in numerous clinical research studies on substance abuse, and a lecturer and writer on psychiatry, psychoanalysis, and substance abuse problems. His studies, publications, and teaching have gained him recognition for his contributions on self-medication factors and self-care deficits in substance use disorders and the importance of modified techniques in group therapy for substance abusers. He is a founding member of the American Academy of Addiction Psychiatry (AAAP) and is a Past-President of this national organization. AAAP honoured him in 2000 by making him the recipient of its Founders Award and Keynote speaker for the annual scientific meeting in recognition of his 'courage in changing the ways we think of and understand addictions'.

Aska Matsunaga completed her BSc Applied Psychology degree at the University of Kent as part of her career path to become a clinical psychologist, and has worked in London treatment services in addictions and adult mental health. She has delivered CBT in group settings and carried out research on methadone maintenance treatment as well as research into cross-cultural anger rumination and aggressive behaviour.

Liz McGrath qualified as a clinical psychologist from University College London, and has over 16 years experience of work in addiction services in Central London.

She completed her training in clinical neuropsychology at the Institute of Psychiatry, London, before going on to train in mindfulness-based approaches at the Centre for Mindfulness Research and Practice in Bangor, Wales. Liz has applied mindfulness-based approaches at the individual, group, team and organizational levels in an inner-London NHS substance misuse service.

Mani Mehdikhani is a principal clinical psychologist and currently works for Greater Manchester West Trust's Specialist Services Network. Mani has worked as both a clinician and as a researcher in the field of addictions and substance misuse. He is a member of the British Psychological Society (BPS) and is also registered with the Health & Care Professions Council (HCPC). Mani regularly teaches on the Addiction modules at both Manchester and Liverpool Universities' Clinical Psychology training courses, and he has an interest in addiction, attachment, evolutionary psychology and personality disorders.

Luke Mitcheson, consultant clinical psychologist, is the Lead Psychologist for the addictions services in the South London and Maudsley NHS Foundation Trust and a consultant working in Lambeth community drug and alcohol services. He is also seconded as a clinical advisor to Public Health England in the Alcohol, Drugs and Tobacco Division.

Fraser Morrison is a clinical psychologist working in the field of Alcohol Related Brain Damage (ARBD). He has significant experience of substance misuse services and has specialized in the area of ARBD in recent years. He is currently completing the British Psychological Society Qualification in Clinical Neuropsychology and has published research specifically in this field of adapting existing therapeutic approaches and investigation of outcome.

Jo M. Nicholson completed her Doctorate of Clinical Psychology in 1997 and worked for 12 years in adult mental health services, mostly within acute psychiatric care settings. She currently specializes in working with people with Hepatitis C at Sheffield Teaching Hospitals. Dr Nicholson has an enduring interest in working with 'hard to reach/hard to engage' groups, and she has a special interest in working with dual diagnosis, personality and substance misuse populations. In addition, she has an interest in service development and change process in NHS settings.

Dominic O'Ryan trained as a clinical psychologist at University College London and has worked as a practitioner and developer of clinical approaches in addiction services in Central London for over 15 years. In addition, he qualified in CBT from the Institute of Psychiatry, London, and in CBT Supervision from Royal Holloway University of London. Dominic has trained and practised in mindfulness-based cognitive therapy and offers mindfulness, acceptance and resilience-based approaches to service users and staff in an inner-London NHS substance misuse service.

Tony Rao is consultant old age psychiatrist at South London and Maudsley NHS Foundation Trust, working in an inner-city area of London with high rates of alcohol misuse in older people. As well as a Visiting Researcher at the Institute of Psychiatry, Tony is Chair of the Royal College of Psychiatrists Working Group on Older People and Substance Misuse. He is involved in policy change for older people with dual diagnosis and provides expertise to advisory bodies and voluntary organizations on substance misuse in older people.

Jenny Svanberg is a consultant clinical psychologist and Lead Psychologist for Substance Misuse in NHS Forth Valley. Her research and clinical interests include the prevention, assessment and treatment of complex difficulties relating to substance use and addiction.

Arlene Vetere is Professor of Family Therapy and Systemic Practice at VID Specialized University, Oslo, Norway. Arlene is a clinical psychologist and systemic family therapist. Professors Vetere and Dallos have co-authored many articles and three books: *Systemic Therapy and Attachment Narratives: Applications across a Range of Clinical Settings* (2009, Routledge), is most relevant to their chapter in this book.

Sarah Wadd is programme director of the Substance Misuse and Ageing Research Team (SMART) at the University of Bedfordshire and is one of the UK's leading experts on substance misuse in older people. Her seminal 'Working with Older Drinkers Study' identified best practice in this area, based on interviews with alcohol practitioners who specialize in working with older people and older people receiving alcohol treatment. She is an expert advisor on substance misuse in older people for the Welsh Government and the UK's Advisory Council on Drug Misuse. Sarah is the academic lead for the £25m Big Lottery-funded 'Drink Wise Age Well' Programme which aims to reduce alcohol-related harm in people aged 50 and over. Her other research studies have included alcohol misuse that co-exists with cognitive impairment in older people and illicit drug and medication misuse in older people, and she has contributed to studies on alcohol-related elder abuse and sight loss. Sarah is a cofounder of the Coalition of Older Adults Affected by Substance Misuse (COAASM), whose members work to reduce discrimination and improve prevention, services and treatment for older adults and families affected by substance misuse.

Kathryn Walsh is currently pursuing clinical psychology doctoral training at the University of Birmingham. Kathryn previously worked as a Research Associate at the School of Psychology, University of Birmingham, in a Brief Intervention National Institute of Health Research funded randomized controlled trial for people with addictions and severe mental health problems. She has published in the area of addictions and mental health and was awarded the first prize in the mental-health and substance-use essay competition 2012 by the *Mental Health and Substance Use* academic journal, where the essay was subsequently published.

Martin Weegmann is a consultant clinical psychologist and group analyst, with 20 years experience in the field of substance misuse. He is a well-known trainer, having delivered workshops and keynote lectures to a range of organizations through the United Kingdom, including organizing seven annual conferences on the theme 'Psychotherapy of Addiction'. Martin has co-edited two books, *Psychodynamics of Addiction* (2002, Wiley) and *Group Psychotherapy and Addiction* (2004, Wiley) and published many chapters and papers. His latest book, *The World within the Group: Developing Theory for Group Analysis* (London, Karnac) was published in 2014. In 2011, he joined the General Services Board of Alcoholics Anonymous, as a 'non-alcoholic trustee'.

Robert West is Professor of Health Psychology and Director of Tobacco Studies at the Cancer Research UK Health Behaviour Research Centre, University College London, UK. Professor West is also Editor-in-Chief of the journal *Addiction*. He has authored more than 500 scientific articles, books and book chapters. He was co-founder of the

NHS stop-smoking services. His research includes evaluations of methods of helping smokers to stop and population surveys of smoking and smoking cessation patterns. He is author of *The SmokeFreeFormula* (Orion), which aims to bring the science of stopping to smokers. For more information, see www.rjwest.co.uk.

Christopher Whiteley, consultant clinical psychologist, is the Trust Deputy Head of Psychology for South London and Maudsley NHS Foundation Trust. His clinical work is with the Trust's specialist HIV Mental Health Team. He previously worked for over 10 years in drug and alcohol treatment services and more recently as a seconded clinical advisor to Public Health England in the Alcohol, Drugs and Tobacco Division.

PART 1

Understanding the Psychology and Treatment of Addictions

1 Addiction: A Comprehensive Approach

JAMIE BROWN AND ROBERT WEST

Cancer Research UK Health Behaviour Research Centre, University College London, UK

CHAPTER OUTLINE

1.1   INTRODUCTION

'Addiction' is a social construct which can be usefully defined as a chronic condition in which there is a repeated powerful motivation to engage in a rewarding behaviour, acquired as a result of engaging in that behaviour, that has significant potential for unintended harm. From this perspective, a broad conception of motivation is at the heart of addiction and requires any theory of addiction to be based on a comprehensive theory of motivation. This approach understands addiction can be driven by many different factors – physiological, psychological, environmental and social – and that it is not useful to focus on one particular factor to the exclusion of all others. PRIME theory aims to provide a conceptual framework within which the major insights provided by more specific theories of choice, self-control, habits, emotions and drives can be integrated.

PRIME theory describes the motivational system as the set of brain processes that energize and direct our actions. The system can be usefully divided into five interacting but distinct sub-systems: (1) response execution; (2) impulses/inhibition; (3) motives (wants and needs); (4) evaluations (beliefs about what is good or bad); and (5) plans (self-conscious intentions). The response execution system co-ordinates what is happening at any given moment. The proximal influences on this are the impulses and inhibitions to perform particular responses. Motives can influence behaviour only through impulses and inhibitions, evaluations can do so only through motives, and plans must operate on either motives or evaluations. These can also each be influenced by the immediate internal or external environment. Important internal sources of influence include identity, self-control, drives and emotional states.

A core proposition is that all the subsystems compete with one another and we simply act in response to the strongest influence at any given moment. In terms of deliberate action, this means that from one moment to the next *we will always act in pursuit of what we most want or need at that moment*. These motives vary according to the current strength of evaluations and plans, but also in response to the internal and external environment. For example, if an intention or belief is not currently generating a sufficiently strong motive for performing (or inhibiting) a particular action, then the system may produce an apparently contradictory action in response to a strong internal drive or external stimulus. The operation of this dynamic, complex system is inherently unstable – reflecting the variety in patterns of addictive behaviour – and requires constant balancing to avoid heading into maladaptive 'chreods'. The motivational system can be changed over time by a range of processes including habituation, associative learning, imitation and explicit memory.

This chapter provide a brief background to the origins of PRIME theory, before describing in more detail the proposed structure of the motivational system, important internal and external sources of influence, the dynamics of the system, and how motivational dispositions change over time. The chapter will finish by summarizing addiction research that has been inspired and informed by PRIME theory.

1.2   EXISTING THEORIES

There is no shortage of theories about addiction. The book *Theory of Addiction* (West & Brown, 2013), in which PRIME theory was first proposed, was originally intended to provide a convenient overview of available theories. During the course of the research for the book, however, it became apparent that theories of addiction tend to focus on one aspect of addiction or rely upon just one level of explanation. In a problem as manifestly complex as addiction, these approaches are unable to provide a sufficiently coherent and nuanced account of the phenomenon. Existing theories span a range of approaches from those that emphasize choice to those that focus on neuropharmacology. We now summarize some important categories of addiction theory and explain in each case why we believe more comprehensive theories are required. For a fuller account, see Chapters 3–7 in West and Brown (2013).

1.2.1   *Choice Theories*

Examples of theories that focus on addiction as the exercise of choice based on desires are Becker's Rational Addiction Theory (Becker & Murphy, 1988) and Skog's Unstable Preference Theory (Skog, 2000; 2003). Others focus on addicts' 'expectancies' (for a review, see Jones, Corbin & Fromme, 2001). Slovic et al. (2002; 2007) have developed a theory of judgement relating feelings to analytical judgements (an 'affect heuristic') and applied this to smoking. There are theories that focus on attentional, or other cognitive, biases (e.g. McCusker, 2001; Mogg, Field & Bradley, 2005; Field & Cox, 2008). A raft of theories argue that the behaviour of addiction can be understood in terms of concepts derived from economic theory, such as temporal discounting (e.g. Bickel, DeGrandpre & Higgins, 1995; Bickel, Miller Kowal, Lindquist & Pitcock, 2007).

A synthesis of these theories describes an individual who chooses in some sense to engage or not engage in the behaviour. The choice involves a cost-benefit analysis: the costs are weighed against the benefits of the behaviour which change over time and the appreciation of which changes over time. The costs and benefits, and indeed aspects of the analysis, may involve mental representations to which one does not have full conscious access. The choice does not need to be rational; it can be influenced by pharmacological and non-pharmacological factors, including one's sense of self and what one wants to be, and possibly by biases in attention to and memory for stimuli related to the addictive behaviour. In this view, the idea that addictive behaviour is driven by a damagingly powerful and repeated motivation is an illusion based on a failure to appreciate that the expressed desire to stop doing something at one time does not reflect the preferences operating at a later time after the attempt at restraint has begun.

An important problem with this view is that it does not accord with the experience of many addicts. At the point where they find themselves about to relapse back to their old ways, they frequently report feeling compulsion that is distinct from simple desire. It is not even that it is a 'strong desire'; it is an urge that is often accompanied by a sincere attempt to resist. Successful restraint does not simply depend upon on analysis leading to a decision to refrain; the implementation of the choice requires self-control and expends mental effort. By focusing on the choice, the approach neglects the panoply of observational and research evidence for the importance of a failure of impulse control in the development and maintenance of addiction.

1.2.2   Compulsion and Self-Control Theories

The so-called 'disease model' of addiction takes the view that addiction involves powerful and overpowering compulsions that are experienced as 'cravings' (e.g. Jellinek, 1960; Gelkopf, Levitt & Bleich, 2002). Examples of theories concerning the failure of impulse control include those that focus on either the dysfunction of inhibitory brain circuitry (Lubman, Yucel & Pantelis, 2004; Dalley, Everitt & Robbins, 2011), or the dysfunction of the prefrontal cortex (Goldstein & Volkow, 2011). A cognitive model of craving has also been proposed (Tiffany & Drobes, 1991). A more general view of addiction as a failure of self-regulation has been proposed by Baumeister (Baumeister et al., 1994; Baumeister & Vohs, 2007; Vohs & Baumeister, 2011). Self-regulation extends beyond impulse control, or the adequate functioning of basic associated mechanisms; instead, it recognizes that failure to self-regulate may also involve a lack of reflective strategies, skills and capacity for self-control. Other examples of theories emphasizing the role of self-regulation in addiction are cognitive control theory (Miller & Cohen, 2001), executive dysfunction theory (Hester & Garavan, 2004; Fernández-Serrano, Pérez-García, Perales & Verdejo-García, 2010; Madoz-Gurpide, Blasco-Fontecilla, Baca-Garcia & Ochoa-Mangado, 2011), and self-determination theory (Deci, Eghrari, Patrick & Leone, 1994; Ryan & Deci, 2000; Deci & Ryan, 2012).

By incorporating theorizing about compulsion and self-control into ideas about choice, many important aspects of addiction are explicable. An addict may be someone for whom the desire to engage in an activity is abnormally strong, or the ability to resist the desire is abnormally weak, or some combination of both. Invoking both avoids the philosophical problem of addicts having 'no choice', which is implied by relying only on regulatory failure, and can explain a great deal about addiction. However, a model relying on choice (even if it acknowledges failures in self-control can sometimes be undermined), still has anomalies. A reliance on choice means that behaviour is still fundamentally centred on analyses of costs and benefits (however irrational), whereas, in reality, sometimes behaviour is simply not related to such analysis; instead it is habitual or automatic (i.e., the behaviour itself is automatic, not just the processes by which choices form). Another difficulty for choice models is that sometimes the priority given to certain behaviours can be out of all proportion to any apparent analysis, even allowing for certain biases or unstable preferences. The field of behavioural pharmacology can address this weakness.

1.2.3   Theories Focusing on the Neural Basis of Reward and Punishment

There are theories that focus on addiction as the development of a habit through instrumental learning (O'Brien, Childress, McLellan & Ehrman, 1992), or through both instrumental and Pavlovian processes (Everitt, Dickinson & Robbins, 2001; Everitt & Robbins, 2005; Everitt et al., 2008). Others, such as the Opponent Process theory, seek to explain the development of pharmacological tolerance and withdrawal symptoms (Solomon & Corbit, 1973; 1974; Solomon, 1980), which may lead to dose escalation and maintenance of drug use to avoid the aversive consequences of abstinence (e.g. Lewis, 1990; Schulteis & Koob, 1996; Koob, Sanna & Bloom, 1998). There are theories that focus on the neural basis of rewards that underpin addiction (e.g. Wise & Bozarth, 1987; Koob & Nestler, 1997; Koob & Le Moal, 2001; Weiss & Koob, 2001; Hyman, Malenka & Nestler, 2006). There are also theories that focus on Pavlovian conditioning in the development of cravings and dependence (e.g. Melchior & Tabakoff, 1984).

Theories focusing on the neural bases of addiction have become more complex over the years. White (1996) has proposed a theory involving multiple learning pathways. A particularly popular theory differentiates the hedonic effects of addictive drugs from their effects on pathways involved in habit learning in the context of cues (Robinson & Berridge, 2003; Berridge & Robinson, 2011). In that theory, it is claimed that tolerance to the hedonic effects of some drugs occurs while the mechanism underpinning the effect of cues on wanting a drug actually sensitize as a result of drug exposure. Instrumental learning and classical conditioning models have been combined in a theory that differentiates the effects of addictive drugs on different parts of the brain's reward system (e.g. Balfour, 2004). More recently, attempts have been made to integrate how the neural bases of learning in addiction ultimately relate to dysfunction in inhibitory circuits (Koob & Volkow, 2010).

The addition of associative learning and response mechanisms, and their neural bases which can be affected directly by drugs, improves the explanatory power of a model of addiction. The synthesis of models previously described already recognized that an individual often chooses to engage in addictive behaviour as a result of a cost-benefit analysis of the alternatives, which may be influenced by biases and changing preferences. The concepts of compulsion and self-control account for the phenomenon whereby addicts sometimes sincerely choose to refrain from a behaviour but fail to enact their choice. Learning mechanisms help explain that sometimes behaviour results from a habit with little conscious decision-making, and also why certain behaviours come to be valued out of proportion to the benefits they confer, even after controlling for processing biases or preferences changing over time according to emerging needs or drives.

1.2.4   Integrated Theories

There are few theories that have attempted to span many of the areas considered above, but two that are important to mention are Orford's Excessive Appetites theory (Orford, 2001) and Blaszczynski's model of pathological gambling (Blaszczynski & Nower, 2002). These two theories are able to capture the experience of addiction and they do so by recognizing the diversity of patterns, feelings and routes to addiction. This diversity presents a major challenge to theory development. A synthetic theory must account for the big observations but also needs to be more than a listing of influences and factors; it must synthesize and add value with a unifying construct that itself generates new ideas.

1.2.5 The Need for a Synthetic Theory

A theory is needed that provides a parsimonious, synthetic and useful description of the nature of addiction that explains the major observations relating to the phenomenon and incorporates the insights of the range of theories that have been proposed to date.

PRIME theory is an attempt to synthesize the insights contained in more specific theories into a coherent account that is set within a general theory of motivation. This chapter provides an outline of the theory. For the sake of conciseness, it is just an exposition – it delves only a little into the evidence and inferences that led to the development of the theory, or the theory's relationship with others in the literature. It is recognized that the ideas need to be expanded, developed, defended and related to other intellectual contributions on which it has drawn. This is attempted in the book, *Theory of Addiction* (West & Brown, 2013).

The theory is pitched at the psychological level of analysis but with a view to providing a 'pegboard' into which can be plugged theories at other levels (including economic theories and neurophysiological theories). When giving a psychological account of motivation, it is impossible to avoid making statements that just sound like common sense. The advance on common sense that is being offered here is bringing these ideas together in a coherent framework, together with non-common-sense ideas that have been developed through formal study and critical observation.

It is painted with a broad brush and does not attempt to capture what is known about the details of drug actions, social forces, and so on. However, it does seek to provide a coherent framework within which existing knowledge and future findings can be integrated.

1.3 THE HUMAN MOTIVATIONAL SYSTEM

PRIME theory is a general theory of motivation, this being defined as the brain processes that energize and direct behaviour. Before focusing on the structure of the motivational system, it is important to consider this in the broader context of behaviour. The proposed system fits usefully within a simple model that describes how capability, opportunity and motivation interact as a system to generate behaviour. This COM-B model takes a general form about the necessary conditions required for a behaviour that has been re-iterated over centuries in one form or another (be it legal systems or consensus meetings among behavioural theorists; Michie, van Stralen & West, 2011). In particular, a person must have the physical and psychological capability to enact a behaviour; they must have the physical and social opportunity to engage in it; and they must be more motivated by a course of action at the relevant moment than some other behaviour. This broad level of analysis serves as a reminder that 'motivational systems' do not exist in vacuums; systems do not become addicted to activities. There are factors beyond the motivational system – for example, knowledge and skills, and the social and cultural milieu which dictate perceptions and availability – that are crucial to understanding certain patterns of addictive behaviour.

1.3.1   *Structure of the Motivational System*

According to PRIME theory, the human motivational system consists of a chain of five interacting subsystems whose initials make the PRIME acronym (see Figure 1.1).

The response subsystem organizes and executes responses. This involves starting, modifying or stopping actions. Responses can arise from reflexes – learned or innate, which are activated directly by internal or external stimuli – or from the output of the subsystem which generates potentially competing or additive impulses and inhibitions. At any given moment, it is the resultant force from this competition which controls our responses, notwithstanding a small subset of particular stimuli that can directly activate responses.

Impulses typically only enter conscious awareness when for some reason they are not immediately translated into action. They are then experienced as 'urges'. It is not uncommon for a course of action to be impossible within an immediate environment, which is why people frequently experience urges. When available to consciousness, the strength can, in principle, be measured using self-report. Impulses and inhibitions are influenced by internal and external stimuli (see Section 1.4) and also by the output of the subsystem that generates motives (also known colloquially as 'desires').

The motive subsystem promotes a consideration of the possible consequences of different courses of action and thereby lies at the heart of purposeful behaviour. When entering consciousness, motives are experienced as feelings of want or need for that thing. Wants involve mental representations of something and associated feelings of anticipated pleasure or satisfaction; needs are feelings of anticipated relief from mental or physical discomfort arising from some actual or imagined event or situation. Wants and needs are influenced by internal and external stimuli, including reminders, physical sensations and drive states. Particularly important are

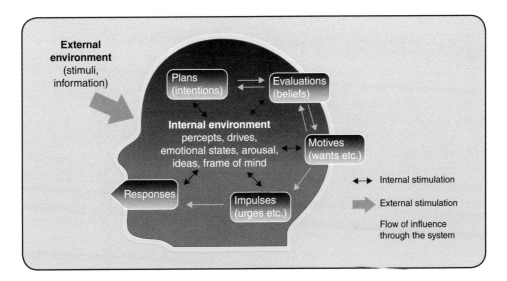

FIGURE 1.1 *Structure of the human motivational system*

Source: West and Brown 2013. Reproduced with permission of John Wiley & Sons Ltd.

generalized positive and negative emotional states such as happiness and sadness, which lead by association to targeted emotional states of liking and disliking. More than one motive can co-exist at one time. If motives do not involve the same course of action, then this competition will create a particular kind of generalized emotional state; a feeling of 'conflict'. This is unpleasant, and like any other adverse emotional state creates a motive to escape or avoid it. When motives co-occur, the one with the greatest valence prevails in generating an impulse or inhibition at a particular moment. This will then compete or combine with any other impulses and inhibitions that are directly generated by internal or external stimuli to start, stop or modify an action. Motives can also be influenced by the subsystem that generates evaluations.

Evaluations are a type of belief. Beliefs are conscious mental representations of the world that are propositional, i.e. expressed through language, as distinct from 'images' that are experienced iconically. The propositions reflect what an individual holds to be true, not true, or what might be true with varying degrees of likelihood, and have feelings of confidence attached to them. Uniquely, evaluations also involve a judgment about the extent to which a thing is also 'good' or 'bad'. Evaluations can be 'global' (generally good or bad), 'aesthetic' (pleasing or displeasing), 'functional' (performing well or badly), 'ethical' (right or wrong) and 'utilitarian' (useful or detrimental). Evaluations are generated by analysis and inference, and internal and external stimuli. Evaluations can only influence behaviour by producing motives, either directly or indirectly (via internal states like anger); they have no direct route to the impulse subsystem. Thus, believing an activity to be a good, or right, or useful thing to do, will not result in the corresponding behaviour unless it also produces a sufficiently strong feeling of wanting or needing to do so. Motives can input back onto evaluations; if a motive for a particular activity is strongly activated, this may cause a re-evaluation of the 'goodness' or 'rightness' of that activity. Evaluations are also influenced by the planning subsystem, which is most distal from the execution of behaviour.

Plans involve a future course of action, at least some degree of commitment, and a representation (however vague) of some starting conditions. Plans are most commonly formed when there is a motive to engage in an act but the time is not right at that moment. This may be because of competing desires or because the conditions when the act would be desirable do not yet exist. Plans are also formed when a course of action is immediately possible but sufficiently complex that plans are required to organize sequencing the behaviour. In each case, a plan will only produce behaviour at a later moment insofar that it is recalled. Remembering a plan at a time in which the starting conditions are met usually generates a positive evaluation of this act (the magnitude of which depends on the commitment with which the plan was formed). The alternative is that a plan is re-evaluated in light of new experience or other more salient current influences within the motivational system, and is thereby modified or abandoned. Insofar that this does not happen and the plan is evaluated positively, then this creates a level of desire to do it, which may generate a corresponding impulse. Whether or not the act is undertaken will depend on competing plans, evaluations, motives and impulses and inhibitions at the same moment.

1.4 INTERNAL AND EXTERNAL SOURCES OF INFLUENCE

1.4.1 *Drives, Emotional States and Arousal*

'Drives' (such as hunger) and 'emotional states' (such as happiness and distress, and liking and disliking) are of fundamental importance. There are a variety of drives, with the most well-known being homeostatic ones, such as hunger and thirst. These involve a motivational tension that is reduced by 'consummatory behaviour'. Drives are affected by internal stimuli that signal physiological needs and external stimuli that amplify or draw attention to, or suppress or draw attention away from, them. Many drives are innate and common to all humans, but drives can also be acquired; for example, chronic exposure to nicotine from cigarettes leads to abnormally low levels of dopamine in the central nervous system whenever nicotine concentrations are depleted. Drives can produce direct impulses to engage in actions that reduce them, which have been learnt through experience. They can also produce impulses indirectly by creating emotional states (see below). Finally, drives can activate motives for courses of action that experience has shown to achieve drive reduction.

Emotional states are either 'generalized' (such as happiness and distress) or 'targeted' (such as liking and disliking). The cause of emotional states is complex, variable between individuals, and often difficult to introspect. Typically, they derive from the experience of stimuli/events that we perceive as affecting our well-being, the well-being of things we care about, our identity, and our sense of what is right and wrong. For many people, important determinants of well-being from one moment to the next are 'hedonic' experiences (pleasure and discomfort): things that give us pleasure tend to make us content, and therefore lead to liking, whereas things that cause discomfort tend to make us distressed and lead to disliking. Thus, targeted emotional states are generated by generalized ones – the difference is that they are directly attached to the mental representation of the perceived cause. Generalized emotional states can directly influence impulses, for example, an instinctive impulse to laugh or cry. They can also create impulses indirectly by acting as rewards and punishments through associative learning. Targeted emotional states lead to motives; most obviously liking leads to wanting and disliking leads to not wanting.

An important link between drives and emotional states is that changes in drive level can produce emotional states: drive reduction can be pleasurable, while an increasing drive or failure to reduce a drive can cause discomfort.

Arousal is the generalized level of energy in which the motivational system resides. The extent of arousal affects the sensitivity of all the elements within the system to other elements and external inputs, such as stimuli perceived by our senses. During arousal, relevant stimuli also become more likely to be perceived, as arousal also causes attention to become more focused. Arousal not only increases the sensitivity of all elements within the system, it also re-parameterizes the priority given to each element of the system by other elements. For example, very high levels of arousal lead to interference by emotional states of analytical thinking being used to arrive at evaluations. The primary determinant of arousal is drives and emotional states. The relationship is bi-directional, which explains how the influence of emotional states and drives can quickly increase.

1.4.2   Self-Control and Identity

We all hold beliefs and images about ourselves. These representations of self, and how we feel about them, constitute our identity. Identity only exists meaningfully when attention is drawn to it, and varies over time with experience, and different aspects will be variously coherent. Identity is a potentially important source of strong motives: aspects of our identity about which we feel strongly generate wanting, or even needing, to behave consistently with that belief or image of our self.

Self-control is defined as acting in accordance with a plan, evaluation or motive derived from a representation of our self in the face of competing desires, impulses and inhibitions arising from other unrelated sources. Self-control is therefore dependent on activating relevant aspects of our identity at the appropriate moments. The strength of attachment to the activated aspects determines the strength of the plans, evaluations, and ultimately wants and needs arising from them. Self-representations that are coherent and have clear boundaries, which mean that they are remembered and applicable to all relevant situations, will have greater control over behaviour. The exercise of self-control requires 'effort' that leads to depleted 'motivational resources' with continued expenditure.

1.5   THE DYNAMICS OF THE SYSTEM

1.5.1   The Moment-to-Moment Control of Behaviour

The motivational system is fundamentally dynamic. In order for a subsystem to influence behaviour, it must do so through impulses and inhibitory forces operating at the time. However, outputs of a particular subsystem exist only when they are generated. This is equally true for 'higher' subsystems like plans and evaluations, as it is for motives and impulses. This places a greater emphasis on the immediate internal and external environment in controlling behaviour than theories which assume motives and impulses are transients but that other components (e.g. attitudes and self-efficacy) have enduring, trait-like, qualities.

Consistency in behaviour lies in more or less stable dispositions for components of the motivational system to respond in particular ways to particular (internal or external) stimuli. When these dispositions are enduring, they are considered to be traits and when they themselves are generated by current stimuli, they are thought of as states.

A key proposition – referred to as the first law of motivation – arising out of the moment-to-moment control of behaviour and the structure of the motivational system is that: 'At every moment we act in pursuit of what we most want or need at that moment.' This law recognizes that stimuli can produce impulses and behaviour directly without motives but concerns itself with deliberate behaviour by specifying the pursuit of action. Under this law of motivation, control over behaviour involves shaping these momentary wants and needs.

Identity is the source of self-control, and identity change is therefore posited to be a key starting point for deliberate behaviour change. Deliberate behaviour change is sustained when the desires arising from the new identity are stronger at each relevant moment than the desires arising from other sources to revert to the previous behaviour pattern, or are able to overwhelm habitual or instinctive impulses.

1.5.2 The Unstable Mind and Chreods

The human mind has evolved to be inherently unstable; the adaptive advantage is extreme adaptability, creativity and sensitivity to inputs and contingencies. The converse is that the system requires constant balancing input to prevent it from spiralling 'out of control' into maladaptive thought processes and behaviour patterns. This includes the motivational system, with the maladaptive patterns of behaviour representing addiction. For most people under most conditions, there are normally enough checks and balances in the system to ensure that it does not descend into these patterns permanently, but it is fiendishly complex to predict with confidence which inputs will lead the system to these maladaptive patterns, and indeed which would subsequently restore balance. Sometimes extreme one-off events are required to put a system into a very different state, whereas at other times a small innocuous event will be sufficient to send the system down a very different path at which point the checks and balances would maintain the new system. There are still other instances where a succession of small events is necessary and progressively leads the system to become firmly established in a new state.

These patterns can be understood in terms of the concepts of chaos theory (a mathematical approach to modelling complex systems, such as weather patterns) or 'epigenetic landscapes' (Waddington, 1977). In chaos theory, systems descend into relatively steady states over the short to medium term but can then switch, apparently unpredictably, to other violently unstable states, or even move in a pseudo-random fashion between them. The idea developed from the discovery that a minuscule difference in the initial parameters of a complex programme designed to model atmospheric conditions eventually leads to massive differences in output. This led to the famous notion of the flapping of butterfly wings in Asia potentially being responsible for storms in America. The 'epigenetic landscape' is a useful pictorial representation of these ideas (see Figure 1.2). The landscapes represent the state of a system at a given moment as the position of a ball on an undulating landscape, and potential

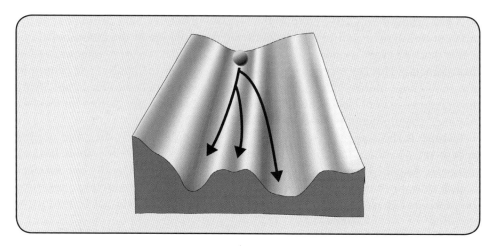

FIGURE 1.2 *Example of an epigenetic landscape*

Source: West and Brown 2013. Reproduced with permission of John Wiley & Sons Ltd.

future states that are represented by later positions on the landscape along which it is moving. The undulations or valleys of the landscapes (called 'chreods') vary in depth and shape and divide at critical periods. The path the ball eventually follows can be radically different as the result of a marginal difference in input at a 'critical period'. At later moments, considerably greater inputs can be insufficient to prevent the ball from continuing along a particular chreod.

A logical corollary of this perspective is that there are no stages to behaviour change. Or, certainly none that are linear and that can be assessed by simple questionnaires. Instead, motivation to change is much more unstable and responsive to the immediate environment. Thus, PRIME theory argues that the most effective use of resources is to put the maximum tolerable pressure on individuals to change at all available moments, rather than stimulating thoughts about what stage of readiness a person is currently occupying.

1.6   CHANGING DISPOSITIONS

The processes of change that operate on dispositions within the motivational system are drawn from the broad psychology literature. They include 'automatic' processes (not requiring, although not necessarily excluding, self-conscious thought), such as habituation (becoming less responsive with repeated occurrences of a stimulus), sensitization (becoming more responsive with repeated occurrences of a stimulus), associative learning (underpinning instrumental/operant and Pavlovian/classical conditioning), and imitation learning (mirroring a behaviour). Reflective processes tend to be based on explicit memory, recollected experiences can be subject to processes of inference (induction and deduction) and analysis (calculation, comparison, judgement and estimation).

1.7   TESTING THE THEORY

The first edition of *Theory of Addiction* presented the original formulation of PRIME theory and was published in 2006 (West, 2006). In the years since, a number of studies have been inspired by the theory, and a great many others have been used to interpret various findings relating to addictive behaviour.

A single-item scale of motivation to quit smoking was developed on the basis of PRIME theory to discriminate between differing levels of motives, evaluation and plans. In a large study of the English population, the scale was linearly and sensitively related to the likelihood of a quit attempt 6 months after the baseline assessment (Kotz, Brown & West, 2013). In a similar study, a simple self-reported rating of the strength of urge to smoke over the previous 24 hours was a better predictor of succeeding at stopping smoking than well-established scales based on patterns of consumption (Fidler, Shahab & West, 2011). This result supports the notion from PRIME theory that a repeated powerful motivation is the central feature of addictive behaviour, and that patterns of consumption are indirect symptoms; consumption is also determined by external factors which are liable to have (on average) less influence on the likelihood of success.

The multifaceted nature of motivation proposed by PRIME theory is supported by the unique contributions that enjoyment and dependence make to the process of smoking cessation. There is evidence that wanting to smoke arises from anticipated enjoyment and thereby deters even the attempt to stop while the day-to-day craving that arises from abstinence is dominant in determining the success once attempts have been initiated (McEwen, West & McRobbie, 2008; Fidler & West, 2011).

The relative influence of wanting, duty and intention in predicting quit attempts among smokers has also been examined (Smit, Fidler & West, 2011). The superiority of wanting over duty in predicting quit attempts supports the distal influence of higher-level constructs as postulated by PRIME theory. The theory is relatively agnostic about the relationship between duty and behaviour, and the study reported a negative association. Finally, the study also found that intention had an effect on attempts that was independent of desire. By contrast, PRIME theory argues that intention should be mediated by generating desires. However, the theory also argues that this mediation occurs in the moment in which a plan is enacted and is therefore undetectable by a simple two-stage longitudinal assessment of future plans at baseline and then later behaviour.

The chaotic nature and instability of the motivational system are reflected in a number of recent findings. Meta-analysis suggests that physicians are more effective in promoting quit attempts by offering assistance to all smokers than by advising smokers to quit and offering assistance only to those who express an interest in doing so (Aveyard, Begh, Parsons &West, 2012). Similarly, population surveys have reported that spontaneous or unplanned attempts to stop smoking are common – somewhere between a quarter and half all attempts – and appear to be associated with greater success compared with planned attempts (West & Sohal, 2006; Sendzik, McDonald, Brown, Hammond & Ferrence, 2011), at least among some groups of smokers (Resnicow, Zhou, Scheuermann, Nollen & Ahluwalia, 2014).

Finally, evidence for the importance of identity in the motivational system has accumulated. Positive smoker identity has proved to be an important barrier to making a quit attempt in the future (van den Putte, Yzer, Willemsen & de Bruijn, 2009; Tombor, Shahab, Brown & West, 2013). Considering the role of identity as a high-level source for generating strong desires to maintain behaviour change, one study found that there was a steep decline in the prevalence of a self-reported attraction to smoking and a smoker identity with the length of time a smoker had been abstinent (Vangeli, Stapleton & West, 2010). The implication is that smokers are more likely to relapse without the ongoing source of resolve provided by a non-smoker identity and consequently the existence of a smoker identity becomes rarer the longer people have successfully abstained.

SUGGESTIONS FOR FURTHER READING

Orford, J. (2001). Addiction as excessive appetite. *Addiction, 96*(1), 15–31. doi:10.1046/j.1360-0443.2001.961152.x

West, R., & Brown, J. (2013). *Theory of addiction* (2nd ed.). Oxford: Wiley-Blackwell.

REFERENCES

Aveyard, P., Begh, R., Parsons, A., & West, R. (2012). Brief opportunistic smoking cessation interventions: A systematic review and meta-analysis to compare advice to quit and offer of assistance. *Addiction, 107*(6), 1066–1073. doi: 10.1111/j.1360-0443.2011.03770.x

Balfour, D. K. J. (2004). The neurobiology of tobacco dependence: A preclinical perspective on the role of the dopamine projections to the nucleus accumbens. *Nicotine and Tobacco Research, 6,* 899–912. doi:10.1080/14622200412331324965

Baumeister, R. F., Heatherton, T. F., & Tice, D. M. (1994). *Losing control: How and why people fail at self-regulation.* San Diego: Academic Press.

Baumeister, R. F., & Vohs, K. D. (2007). Self-regulation, ego depletion, and motivation. *Social and Personality Psychology Compass, 1*(1), 115–128. doi: 10.1111/j.1751-9004.2007.00001.x

Becker, G. S., & Murphy, K. M. (1988). A theory of rational addiction. *Journal of Political Economy, 96,* 675–700.

Berridge, K. C., & Robinson, T. E. (2011). Drug addiction as incentive sensitization. In J. Poland & G. Graham (Eds.), *Addiction and responsibility* (pp. 21–54). Cambridge, MA: MIT Press.

Bickel, W. K., DeGrandpre, R. J., & Higgins, S. T. (1995). The behavioral economics of concurrent drug reinforcers: A review and reanalysis of drug self-administration research. *Psychopharmacology (Berl), 118*(3), 250–259.

Bickel, W. K., Miller, M. L., Yi, R., Kowal, B. P., et al. (2007). Behavioral and neuroeconomics of drug addiction: Competing neural systems and temporal discounting processes. *Drug and Alcohol Dependence, 90, Suppl. 1,* S85. doi:http://dx.doi.org/10.1016/j.drugalcdep.2006.09.016

Blaszczynski, A., & Nower, L. (2002). A pathways model of problem and pathological gambling. *Addiction, 97*(5), 487–499. doi:10.1046/j.1360-0443.2002.00015.x

Dalley, J. W., Everitt, B. J., & Robbins, T. W. (2011). Impulsivity, compulsivity, and top-down cognitive control. *Neuron, 69*(4), 680–694. doi:http://dx.doi.org/10.1016/j.neuron.2011.01.020

Deci, E. L., Eghrari, H., Patrick, B. C., & Leone, D. R. (1994). Facilitating internalization: The self-determination theory perspective. *Journal of Personality, 62*(1), 119–142. doi:10.1111/j.1467-6494.1994.tb00797.x

Deci, E. L., & Ryan, R. M. (2012). Overview of self-determination theory. In R. M. Ryan (Ed.), *The Oxford handbook of human motivation* (pp. 85–110). Oxford: Oxford University Press.

Everitt, B. J., Belin, D., Economidou, D., Pelloux, Y., et al. (2008). Neural mechanisms underlying the vulnerability to develop compulsive drug-seeking habits and addiction. *Philosophical Transactions of the Royal Society B: Biological Sciences, 363*(1507), 3125–3135. doi:10.1098/rstb.2008.0089

Everitt, B. J., Dickinson, A., & Robbins, T. W. (2001). The neuropsychological basis of addictive behaviour. *Brain Research Reviews, 36*(2–3), 129–138. doi:http://dx.doi.org/10.1016/S0165-0173(01)00088-1

Everitt, B. J., & Robbins, T. W. (2005). Neural systems of reinforcement for drug addiction: from actions to habits to compulsion. *Nature Neuroscience, 8*(11), 1481–1489. doi:10.1038/nn1579

Fernández-Serrano, M. J., Pérez-García, M., Perales, J. C., & Verdejo-García, A. (2010). Prevalence of executive dysfunction in cocaine, heroin and alcohol users enrolled in therapeutic communities. *European Journal of Pharmacology, 626*(1), 104–112. doi:http://dx.doi.org/10.1016/j.ejphar.2009.10.019

Fidler, J. A., Shahab, L., & West, R. (2011). Strength of urges to smoke as a measure of severity of cigarette dependence: Comparison with the Fagerström Test for Nicotine Dependence and its components. *Addiction, 106*(3), 631–638. doi:10.1111/j.1360-0443.2010.03226.x

Fidler, J. A., & West, R. (2011). Enjoyment of smoking and urges to smoke as predictors of attempts and success of attempts to stop smoking: A longitudinal study. *Drug and Alcohol Dependence, 115*(1–2), 30–34. doi:http://dx.doi.org/10.1016/j.drugalcdep.2010.10.009

Field, M., & Cox, W. M. (2008). Attentional bias in addictive behaviors: A review of its development, causes, and consequences. *Drug Alcohol Dependence, 97*(1–2), 1–20. doi:10.1016/j.drugalcdep.2008.03.030

Gelkopf, M., Levitt, S., & Bleich, A. (2002). An integration of three approaches to addiction and methadone maintenance treatment: The self-medication hypothesis, the disease model and social criticism. *Israel Journal of Psychiatry and Related Sciences, 39*(2), 140–151.

Goldstein, R. Z., & Volkow, N. D. (2011). Dysfunction of the prefrontal cortex in addiction: Neuroimaging findings and clinical implications. *Nature Reviews Neuroscience, 12*(11), 652–669. doi:10.1038/nrn3119.

Hester, R., & Garavan, H. (2004). Executive dysfunction in cocaine addiction: Evidence for discordant frontal, cingulate, and cerebellar activity. *The Journal of Neuroscience, 24*(49), 11017–11022. doi: 10.1523/jneurosci.3321-04.2004

Hyman, S. E., Malenka, R. C., & Nestler, E. J. (2006). Neural mechanisms of addiction: The role of reward-related learning and memory. *Annual Review of Neuroscience, 29*, 565–598. doi:10.1146/annurev.neuro.29.051605.113009

Jellinek, E. M. (1960). *The disease concept of alcoholism*. New Brunswick, NJ: Hillhouse Press.

Jones, B. T., Corbin, W., & Fromme, K. (2001). A review of expectancy theory and alcohol consumption. *Addiction, 96*(1), 57–72. doi:10.1080/09652140020016969

Koob, G. F., & Le Moal, M. (2001). Drug addiction, dysregulation of reward, and allostasis. *Neuropsychopharmacology, 24*(2), 97–129. doi:10.1016/S0893-133X(00)00195-0

Koob, G. F., & Nestler, E. J. (1997). The neurobiology of drug addiction. *The Journal of Neuropsychiatry and Clinical Neurosciences, 9*(3), 482–497. doi:http://dx.doi.org/10.1176/jnp.9.3.482

Koob, G. F., Sanna, P. P., & Bloom, F. E. (1998). Neuroscience of addiction. *Neuron, 21*(3), 467–476. doi:10.1016/S0896-6273(00)80557-7

Koob, G. F., & Volkow, N. D. (2010). Neurocircuitry of addiction. *Neuropsychopharmacology, 35*(1), 217–238. doi: 10.1038/npp.2009.110

Kotz, D., Brown, J., & West, R. (2013). Predictive validity of the Motivation To Stop Scale (MTSS): A single-item measure of motivation to stop smoking. *Drug Alcohol Dependence*, *128*(1–2), 15–19. doi:10.1016/j.drugalcdep.2012.07.012

Lewis, M. J. (1990). Alcohol: mechanisms of addiction and reinforcement. *Advances in Alcohol and Substance Abuse*, *9*(1–2), 47–66. doi:10.1300/J251v09n01_04

Lubman, D. I., Yucel, M., & Pantelis, C. (2004). Addiction, a condition of compulsive behaviour? Neuroimaging and neuropsychological evidence of inhibitory dysregulation. *Addiction*, *99*(12), 1491–1502. doi:10.1111/j.1360-0443.2004.00808.x

Madoz-Gurpide, A., Blasco-Fontecilla, H., Baca-Garcia, E., & Ochoa-Mangado, E. (2011). Executive dysfunction in chronic cocaine users: An exploratory study. *Drug Alcohol Dependence*, *117*(1), 55–58. doi: 10.1016/j.drugalcdep.2010.11.030

McCusker, C. G. (2001). Cognitive biases and addiction: An evolution in theory and method. *Addiction*, *96*(1), 47–56. doi:10.1046/j.1360-0443.2001.961474.x

McEwen, A., West, R., & McRobbie, H. (2008). Motives for smoking and their correlates in clients attending stop smoking treatment services. *Nicotine & Tobacco Research*, *10*(5), 843–850. doi:10.1080/14622200802027248

Melchior, C. L., & Tabakoff, B. (1984). A conditioning model of alcohol tolerance. *Recent Developments in Alcohol, 2*, 5–16.

Michie, S., van Stralen, M. M., & West, R. (2011) The Behaviour Change Wheel: A new method for characterising and designing behaviour change interventions. *Implementation Science, 6*, 42. doi:10.1186/1748-5908-6-42

Miller, E. K., & Cohen, J. D. (2001). An integrative theory of prefrontal cortex function. *Annual Review of Neuroscience*, *24*(1), 167–202. doi:10.1146/annurev.neuro.24.1.167

Mogg, K., Field, M., & Bradley, B. P. (2005). Attentional and approach biases for smoking cues in smokers: An investigation of competing theoretical views of addiction. *Psychopharmacology, 180*, 333–341. doi:10.1007/s00213-005-2158-x

O'Brien, C. P., Childress, A. R., McLellan, A. T., & Ehrman, R. (1992). A learning model of addiction. *Research Publications – Association for Research in Nervous and Mental Disease, 70*, 157–177.

Orford, J. (2001). Addiction as excessive appetite. *Addiction*, *96*(1), 15–31. doi:10.1046/j.1360-0443.2001.961152.x

Resnicow, K., Zhou, Y., Scheuermann, T. S., Nollen, N. L., & Ahluwalia, J. S. (2014). Unplanned quitting in a triethnic sample of U.S. smokers. *Nicotine & Tobacco Research*, *16*(6), 759–765. doi:10.1093/ntr/ntt272

Robinson, T. E., & Berridge, K. C. (2003). Addiction. *Annual Review of Psychology*, *54*(1), 25–53. doi:10.1146/annurev.psych.54.101601.145237

Ryan, R. M., & Deci, E. L. (2000). Self-determination theory and the facilitation of intrinsic motivation, social development, and well-being. *American Psychologist*, *55*(1), 68–78.

Schulteis, G., & Koob, G. F. (1996). Reinforcement processes in opiate addiction: A homeostatic model. *Neurochemical Research*, *21*(11), 1437–1454. doi:10.1007/BF02532385

Sendzik, T., McDonald, P. W., Brown, K. S., Hammond, D., & Ferrence, R. (2011). Planned quit attempts among Ontario smokers: Impact on abstinence. *Addiction*, *106*(11), 2005–2013. doi:10.1111/j.1360-0443.2011.03498.x

Skog, O. J. (2000). Addicts' choice. *Addiction*, *95*(9), 1309–1314. doi:10.1046/j.1360-0443.2000.95913091.x

Skog, O. J. (2003). Addiction: Definition and mechanisms. In R. E. Vuchinich, & N. Heather (Eds.), *Choice, behavioural economics and addiction* (pp. 157–175). Amsterdam: Pergamon.

Slovic, P., Finucane, M., Peters, E., & MacGregor, D. G. (2002). The affect heuristic. In T. Gilovich, D. Griffin, & D. Kahneman (Eds.), *Intuitive judgment: Heuristics and biases*. New York: Cambridge University Press.

Slovic, P., Finucane, M. L., Peters, E., & MacGregor, D. G. (2007). The affect heuristic. *European Journal of Operational Research, 177*(3), 1333–1352. doi:http://dx.doi.org/10.1016/j.ejor.2005.04.006

Smit, E. S., Fidler. J. A., & West, R. (2011). The role of desire, duty and intention in predicting attempts to quit smoking. *Addiction, 106*(4), 844–851. doi:10.1111/j.1360-0443.2010.03317.x

Solomon, R. L. (1980). The Opponent-Process Theory of acquired motivation: The costs of pleasure and the benefits of pain. *The American Psychologist, 35*(8), 691–712.

Solomon, R. L., & Corbit, J. D. (1973). An Opponent-Process Theory of motivation. II. Cigarette addiction. *Journal of Abnormal Psychology, 81*(2), 158–171.

Solomon, R. L., & Corbit, J. D. (1974). An Opponent-Process Theory of motivation. I. Temporal dynamics of affect. *Psychological Review, 81*(2), 119–145.

Tiffany, S. T., & Drobes, D. J. (1991). The development and initial validation of a questionnaire on smoking urges. *British Journal of Addiction, 86*(11), 1467–1476. doi:10.1111/j.1360-0443.1991.tb01732.x

Tombor, I., Shahab, L., Brown, J., & West, R. (2013). Positive smoker identity as a barrier to quitting smoking: Findings from a national survey of smokers in England. *Drug and Alcohol Dependence, 133*(2), 740–745. doi:http://dx.doi.org/10.1016/j.drugalcdep.2013.09.001

van den Putte, B., Yzer, M., Willemsen, M. C., & de Bruijn, G.-J. (2009). The effects of smoking self-identity and quitting self-identity on attempts to quit smoking. *Health Psychology, 28*(5), 535–544. doi:10.1037/a0015199

Vangeli, E., Stapleton, J., & West, R. (2010). Residual attraction to smoking and smoker identity following smoking cessation. *Nicotine & Tobacco Research, 12*(8), 865–869. doi:10.1093/ntr/ntq104

Vohs, K. D., & Baumeister, R. F. (2011). *Handbook of self-regulation: Research, theory, and applications.* New York: The Guilford Press.

Waddington, C. (1977). *Tools for thought: How to understand and apply the latest scientific techniques of problem solving.* New York: Basic Books.

Weiss, F., & Koob, G. F. (2001). Drug addiction: Functional neurotoxicity of the brain reward systems. *Neurotoxicity Research, 3*(1), 145–156.

West, R. (2006). *Theory of addiction* (1st ed.). Oxford: Blackwell Publishing.

West, R., & Brown, J. (2013). *Theory of addiction* (2nd ed.). Oxford: Wiley-Blackwell.

West, R., & Sohal, T. (2006). 'Catastrophic' pathways to smoking cessation: Findings from national survey. *British Medical Journal, 332*, 458–460. doi:http://dx.doi.org/10.1136/bmj.38723.573866.AE

White, N. M. (1996). Addictive drugs as reinforcers: Multiple partial actions on memory systems. *Addiction, 91*(7), 921–950. doi:10.1046/j.1360-0443.1996.9179212.x

Wise, R. A., & Bozarth, M. A. (1987). A psychomotor stimulant theory of addiction. *Psychological Review, 94*(4), 469–492.

2 An Attachment-Informed Approach to Working with Addiction

DAVID CURRAN[1] AND MANI MEHDIKHANI[2]

[1]Queens University Belfast, Northern Ireland
[2]Greater Manchester West Trust's Specialist Services Network Manchester UK

CHAPTER OUTLINE

2.1 INTRODUCTION TO ATTACHMENT

Attachment theory, particularly as it pertains to child development, is often closely associated with the work of John Bowlby and Mary Ainsworth (Bretherton, 1992; Höfler & Kooyman, 1996). From its inception, Bowlby broadly drew his inspiration from the fields of ethology (attachment as an evolutionarily adaptive behaviour; animal models of imprinting), cognitive and information processing, developmental psychology (touching on the works of Piaget and others), and psychoanalysis (particularly object relation theory) (Bretherton, 1992) to develop the key tenets of attachment theory. In turn, attachment theory has come to touch on, and in many cases transform, these and other related fields of studies.

Bowlby argued that far from being 'immature psychological defences' (as they were commonly understood in the psychoanalytic discourse of the mid-1950s), what are now described as attachment behaviours in children (e.g. crying, clinging, etc.) were in fact the end-product of an evolutionary process whose outcome was to ensure that offspring were able to adjust their proximity to an attachment figure. As Wallin (2007, p. 11) has noted: 'Bowlby understood that the primal nature of attachment as a motivational system is rooted in the infant's absolute need to maintain physical proximity.' This is because in many animal systems (including mammalian and primate), a degree of parental care and investment in the offspring is thought to be crucially important to their survival and future reproductive success (Trivers, 1972; Wallin, 2007). Later refinement of the theory introduced the concept of 'felt security' (comforting availability) highlighting not just proximity to the caregiver but the offspring's internal experiences related to the caregiver (mood, fantasies, perception of the caregiver's past availability, etc.; Wallin, 2007). Bowlby overturned the then conventional thinking of the time, partly based on Freudian and Behaviourist views, that it was the parent's gratification of a child's physiological needs that leads to the child forming a 'dependence' on the parent. He also suggested that the 'good object' of psychoanalytic theory was in reality the 'internal working model' (IWM or cognitive/affective schema) a person has of an attachment figure that is perceived as being both accessible and attentive to one's needs. Bowlby thus saw attachment as a biological drive and talked of an attachment behaviour system.

Mary Ainsworth, a developmental psychologist and researcher, has been described as the other key early figure in developing our understanding of attachment in children. Ainsworth and her colleagues are best known for developing an experimental research methodology known as the 'Strange Situation' which examined key processes in mother and infant attachment (Ainsworth, Blehar, Waters & Wall, 1978). These experimental procedures involved separating and bringing back together mothers and their 12-month-old infants in a specially constructed laboratory setting. They found that around 60% of the infants behaved in a normative manner (as predicted by Bowlby's theory) in that, although distressed by the absence of the mother, the infants actively sought the mother on her return and were soothed by her. These children were deemed to be secure in their attachment. Another group of children showed signs of extreme upset in the sudden realization of the absence of the mother. On being reunited, they showed ambivalence about the return of the parent simultaneously seeking comfort and showing anger for being abandoned. This attachment pattern was called anxious-resistant. A third group of children showed no upset or distress when the parent left the room and tended to avoid contact with the parent on their return; this third group were described as having an avoidant style of attachment. A fourth category of attachment was later suggested by Main and Solomon (1990), namely, that of disorganized/disoriented attachment. It is thought that children with this type of attachment style may both seek contact with an attachment figure and at the same time fear them due to past episodes of neglect or physical abuse by caregivers.

From the above it emerged that there may be a number of different styles or patterns of early attachment, and that they might be linked to parents' sensitivity and responsiveness to their children's needs (in their first year of life). Among Ainsworth's key contributions in this area was the concept of the 'secure base'. It has been suggested that the attachment figure provides a secure base from which a child is able to explore their environment and to act as a safe haven to return to for comfort in times of high anxiety or distress (Bowlby, 1988; Wallin, 2007). This use of the attachment figure as a base to safely explore the environment is seen to be part of the exploratory behavioural system which is connected to the attachment system (Wallin, 2007). It has been suggested that the securely attached person can experience attachment insecurity as a result of subsequent life events and changes in the relationship with both early and later romantic attachment figures (Thompson, Lamb & Estes, 1982). This is one reason Bowlby used the term 'Working' model, in order to highlight the fact that the processes involved in a person's cognitive representation of the self and others are dynamic and can alter depending on experiences occurring in the context of future relationships. Nevertheless, although secure or insecure attachment cannot guarantee either a positive or negative life outcome (Fagot & Kavanagh, 1990), early secure attachment may position a person to recover more quickly from future adversity.

The work of Mary Main arguably launched what Karen (1994) has termed the 'second revolution in attachment studies'. Main and colleagues developed the Adult Attachment Interview which paved the way for an exploration of attachment experiences beyond childhood (Main, Kaplan & Cassidy, 1985). While the research stream by Bowlby, Ainsworth, and to some extent Main, focused on parent-child attachment, in the 1980s, researchers began to consider the impact of attachment experiences in adulthood. This other line of enquiry, into adult attachment (initiated by researchers such as Hazan & Shaver, 1987) considered that past attachment experiences might extend into adulthood and with respect to romantic relationships. Hazan and Shaver (1987) noting the parallels with attachment processes in children (e.g. secure base effect, engagement in intimate contact, etc.), viewed the bond between romantic partners as an extension of the same attachment behavioural system as envisaged by Bowlby. The line of enquiry by Kim Bartholomew (1997) further elaborated and refined earlier investigations into adult attachment patterns.

Where Bartholomew departs from the other models of adult attachment is in the formulation of a four-category model based on two dimensions (Griffin & Bartholomew, 1994; Bartholomew, 1997). Bartholomew's four-category model was based on Bowlby's concept of the Internal Working Model (IWM) and assumed that people hold some combination of either positive or negative views towards the self and towards the other (e.g. those who hold a positive view of both the self and the other are said to be securely attached). Another group of researchers (Brennan, Clark & Shaver, 1998) have proposed a similar four-category and two-dimensional model, with the two dimensions based on attachment-related anxiety and attachment-related avoidance (e.g. those who have both low attachment-related anxiety and low attachment-related avoidance are said to be securely attached).

The work of Fonagy and his colleagues over the past two decades has further enhanced our understanding of the mechanisms by which difficult attachment experiences with a primary carer in childhood can impact on psychological well-being and lead to a range of difficulties in later life. The concept of mentalization (or reflective function) has been identified as key mediating variables in this relationship (see Section 2.2.1 on Parenting). Sensitive and responsive caregivers who model self-awareness and encourage their child to be aware of their own thoughts and feelings, and to think about the internal worlds of others, will help foster a good capacity to mentalize (Fonagy, Target, Steele, & Steele, 1998).

2.2 ATTACHMENT AND PSYCHOPATHOLOGY

As has been noted, secure attachment to a primary caregiver in childhood may confer a degree of immunity against the emergence of psychopathology in later life. The potential for attachment experiences in childhood to influence psychological functioning in adulthood is well established, with a strong relationship found between attachment style and various forms of psychopathology (Shorey & Snyder, 2006). Mickelson, Kessler and Shaver (1997) using a nationally representative sample of American adults, found elevations in insecure attachment was associated with DSM-III-R mood and anxiety disorders. A recent review of over 200 studies, which used a variety of methodologies and both clinical and non-clinical samples, concluded that there was strong evidence for an association between insecure attachment styles and the full range of common mental health problems across the continuum in terms of severity of presentation from mild to severe (Mikulincer & Shaver, 2007).

Strong evidence also exists for a relationship between insecure attachment styles and most forms of personality disorder (Meyer & Pilkonis, 2001; 2005). In their factor analytic twin study, Crawford et al. (2007) identified two overarching personality dimensions: 'emotional dysregulation' (highly correlated with neuroticism) and 'inhibitedness' (strongly correlated with low extraversion/openness to experience) which were found to be particularly pronounced in individuals with insecure attachment styles. Anxious attachment was associated with 'emotional dysregulation' and avoidant attachment was related to 'inhibitedness'. Crawford et al. (2007) have suggested that most forms of Axis II disturbance are strongly influenced by either anxious or avoidant attachment styles. Many have pointed to the interpersonal difficulties so evident in personality disorder as a key factor in this relationship (Steele & Siever, 2010).

The pathway by which attachment insecurity exerts an influence on Axis I and II disorders is thought to be complex. Contemporary views in attachment research, acknowledge the range of factors which can interact and influence the emergence of mental health problems (Fonagy & Luyten, 2009; van IJzendoorn, Caspers, Bakermans-Kranenburg, Beach & Philibert, 2010; Nolte, Guiney, Fonagy, Mayes, & Luyten, 2011). Attempts to understand the nature of this relationship have pointed to the potential importance of common third factors, such as experiences of parenting (Brennan & Shaver, 1998), or experiences of childhood abuse (Johnson et al., 2001). There is also a general consensus that attachment insecurities can exert profound effects in terms of an individual's capacity to effectively regulate their emotions, and engage in helpful and fulfilling relationships. Maintaining good psychological health and well-being is likely to be challenged when faced with such difficulties.

2.2.1 *Parenting*

The potential for parenting style to influence the formation of secure attachment or otherwise has been explored by several authors, and this relationship is likely to be reciprocal in nature. Even without the experience of trauma, abuse, or neglect, differences in parenting practices have been noted to have the potential to significantly impact on subsequent patterns of coping in adult life. This can be accentuated when there is some form of parental psychopathology, or when a parent has their own unresolved childhood trauma experiences (Sher, Grekin & Williams, 2005). Parenting practices are also thought to influence the transgenerational transmission of attachment styles. The tendency for attachment patterns to be transmitted across generations is well recognized (Main et al., 1985; van IJzendoorn, 1995). Though the mechanism by which such transmission occurs is unclear, both conscious (e.g. parenting behaviour/style), and unconscious (e.g. unresolved loss/trauma on the part of the parent) factors have been identified as influential (Wallin, 2007). In a model put forward by Rholes, Simpson, Blakely, Lanigan and Allen (1997), parental insecure attachment can result in the development of maladaptive parenting styles which can have a direct influence on the attachment experience of the child.

Fonagy (2001) has highlighted mentalization (or reflective function) as an important mediating variable in the transgenerational transmission of attachment styles, and the importance of the 'mentalizing capacity' on the part of the parent. Individuals with a good mentalizing capacity will be able to reflect on their own internal world as well as the internal world of others. The potential for 'emotionally cold parenting' to impede emotional regulation capacity has also been highlighted by several authors (Turner & Paivio, 2002; Polusny, Dickinson, Murdoch & Thuras, 2008).

Using the dimensions of responsiveness (the degree to which the parent responds to the needs/wishes of the child), and demandingness (parental expectations in terms of compliance to rules, and behaviour more generally), Baumrind (1971; 1991) identified three parenting typologies: authoritative, authoritarian and permissive. Using the same two dimensions, Maccoby and Martin (1983) identified a fourth possible parenting style – neglectful (low responsiveness and undemanding). Children exposed to this type of disengaged/unresponsive parenting were more likely to have academic and conduct problems and impaired psychosocial development. Baumrind (1971; 1991) found the children of authoritarian parents (low responsiveness, high demand-ingness) were more likely to be irritable, moody, and distrustful of others, and in adolescence to have poorer social and cognitive outcomes. Permissive parenting (high responsiveness, low demandingness) was associated with dependent children, who were more likely to be demanding, impulsive and aggressive. In contrast, children of authoritative parents (moderate responsiveness and demandingness) seemed to fare best. These children were exposed to firm (not rigid) and responsive (not indul-gent) parenting and were typically found to be more friendly and socially competent, and better equipped for dealing with their environment. It has been suggested that authoritative parenting shares similar qualities and characteristics to the approach thought to foster secure attachment (Karavasilis, Doyle & Markiewicz, 2003).

2.2.2   Trauma

A growing body of research has enhanced our understanding of the interplay between traumatic experiences and attachment relationships (e.g. Schore, 2001; Nolte et al., 2011). The interaction between the variables is likely to be ongoing and dynamic in nature throughout childhood. Findings from the Adverse Childhood Experiences study (ACE Study; Felitti et al., 1998) make it clear that there are significant long-term ramifications accruing from such exposure. As noted previously in this chapter, secure attachment is likely to serve a protective function, lead to increased resilience, and potentially moder-ate the impact of exposure to trauma (Gunnar & Quevedo, 2007; Breidenstine, Bailey, Zeanah & Larrieu, 2011). Such exposure may also increase vulnerability to psychological difficulties in later life (Gunnar & Quevedo, 2007; Luyten & Van Houdenhove, 2013).

Some authors interested in the cumulative effects of childhood adversity have considered concepts such allostasis and the 'allostatic load model' as potentially use-ful explanatory mechanisms in understanding the response to early trauma (Ganzel, Morris & Wethington, 2010). Allostasis seeks to help us understand how the body manages stress and regulates physiological and psychological 'wear and tear'. In this model, the human body is recognized as adaptable, however, when exposed to a high level of allostatic load (or overload), there are potential impacts on neurobiology, neuroendocrinology and brain development (McEwen & Wingfield, 2003; Nolte et al., 2011). Thus, high levels of childhood adversity (repeated stress or trauma) may interact with other factors such as attachment to influence the development of later psychopathology (Fonagy & Luyten, 2009; van IJzendoorn et al., 2010; Nolte et al., 2011; Luyten, Van Houdenhove, Lemma, Target & Fonagy, 2012).

2.3   ATTACHMENT AND ADDICTION

There is a growing field of research dedicated to exploring how attachment might influence the development of addiction. A range of difficulties have been identi-fied in individuals who have experienced attachment issues, such as interpersonal functioning deficits, alexithymia, and emotion regulation problems, and other forms of psychological distress. Emotion regulation difficulties are a core feature of both insecure attachment styles and substance use disorders, and have been of particular interest to some researchers (Newcomb, 1995; Weinberg, Rahdert, Colliver & Glantz, 1998; Magai, 1999; Belsky, 2002).

Children learn how to regulate their emotional state through their relationship with a sensitive and responsive caregiver. When a child is in distress, the caregiver will help to calm and soothe, attending to both their physical and emotional needs. Over time the child will gradually learn to use strategies to self-regulate (self-soothe) when faced with distress. Attachment theorists posit that childhood attachment experiences become 'internalized' and the cognitive-motivational schemata (IWMs) that develop are highly influential in terms of subsequent exposure to stress. When a child has been exposed to unhelpful attachment experiences, they are more likely to develop and engage in maladaptive strategies for managing distress such as avoidance or anxiety (Mallinckrodt & Wei, 2005), and be more vulnerable to the development of stress-related disorders (Gunnar & Quevedo, 2007; Luyten & Van Houdenhove, 2013).

2.3.1   *Emotion Regulation*

Bateman and Fonagy (2008) have suggested that substance misuse may be an attempt to ameliorate experiences of 'dysregulation' of emotional state. It is the potential for substances to help regulate emotions which has led some theorists to attempt to understand Substance Use Disorder (SUD) within an attachment framework (e.g. Zinberg, 1975; Höfler & Kooyman, 1996), with some going so far as to explicitly conceptualize SUD as an attachment disorder (Flores, 2004; Khantzian, 2012). It has been noted that many individuals with a SUD have difficulties establishing and maintaining mutually satisfying relationships (a by-product of their own attachment histories). A number of other authors have suggested that individuals with insecure attachment histories may seek external means to assist with emotional regulation, rather than seeking support from others (Brennan & Shaver, 1995; Cooper, Shaver & Collins, 1998; Finzi-Dottan, Cohen, Iwaniec, Sapir & Weizman, 2003; McNally, Palfai, Levine, & Moore, 2003). Some individuals may reach a point where they seek to avoid intimacy or rejection from others. As a result, when psychological distress is experienced, they can look to external sources (or substances) as a means of managing their emotional state (Flores, 2004). Substances will differ in their physiological and psychological effects (Suh, Ruffins, Robins, Albanese & Khantzian, 2008), but all have the potential to up- or down-regulate affect. Zinberg (1975) suggested that substances can take on 'surrogacy' qualities, and provide a valid alternative method of attaining a form of security, as opposed to relating to others. Ultimately the substance becomes an effective strategy for managing difficult emotions, thus negating the need for closeness or emotional support from others.

From a theoretical perspective it has been proposed that, over time, individuals can come to form an attachment relationship with a given substance (Zinberg, 1975), especially when a substance comes to fulfil important functions such as containment of psychological distress (Reading, 2002). Reading has proposed that a substance can also come to be experienced as providing a 'secure base' and satisfying psychological needs. Given a substance's capacity to regulate an individual's emotional state (e.g. anxiety reduction, elevation of mood), continued use can be encouraged and the potential for a more dependent pattern of use can emerge (Zinberg, 1975). It is also possible that with repeated use, the relationship with the substance can become incorporated into an individual's IWM. Subsequently the attachment behavioural system may be activated by separation (abstinence from substance), and continued substance use becomes the means to return to the secure base experience (Höfler & Kooyman, 1996).

2.3.2 *Alexithymia*

The term alexithymia was first introduced by Sifneos (1977) and is characterized by marked deficits in terms of emotional insight and reflective capacity (Thorberg & Lyvers, 2010). Other core features of the construct include an externally orientated thinking style, and a significant lack of imaginal capacity (Bagby et al., 2009). Attempts to understand the development of alexithymia have suggested that early attachment experiences are a potentially influential mechanism (De Rick & Vanheule, 2007; Thorberg & Lyvers, 2006; Thorberg et al., 2009; Thorberg et al., 2011).

In a SUD population, De Rick and Vanheule (2007) found that individuals with insecure attachment styles were more likely to experience difficulties with alexithymia (difficulties verbalizing/communicating emotions). As with emotion dysregulation, alexithymia has been identified as a significant risk factor for the development of a range of mental health problems. In individuals with alcohol dependence, it has been found that those who also experience alexithymia will have a more severe clinical profile and a poorer long-term prognosis (Loas, Fremaux, Otmani, Lecercle & Delahousse, 1997; Sakuraba, Kubo, Komoda & Yamana, 2005). Additionally, Thorberg et al. (2011) have found a strong relationship between alexithymia and cravings for alcohol. They posit that an awareness of such difficulties is important in terms of treatment planning, and have suggested the routine assessment of such difficulties especially when attachment difficulties are suspected.

2.3.3 *Interpersonal Difficulties*

Existing research would offer support to the view that substance-misusing individuals with insecure attachment styles experience greater difficulties with regards to interpersonal relationships, which will have implications for psychological well-being (Thorberg & Lyvers, 2006; 2010). Doumas et al. (2006) found fearful and preoccupied attachment styles in particular were related to interpersonal functioning difficulties.

Particular forms of attachment insecurity will impact on interpersonal functioning in different ways. Individuals who have a predominantly avoidant (or dismissing) attachment style (the style most commonly reported in individuals with addiction problems) often score highly on measures of emotional suppression and have difficulty in forming and maintaining friendships. Close or intimate relationships are also often found to be difficult with individuals wary of forming relationships which have depth or could be emotionally demanding (Howe, 2011). Those with an anxious (or preoccupied) attachment style will often be characterized by feelings of low self-esteem and anxiety. They typically will have experienced others in the past as unpredictable and inconsistent. As a result, they will seek to maintain a high level of emotional involvement and emotional dependence on others in relationships, and this can inevitably put relationships under strain. However, such individuals are more likely to remain in relationships even when they are unhelpful (Davila & Bradbury, 2001). Those with a fearful avoidant attachment style (or unresolved state of mind) are also at high risk in terms of interpersonal functioning. Typically they will fear intimacy, and being socially isolated, and will cycle between seeking out emotional involvement with others, only to be overwhelmed by anxieties about rejection which lead to withdrawal from these same relationships (Howe, 2011).

2.3.4   Co-Morbid Mental Health Problems

Research focused on SUD populations would suggest insecure attachment styles are associated with higher levels of psychological difficulties, particularly anxiety and depression (Schindler et al., 2005; Doumas et al., 2006; De Rick & Vanheule, 2007; De Rick et al., 2009). Evidence emerging from some of these studies would suggest that the presence of such mental health issues is independent of the severity, onset and duration of the SUD (Schindler et al., 2005; De Rick, Vanheule & Verhaeghe, 2009). This lends support to the notion that substances can come to be used as a means of managing psychological distress (or regulating emotion).

2.4   ATTACHMENT STYLES IN CLINICAL SAMPLES

Existing research in substance-misusing populations would indicate that a higher proportion of insecure attachment styles are evident within clinical samples (Schindler et al., 2005; Doumas, Blasey & Mitchell, 2006), which has led some to postulate that insecure attachment may initiate the pathway for substance misuse in later life (Vungkhanching, Sher, Jackson & Parra, 2004). Schindler et al. (2005) reviewed the findings of 11 studies which explored the relationship between SUD and specific attachment styles in largely university and community samples. The studies varied in terms of the assessment methods employed (e.g. Adult Attachment Interview (AAI) by Main, Goldwyn & Hesse, 2003; Hazan and Shaver Self-Report (HSSR) by Hazan & Shaver, 1987) and self-report measures (Bartholomew 1990), and in several of the studies the SUD–attachment relationship was not the primary focus. Schindler et al. (2005) found the strongest empirical link existed between fearful/avoidant attachment styles and substance-related difficulties.

More recent studies have sought to explore this relationship in individuals engaged in treatment for substance-related difficulties, with evidence for a variety of attachment difficulties emerging. Across studies, the majority of individuals have been found to be experiencing some level of impairment to their attachment system (De Rick et al., 2009). In an inpatient sample, Francis, Kaiser and Deaver (2003) found a dismissing attachment style (44.2%) to be predominant, with only 18.6% classified as having a secure attachment style. When compared to a control group, fearful and preoccupied attachment styles were also more evident in this sample. Other studies have found the preoccupied (or anxious-ambivalent) attachment styles (corresponding categories in the three- and four-category attachment models) to be prominent in substance-misusing populations (Schindler et al., 2005; Molnar, Sadava, DeCourville & Perrier, 2010). However, as with non-clinical populations, the most consistent finding has been the presence of the fearful (or 'avoidant') attachment style (Schindler et al., 2005; Doumas et al., 2006). This is of importance given that individuals with this particular pattern of attachment insecurity (characterized by high levels of anxiety and avoidance in relationships), are more likely to desire closeness in relationships with others but encounter difficulties with regards to trusting and relying on others (Shaver & Mikulincer, 2002). In addition, they are less likely to possess the deactivating strategies, associated with dismissive attachment styles, which can help to defend against psychological distress. This increases the likelihood that they will seek to regulate their emotional state through the use of substances.

While the evidence base is inconsistent, there is also a suggestion that the degree of impairment to the attachment system is predictive of the severity and duration of substance misuse (Schindler et al., 2005). In individuals with alcohol problems, Thorberg et al. (2011) found insecure attachment to be predictive of more strongly held alcohol-related cognitions.

2.5 ASSESSMENT AND FORMULATION THROUGH AN ATTACHMENT LENS

A key aim of the assessment process will be to arrive at a shared understanding or formulation of the client's difficulties. The methods by which attachment can be assessed are varied and include the clinical interview (judgements based on attachment narrative and autobiographical memory), psychometric measures, and information gleaned from counter-transferential responses.

As has been noted, individuals with difficult attachment histories can experience problems regulating their emotional state, recognizing and expressing their feelings, and forming and maintaining relationships (Doumas et al., 2006; Powers et al., 2006; Thorberg & Lyvers, 2006; 2010). The presence of such difficulties is important to determine at the point of assessment, as this will help to inform the formulation and will be useful in terms of devising an individually tailored treatment plan.

2.5.1 The Clinical Interview

The clinical interview usually provides the first opportunity to gather information regarding an individual's formative experiences and establish a sense of their early attachment relationships. In exploring a person's narratives, it is important for the clinician to keep in mind the relationship between the client's addictive behaviours and the impact of disruption to attachment processes in the context of developmental attachment milestones.

As previously highlighted, in the early stages of attachment development (during infancy), a number of both relational and external factors can affect the stability of the affectional bond between caregiver and child; these include parenting style, trauma, parental mental health, employment patterns, anti-social behaviour (including criminality) and substance misuse / dependence. Other significant life events (such as the loss of a parental figure through death or divorce, poverty, parental illness or hospitalization, etc.), parental satisfaction (or dissatisfaction) with the marital relationship, and child care arrangements (nursery and pre-school) also exert an influence on both attachment classification and stability.

During late childhood / early adolescence, negative life events can continue to exert a powerful influence on attachment styles. This in many ways may be the critical attachment stage in a client's addiction career. At this stage there is a gradual transition from the parent as the primary attachment figure to greater emotional investment in close friends and potential romantic partners (Hazan & Shaver, 1987). Höfler and Kooyman (1996, p. 517) have argued that alcohol and other narcotic substances may come to be implicitly represented by lonely, isolated and unloved adolescents as providing 'a secure base allowing conflict-free proximity seeking'. There is some evidence that substance use among later addicts frequently commences in early to mid-adolescence and that the earlier the age of onset of use, the more problematic the addictive behaviour becomes later on in life (see Warner & White, 2003).

When seeking to explore a client's attachment history, both how information is relayed by the client (process) and what is actually said (content) should be considered carefully. When asked about early experience of primary caregivers, how much detail (or psychological depth) is offered in the account provided? Are stories excessively brief / succinct with an emphasis on normalizing their experience? Does retelling the story evoke strong emotion or no emotional expression? There are a number of problems with relying purely on client's attachment narratives. Memories (including attachment memories), as we now well understand, are constructed, tend to be subject to revision in light of later events and information, and are subject to cognitive bias. To counter this, if possible, it may also be useful to obtain 'collateral' information from the clients' partners, parents and siblings about their early history. As part of this process it may also be helpful to undertake a genogram or family tree (Bowlby, 1994). This can be used not only to explore relationships with a person's extended family but to also explore patterns in the person's relationship history.

According to Bowlby (1994, p. 169), another 'major difficulty in the process of assessment is that the information given may omit vital facts or falsify them'. Both the client and their attachment figures may be invested in this process (either unwittingly or deliberately). For parents, it may be painful to recall or admit to episodes of rejection (or threats to abandon), neglect or abuse, suicide attempts, parental conflict or aggression, etc. They may view the assessment as criticism or an attempt to fix blame. The clients may also feel that they were to blame for such episodes, feel protective towards the parent, and collude with them in 'keeping the family secret', rather than attributing their problems to some other cause (Bowlby, 1994). It is important that clinicians be aware of the above dynamic and also be careful not to turn the interview into an opportunity for the client to apportion the blame for their difficulties onto their attachment figures.

2.5.2 Psychometric Approaches

Two principal traditions exist with regard to the assessment of adult attachment using psychometric measures. One approach is influenced by developmental theory and is particularly interested in how adults' representation of attachment is influenced by childhood relationships with primary caregivers. Main and her research group developed the Adult Attachment Interview (George, Kaplan & Main, 1985) for this purpose. This approach was closely tied to the work initiated by Ainsworth (including the use of the three-category approach pioneered by her own research group) and came from a clinical background with a focus on the use of interviews or behavioural observations (Bartholomew & Shaver, 1998). The psychometric measures and methodologies most associated with the above approach include the Strange Situation, AAI, and AAI Q-Sort (Waters & Deane, 1985).

The other approach focuses on adult attachment orientation, using self-report measures such as the Relationship Questionnaire (RQ; Bartholomew & Horowitz, 1991), the Relationship Scale Questionnaire (RSQ; Griffin & Bartholomew, 1994) and Experiences in Close Relationships Revised (ECR-R; Fraley, Waller, & Brennan, 2000). The different developmental trajectories leading adults towards feeling more or less secure are influenced by factors such as the loss of key attachment figures, the quality of peer and romantic relationships and the formation of therapeutic alliances with health professionals among others (Reading, 2002). It is argued then that one's IWM of a parent can diverge from those of the romantic partner so that 'a person may feel and act one way in one kind of relationship and a different way in another' (Bartholomew & Shaver, 1998, p. 41). Additionally, Flores (2004, p. 145) has suggested that the four-category model (Bartholomew, 1990) may be the most 'accurate' and useful method in an addictions milieu.

2.5.3 Transference and Counter-Transference

One of the key ideas common to both psychodynamic and attachment approaches is that as adults we tend to replicate (aspects of) early relationships with our caregivers in the context of later relationships. It is these behaviours which in therapy are often referred to as the client's transference. It is suggested here that these behaviours and the corresponding therapist responses (their counter-transference) may provide information regarding the clients' attachment profile (Ligiero & Gelso, 2002). Clinicians working in addictions settings, particularly in multidisciplinary teams, may also wish to explore the counter-transferential responses of their colleagues to the client.

Exploring the client's history of contact with services may prove helpful in understanding their attachment style; are they less interested in the treatment and their recovery, and more preoccupied with maintaining a contact relationship with their worker? Have they repeatedly presented to and been discharged from the service? Has the client remained in the service for a long period? Does the client make frequent complaints about their worker or become aggressive? Clues to a client's attachment orientation may also emerge from an exploration of the manifest content versus the latent content of their communication with their therapist. It is quite common for clients to begin a session with a story (often a complaint) ostensibly about another professional in a 'caregiving' role (e.g. their GP or some other healthcare professional). Hidden behind the manifest content of such a story is a parallel complaint about the 'caregiver' (psychologist, counsellor or key worker) sitting in front of the client. Such narratives often contain a number of attachment-related kernel statements about not receiving special or perfect care; complaints about 'feeling let down' (what has been referred to as 'attachment injury'; Vetere, 2011), fears that they are wasting the clinician's time, worries about being discharged (rejected or abandoned), complaints that they are not being 'listened to' by their clinicians, that they have to 'tell their stories' multiple times to different professionals, that clinicians do not 'really care' and are only 'doing it for the money', etc.). The above may help determine key information about the client's attachment profile.

2.6   TREATMENT IMPLICATIONS

Attachment difficulties operate on a continuum and may be present to greater or lesser extents in different individuals. At the extreme end of the spectrum, adults with a history of insecure attachment are likely to experience difficulties in a range of domains, including: interpersonal functioning; recognizing, identifying, and expressing affect; emotional literacy and capacity to manage negative emotions; low self-esteem and other mental health issues; and loss/trauma issues related to previous (formative) relationships. An effective intervention will seek to address and assist with such difficulties.

Engaging and retaining the client in therapy will form the basis of any intervention. It has been suggested that even for those with difficult early attachment experiences, it is possible to attain 'earned secure attachment' through achieving a 'significant emotional relationship' with another person at a subsequent point in life, and for some this could be through some form of therapy relationship (Siegel, 2001).

2.6.1   *Therapeutic Alliance*

From an attachment perspective, a key function of any therapeutic encounter will be to create a safe, containing environment. With this 'secure base' established, the clinician is then able to manage the client's psychological distress, and allow the client the space and time to begin to explore and discover more adaptive ways of managing their difficulties. High rates of treatment attrition, client disengagement and relapse are commonly encountered by services delivering treatment to those with SUD (De Rick & Vanheule, 2007). One factor which has been found to be a modest but consistent predictor of successful engagement and retention in treatment is the quality of the therapeutic alliance (Meier, Barrowclough & Donmall, 2005). While the formation of an effective working relationship is an essential ingredient in any form of psychotherapy, the emotional demands involved in forming and maintaining an effective therapeutic alliance may prove challenging for those with problematic attachment histories (Khantzian, 2012).

Previous psychotherapy research has highlighted how therapeutic alliance can be influenced by the quality of other significant relationships (past and present) in the life of the client. In general, clients who have secure attachment histories, and a history of successful relationships are more likely to establish a productive and positive therapeutic alliance (Gelso & Carter, 1985; Kokotovic & Tracey, 1990; Paivio & Patterson, 1999; Eames & Roth, 2000; Kanninen, Salo, & Punamaki, 2000; Mallinckrodt, 2000; Lecomte et al., 2008).

Another key element influencing the development of an effective therapeutic alliance is the clinician's own attachment style (Mikulincer & Shaver, 2007). As Reading (2002) has noted, 'The attachment needs and dynamics of both patient and therapist are inevitably implicated in the psychotherapeutic encounter.' Meyer and Pilkonis (2001) have suggested that the therapist's attachment style affects both the strength and the speed with which a working relationship is formed. Reading (2002) has further argued that there are at least two key differences in cognitive behavioural and attachment models of addiction. In the former approach, lapses are thought to be related to times of reduced vigilance and a poor sense of self-efficacy, or the absence of alternative adaptive coping strategies. However, the attachment model suggests that the person continues to have a conscious awareness of the high-risk situations that typically bring on lapses, but that these become less salient. Instead, here the attachment model sees the person's choice to use drugs as a means of accessing a secure base effect at times of heightened anxiety. A second related area of difference is highlighted by the fact that cognitive behavioural approaches rarely address the positive aspects of a person's substance use. This can lead the therapist to align themselves with the client's desire to give up their addiction leading to a 'lopsided posture' in which they neglect the bond between the client and their drugs. Once established the therapeutic relationship alliance offers an alternative 'secure base' to that sought through the drug of choice.

2.6.2   *Enhancing Skills*

Deficits in emotion regulation and interpersonal functioning will often be specifically identified as treatment targets in any attachment-informed intervention. Identifying individuals who are experiencing emotional and interpersonal difficulties, and targeting these specific issues may reduce the likelihood of disengagement, and ultimately lead to more positive treatment outcomes (De Rick & Vanheule, 2007). From this perspective, the development of an effective therapeutic alliance is an integral part of the recovery journey.

A variety of manualized treatment programmes can be found, which focus on enhancing emotion regulation skills and equipping clients with techniques to manage psychological distress. Mentalization Based Treatment (MBT) has been developed by Bateman and Fonagy (2007) specifically with a view to targeting and addressing deficits resulting from attachment insecurities, such as poor interpersonal functioning and difficulties with emotion regulation. A variety of techniques are used to develop an individual's awareness of their own thoughts and feelings, and of the thoughts and emotional worlds of others. Doumas et al. (2006) have noted that the potential benefit of adopting a cognitive behavioural approach which focuses initially on the development of more adaptive emotional regulation strategies will be helpful. In particular, any training packages to develop new coping and social skills will have potential in terms of helping to challenge negative cognitions about the self and others. Doumas et al. (2006) also suggest explicitly targeting therapeutic work which will increase comfort with intimacy and encouraging social interaction. Woodford (2012) has also detailed strategies aimed at enhancing levels of emotional literacy.

Other treatment packages such as Dialectic Behaviour Therapy (DBT) have been adapted for use with SUD populations (Dimeff & Linehan, 2008). DBT combines cognitive behavioural strategies to enhance skills to regulate affect as well as techniques for improving interpersonal effectiveness in relationships. Another core element of DBT is the practice of mindfulness (discussed in greater detail in Chapter 6 in this volume). Again, this can assist the client in the management of difficult emotions, and there is growing evidence for its effectiveness with this population (Appel & Kim-Appel, 2009).

Group work has traditionally been a popular approach in the field of addiction treatment, and there is widespread recognition and acknowledgement of the potential benefits of 'curative group processes' (Yalom, 1995). In particular, the potential to improve interpersonal relationship skills and learning have been highlighted (Hill & Harris, 2011). Involvement in different forms of group psychotherapy has the potential to impact positively in terms of changes to both attachment style and interpersonal functioning (Kinley & Reyno, 2013).

Flores (2004) has highlighted the potential benefits of '12 Step' approaches (e.g. Alcoholic Anonymous (AA) or Narcotics Anonymous (NA)) in the treatment of individuals who have difficult attachment histories. He has suggested that for some clients the damage (disruption to the attachment system) may have been too severe, or may have occurred too early in their development, for individual therapy to be truly curative. In such circumstances, mutual aid support groups such as AA have the potential to form a long-term, if not a lifelong, 'holding environment' (Flores, 2004).

Furthermore, it has been argued that adherents of the 12 Step approach have (perhaps) inadvertently incorporated the main precepts of an attachment-based approach into their model (Flores, 2004). Here working therapeutically with addiction using attachment as a framework means that in large part the role for the psychologist or therapist is to help ease the path of the addicted client towards accessing such groups and to ensure that they maximize their success in this recovery process. This is not an easy task. As Jenkins and Tonigan (2011) have noted, the clients' own attachment orientation will predict their engagement with such groups, for example, in contrast to those with high attachment anxiety, clients with high attachment avoidance tend to be less likely to obtain a sponsor, to engage in going through the steps, and to attend meetings.

2.6.3   Addressing Issues of Loss

As has been noted, often individuals with difficult attachment experiences will have encountered other forms of childhood adversity. When this is the case, the likelihood of the presence of other problems such as personality disorder and complex PTSD is increased. In such circumstances, an important part of treatment will be providing the client with an opportunity to process trauma-related memories, and grieve for early losses (de Zulueta, 2009). Care should be exercised with the timing of such interventions, and clinicians should ensure they avail themselves of appropriate training and supervisory support.

2.7   CONCLUSION

There has been increasing interest in the concept of attachment in the field of addiction research and treatment. Difficult attachment histories are commonplace in client narratives, and traditional treatment endeavours have largely ignored their presence. A number of treatment approaches which have typically been used to assist in the treatment of personality-based difficulties, and which target deficits associated with attachment insecurities, such as poor interpersonal functioning and difficulties with emotion regulation (e.g. DBT, MBT mindfulness) are increasingly being used in addiction settings. Recognizing the presence of difficult early attachment experiences and incorporating these into case formulations have the potential to assist in the tailoring of treatment packages and improve treatment outcomes.

SUGGESTIONS FOR FURTHER READING

Bowlby, J. (1980). *Attachment and loss* (vol. 3). London: Hogarth.

Bowlby, J. (1988). *A secure base: Parent-child attachment and healthy human development*. New York: Basic Books.

Bowlby, J. (1994). *The making and breaking of affectional bonds*. New York: Routledge. (Original work published 1979).

Cassidy, J., & Shaver, P. R. (2008). *Handbook of attachment: Theory, research, and clinical applications* (2nd ed.). London: Guilford Press.

Fabes, R., & Martin, C. L. (2000). *Exploring child development: Transactions and transformations*. Boston: Allyn and Bacon.

Howe, D. (2011). *Attachment across the lifecourse*. London: Palgrave.

Ma, K. (2006). Attachment theory in adult psychiatry. Part 1: conceptualisations, measurement and clinical research finding. *Advances in Psychiatric Treatment, 12*, 440–449. doi:10.1192/apt.12.6.440

Mallinckrodt, B., Gantt, D., & Coble, H. (1995). Attachment patterns in the psychotherapy relationship: Development of a client attachment to therapist scale. *Journal of Counselling Psychology, 42*(3), 307–317. doi:10.1037/0022-0167.42.3.307

Wallin, D. J. (2007). *Attachment in psychotherapy*. London: Guilford Press.

REFERENCES

Ainsworth, M. D. S., Blehar, M. C., Waters, E., & Wall, S. (1978). *Patterns of attachment: A psychological study of the strange situation*. Hillsdale, NJ: Lawrence Erlbaum Associates.

Appel, J., & Kim-Appel, D. (2009). Mindfulness: Implications for substance abuse and addiction. *International Journal of Mental Health and Addiction, 7*(4), 506–512. doi:10.1007/s11469-009-9199-z

Bagby, R. M., Quilty, L. C., Taylor, G. J., Grabe, H. J., Luminet, O., Verissimo, R., et al. (2009) Are there subtypes of alexithymia? *Personality and Individual Difference, 47*(5), 413–418. doi:10.1016/j.paid.2009.04.012

Bartholomew, K. (1990). Avoidance of intimacy: An attachment perspective. *Journal of Social and Personal Relationships, 7*, 147–178. doi:10.1177/0265407590072001

Bartholomew, K. (1997). Adult attachment processes: Individual and couple perspectives. *British Journal of Medical Psychology, 70*, 249–263. doi:10.1111/j.2044-8341.1997.tb01903.x

Bartholomew, K., & Horowitz, L. (1991). Attachment styles among young adults: A test of a four category model. *Journal of Personality and Social Psychology, 61*(2), 226–244. doi:10.1037/0022-3514.61.2.226

Bartholomew, K., & Shaver, P. R. (1998). Methods of assessing adult attachment: Do they converge? In J. A. Simpson, & W. S. Rholes (Eds.), *Attachment theory and close relationships* (pp. 25–45). New York: Guilford Press.

Bateman, A. W., & Fonagy, P. (2007). *Mentalization-based treatment for borderline personality disorder: A practical guide*. Oxford: Oxford University Press.

Bateman, A. W. & Fonagy, P. (2008). Comorbid antisocial and borderline personality disorders: Mentalization-based treatment. *Journal of Clinical Psychology, Special Issue: Treating Comorbid Personality Disorders, 64*(2), 181–194. doi:10.1002/jclp.20451

Baumrind, D. (1971). Current patterns of parental authority. *Developmental Psychology, 4*(1), 1–103. doi:10.1037/h0030372

Baumrind, D. (1991). The influence of parenting style on adolescent competence and substance use. *Journal of Early Adolescence, 11*, 56–95. doi:10.1177/0272431691111004

Belsky, J. (2002). Developmental origins of attachment styles. *Attachment & Human Development, 4*, 166–170. doi:10.1080/14616730210157510

Bowlby, J. (1980). *Attachment and loss* (vol. 3). London: Hogarth.

Bowlby, J. (1988). *A secure base: Parent-child attachment and healthy human development*. New York: Basic Books.

Bowlby, J. (1994). *The making and breaking of affectional bonds*. New York: Routledge. (Original work published 1979).

Breidenstine, A. S., Bailey, L. O., Zeanah, C. H., & Larrieu, J. A. (2011). Attachment and trauma in early childhood: A review. *Journal of Child & Adolescent Trauma, 4*, 274–290. doi:10.1080/19361521.2011.609155

Brennan, K. A., Clark, C. L., & Shaver, P. R. (1998). Self-report measurement of adult attachment: An integrative overview. In J. A. Simpson, & W. S. Rholes (Eds.), *Attachment theory and close relationships* (pp. 46–76). New York: Guilford Press.

Brennan, K. A., & Shaver, P. R. (1998). Attachment styles and personality disorders: Their connections to each other and to parental divorce, parental death, and perceptions of parental caregiving. *Journal of Personality, 66*(5), 835–878. doi:10.1111/1467-6494.00034

Brennan, K. A. & Shaver, P. R. (1995). Dimensions of adult attachment, affect regulation, and romantic relationship functioning. *Personality & Social Psychology Bulletin, 21*(3), 267–283. doi: http://journals.sagepub.com/doi/abs/10.1177/0146167295213008

Bretherton, I. (1992). The origins of attachment theory: John Bowlby and Mary Ainsworth. *Developmental Psychology, 28*, 759–775. doi:10.1037/0012-1649.28.5.759

Cooper, M. L., Shaver, P. R., & Collins, N. L. (1998). Attachment styles, emotion regulation, and adjustment in adolescence. *Journal of Personality and Social Psychology, 74*, 1380–1397. doi:10.1037/0022-3514.74.5.1380

Crawford, T. N., Livesley, W. J., Jang, K. L., et al. (2007). Insecure attachment and personality disorder: A twin study of adults. *European Journal of Personality, 21*, 191–208. doi:10.1002/per.602

Davila, J., & Bradbury, T. N. (2001). Attachment insecurity and the distinction between unhappy spouses who do and do not divorce. *Journal of Family Psychology, 15*, 371–393. doi:10.1037/0893-3200.15.3.371

De Rick, A., & Vanheule, S. (2007). Attachment styles in alcoholic inpatients. *European Addiction Research, 13*, 101–108. doi:10.1159/000097940

De Rick, A., Vanheule, S., & Verhaeghe, P. (2009). Alcohol addiction and the attachment system: An empirical study of attachment style, alexithymia, and psychiatric disorders in alcoholic inpatients. *Substance Use & Misuse, 44*, 99–114. doi:10.1080/10826080802525744

de Zulueta, F. (2009). Post-traumatic stress disorder and attachment: Possible links with borderline personality disorder. *Advances in Psychiatric Treatment, 15*, 172–180. doi:10.1192/apt.bp.106.003418

Dimeff, L. A., & Linehan, M. M. (2008). Dialectical behavior therapy for substance abusers. *Addiction Science & Clinical Practice, 4*(2), 39–47.

Doumas, D. M., Blasey, C. M., & Mitchell, S. (2006). Adult attachment, emotional distress, and interpersonal problems in alcohol and drug dependency treatment. *Alcoholism Treatment Quarterly, 24*(4), 41–54. doi:10.1300/J020v24n04_04

Eames, V., & Roth, A. (2000). Patient attachment orientation and the early working alliance: A study of patient and therapist reports of alliance quality and ruptures. *Psychotherapy Research, 10*(4), 421–434. doi:10.1093/ptr/10.4.421

Fagot, B. I., & Kavanagh, L. (1990). The prediction of antisocial behaviour from avoidant attachment classifications. *Child Development, 61*, 864–873. doi:10.1111/j.1467-8624.1990.tb02828.x

Felitti, V. J., Anda, R. F., Nordenberg, D., Williamson, D. F., Spitz, A. M., Edwards, V., et al. (1998). Relationship of childhood abuse and household dysfunction to many of the leading causes of death in adults: The adverse childhood experiences (ACE) study. *American Journal of Preventive Medicine, 14*(4), 245–258. doi:10.1016/S0749-3797(98)00017-8

Finzi-Dottan, R., Cohen, O., Iwaniec, D., Sapir, Y., & Weizman, A. (2003). The drug-user husband and his wife: Attachment styles, family cohesion and adaptability. *Substance Use and Misuse, 38*, 271–292. doi:10.1081/JA-120017249

Flores, P. J. (2004). *Addiction as an attachment disorder.* New York: Jason Aronson.

Fonagy, P., & Luyten, P. (2009). A developmental, mentalization-based approach to the understanding and treatment of borderline personality disorder. *Development and Psychopathology, 21*(4), 1355–1381. doi:10.1017/S0954579409990198

Fonagy, P., Target, M., Steele, H., & Steele, M. (1998). *Reflective-functioning manual for application to adult attachment interviews* (vol. 5). London: University College London.

Fraley, R. C., Waller, N. G., & Brennan, K. A. (2000). An item-response theory analysis of self-report measures of adult attachment. *Journal of Personality and Social Psychology, 78,* 350–365. doi:10.1037/0022-3514.78.2.350

Francis, D., Kaiser, D., & Deaver, S. P. (2003). Representations of attachment security in the bird's nest drawings of clients with substance abuse disorders. *Art Therapy: Journal of the American Art Therapy Association, 20*(3), 125–137. doi:10.1080/07421656.2003.10129571

Ganzel, B. L., Morris, P. A., & Wethington, E. (2010). Allostasis and the human brain: Integrating models of stress from the social and life sciences. *Psychological Review, 117,* 134–174. doi:10.1037/a0017773

Gelso, C., & Carter, J. (1985). The relationship in counselling and psychotherapy; Components, consequences, and theoretical antecedents. *The Counseling Psychologist, 13,* 155–244. doi:10.1177/0011000085132001

George, C., Kaplan, N., & Main, M. (1985). *The adult attachment interview.* Berkeley: University of California.

Griffin, D. W., & Bartholomew, K. (1994). Models of the self and other: Fundamental dimensions underlying measures of adult attachment. *Journal of Personality and Social Psychology, 67*(3), 430–445. doi:10.1037/0022-3514.67.3.430

Gunnar, M., & Quevedo, K. (2007). The neurobiology of stress and development. *Annual Review of Psychology, 58,* 145–173. doi:10.1146/annurev.psych.58.110405.085605

Hazan, C., & Shaver, P. (1987). Romantic love conceptualized as an attachment process. *Journal of Personality and Social Psychology, 52*(3), 511–524. doi:10.1037/0022-3514.52.3.511

Hill, R., & Harris, J. (2011). *Principles and practice of group work in addictions.* Hove: Routledge.

Höfler, D. Z., & Kooyman, M. (1996). Attachment transition, addiction and therapeutic bonding: An integrative approach. *Journal of Substance Abuse Treatment, 13*(6), 511–519. doi:10.1016/S0740-5472(96)00156-0

Howe, D. (2011). *Attachment across the lifecourse.* London: Palgrave.

Jenkins, C. O. E., & Tonigan, J. S. (2011). Attachment avoidance and anxiety as predictors of 12-Step group engagement. *Journal of Studies on Alcohol and Drugs, 72*(5), 854–862.

Johnson, J. G., Cohen, P., Smailes, E. M., Skodol, A. E., Brown, J., & Oldham, J. M. (2001). Childhood verbal abuse and risk for personality disorders during adolescence and early adulthood. *Comprehensive Psychiatry, 42,* 16–23. doi:10.1053/comp.2001.19755

Kanninen, K., Salo, J., & Punamaki, R. L. (2000). Attachment patterns and working alliance in trauma therapy for victims of political violence. *Psychotherapy Research, 10*(4), 435–449. doi:10.1093/ptr/10.4.435

Karavasilis, L., Doyle, A., & Markiewicz, D. (2003). Associations between parenting style and attachment to mother in middle childhood and adolescence. *International Journal of Behavioral Development, 27,* 153–164. doi:10.1080/0165025024400015

Karen, R. (1994). *Becoming attached: First relationships and how they shape our capacity to love.* New York: Oxford University Press.

Khantzian, E. J. (2012). Reflections on treating addictive disorders: A psychodynamic perspective. *The American Journal on Addictions, 21,* 274–279. doi:10.1111/j.1521-0391.2012.00234.x

Kinley, J. L., & Reyno, S. M. (2013). Attachment style changes following intensive short-term group psychotherapy. *International Journal of Group Psychotherapy, 63,* 53–75. doi:10.1521/ijgp.2013.63.1.53

Kokotovic, A. M., & Tracey, T. J. (1990). Working alliance in the early phase of counselling. *Journal of Counselling Psychology, 37,* 16–21. doi:10.1037/0022-0167.37.1.16

Lecomte, T., Spidel, A., Leclerc, C., MacEwan, G. W., Greaves, C., & Bentall, R. P. (2008). Predictors and profiles of treatment non-adherence and engagement in services problems in early psychosis. *Schizophrenia Research, 102*(1), 295–302. doi:10.1016/j.schres.2008.01.024

Ligiero, D. P., & Gelso, C. J. (2002). Countertransference, attachment, and the working alliance: The therapist's contribution. *Psychotherapy: Theory, Research, Practice, Training, 39*(1), 3–11. doi:10.1037/0033-3204.39.1.3

Loas, G., Fremaux, D., Otmani, O., Lecercle, C., & Delahousse, J. (1997). Is alexithymia a negative factor for maintaining abstinence? A follow-up study. *Comprehensive Psychiatry, 38*(5), 296–299. doi:10.1016/S0010-440X(97)90063-8

Luyten, P., & Van Houdenhove, B. (2013). Common and specific factors in the psychotherapeutic treatment of patients suffering from chronic fatigue and pain disorders. *Journal of Psychotherapy Integration, 23*(1), 14–27. doi:10.1037/a0030269

Luyten, P., Van Houdenhove, B., Lemma, A., Target, M., & Fonagy, P. (2012). A mentalization-based approach to the understanding and treatment of functional somatic disorders. *Psychoanalytic Psychotherapy, 26*, 2, 121–140. doi:10.1080/ 02668734.2012.678061

Maccoby, E. E., & Martin, J. A. (1983). Socialization in the context of the family: Parent-child interaction. In E. M. Hetherington (Ed.), *Handbook of child psychology*: vol. 4, *Socialization, personality, and social development* (pp. 1–101). New York: John Wiley & Sons, Inc.

Magai, C. (1999). Affect, imagery and attachment: Working models of interpersonal affect and the socialization of emotion. In J. Cassidy, & P. R. Shaver (Eds.), *Handbook of attachment* (pp. 787–802). New York: Guilford Press.

Main, M., Goldwyn, R., & Hesse, E. (2003). Adult attachment scoring and classification systems. Unpublished manuscript, University of California at Berkeley.

Main, M., Kaplan, N., & Cassidy, J. (1985). Security in infancy, childhood, and adulthood: A move to the level of representation. In I. Bretherton, & E. Waters (Eds.), *Growing points in attachment theory and research. Monographs of the Society for Research in Child Development* (no. 50, pp. 66–106). Chicago: University of Chicago Press.

Main, M., & Solomon, J. (1990). Procedures for identifying disorganized/disoriented infants during the Ainsworth Strange Situation. In M. Greenberg, D. Cicchetti, & M. Cummings (Eds.), *Attachment in the preschool years* (pp. 121–160). Chicago: University of Chicago Press.

Mallinckrodt, B. (2000). Attachment, social competencies, social support, and interpersonal process in psychotherapy. *Psychotherapy Research, 10*(3), 239–266. doi:10.1093/ptr/10.3.239

Mallinckrodt, B., & Wei, M. (2005). Attachment, social competencies, social support, and psychological distress. *Journal of Counselling Psychology, 52*, 358–367. doi:10.1037/0022-0167.52.3.358

McEwen, B. S., & Wingfield, J. C. (2003). The concept of allostasis in biology and biomedicine. *Hormone & Behaviour, 43*(1), 2–15. doi:10.1016/S0018-506X(02)00024-7

McNally, A. M., Palfai, T. P., Levine, R. V., & Moore, B. M. (2003). Attachment dimensions and drinking-related problems among young adults: The mediational role of coping motives. *Addictive Behaviour, 28*(6), 1115–1127. doi:10.1016/S0306-4603(02)00224-1

Meier, P., Barrowclough, C., & Donmall, M. (2005). The role of the therapeutic alliance in the treatment of substance misuse: a critical review of the literature. *Addiction, 100*, 304–316. doi:10.1111/j.1360-0443.2004.00935.x

Meyer, B., & Pilkonis, P. A. (2001). Attachment style. *Psychotherapy: Theory, Research, Practice, Training, 38*(4), 467–472. doi:10.1037/0033-3204.38.4.466

Meyer, B., & Pilkonis, P. A. (2005). An attachment model of personality disorder. In M. F. Lenzenweger, & J. F. Clarkin (Eds.), *Major theories of personality disorder* (pp. 231–281). New York: Guilford Press.

Mickelson, K. D., Kessler, R. C., & Shaver, P. R. (1997). Adult attachment in a nationally representative sample. *Journal of Personality and Social Psychology, 73*, 1092–1106. doi:10.1037/0022-3514.73.5.1092

Mikulincer, M., & Shaver, P. R. (2007). *Attachment in adulthood: Structure, dynamics, and change*. New York: Guilford Press.

Molnar, D., Sadava, S., DeCourville, N., & Perrier, C. (2010). Attachment, motivations, and alcohol: Testing a dual-path model of high-risk drinking and adverse consequences in transitional clinical and student samples. *Canadian Journal of Behavioural Science, 42*, 1–13. doi:10.1037/a0016759

Newcomb, M. D. (1995). Identifying high-risk youth: Prevalence and patterns of adolescent drug abuse. In E. Rahdert, & D. Czechowicz (Eds.), *Adolescent drug abuse: clinical assessment and therapeutic interventions* (pp. 7–38). NIDA Research Monograph Series 156, Rockville, MD.

Nolte, T., Guiney, J., Fonagy, P., Mayes, L. C., & Luyten, P. (2011). Interpersonal stress regulation and the development of anxiety disorders: an attachment-based developmental framework. *Frontiers in Behavioral Neuroscience, 5*(55). doi:10.3389/fnbeh.2011.00055

Paivio, S. C., & Patterson, L. A. (1999). Alliance development in therapy for resolving child-hood abuse issues. *Psychotherapy: Theory, Research, Practice, Training, 36*, 343–354. doi:10.1037/h0087843

Polusny, M. A., Dickinson, K. A., Murdoch, M., & Thuras, P. (2008). The role of cumulative sexual trauma and difficulties identifying feelings in understanding female veterans' physical health outcomes. *General Hospital Psychiatry, 30*(2), 162–170. doi:10.1016/j.genhosppsych.2007.11.006

Powers, S. I., Pietromonaco, P. R., Gunlicks, M., & Sayer, A. (2006). Dating couples' attachment styles and patterns of cortisol reactivity and recovery in response to a relationship conflict. *Journal of Personality and Social Psychology, 90*(4), 613–628. doi:http://dx.doi.org/10.1037/0022-3514.90.4.613

Reading, B. (2002). The application of Bowlby's attachment theory to the psychotherapy of the addictions. In M. Weegman, & R. Cohen (Eds.), *The psychodynamics of addiction* (pp. 3–12). London: Whurr.

Rholes, W. S., Simpson, J. A., Blakely, B. S., Lanigan, L., & Allen, E. A. (1997). Adult attachment styles, the desire to have children, and working models of parenthood. *Journal of Personality, 65*, 357–385. doi:10.1111/j.1467-6494.1997.tb00958.x

Sakuraba, S., Kubo, M., Komoda, T., & Yamana, J.-I. (2005). Suicidal ideation and alexithymia in patients with alcoholism: A pilot study. *Substance Use & Misuse, 40*(6), 823–830. doi:10.1081/JA-200030702

Schindler, A., Thomasius, R., Sack, P. M., Gemheinhardt, B., Kustner, U., & Eckert, J. (2005). Attachment and substance use disorders: A review of the literature and a study in drug dependent adolescents. *Attachment & Human Development, 7*(3), 207–228. doi:10.1080/14616730500173918

Schore, A. (2001). The effects of a secure attachment relationship on right brain development, affect regulation, and infant mental health. *Infant Mental Health Journal, 22*, 201–269. doi:10.1002/1097-0355(200101/04)22:1<201::AID-IMHJ8>3.0.CO;2-9

Shaver, P. R., & Mikulincer, M. (2002). Attachment-related psychodynamics. *Attachment & Human Development, 4*, 133–161. doi:10.1080/14616730210154171

Sher, K. J., Grekin, E. R., & Williams, N. A. (2005). The development of alcohol use disorders. *Annual Review of Clinical Psychology, 1*, 493–523. doi:10.1146/annurev.clinpsy.1.102803.144107

Shorey, H. S., & Snyder, C. R. (2006). The role of adult attachment styles in psychopathology and psychotherapy outcomes. *Review of General Psychology, 10*(1), 1–20. doi:10.1037/1089-2680.10.1.1

Siegel, D. J. (2001). Toward an interpersonal neurobiology of the developing mind: Attachment relationships, "mindsight," and neural integration. *Infant Mental Health Journal, 22*(1–2), 67–94. doi:10.1002/1097-0355(200101/04)

Sifneos, P. E. (1977). The phenomenon of 'alexithymia'. *Psychotherapy and Psychosomatics, 28*, 47–57.

Steele, H., & Siever, L. (2010). An attachment perspective on borderline personality disorder: Advances in gene–environment considerations. *Current Psychiatry Reports, 12*, 61–67. doi:10.1007/s11920-009-0091-0

Suh, J. J., Ruffins, S., Robins, C. E., Albanese, M. J., & Khantzian, E. J. (2008). Self-medication hypothesis: Connecting affective experience and drug choice. *Psychoanalytic Psychology, 25*(3), 518–532. doi:10.1037/0736-9735.25.3.518

Thompson, R. A., Lamb, M. E., & Estes, D. (1982). Stability of infant mother attachment and its relationship to changing life circumstances in an unselected middle class sample. *Child Development, 53,* 144–148.

Thorberg, F. A., & Lyvers, M. (2006). Attachment, fear of intimacy and differentiation of self among clients in substance disorder treatment facilities. *Addictive Behaviors, 31,* 732–737. doi:10.1016/j. addbeh.2005.05.050

Thorberg, F. A., & Lyvers, M. (2010). Attachment in relation to affect regulation and interpersonal functioning among substance use disorder inpatients. *Addiction Research & Theory, 18*(4), 464–478. doi:10.3109/16066350903254783

Thorberg, F. A., Young, R. M., Sullivan, K. A., & Lyvers, M. (2009). Alexithymia and alcohol use disorders: A critical review. *Addictive Behaviors, 34*(3), 237–245.

Thorberg, F. A., Young, R. M., Sullivan, K. A., et al. (2011). Alexithymia, craving and attachment in a heavy drinking population. *Addictive Behaviours, 36,* 427–430. doi:10.3109/16066359.2011.5 80065

Trivers, R. L. (1972). Parental investment and sexual selection. In B. Campbell (Ed.), *Sexual selection and the descent of man, 1871–1971* (pp. 136–179). Chicago: Aldine.

Turner, A. M., & Paivio, S. C. (2002). Relations among childhood trauma, alexithymia, social anxiety, and social support. Poster presented at the American Psychological Association, Chicago.

Van IJzendoorn, M. H. (1995). Adult attachment representations, parental responsiveness and infant attachment; A meta-analysis on the predictive validity of the Adult Attachment Interview. *Psychological Bulletin, 117,* 387–403. doi:10.1037/0033-2909.117.3.387

Van IJzendoorn, M. H., Caspers, K., Bakermans-Kranenburg, M. J., Beach, S. R. H., & Philibert, R. (2010). Methylation matters: Interaction between methylation density and 5HTT genotype predicts unresolved loss or trauma. *Biological Psychiatry, 68,* 405–407. doi:10.1016/j. biopsych.2010.05.008

Vetere, A. (2011). Working within and between: Couples therapy and substance misuse. Paper presented at British Psychological Society, Division of Clinical Psychology, Addictions Faculty, CPD day, London, 27 July.

Vungkhanching, M., Sher, K. J., Jackson, K. M., & Parra, G. R. (2004). Relation of attachment style to family history of alcoholism and alcohol use disorders in early adulthood. *Drug & Alcohol Dependence, 75*(1), 47–53. doi:10.1016/j.drugalcdep.2004.01.013

Wallin, D. J. (2007). *Attachment in psychotherapy.* London: Guilford Press.

Warner, L. A., & White, H. R. (2003). Longitudinal effects of age at onset and first drinking situations on problem drinking. *Substance Use & Misuse, 38,* 1983–2016. doi:10.1081/JA-120025123

Waters, E., & Deane, K. (1985). Defining and assessing individual differences in attachment relationships: Q-methodology and the organization of behavior in infancy and early childhood. In I. Bretherton, & E. Waters (Eds.), *Growing pains of attachment theory and research: Monographs of the Society for Research in Child Development* (no. 50, Serial No. 209 (1-2), pp. 41–65). Chicago: University of Chicago Press.

Weinberg, N. Z., Rahdert, E., Colliver, J. D., & Glantz, M. D. (1998). Adolescent substance abuse: A review of the past 10 years. *Journal of the American Academy of Child and Adolescent Psychiatry, 37*(3), 252–261. doi:10.1097/00004583-199803000-00009

Woodford, M. S. (2012). *Men, addiction & intimacy.* Hove: Routledge.

Yalom, I. D. (1995). *The theory and practice of group psychotherapy.* New York: Basic Books.

Zinberg, N. (1975). Addiction and ego function. *Psychoanalytic Study of the Child, 30,* 567–588.

Interventions

ALEX COPELLO AND KATHRYN WALSH

University of Birmingham, Birmingham, UK

CHAPTER OUTLINE

3.1 INTRODUCTION

Most attempts to conceptually explain and understand addiction problems tend to focus on the individual substance user and on internal individual processes, either physical, such as tolerance and withdrawal, or psychological, including, for example, motivation, individual behaviour or cognition. Much less attention has focused on the social context within which addiction takes place (Copello & Orford, 2002). Alcohol and drug problems affect and cause harm to many people as well as the individual user, and in turn the social context can influence continued substance use behaviour or change. Hence, addiction models that ignore the influence of the social environment can offer at best partial explanations and are limited.

In this chapter we take a contrasting view to the more familiar individual models and focus specifically on the social context of the substance user, including their families and close friends. We do this from a number of perspectives. First, we consider the types of social contexts and networks of alcohol and drug users entering treatment, before exploring what research has shown in terms of the impact that addiction problems can have on those concerned, i.e. the significant people close to those with the alcohol or drug problem. Families have been studied to a greater extent than other people such as friends in research, so we explore models that have been put forward to explain the impact and consequences of addiction problems on families. We describe the Stress-Strain-Coping-Support (SSCS) model as a psychological way of understanding these problems before we turn to the practical aspects of treatments that attempt to either involve, or provide help directly to, both families and also wider social networks. Finally, we consider the implementation and the development of family-responsive addiction services.

3.2 THE COMPOSITION OF ALCOHOL AND DRUG USERS' SOCIAL NETWORKS

When attempting to understand the social environment of people experiencing serious alcohol and drug problems, there is some, although limited, evidence about the composition of social networks of treatment populations. The UK Alcohol Treatment Trial (UKATT), the largest trial of psychosocial treatment for alcohol problems conducted in the UK, systematically collected data on the social network composition of those entering the trial using the Important People and Activities (IPA; Beattie et al., 1993), a validated questionnaire measure of social networks and social support. Participants entering the UKATT trial were asked about the people they had spent most time with over the previous three months (aged at least 12 years old). They named these 'important' people and described each of them using demographic and drinking-related characteristics. A secondary analysis of this data revealed that, overall, 4,677 important people were named by 740 participants entering routine alcohol treatment in UK services and consenting to participate in UKATT. All participants could name at least one important person; the highest number named was 12. Participants could most frequently name

10 people, and the mean number named across the whole sample was 6.5. The measure also looks more closely at the four most important people nominated by each participant. Here, the majority of people entering alcohol treatment named their partner as the most important person, although other family members were also a popular choice. Parents, children and siblings were mentioned as important within the four most important categories. Very few participants named their partner as least important person of the four. Other members of close family were predominantly named as second or third most important, and friends were commonly named as third or fourth.

In a study of clients in Opiate Substitution Treatment (OST) in the UK National Health Service (Day et al., 2013b) 118 participants were interviewed using a shorter adaptation of the IPA measure, the Important People Drug and Alcohol Interview (IPDA; Zywiak et al., 2009), and they identified a total of 820 network members with a mean network size of 6.9 people. Of this group, 378 (46%) were immediate family members; 189 (23%) friends; 97 (12%) extended family members; 51 (6%) treatment professionals or members of self-help groups; 47 (6%) sexual partners; 16 (2%) colleagues from work; and 42 (5%) others. The study revealed that two-thirds of the social network of clients was made up of family members, with the remaining third made up of mostly friends and a smaller number of self-help group members, or professionals.

The above two studies provide some useful information. They appear to challenge the notion that people entering treatment for alcohol and or drug problems are isolated or lack potential sources of social support. On the other hand, they also suggest that a number of people can potentially be affected and harmed by the impacts of the problem. In addition, despite some apparent differences between the two groups, such as the higher number of partners proportionately reported by the alcohol treatment sample, the largest composition of the networks appears to comprise family members.

While informative, the data arising from the two studies also has some limitations. First, it is only based on people entering, or within, treatment and consenting to take part in research. The extent to which these findings can be generalized to wider populations of those with alcohol and drug problems remains unclear, although it is unlikely that treatment groups will differ greatly from the findings presented. The data, however, is limited in helping to understand the social networks of those people not in treatment. These are by far the largest group of people with alcohol and drug problems and are those where social networks might both experience serious unidentified harms, and also have the potential to be influential in relation to the person's addictive and treatment-seeking behaviour.

3.3   IMPACTS OF ADDICTIONS ON OTHERS

An alternative yet complementary perspective involves looking at the experience from the point of view of those affected. To date, literature on the adverse effects of alcohol has primarily focused on the harms caused by alcohol to the drinker themselves (Laslett et al., 2011). People's health and well-being are affected by those around them (Ferris, Laslett, Livingstone, Room & Wilkinson, 2011), yet until recently, there had been relatively little consideration given to the harms people may experience as a result of someone else's drinking. The limited data that is available has generally focused on more tangible impacts, for example, the number of deaths caused by drivers under the influence of alcohol. For less tangible impacts on those other than the drinker, data is limited. Although it appears well known that these impacts do occur, any attempt to quantify them has only recently begun. The specific ways in which others are affected, the severity of the impact, and how much time and money individuals spend responding to the drinking of others are additional questions to which little research has been devoted (Room et al., 2010).

In 2008, the 'Harm to Others' survey was conducted with 2,600 people in Australia (Laslett et al., 2010) and 3,068 in New Zealand (Casswell, You & Huckle, 2011), and the project has since obtained funding from the World Health Organization for replication across several countries, including, among others, some African countries, Chile and India. This cross-sectional general population survey attempted to ascertain how many of those surveyed had been affected by somebody else's drinking in the past 12 months. It allowed respondents to identify the drinker whose alcohol consumption had impacted on them the most and to describe in detail exactly how they had been affected, and how often.

At their most inclusive, figures suggest that around 70% of people have experienced 'some level of inconvenience' in the past year as a result of someone else's drinking, with 43% reporting a fairly serious degree of abuse, threat or damage from a stranger (Laslett et al., 2011). When the criteria are refined to the drinking of someone known to the individual, for example, their partner, a family member, a friend or a co-worker, the figure is lower.

Just over a quarter (28%) of Australian adults reported being negatively affected by the drinking of someone they knew. Younger respondents were more likely to report that they had been affected, and compared to males, females were almost twice as likely. Seven per cent of respondents reported living with a problematic drinker in the past year; often their partner or a family member. In New Zealand, however, this figure was considerably higher, with 1 in 4 reporting that the heavy drinker was part of their household (Casswell et al., 2011).

People can be affected by another person's drinking in many ways. Nearly three-quarters of people report being affected by a stranger's drinking, and these impacts can often be seen as more of an acute inconvenience, for example, street noise or having to avoid a public place (Laslett et al., 2010). The impact from drinkers known to the person, however, is generally more serious and prolonged. It can also depend on the nature of their relationship. For example, the partner most frequently reports that drinking causes serious arguments within the relationship, whereas family members are more likely to report feeling emotionally hurt or neglected, and friends report that the drinker has negatively affected a social occasion (Laslett et al., 2010). Having a heavy drinker around can lead to a range of difficult situations for the person affected, and can also be linked to a spectrum of problems with their own well-being, mental health and quality of life.

Having at least one heavy drinker in a person's social circle, whether this is a relative or a friend, can significantly increase the likelihood of experiencing anxiety or depression (Ferris et al., 2011). Exposure to heavy drinkers has also been shown to reduce personal well-being (measured by the Personal Wellbeing Index Scale – PWI; International Wellbeing Group, 2006) and utility health scores (measured by the EuroQuol-5 dimension (EQ5D); The EuroQol Group, 1990), particularly in relation to areas such as reduction in usual activities, increased pain and discomfort, and higher levels of anxiety and depression. Furthermore, as the perceived severity of the exposure and impact of someone else's drinking increases, there is a corresponding reduction in the respondent's quality of life (Laslett et al., 2010; Casswell et al., 2011).

The high level of symptoms has also been shown in a series of US studies based on medical records of health care utilization. When comparing family members of people with substance use problems to family members of persons without substance use problems (Ray, Mertens & Weisner, 2007; 2009), and to family members of diabetes and asthma sufferers (Ray, Mertens & Weisner, 2009), those with a substance-using relative were significantly more likely to be diagnosed with a list of physical and psychological conditions, most commonly depression and problematic substance use themselves. Furthermore, family members of substance users consistently reported higher health service-related costs than their comparisons, in particular, relating to mental health care, contact with substance use services and hospital emergency department presentations (Ray et al., 2009).

It is not surprising that having a family member with an addiction can potentially be disempowering and demoralizing. People may feel ashamed of, or embarrassed by, the family member and may try to conceal or minimize the issue due to a fear of judgement, blame or criticism from others, including their own relatives, their social network and the wider society. Such feelings of shame or embarrassment resulting from having a family member with addiction problems may create unique burdens which can result in isolation and potential loss of social support for the affected family members. Figures from a study by Ahmedani et al. (2013) suggest that around 50% of family members feel embarrassed by their relative's ADMC (alcohol, drug or mental health condition), twice the number of family members who feel embarrassed as a result of a relative's general medical condition, such as cancer or heart problems. These figures, however, included people affected by several conditions in the family, one of which was alcohol and drug problems, but also included mental health and serious memory problems. Unfortunately, the sample size in this study would not allow individual condition analysis. Nevertheless, family members often experience feelings of embarrassment as a result of their relative's addiction problems. This may not only lead to concealment of the condition, but also impose barriers to care for both of the family members and perhaps prolong the duration of the problems and their related consequences (Ahmedani et al., 2013).

The review of the available evidence in this section clearly supports the notion that the impacts of addiction problems on others, including family members, can be serious and long-lasting. The experience is complex, combining high levels of stressful circumstances with the likely presence of physical and psychological symptoms of stress and a feeling of shame and embarrassment leading to isolation, stigma and loss of support, as well as lack of contact with potentially helpful services. Before we focus on forms of help and interventions, we discuss the Stress-Strain-Coping-Support Model as a way of understanding these experiences.

3.4 THEORETICAL MODELS OF ADDICTION AND THE FAMILY: STRESS-STRAIN-COPING-SUPPORT

Models of addiction often typecast the family members of those with substance use problems in a negative way, suggesting that addiction is a result of long-standing family 'dysfunction' or 'instability', blaming the family member for their relatives' problems. The Stress-Strain-Coping-Support (SSCS) model, however, draws on the work of Orford and colleagues in Mexico, England and Australia, and is further informed by the emerging 'harm to others' literature, to provide an alternative viewpoint. The SSCS model perceives family members as ordinary people who are finding it difficult to cope with stressful circumstances that are not of their making, and avoids any attribution of blame to the family member for the development or maintenance of the problem (Orford, Velleman, Natera, Templeton & Copello, 2013). It is empowering in the sense that it gives back some of the control to family members that is often lost in other models, and believes that family members, perhaps with some additional support, have the inherent ability to improve their own health and well-being, and have a positive impact on their relative's substance use. In essence, and in its simplest form, the model implies that if stress is not satisfactorily coped with, then strain is likely to be evident in the form of some departure from health and well-being; and that support and information are key in helping people to cope with this stress (Orford, Copello, Velleman & Templeton, 2010a). The building blocks of the model described in more detail below therefore include: stressful experiences, coping responses, available information and knowledge, support and the potential for resulting strain in the form of symptoms.

Despite individual differences, the model assumes that the core experience of family members is fundamentally the same. Substance use in the family can cause family bonds and relationships to deteriorate and family life to be threatened, possibly leading to situations where family members worry about their relatives, where there may be conflict over money and possessions, and where there is potential for hostility and aggression (Orford et al., 2013). Each of these, in addition to a much longer list of difficult situations, has the potential to cause *stress* for the family member; regardless of their gender, age or socio-cultural group.

This stress in turn is capable of putting substantial *strain* on the family member. Research across countries suggests that addiction in the family is generally stressful enough to put the family members' physical, mental and general health at risk (Orford 1990; Wiseman, 1991; Ray et al., 2007; Orford et al., 2013). Family members may report signs of ill health which they attribute, or think may be attributed to, the relative's addiction, including sleep problems, weight changes, and an increase in both psychological symptoms (e.g. anxiety, depression) and physical symptoms (e.g. hypertension, pains, migraine). Furthermore, in addition to the strain put on the family members' health, other domains of life can be affected by the stress, such as their work or career, and their friendship network (Orford et al., 2010a).

Family members become faced with the often challenging task of trying to understand what is going on and deciding how to deal with and respond to the situation (Orford et al., 2010a). They want to find the best way of *coping*, and there is not necessarily any right or wrong answer, although some are considered by family members to be counterproductive. Qualitative interviews with affected family members (Orford, Velleman, Copello, Templeton & Ibanga, 2010bb) have suggested that there are three broad methods of coping. However, it is worth noting that there are no distinct boundaries between these, and overlap often occurs. Family members often reported 'putting up with' their relatives' substance use, for example, giving them money through fear they will commit crime. Some reported 'standing up to it' in an attempt to regain some of the control over family life that has been lost, while others withdrew from the situation and tried to 'gain independence' from the relative by putting distance between them, for example, leaving, or asking them to leave.

Family members are usually unsure about what to do and struggle to find the best way of coping, and therefore welcome any *support*, help and advice. Good social support is an important resource for coping and this plays an important role in the model (Orford et al., 2010a). When it occurs, social support is highly valued, however, it has been suggested that this may be rare (Orford et al., 2010a). The emotional support of people who have been through similar situations themselves can be appreciated, as well as the provision of accurate information and practical support. Family members perceive the feeling of 'being backed up' in their ways of coping as helpful, as opposed to having support from somebody who criticizes their coping methods.

As previously mentioned, affected family members may not seek support as a result of the embarrassment or shame they may feel if others knew about the addiction (Ahmedani et al., 2013; Orford et al., 2010b). Unfortunately, this may be reinforced through negative experiences with both personal and professional support systems. Family members have described receiving unsympathetic or unhelpful advice from family and friends (Orford et al., 2010b), and have reported feeling that they may have received inadequate support or information from professionals who were often unwilling or unable to talk through various coping strategies. Some have even reported feeling blamed by professionals; that the professional was implying that the relative's addiction was the family members' fault (Orford et al., 2010b).

The overall experience of family members suggests that their own social networks are often neither helpful nor supportive (Orford et al., 2010b). Social support needs to recognize the multi-layered nature of the stress, the complexity of the various coping strategies, and the confusion and mixed feelings that may be felt towards the relative (Orford et al., 2010b).

3.5 FROM MODELS TO INTERVENTIONS

The discussion up to this point supports the idea that, in addition to the harm caused by alcohol and drug problems to the person using substances, those affected close to the user also have important psychological needs. These needs can potentially be addressed and alleviated either through interventions delivered directly to those affected or through their involvement in the treatment for the relative with the addiction problem. Each of these two areas is described in the next sections with specific reference to two types of evidence-based interventions.

3.5.1   Supporting Family Members in Their Own Right: The 5-Step Method

From the literature reviewed so far, it becomes clear that one way to attempt to reduce the harm caused by addiction problems to others involves the provision of direct psychological help to those who are affected, irrespective of whether the relative with the addiction problem is in treatment or even considering help at all. An example of such an approach is the development and evaluation of the 5-Step Method to help family members in their own right (Copello, Templeton, Orford & Velleman, 2010a). Based on the Stress-Strain-Coping-Support Model (SSCS) discussed, the method aims to systematically provide help to family members affected by the addiction problem of a close relative. The five steps of the method are: (1) active listening to elicit the family member's experience; (2) provision of targeted and specific information; (3) an exploration of coping responses; (4) establishing and enhancing social support; and (5) discussing any additional needs. Table 3.1 illustrates how the steps of the approach map onto the components of the SSCS model.

In a number of research studies, the delivery of the method to individual family members has been evaluated and has shown promise in terms of reductions of symptoms of stress and changes in important aspects of coping behaviours, either when delivered over a series of sessions or as one individual session supported by a

Table 3.1 *Contents of the 5-Step Method mapped onto the Stress-Strain-Coping-Support Model*

5-Step Method	Components of SSCS model
Step 1 Listen, reassure and explore concerns. Elicit the family member's story and experiences. Active listening.	Stress and strain
Step 2 Provide specific targeted information	Need for understanding and increased knowledge
Step 3 Explore coping responses by eliciting advantages and disadvantages of various coping responses as perceived by family member	Coping
Step 4 Establish current support and ways of enhancing support for family member	Social support
Step 5 Discuss further needs for family member, involving the relative or the rest of the family	Additional needs

Source: Adapted from Copello, Templeton, Orford and Vellema, 2010a.

self-help manual (see Copello, Templeton, Orford & Velleman, 2010b, for a summary of the evidence). The method is somewhat unique in the focus on family members in their own right, an area that has not been developed as much, when compared to approaches that aim to use families as a way of supporting the relative with the addiction problem, or bringing the user into treatment (Copello, Velleman & Templeton, 2005; Copello, Templeton & Velleman, 2006).

While the elements of the approach are not novel per se, the theoretical framework allows those delivering the method to follow a structured approach, discussing and eliciting from the affected family member their experiences of stress, need for information, coping behaviours, social support and their hopes and expectations for the future. In contrast to other approaches, the method is brief, structured and focused, and starts from the premise that family members are ordinary people caught up in highly stressful situations, and trying to work out ways to respond to these realities, as opposed to suffering from deficiencies or causing the addiction problem themselves. Based on this understanding, the style of the person delivering the method should be supportive, non-judgemental and avoid some of the more unhelpful language, for example, 'enabling', 'collusion' and similar terms that unfortunately are commonly used to describe family members' responses, and are often experienced as critical by family members.

The method is based on the premise that all behaviours and responses can be ultimately understood as dilemmas, and a clear exploration of the advantages and disadvantages of each coping behaviour (or dilemma) can lead to a more considered and informed response by the family member. It is also based on the assumption that each family is unique, and as such there is no universally 'right' or 'wrong' response, given that each action will lead to impacts on a range of outcomes for different family members, including the user of substances, the family member and, where relevant, the rest of the family. It is unlikely that one coping action will lead consistently to the same set of outcomes in all these areas of family life across different families and circumstances. For example, in a family unit that includes two partners and their children, the action of a partner purchasing an alcoholic drink for the relative with an alcohol problem may be detrimental for the continued consumption of alcohol of the relative, and also the emotional experience of the family member who may feel used and that his/her action is not helping. Yet, that action may reduce the likelihood, or indeed prevent, an aggressive confrontation between partners that in turn may reduce the children's exposure to family conflict and potential violence. Hence, given such a complex set of interactions and potential consequences, simplistic explanatory models and advice may not be enough to help the family member deal with such scenario and the attempts to resolve this challenging dilemma. The 5-Step Method proposes a careful exploration of all the potential advantages and disadvantages of responses to such a scenario in order to empower and support the family member to reach a more informed decision on how to respond.

To date, the 5-Step Method has been fairly popular, and increasingly teams and services are requesting training in the approach. The approach benefits from the fact that it is based on evidence from the underlying theoretical SSCS model that informed its development, and there is also some evidence of effectiveness through a series of fairly robust research studies (Copello et al., 2010b). Two main challenges remain for the 5-Step Method to make a more significant impact on routine practice. One is increased dissemination and further implementation in routine services. While some services have shown interest and commitment to train the workforce on the approach, significant challenges remain in terms of maintenance of delivery over time, including supervision and systems that support continued sustained practice. The second is the further testing of the method against less-structured supportive interventions, or a more traditional control condition, in order to establish the most important components of the method.

3.5.2   *Involving Families and Wider Social Networks in Treatment to Support Alcohol- and Drug-Users*

While it is likely that family members may benefit from increased involvement in the help that the relative with the addiction problem is receiving from treatment agencies, and this is often expressed as a wish by many family members, the emphasis and tradition of these approaches come from a different conceptual standpoint to the one discussed so far. The conceptual underpinning of these approaches is the positive influence of social, as well as more addiction-specific (or abstinence-related), support for the improvement and eventual resolution of addictive behaviour.

That the social environment of those with alcohol problems, for example, is an important factor has been shown in research to date. General social support, alcohol-specific social support and the drinking behaviour of the social network members have all been shown to be unique predictors of positive alcohol treatment outcomes (for examples, see Havassy, Hall & Wasserman, 1991; Beattie et al., 1993; Longabaugh, Wirtz, Zweben & Stout, 1998; Mohr, Averna, Kenny & Del Boca, 2001; Wasserman, Stewart & Delucchi, 2001; McCrady, 2004). What has been more challenging is the question of whether these factors can be incorporated into treatment interventions for those seeking help with alcohol and drug problems and act as intervention mechanisms of positive change.

Approaches focused on the development of positive social support for change have drawn not only on families, but also on wider social networks, including friends, and other close people affected and concerned enough about the problem to take action and become involved in these types of interventions.

Developed in the UK, the Social Behaviour and Network Therapy (SBNT) is one such treatment approach that aims to use, and where possible, develop and enhance social support for a positive change in addictive behaviour (Copello, Orford, Hodgson, Tober & Barrett, 2002). The original intervention was initiated to respond to those presenting for alcohol problem treatment (Copello, Orford, Tober & Hodgson, 2009), and was developed and tested as part of the UK Alcohol Treatment Trial (UKATT) conducted in UK alcohol treatment services. SBNT was found to be as effective and cost-effective as the more-established Motivational Enhancement Therapy (MET) in the UKATT trial, both treatments leading to significant reductions in alcohol consumption and improvements in mental health (UKATT Research Team, 2005aa) and leading to significant savings (UKATT Research Team, 2005bb). The possibility of delivering the intervention to drug users was later tested and established in a feasibility trial (Copello, Williamson, Orford & Day, 2006).

The aim of the intervention is described in more detail in a published treatment manual that was used within UKATT to train therapists (Copello et al., 2009). The intervention starts with the social network identification of the client with the addiction problem coming into a service. Networks, as already discussed, commonly include a mixture of family members, as well as friends and colleagues. Early in the intervention it is important to establish who the client perceives to be potentially important and helpful, and, if necessary and appropriate, and with the agreement of the client, invite network members to future treatment sessions. Thereafter, using a mixture of core and elective session topics, the therapist and client (and network members if involved) work collaboratively to establish and enhance a good level of positive support for a positive change in substance use. Motivational techniques, communication and coping mechanisms, social support, and crucially, given the nature of substance misuse, developing a network-based relapse management plan are all central to the intervention. The therapeutic approach also has scope to address client-focused elective areas, for example, educational requirements and the development of shared positive activities as alternatives to substance use.

The way of working inherent in SBNT offers different options and possibilities for those delivering treatment. Engaging with the social environment of the substance user can open up new possibilities and the opportunity to tap into the provision of ongoing support outside of the treatment setting. Fostering and enhancing natural support systems can provide a long-term sustained mechanism for change and maintenance of change that have the potential to act beyond the treatment episode. Support can also be drawn from recovery groups and self-help where this is seen as important for and by the client. In our experience, through training and development of the approach, we have found that perhaps the most significant challenge in those delivering treatment is making a shift from an individual focus of treatment to one that incorporates and works with people within their natural social environment, a contrast to working within the vacuum and the privacy of the treatment room. This way of working, however, raises a number of significant challenges (e.g. Lee, Christie, Copello & Kellett, 2012).

At the time of writing, two research studies are underway to further test SBNT with two different client groups. An adapted, somewhat briefer version of the approach is being tested in UK National Health Services adult drug treatment teams with clients attending opiate substitution therapy. In this trial, SBNT is being compared to treatment as usual, using random allocation (Day et al., 2013a). In addition, an adapted version of SBNT is being tested with young people (ages 12–18) entering treatment for drug and alcohol problems. It is hoped that these two studies will help to further aid understanding of some of the processes that may be helpful to support those with significant addictions in their quest to develop lives away from reliance on and problematic use of alcohol and drugs.

3.6   CONCLUSION

We started this chapter by attempting to make the case that addiction problems affect many more people than only the person using the substances. We aimed to present some of the accumulating evidence that supports this view and highlighted some of the significant impacts in terms of psychological and physical health that can result. On the basis of the evidence presented, it is possible to suggest that for every person with an addiction problem, there is at least a minimum of one other person significantly affected who may benefit from psychological help. The latter's needs are often hidden and unrecognized and the services available do not reflect this level of need. The figures available suggest that these impacts constitute a major, but possibly neglected, public health problem. Despite the increased recognition in some countries, and policies of the needs of families and closely affected others (Velleman, 2010), there is still some way to go if we are to offer a positive, comprehensive and effective response. The accumulation of data offered by studies such as the 'harm to others' programme of research can start to map out and identify these harms as a precursor to developing more effective responses.

The two methods discussed in more detail in this chapter are examples of attempts to respond to others' needs within existing specialist service provision, and can go some way to deal with and respond to reduce the harms to others. Service delivery, however, remains predominantly oriented towards the focal alcohol or drug client, despite the evidence of needs of affected others and available interventions to support families. Family-focused work should be informed by the evidence that an effective response to the needs of family members, and others affected has the potential to significantly reduce harm and health problems in this group, and that involving family members in supporting the treatment of the user can also improve outcomes.

Given the high prevalence of these problems, it is unlikely that only a specialist response will be enough, as family members affected will continue to access other services when experiencing symptoms, such as primary care or mental health service systems, where the nature of the problem may not be acknowledged or openly discussed unless those involved in those services are adequately trained to identify and respond to these needs. While we continue to identify more precisely the harms, we also need to continue to develop adequate ways to reduce or minimize those harms. This sets our challenge for the future.

SUGGESTIONS FOR FURTHER READING

Casswell, S., You, R.Q., & Huckle, T. (2011). Alcohol's harm to others: Reduced wellbeing and health status for those with heavy drinkers in their lives. *Addiction, 106,* 1087–1094. doi:10.1111/ j.1360-0443.2011.03361.x

Copello, A., Orford, J., Hodgson, R., Tober, G., & Barrett, C. On behalf of the UKATT Research Team. (2002). Social Behaviour and Network Therapy: Basic principles and early experiences, *Addictive Behaviors, 27,* 345–366. doi:http://dx.doi.org/10.1016/S0306-4603(01)00176-9

Copello, A., Orford, J., Tober, G., & Hodgson, R. (2009). *Social behaviour and network therapy for alcohol problems.* London: Brunner Routledge.

Copello, A., Templeton, L., Orford, J., & Velleman, R. (2010). The 5-Step Method: Principles and practice. *Drugs: Education, Prevention and Policy, 17*(S1), 86–99. doi:10.3109/09687637.2010.515186

Day, E., Copello, A., Karia, M., Roche, J., Grewal, P., George, S., et al. (2013). Social network support for individuals receiving opiate substitution treatment and its association with treatment progress. *European Addiction Research, 19,* 211–221. doi:10.1159/000343827

Laslett, A-M., Catalano, P., Chikritzhs, Y. Dale, C., Doran, C., Ferris, J., et al. (2010). *The range and magnitude of alcohol's harm to others.* Fitzroy, VIC: AER Centre for Alcohol Policy Research, Turning Point Alcohol and Drug Centre, Eastern Health.

Orford, J., Copello, A., Velleman, R., & Templeton, L. (2010). Family members affected by a close relative's addiction: The stress-strain-coping-support model. *Drugs: Education, Prevention and Policy, 17*(1), 36–43. doi:10.3109/09687637.2010.514801

Orford, J., Natera, G., Copello, A., Atkinson, C., Mora, J., Velleman, R., et al. (2005). *Coping with alcohol and drug problems. The experiences of family members in three contrasting cultures.* London: Brunner-Routledge.

REFERENCES

Ahmedani, B. K., Kubiak, S. P., Kessler, R. C. de Graaf, R., Alonso, J., Bruffaerts, R., et al. (2013). Embarrassment when illness strikes a close relative: A World Mental Health Survey Consortium Multi-site Study. *Psychological Medicine, 43,* 2191–2202. doi:10.1017/S003329171200298X

Beattie, M., Longabaugh, R., Elliot, G., Stout, R., Fava, J., & Noel, N. (1993). Effects of the social environment on alcohol involvement and subjective well-being prior to alcoholism treatment. *Journal of Studies on Alcohol, 54,* 283–296.

Casswell, S., You, R.Q., & Huckle, T. (2011). Alcohol's harm to others: Reduced wellbeing and health status for those with heavy drinkers in their lives. *Addiction, 106,* 1087–1094. doi:10.1111/j.1360-0443.2011.03361.x

Copello, A., & Orford, J. (2002). Addiction and the family: Is it time for services to take notice of the evidence? *Addiction, 97,* 1361–1363. doi:10.1046/j.1360-0443.2002.00259.x

Copello, A., Orford, J., Hodgson, R., Tober, G., & Barrett, C. On behalf of the UKATT Research Team. (2002). Social Behaviour and Network Therapy: Basic principles and early experiences, *Addictive Behaviors, 27,* 345–366. doi:http://dx.doi.org/10.1016/S0306-4603(01)00176-9

Copello, A., Orford, J., Tober, G., & Hodgson, R. (2009). *Social behaviour and network therapy for alcohol problems.* London: Brunner Routledge.

Copello, A., Templeton, L., Orford, J., & Velleman, R. (2010a). The 5-Step Method: Principles and practice. *Drugs: Education, Prevention and Policy, 17*(S1), 86–99. doi:10.3109/09687637.2010.515186

Copello, A., Templeton, L., Orford, J., & Velleman, R. (2010b). The 5-Step Method: Evidence of gains for affected family members. *Drugs: Education, Prevention and Policy, 17*(S1), 100–112. doi:10.3109/09687637.2010.514234

Copello, A., Templeton, L., & Velleman, R. (2006). Family intervention for drug and alcohol misuse: Is there a best practice? *Current Opinion in Psychiatry, 19,* 271–276. doi:10.1097/01.yco.0000218597.31184.41

Copello, A., Velleman, R., & Templeton, L. (2005). Family interventions in the treatment of alcohol and drug problems, *Drug and Alcohol Review, 24*(4), 369–385. doi:10.1080/09595230500302356

Copello, A., Williamson, E., Orford, J., & Day, E. (2006). Implementing and evaluating Social Behaviour and Network Therapy in drug treatment practice in the UK: A feasibility study. *Addictive Behaviors, 31,* 802–810. doi:10.1016/j.addbeh.2005.06.005

Day, E., Copello, A., Seddon, J., Christie, M., Bamber, D., Powell, C., et al.. (2013a). Pilot study of a social network intervention for heroin users in opiate substitution treatment: Study protocol for a randomized controlled trial. *Trials, 14,* 264. doi:10.1186/1745-6215-14-264 http://www.trialsjournal.com/content/14/1/264

Day, E., Copello, A., Karia, M., Roche, J., Grewal, P., George, S., et al. (2013b). Social Network Support for Individuals receiving opiate substitution treatment and its association with treatment progress. *European Addiction Research, 19,* 211–221. doi:10.1159/000343827

EuroQol Group. (1990). EuroQol: A new facility for the measurement of health-related quality of life. *Health Policy, 16*, 199–208.

Ferris, J. A., Laslett, A., Livingstone, M., Room, R., & Wilkinson, C. (2011). The impacts of others' drinking on mental health. *Medical Journal of Australia, 195*(3), 22–26.

Havassy, B., Hall, S., & Wasserman, D. (1991). Social support and relapse: commonalities among alcoholics, opiate users, and cigarette smokers. *Addictive Behaviors, 16*, 235–246. doi:http://dx.doi.org/10.1016/0306-4603(91)90016-B

International Wellbeing Group. (2006). *Personal wellbeing index* (4th ed.). Deakin University, Melbourne: Australian Centre on Quality of Life.

Laslett, A-M., Catalano, P., Chikritzhs, Y., Dale, C., Doran, C., Ferris, J., et al. (2010). *The range and magnitude of alcohol's harm to others*. Fitzroy, VIC: AER Centre for Alcohol Policy Research, Turning Point Alcohol and Drug Centre, Eastern Health.

Laslett, A-M., Room, R., Ferris, J., Wilkinson, C., Livingstone, M., & Mugavin, J. (2011). Surveying the range and magnitude of alcohol's harm to others in Australia. *Addiction, 106*, 1603–1611. doi:10.1111/j.1360-0443.2011.03445.x

Lee, C., Christie, M., Copello, A., & Kellett, S. (2012). Barriers and enablers to implementation of family-based work in alcohol services: A qualitative study of alcohol worker perceptions. *Drugs: Education, Prevention, and Policy, 19*(3), 244–252. doi:10.3109/09687637.2011.644599

Longabaugh, R., Wirtz, P., Zweben A., & Stout, R. (1998). Network support for drinking, alcoholics anonymous and long-term matching effects. *Addiction, 93*, 1313–1333. doi:10.1046/j.1360-0443.1998.93913133.x

McCrady, B. (2004). To have but one true friend: Implications for practice of research on alcohol use disorders and social networks. *Psychology of Addictive Behaviors, 18*, 113–121. doi:10.1037/0893-164X.18.2.113

Mohr, C., Averna, S., Kenny, D., & Del Boca, F. (2001). 'Getting by (or getting high) with a little help from my friends': An examination of adult alcoholics' friendships. *Journal of Studies on Alcohol and Drugs, 62*, 637–645.

Orford, J. (1990). Alcohol and the family: An international review of the literature with implications for research and practice. In L. T. Kozlowski, H. M. Annis, H. D. Cappell, F. B. Glaser, M. S. Goodstadt, Y. Israel, et al. (Eds.), *Research advances in alcohol and drug problems* (vol. 10, pp. 81–155). New York: Plenum Press.

Orford, J., Copello, A., Velleman, R., & Templeton, L. (2010a). Family members affected by a close relative's addiction: The stress-strain-coping-support model. *Drugs: Education, Prevention and Policy, 17*(1), 36–43. doi:10.3109/09687637.2010.514801

Orford, J., Velleman, R., Copello, A., Templeton, L., & Ibanga, A. (2010b). The experiences of affected family members: A summary of two decades of qualitative research. *Drugs: Education, Prevention and Policy, 17*(1), 44–62. doi:10.3109/09687637.2010.514192

Orford, J., Velleman, R., Natera, G., Templeton, L., & Copello, A. (2013). Addiction in the family is a major but neglected contributor to the global burden of adult ill-health. *Social Science and Medicine, 78*, 70–77. doi:doi.org/10.1016/j.socscimed.2012.11.036

Ray, G. T., Mertens, J. R., & Weisner, C. (2007). The excess medical cost and health problems of family members of persons diagnosed with alcohol or drug problems. *Medical Care, 45*, 116–122.

Ray, G. T., Mertens, J. R., & Weisner, C. (2009). Family members of persons with alcohol or drug dependence: Health problems and medical cost compared to family members of persons with diabetes and asthma: Family members of persons with AODD. *Addiction, 104*(2), 203–214. doi:10.1111/j.1360-0443.2008.02447.x

Room, R., Ferris, J., Laslett, A., Livingstone, M., Mugavin, J., & Wilkinson, C. (2010). The drinker's effect on the social environment: A conceptual framework for studying alcohol's harm to others. *International Journal of Environmental Research and Public Health, 7*, 1855–1871. doi:10.3390/ijerph7041855

UKATT Research Team. (2005a). Effectiveness of treatment for alcohol problems: Findings of the randomised UK Alcohol Treatment Trial. *British Medical Journal, 331,* 541–544. doi:http://dx.doi.org/10.1136/bmj.331.7516.541

UKATT Research Team. (2005b). Cost-effectiveness of treatment for alcohol problems: Findings of the randomised UK Alcohol Treatment Trial. *British Medical Journal, 331,* 544–558. doi:http://dx.doi.org/10.1136/bmj.331.7516.544

Velleman, R. (2010). The policy context: Reversing a state of neglect. *Drugs: Education, Prevention and Policy, 17*(1), 8–35. doi:10.3109/09687637.2010.514796

Wasserman, D., Stewart, A., & Delucchi, K. (2001). Social support and abstinence from opiates and cocaine during opioid maintenance treatment. *Drug Alcohol Dependencce, 65,* 65–75. doi:http://dx.doi.org/10.1016/S0376-8716(01)00151-X

Wiseman, J. P. (1991). *The other half: Wives of alcoholics and their social-psychological situation.* New York: Aldine de Gruyter.

Zywiak, W., Neighbors, C., Martin, R. Johnson, J., Eaton, C., & Rohsenow, D. (2009). The Important People Drug and Alcohol interview: Psychometric properties, predictive validity, and implications for treatment. *Journal of Substance Abuse Treatment, 36,* 321–330. doi:http://dx.doi.org/10.1016/j.jsat.2008.08.001

4   Working Systemically with Alcohol Misuse

ARLENE VETERE[1] AND RUDI DALLOS[2]

[1]VID Specialized University, Oslo, Norway
[2]Plymouth University, Plymouth, UK

CHAPTER OUTLINE

4.1   INTRODUCTION

> Many of the most intense emotions arise during the formation, the maintenance, the disruption and the renewal of attachment relationships. The formation of a bond is described as falling in love, maintaining a bond as loving someone, and losing a partner as grieving over someone. Similarly, threat of loss arouses anxiety, and actual loss gives rise to sorrow, whilst each of these situations is likely to arouse anger. The unchallenged maintenance of a bond is experienced as a source of security and the renewal of a bond as a source of joy.
>
> (Bowlby, 1980, p. 12)

The quotation above, from Bowlby's work, reminds us that threat of loss, rejection and abandonment arouses the same difficult emotional responses as actual abandonment, such as when a partner threatens, 'I'm leaving, I've had enough', or a parent shouts in frustration and anger, 'I wish you'd never been born.' The quotation also begins to make clear that if anger is part of the response to perceived or actual rejection, then others are likely to become organized and preoccupied by the anger, and tend to lose curiosity about what else the person may be experiencing, such as hurt feelings, and sadness, and so on. Finally, the quotation helps us see that the renewal of relationships is as important as the initial 'falling out'. Thus, in our therapeutic work, we pay as much attention to how people resolve and heal relationship dilemmas and hurts, as we do to the reasons and ways that they experience disappointments and hurts. If alcohol is used to comfort and soothe in the face of hurt and feeling oneself to be a disappointment to others, and to numb unbearable feelings of shame and sadness, it can then paradoxically make it more likely that alcohol will be used as the solution in future, in response to others' continued disappointment in their use of alcohol.

Bowlby (1973, p. 407) has also written about our lifelong need for a 'secure base' in our close relationships, experienced as trust and felt security:

> For not only young children, it is now clear, but human beings of all ages are found to be at their happiest and to be able to deploy their talents to best advantage when they are confident that, standing behind them are one or more trusted persons who will come to their aid should difficulties arise. The person trusted provides a secure base from which his (or her) companion can operate.

In our therapeutic work with people whose drinking is problematic, the question of trust is paramount. They may have come to trust alcohol to help them deal with their emotions, and to protect them from intolerable emotion. The idea that other people can be trusted may be frightening, if they have learned through previous adverse experiences that people cannot be trusted, i.e. they let you down, they hurt you, and they harm you. If people have experienced the pairing of seeking of care and comfort with rejection, fear or abuse, then this seeking of care becomes frightening. This poses not only a problem for them and their families, but also for the alcohol service practitioners, since attempts to 'help' may trigger non-conscious negative expectations. Such dilemmas need a delicate and persistent response from practitioners, and we shall explore in this chapter how attachment narrative therapy (ANT) and systemic thinking can inform practice in community alcohol services. We wish to advance the argument that a singular focus in community alcohol services on the individual of the drinker both misses the opportunity to support family members and to see them as a resource, thus helping to motivate the problem drinker into treatment.

4.2 FAMILY LIFE

Velleman, Copello and Maslin (1998) have explored the impact of problem drinking in family life, for different family relationships, roles and tasks of daily living. The impact is both deep and far-reaching, and can linger on into the future once the problem drinking has ceased. Family members' fear that the problem drinking will resume can colour relationships and impair the re-establishment of trust for years, if not challenged and helped.

Family rituals, such as birthday and coming-of-age celebrations, festivals and holidays may conventionally include the use of alcohol to foster a good occasion. But for some families they can be marred by the presence of alcohol, for example, fear that the problem drinker will get drunk and embarrass or shame others, or behave in ways that shame the drinker. More broadly, there can be other fears, such as, that a younger person may make themselves vulnerable when drunk to the predatory behaviour of others. Shame and shaming are complex – they can be a private and/or public response, and can be both felt experiences and behavioural practices designed to shame and ostracize. The dilemma of shame is that the person shamed feels themselves to be the mistake, rather than having made a mistake, thus making them vulnerable to drinking again to relieve the feelings of shame.

One consequence can be that many activities, such as celebrations and festivities, might be dreaded and even avoided by family members for fear of drunkenness and social embarrassment, leading to a slow closing down of social support networks and a growing isolation for the family. Fear of drinking resuming in the future, once it has ceased, can linger on for years, and make it harder to accept social invitations. Money spent on alcohol may drain family resources, and similarly, keeping the drinker short of money as a way of trying to control drinking, or not inviting people home can contribute to the social isolation. In such circumstances, a service response needs to consider the needs of all family members through providing support, therapy and consultation services, to help them re-grow their social support networks, so crucial for well-being in our communities.

Family members' roles can be changed by drinking in predictable and unpredictable ways. For example, if a parent is drunk, a child may need to take over some parental caretaking responsibilities for other children, and when the parent is sober, they may need to step down from those responsibilities. Such experience with caretaking responsibilities in our families of origin can lead to social competence and a developed sense of compassion, but equally can be overwhelming for the children concerned if the responsibilities overwhelm their capacity to manage. Similarly such changes in role for the children may mean there are times when adult accessibility for comfort and reassurance is restricted and unpredictable. This could lead children to cope by learning to deactivate their own emotional responses and to suppress the expression of their emotional needs for containment and comfort.

Family routines can be affected adversely by problem drinking. Routines are important in families as they provide structure and predictability that give rise to a sense of stability. For example, a parent may forget to collect children from school, or meals may not be prepared on a regular basis. It may not be possible for children to bring their friends home to play for fear of what state their parent may be in, and so on. Communication in families can be affected by problem drinking, in terms of what it is safe to say and when and how to say it. Family members may say things to others they have cause to regret when sober. If there are patterns of binge drinking, there may be differences in what is talked about during periods of drinking and of sobriety, and the person who is drinking may well forget what they said, whereas others do not. This creates a context where feelings can be hurt, resentments and frustrations can build, and behaviours and intentions can be misunderstood, but the context of drinking has made it near impossible to speak about these hurts and disappointments for fear of further conflict or a return to drinking.

Other chapters in this book outline the personal and social costs of heavy drinking, to include physical health problems, violence in relationships, vulnerability to depression, anxiety and suicide, adverse effects on children's well-being, and difficulties at work and public disorder. A family-wide therapeutic response can impact directly on people's lives to both support the drinker into treatment and to help maintain recovery, and to address the mutual impact of causes and consequences in our complex relationship to alcohol.

4.3   FAMILY SYSTEMS APPROACHES

Family systems therapies emphasize the current interactional determinants of problem drinking in the approach to formulation. Formulation and intervention are designed to be collaborative, to use people's own words and understand their views of change, their intentions and values, and to even-handedly address the dilemmas around drinking without confronting denial directly. As hidden shame is so much a feature of drinking that is maintained by affect regulation problems, and ambivalence about alcohol use is expected, any initial denial expressed is understood and explored using a consultation approach. The responsibility for changing drinking patterns rests with the problem drinker and family, with the therapist taking responsibility for creating a context of safety within which change can occur and be supported. The therapist seeks to explore the costs and benefits of problem drinking within the family, for relationships and for individuals. A systemic approach recognizes the impact both for individuals *and* for their relationships (Vetere & Dallos, 2003).

Systemic formulation takes account of patterns in communication, patterns in relationships, patterns over time and life cycle issues, community responses, social discourses around drinking and social support (Vetere & Henley, 2001). Special attention is given to working with violence and abuse in family relationships (Cooper & Vetere, 2005).

4.3.1   Patterns in Communication

As described above, a systemic approach explores sober versus drinking patterns of communication in the family, with special emphasis on the role of alcohol use in affect regulation. Family members may accuse the problem drinker of telling lies about whether they have been drinking, how much, when and where, and so on. This risks further shaming and blaming in relationships. The focus in the therapeutic work is on responsibility, not blame, and on straight talking, i.e. what makes it safe to be clear and direct about what you have been doing and why. So, for example, if a family member hides their beer cans in the bathroom cabinet, we explore what helps them and others move to a position where they can talk about the drinking. Since people hide their drinking to protect themselves and others, the therapeutic work promotes safety, by softening the blaming, affirming needs and wishes, promoting listening and understanding, and supporting accountability.

Anger can often be a response to feeling blamed and shamed. It can also be a response to fearing rejection and abandonment. Bowlby (1980) described two patterns of anger triggered by attachment threat: the anger of hope and the anger of despair. The anger of hope is expressed as a desperate attempt to seek attention from a loved one, for example, by shouting, 'What do I have to do to get you to pay attention to me?'. The anger of despair, in contrast, is usually expressed as contempt for the loved one, 'You're rubbish and a waste of space!'. Both patterns of anger expression, according to Bowlby, show a wish for a continuing relationship connection with the loved one.

Empathy within the therapeutic relationship is crucial for exploring the meaning of significant human experiences and for helping to organize and integrate experiences into a coherent narrative. The therapist slows down the pace of the dialogue, to enable processing of emotionally powerful material and experiences, in ways that reaffirm and clarify people's experiences. Comforting and soothing are offered in response to difficult experiences and interactions that pave the way for family members to take emotional risks in how they reach out to one another in their attempts to resolve and heal hurt.

4.3.2   Patterns in Relationships

Interactional responses to problem drinking can polarize into patterns of complementarity and patterns of symmetry in intimate relationships. For example, symmetrical relationships are characterized by both overt and covert competitiveness, such as over who is right and who is wrong, whose needs take precedence, who needs most looking after, and so on, whereas complementary patterns have someone in a more dominant position, with the other in a subjugated position, for example, on matters of moral propriety, on who is right, who is the carer, and so on. These patterns can be benign in their impact on well-being, but where they constrain and limit both personal and relationship development, they can be helped to evolve into more mutual and reciprocal patterns of interaction, that promote secure bonding.

Power and control in relationships can intersect with attachment security in ways that leave people exposed and vulnerable, for example, having to rely on someone who treats you unkindly. Both symmetrical and complementary patterns are prone to escalation and in alcoholic systems we can see a combination of both in play; the partner may become angry and accuse or criticize, which can lead to mutual blaming and anger – and sometimes to physical violence. This can turn to expressions of remorse by the drinking partner and attempts for their partner to step into a care-giving and controlling mode, such as monitoring the drinking, taking away drink, advising and 'nagging'. These patterns are fuelled in turn by each partner's own attachment histories and also by the influence of the alcohol which is likely to reduce cognition and reflection and increase emotional instability.

When family members themselves become angry, this is likely to further fuel the emotional arousal of the drinking member. For example, family members will sometimes speak of cruelty, such as spitting food at a partner when drunk, to express frustration and make them stop drinking. Occasionally we will encounter relationship patterns where the problem drinker is accused of personal qualities and intentions that are disowned by other family members. Both types of responses are likely to fuel unhelpful arousal and potentially to make the drinker feel more alone, their attachment needs unmet, and with a longing for another drink to help them feel 'better'. Sometimes these patterns are more extreme, such as scapegoating. In our experience as relationship therapists, these issues are in some ways harder to address, as the non-drinker may be occupying the 'high moral ground' with the drinker so shamed that they are unable to assert their own experience and felt needs. In these circumstances, a mix of individual therapy/key worker support, with relationship therapy to follow, helps manage the impact of problem drinking. This is particularly important when the drinking has stopped, as that is often when couples will 'go to the wire' and address whether they still want to be together, and the non-drinking partner may feel entitled to extract 'pay back' by not giving up practices of blaming and shaming. These practices of blaming and shaming often develop as an attempt to stop the drinking, and escalate into symmetrical patterns of interaction as repeated attempts to solve the problem of the drinking.

4.3.3 *Patterns over Time and Life Cycle Issues*

When people seek treatment to help with stopping the drinking, for themselves and their family members, it is always helpful to ask the question, 'why now?'. Very often, life-cycle events and transitions in family life will prompt a review or re-evaluation of life choices. For example, we met a recently retired couple who had been looking forward to spending more time with their many grandchildren. Their three grown-up children had long been worried about the extent of their mother's drinking and the impact on her health, and had recently given her an ultimatum. They told her she could not see her grandchildren until she stopped drinking, as they did not want their children exposed to her when she was inebriated. This caused a crisis in family relationships, and particularly in her relationship with her husband. This prompted them to seek consultation with us in the family therapy service.

Transitions in the family life cycle often provide opportunities for change and for the revision of intergenerational scripts. If drinking has been taking place over a number of years, family members will organize themselves around the drinking and the drinker for protection, and to ensure the daily tasks of family life are managed. The resultant family structure and patterns of interaction, described above, are often referred to as 'problem-determined systems' (Anderson, Goolishian & Winderman, 1986). This description attempts to capture family members' intentions to protect and look after each other, even when the solutions to the problem of drinking appear to make matters worse. This recognition by the therapist, of family members' attempts to help and protect, even when they are unsuccessful, is a softer formulation of the resultant problematic patterns, and may help family members feel less blamed for the difficulties, from which they so often struggle to free themselves.

Family members' willingness to seek help with these 'stuck' and repetitive relationship patterns often depends on their attachment strategies. For example, in some families, there has been an 'avoidant' culture of self-reliance that mitigates against seeking help, in others with 'anxious-ambivalent' patterns there may have been a highly emotionally charged pattern of seeking 'help' but in order mainly to provide a coalition to offer confirmation of their anger. Systemic therapists have also referred to these processes as the 'relationship to help' (Reder & Fredman, 1996). This is the idea that people are more or less willing to seek outside help for emotional and relational difficulties depending on sub-cultural discourses about the acceptability of speaking outside the family, and past experiences of seeking help. This can be a matter of pride and shame in families, so we never underestimate the courage it takes for the problem drinker and family members to seek help for the drinking and its consequences.

Attachment theory posits that our beliefs and expectations about ourselves and others evolve in the context of our early relationships and are reinforced, maintained and changed in the context of our later intimate relationships. Our view of ourselves as loveable and worthy of others' care and attention, and our view of others as deserving of care and attention, can influence why and how we drink. In our experience, many of the people we work with have not been helped to understand and regulate their affect as children growing up, they have not been taught to soothe and comfort themselves when unhelpfully aroused. Further to this, many children have seen their parents use alcohol to deal with their feelings. This combined with a view of self as undeserving of care can lead to a reliance on alcohol, rather than people. The introduction of alcohol as a mechanism for coping with unhelpful physiological arousal may have been ironic, in that exposure to alcohol in the home, or with peers when growing up, may have made the benefits for short-term affect regulation clear. Some children grow up with a 'corrective script' in which they are determined not to employ alcohol as they saw their parents doing. However, faced with distress, rejection or failure, they may find themselves implicitly turning to the bottle as a source of comfort that has been unconsciously 'programmed'. Once they drink, the reduction of anxiety and the blotting out of unbearable feelings and somatic states (tension, aches and pains) are a powerful negative reinforcer, despite the more sober reflection that it is not a long-term solution.

4.4   WORKING THERAPEUTICALLY WITH VIOLENCE AND ABUSE

When violent behaviour has taken place in the family, we work for safety as our first priority (Cooper & Vetere, 2005). We use a visible safety methodology in our practice, so our work with safety is known and understood by all involved – both family members and other practitioners in the professional system. Our safety methodology has been described extensively elsewhere, but suffice to say here, that we use no-violence contracts and safety plans. We pay attention to the effects on children and adults of exposure to others' violent behaviour, and in particular, hidden and masked trauma responses. We liaise closely with the professional system, and address anxiety in the family-professional network. If this anxiety is left unattended, it can lead people to disrupt therapeutic work for fear that safety is not being taken seriously. The relationship between explanations for violence and accountability for behaviour that harms others, as well as responsibility for safety, is managed carefully, so that explanation is not seen to diminish or elide responsibility for harm. As mentioned above, sometimes family members use coercion and control to try to stop the drinking, and often these coercive behaviours become frankly abusive.

Anger can often be triggered in family interaction in the context of attachment threat. Research by Crittenden (2006), building on Bowlby's earlier work, has identified the development of attachment strategies, used by children, young people and adults, to help with affect regulation. At their extremes, they can be described as avoidant strategies or preoccupied strategies, on a continuum of protective and defensive processes. It is helpful to consider how anger might be expressed in response to attachment threat in the context of reliance on one of these coping strategies.

Avoidant strategies involve the use of deactivating strategies to help dismiss the impact of unhelpful physiological arousal – almost as if we try to persuade ourselves we are alright when clearly we are not! Avoidant strategies are thought to develop in childhood as a result of learning that expressing emotion cannot reliably elicit comfort, reassurance or caring. Affect is inhibited and physiological discomfort and emotional distress are denied, and in more extreme instances, distorted or falsified, such as pretending to smile and be happy when unhappy and upset. This can lead to a denial of the need for others' comfort and reassurance, and a somewhat compulsive reliance on the self. As with any coping strategy, it has its limits, and the degree of upset or attachment threat a person is subject to may exceed the capability of this strategy, and anger may 'break through'. It can be experienced as an intrusion, and may be a source of shame if it breaks a family rule about not expressing 'negative' emotion. This rule may have developed out of a family history where anger was dangerous and heralded aggression and physical violence. The 'angry intrusion' can come as a surprise, if not a shock to others, who believed the person to be 'alright'. The developmental outcome might be that family members who have not been helped to develop more balanced strategies for managing upset and distress may feel helpless, frustrated and shamed in the face of the anger. In this case, rather than being able to think about what the anger may mean, and in particular about what vulnerabilities and needs it is indirectly expressing, they may retreat and attempt to supress it. One typical avenue leads to a possible pathologizing of the drinking and the anger, for example, that he is an 'alcoholic' and cannot help it, or that she has a 'dependent personality'. Both of these at one level can be seen as 'non-blaming' but they also ultimately distract attention from the consideration of drinking as a source of comfort and self-regulation.

Preoccupied strategies are thought to develop in a context where care taking is unreliable and unpredictable. The child cannot predict when their distress will elicit a warm and comforting response and learns to persist in their demands for comfort and attention until a response is elicited – in many ways this is like being maintained on an intermittent reinforcement schedule for the child. As a result of this inability to predict, the child learns they cannot rely on what is said, but increasingly must rely on unregulated affective information. The child tends to split their feelings of anger and vulnerability as a self-protective strategy, so they might display one and suppress the other. Emotional expression becomes exaggerated in the absence of cognitive strategies for understanding and regulating affect, such that explanations become simplified in the attempt to manage the complexity and overwhelming nature of unregulated arousal. In this context, strategies for processing negative affect and understanding its consequences on others are limited, such that reliance on alcohol as a more predictable source of comfort and the management of feelings takes hold.

4.5 ENGAGEMENT AND THE THERAPEUTIC RELATIONSHIP

The outcome research literature (summarized in NICE, 2011) supports the role of relatives in confronting the drinking and supporting entry to therapy. However, where a person has developed a primary attachment to alcohol, then therapy may be perceived as a threat rather than a new attachment. In these circumstances we have found it helpful to offer a consultation process as a prelude to relationship therapy. This provides an opportunity to build a relationship with the person without this being potentially undermined too early on in a meeting with the family, where the feared and perhaps typical processes, such as humiliation, may lead the person to think that we are siding with the non-drinking relatives. Thus, a consultation process allows people to 'put their toe in the water' and gradually come to see that talking with us is not experienced as a threat, i.e. a source of shaming, judgemental interaction, and so on. In effect, we start to become a transitional attachment figure for them.

We form a therapeutic triangle between ourselves as relationship therapists, the family and the alcohol key worker. In our view, the alcohol key worker is primary in forming a bridge between the client/s and ourselves, and acts as the stable third in the triangle. The alcohol key worker can help in managing clients' fear and anxiety engendered at the thought of confronting the impact of problem drinking on family members and on family relationships. It seems there is more variation in successful treatment outcome between therapists working in the same modality than across outcomes in different modalities (Lambert, 2004). Thus, differences in treatment effectiveness might be attributed to a key worker/therapist's ability to maintain a facilitative stance in the face of a client's defensiveness or hostility. This emphasizes the central role of the therapeutic alliance in change processes, and suggests that organizational support for key workers and therapists is crucial. The development of a stable therapeutic triangle is the goal, and this forms the secure base within which containment, safety, reflection and relational risk-taking can emerge and grow.

4.6 CONCLUSION

In conclusion, attachment theory has some key implications for systemic practice with couples and families. It recognizes the importance in our therapeutic work of helping clients name their emotional experiences as a prelude to illuminating understanding and re-processing emotional material and lived experience. It facilitates therapeutic work that encourages the development of empathy, and curiosity about the others' experience, based in the felt experience of being listened to, understood, and soothed and calmed. It emphasizes the central role of comforting, reassurance and soothing in managing and regulating affect and unhelpful arousal. It emphasizes the importance of reflection and calm consideration in order to think clearly, to speak straightforwardly about emotional matters, and to make good decisions. And finally, it promotes integration of our representations of affect, cognition and action by supporting our capacity to narrate our experiences in a coherent manner.

SUGGESTIONS FOR FURTHER READING

Cooper, J., & Vetere, A. (2005). *Domestic violence and family safety: A systemic approach to working with violence in families*. Chichester: John Wiley & Sons. Ltd.

Dallos, R., & Vetere, A. (2009). *Systemic therapy and attachment narratives: Applications in a range of clinical settings*. London: Routledge.

Gill, R. (Ed.). (2014). *Addictions from an attachment perspective*. London: Karnac.

Rowe, C., & Liddle, H. (2002). Substance abuse. In D. Sprenkle (Ed.), *Effectiveness research in marriage and family therapy*. Alexandria, VA: AAMFT.

Vetere, A., & Dallos, R. (2003). *Working systemically with families: Formulation, intervention and evaluation*. London: Karnac.

REFERENCES

Anderson, H., Goolishian, H., & Winderman, I. (1986). Problem determined systems: Toward transformation in family therapy. *Journal of Strategic and Family Therapy, 4,* 1–13.

Bowlby, J. (1973). *Attachment and loss.* vol. 2: *Separation, anxiety and anger.* London: Hogarth Press.

Bowlby, J. (1980). *Attachment and loss.* vol. 3: *Loss.* New York: Basic Books.

Cooper, J., & Vetere, A. (2005). *Domestic violence and family safety: A systemic approach to working with violence in families.* Chichester: John Wiley & Sons, Ltd.

Crittenden, P. (2006). A dynamic-maturational model of attachment. *Australian and New Zealand Journal of Family Therapy, 27,* 105–115. doi:10.1002/j.1467-8438.2006.tb00704.x

Lambert, M. (Ed.). (2004). *Bergin and Garfield's handbook of psychotherapy and behavior change* (5th ed.). New York: John Wiley & Sons, Inc.

NICE. (2011). *Alcohol-use disorders: Diagnosis, assessment and management of harmful drinking and alcohol dependence.* NICE Clinical Guideline 115. www.nice.org.uk/guidance/CG115

Reder, P., & Fredman, G. (1996). The relationship to help: Interacting beliefs about the treatment process. *Clinical Child Psychology and Psychiatry, 1,* 457–467.

Velleman, R., Copello, A., & Maslin, J. (Eds.). (1998). *Living with drink: Women who live with problem drinkers.* London: Longman.

Vetere, A., & Dallos, R. (2003). *Working systemically with families: Formulation, intervention and evaluation.* London: Karnac.

Vetere, A., & Henley, M. (2001). Integrating couples and family therapy into a community alcohol service: A pan-theoretical approach. *Journal of Family Therapy, 23,* 85–101. doi:10.1111/1467-6427.00170

5 'Dangerous Desires and Inanimate Attachments': Modern Psychodynamic Approaches to Substance Misuse

MARTIN WEEGMANN[1] AND EDWARD J. KHANTZIAN[2]

[1]NHS and Independent Practice, London, UK
[2]Department of Psychiatry, Harvard Medical School, Cambridge, MA, USA

CHAPTER OUTLINE

5.1 INTRODUCTION

Although psychodynamic approaches to addiction have not been prominent in the field compared with a range of other psychosocial models, it is our contention that such approaches offer a unique and subtle complement to our understanding of the nature of addition and addictive suffering: an understanding in depth. We regard this approach as complementary to, rather than competing with, other approaches such as motivational enhancement, relapse prevention, 12 Step facilitation, and so on. A psychodynamic perspective is of great value to clinicians in their efforts to reach an emotionally hard-to-reach population of clients; and formal psychoanalytic therapy (and, more commonly, psychodynamically-informed therapy) can be of considerable help to many clients as they forge the psychic journey that underpins recovery. Not only this, but psychodynamic understanding is a solid resource to the clinician, regardless of the approach they use, as a way of better containing the complicated and uncomfortable emotions and reactions they can feel in response to their clients.

Laying out our general convictions, we think that it is difficult to comprehend the nature of addictive suffering, as well as the successful overcoming of such suffering, without the following:

- Postulating some notion of the 'internal world', with an intricate layering of affect, cognition, memory and learning. Addiction represents a life lived *in extremis*, requiring a corresponding concept of 'extreme internal worlds'.

- An understanding of 'irrationality', by which we mean that thinking, action and judgment become disconnected, short-term and self-defeating (see Sutherland's (2007 [1992]) interesting exploration of concept of the dimension of irrationality in all human affairs).

- An appreciation of powerful psychological forces, if one wills, including unconscious, in which individuals are caught between quite different positions and motivations. Indeed, the very term 'psycho-dynamic' has from its inception been concerned with such forces and their configurations, which are hard to describe except perhaps by metaphors. Thus individuals with addiction often present as torn individuals, struggling with 'different selves' and contradictory 'self states', as captured by such popular expressions as 'like Jekyll and Hyde', 'it wasn't me', or 'I'm out of character when using'.

- An understanding of the serious dysregulations of life, emotion and relationships associated with substance misuse. This requires thinking about predisposing addictive vulnerabilities and the devastating, traumatizing consequences of immersion in a world of using. Chronic substance misuse has an enveloping effect on individuals, subsuming more and more aspects of their lives, from which people protect themselves by complicated rationales and defences. Unfortunately, blunted empathy, for self and others, and denial of one's wider needs are a concomitant of this envelopment (Weegmann & Khantzian, 2011).

- Acknowledging the complicated emotions, reactions and strains that are aroused in workers who help those with substance misuse, traditionally called 'counter-transferences', and which are seldom explicitly addressed by other approaches.
- An in-depth understanding of the process by which individuals can and do exit addictive careers, re-building damaged selves. A concept of 'internal recovery' is proposed to describe this process of psychic change.

Early psychoanalytic and psychodynamic treatments rested principally on a passive model of interaction by the therapist in which she/he was detached, remote and depended mainly on interpretive interventions. We do not shrink from criticism of such approaches which have suffered from old-fashioned, Freudian formulations, obscure language and speculative concepts, usually focused on the entirely regressive and self-destructive aspects of the disorder. By contrast, contemporary psychodynamic theory and practice place greater emphasis on the centrality of emotions, self-regulation, interpersonal relations, self-care, the treatment alliance and here-and-now observations. Emphasis is placed on active support, empathy, a focus on recurrent themes that occur in and out of therapy, and an emphasis on developmental factors to understand current emotional and relational difficulties clients experience in treatment that parallel experiences outside of treatment (Weegmann & Khantzian, 2011). Collaborative, active and phase-appropriate therapy is important in the assessment and treatment of addictive disorders. In their contribution to the American textbook, *Psychotherapy for the Treatment of Substance Misuse*, Lighdale, Mack and Frances (2011, p. 243) state:

> Application of psychodynamic understanding – including attention to the unconscious, child development, ego function, affect regulation and efforts to enhance self-esteem and deal with shame and other narcissistic vulnerability – widens the range of patients who can be treated.

Similarly, colleagues in the United Kingdom have explored the rich variety of ways in which such understanding can help (Weegmann & Cohen, 2002).

We begin by highlighting three different psychodynamic traditions, followed by our integrative view of addiction as a disorder of self-regulation.

5.2 PRIMITIVE EMOTIONAL STATES: KLEINIAN VIEWS

Just as Freud saw the child within the adult, Melanie Klein saw the infant within the child (Segal, 1973). What happens from the earlier stages of development onwards constitutes developmental templates through which the growing infant makes sense of the world and manages rudimentary emotional life. Klein was centrally concerned with the earliest forces, as it were, of mental life and what it is that enables small steps to integration and growth to proceed. Her, albeit cumbersome, terms to characterize struggles around growth were the 'paranoid-schizoid position', marked by threats, persecutory anxieties and all-good/all-bad polarities and the 'depressive position', in which the infant is able to experience a more mixed world and to experience early forms of guilt and initiate reparative efforts. She posited 'positions' rather than stages, because of the to-and-fro movement between them, continuing to a degree throughout life and in response to stress, when we are all capable of 'reverting' in our response and coping.

Space does not permit a full review of the Kleinian tradition, in relation to substance misuse, but we venture the following hypotheses:

1) Addiction increasingly creates, or re-creates, early emotional states. It reinforces a primitivization of emotions, returning people, as it were, to more paranoid-schizoid functioning; a battle ensues between omnipotent ways of dealing with the world, assisted by drugging versus the desire to change (English, 2009).

2) Drug use is anti-growth, with addiction seen as a form of psychic evasion and evacuation of pain. Developmental 'short-cuts' in the form of 'fixes', 'rushes' and 'highs' impair or halt maturation (Hyatt-Williams, 1978).

3) There is often a wavering of positions, in which addicted individuals at one point see the damage they are doing, struggling to resist its intense pull, while at another point succumb to it, rejecting the need for change or any consideration of reality. This reflects a deep, powerful form of ambivalence, more malignant than the 'motivational dilemmas' postulated by motivational interviewing approaches. It is an added reason why presumed 'change for the better' (e.g. stopping use) can lead to a paradoxical counter-reaction (e.g. returning to use), as change is felt to be dangerous. This wavering of psychic positions is often seen between and within sessions, with moment-to-moment shifts in motivation and the expression of contradictory aims.

4) Dependence on drugs is a striking enactment of what one distinguished Kleinian analyst calls 'psychic retreats' (Steiner, 1993). Psychic retreats are defined as pathological organizations based on powerful avoidances, whose functioning and maintenance feel like a matter of survival to the person concerned. Related terms come to mind: sanctuaries, bastions, refuges. Interestingly, however, some of the terms that refer to avoidances can also refer in our field to places of healing, constituting a different kind of retreat. While not referring specifically to addiction, Steiner (1993, p. 2) writes of such retreats, 'Whether idealised or persecutory, it is clung to as preferable to even worse states which the patient is convinced they are the only alternatives.' One of the tragedies of drug addiction is how the seeking of retreats can become a way of extreme and habituated life;

5) The process of recovery from addiction involves a process of repair – to self, body, spirit and relationships. Reparation is central to the depressive position and psychic integration. Reparation is fragile and personalities can easily revert to simpler, more primitive postures. In the analysis of a violent man,

Anderson (1997) refers to an 'internal tyranny' which would periodically assert itself, with rapid shifts in which his client could make progress, only to 'put the boot in' at a subsequent stage. Thus, guilt is difficult to experience and old ways are difficult to relinquish.

CASE STUDY 5.1   PETER

Peter sought help for his problems from a psychologist, acknowledging that his life was 'mortgaged' to self-destruction and self-neglect. He was ashamed of this and was worried that he had left it 'too late to change'. Peter easily undermined his own progress, throwing caution to the wind. In one session, he observed, 'I can put it this way, the nearest thing I can find to being at ease, really at ease, is by using. And OK. I hate where it leads me the day after, but I keep going back, by which time it's a classic "fuck it".' He was puzzled by the seeming commitment by his therapist, offering the (serious?) joke, 'You've either got to be mad or very brave to deal with me.' There was an appreciative side to him also, in his comment that 'I almost gave up on trying to understand myself over the years – you know, just became an unquestioning addict.'

COMMENT

The psychologist was aware that Peter's state of motivation and goals were forever oscillating and that this was evident in the consulting room, where Peter turned to his psychologist both as a symbolic ally against drugs, while undoing and even mocking the help offered at one and the same time. Drug misuse had indeed constituted a form of psychic retreat for Peter, from the wider demands, responsibilities and potential of the world and self, hence the 'unquestioning addict'. His therapy illustrated just how precarious was his struggle to get beyond the 'addict' which dominated his life, internal and external.

5.3   COMFORTING SELF-OBJECTS: KOHUTIAN VIEWS

Kohut (1971; 1977) appreciated how troubled early parenting interactions around admiring, being admired, comfort and soothing left individuals so affected to suffer with troubled self-states and poor self-esteem. Although he did not systemically consider how these formulations related to the development of substance use disorders, he offered important observations about how self-disturbances could predispose to, and result in, dependence on substances. Kohut and subsequent recent investigators have emphasized how the addictively prone suffer from a lack of inner cohesion, fragmentation, feelings of powerlessness and helplessness. Originally Kohut (1971, p. 46) had stressed that substances were not sought out as substitutes for loved or loving objects, but were adopted as a 'replacement for a defect in psychological structure'. Subsequently he emphasized disturbances in the organization of self-structures characterized by states of disempowerment, helplessness, and low self-regard resulting in defences of grandiosity, disavowal of need and self-sufficiency, alternating with exaggerated needs for comfort and validation from others. Based on this latter conceptualization, he proposed that substance users resort to their drugs to lift these defences and allow self-soothing and revitalization of a better sense of well-being that they are otherwise so devoid of. Balint (1968, p. 56) anticipated this view when he described alcoholics' dependency as a 'basic fault'. He proposed:

> [It was] something wrong in the mind, a kind of deficiency which must be put right ... [to establish a sense of] ... harmony—a feeling that everything is now well between them and their environment—and ... the yearning for this feeling of harmony is the most important cause of alcoholism or, for that matter, any form of addiction.

Dodes (1996; 2002) and Director (2005) have extended these ideas to explain recurrent relapse and the compulsive nature of addiction. Khantzian (2003) clarifies the repetitive nature of addictive behaviour as a means to control addictive suffering. Dodes explained how feelings of helplessness and related narcissistic rage were key in the relapse and use of drugs, and Director described emotional states of powerlessness and unimportance and reactive attitudes of omnipotence leading to repeated relapse.

Little wonder that low to moderate doses of alcohol release restricted, self-sufficient individuals from their constricting defences, or stimulants activate and enliven those suffering with their states of emptiness, feeling vacuous, or impotent; and similarly boost or augment defensive postures of grandiosity and invincibility. Opiates, and heavy doses of alcohol on a different basis, cause individuals struggling with threatening and disorganizing aggression and rage to discover how these agents can feel like a magical elixir to produce a state of comfort and containment when otherwise it is elusive. Whether it is an incomplete and impoverished sense of self, intense disorganizing affect, or restricting and immobilizing defences, it is not surprising that the powerful feeling-altering properties of addictive drugs can become so alluring and compelling for those whose sense of self and self-regard are insufficient or underdeveloped.

CASE STUDY 5.2   MARY

Mary was asked to write an imaginative 'Letter to Alcohol' as part of her therapy. Among the things expressed included, 'When I drink you ... the buzz you give me feels like protection ... I can control and use you to help me, like a liquid talisman. It makes me feel so calm and peaceful ... without you I feel so alone, bereft.'

Mary went on, in the letter, to describe chronic shyness as teenager and how the discovery of alcohol lifted her confidence, enabling social interaction and assertion.

COMMENT

The letter suggests that self-soothing is part of the compelling attraction of alcohol for Mary. Developmentally it seemed that her resources of self were felt to be wanting and that alcohol did at the time, and subsequently, lift those resources and was increasingly incorporated into her coping with life. We underestimate the 'comforting' effects of substances at our peril, even as they co-exist with familiar negative consequences. The letter reads somewhat as a 'love letter', a tribute, and notwithstanding the physiological dimensions of tolerance and drink dependence, provides a useful insight into how she relates to her substance at an experiential level. Incorporated into her narcissistic economy as it were, the threat of change and managing without alcohol are considerable.

5.4   INANIMATE ATTACHMENTS: BOWLBIAN VIEWS

Attachment theory is celebrated for its productivity and influence, reaching far beyond the confines of psychoanalysis; it not only offers a theory of attachments, but also one of motivation, cognitive appraisal, psychobiology and information processing. A complex disorder, addiction affects all of these domains. Here we enumerate four substantive contributions of attachment theory to addictions, and are informed in this respect by the seminal contributions of Flores (2003) in the United States, and Reading (2002) in the United Kingdom.

1) *Misattachment to drugs.* In their relationships to drugs, people with substance misuse can truly be said to develop 'alternative attachments' which are strong, passionate and consuming. In this sense, there is a psychic 'take over' which distorts thinking, feeling and acting, not to mention the 'commandeering' of aspects of brain functions, including learning, reward and memory. The interpersonal consequences of addiction are devastating, summed up in its extremes in the Narcotics Anonymous (NA) saying, 'We don't make relationships, we take hostages.' Features associated with ordinary attachment needs have similarities and parallels with attachment to inanimate substances, such as proximity maintenance, homeostasis, separation distress, and so on. In an evocative turn of phrase, Reading (2002) refers to the transfer by which 'affectional bonds' are replaced by 'addictional bonds'.

2) *Internal working models.* As mediators of attachment experiences, Bowlby (1973, p. 203) explains, 'Each individual builds working models of the world and of himself in it, with the aid of which he perceives events, forecasts the future, and constructs his plans.' Again, in parallel to ordinary processes

of attachment, the user develops an alternative internal working model of the drug, as to what can be expected, what is sought, and so on. Drug experiences and memories gain in salience and, just as Bowlby suggested, a hierarchy of internal working models, so Reading (2012, unpublished) argues that '[the] drug insinuates itself ever higher in the individual's hierarchy of internal working models with a corresponding relegation of person-to-person models to lower status within the hierarchy'.

3) *Attachment disorders.* The issue of predisposition and early vulnerability to addictive disorders is enormously complex, with attachment theory offering an excellent basis for research. As this is explored elsewhere in the book, we simply comment that there is seldom an easy either/or explanation with respect to addictive vulnerability, and that developmental pathways into addiction are highly varied (Khantzian, Mack & Schatzberg, 1974). Over time, there is, however, invariably an inverse relation between substance abuse and healthy interpersonal attachments.

4) *Recovery and discovery.* Attachment-Oriented Therapy (ORT) uses the paradigm of attachment theory as a framework for helping those with substance misuse to rebuild their lives, referring to the graded ways in which attachment to drugs and drug mechanisms can be replaced by, hopefully, healthier, human attachments of various sorts.

CASE STUDY 5.3 CARL

Carl is a 49-year-old orthopaedic surgeon whose licence was suspended after colleagues discovered and reported that beyond his heavy drinking he had resorted to periodic use of an anaesthetic inhalant. He explained that he had resorted to the agent because it was easier to disguise, versus the alcohol, his need to escape persistent feelings of dysphoria. He also added that he thought his use of alcohol in early adolescence was motivated by similar feelings which he discovered were temporarily relieved by alcohol.

As a child, he describes a sense of persistent feelings of being disconnected and lonely. Although he feels his mother was well intentioned, he always sensed an emotional vacuum. Carl attributed his mother's emotional shallowness to the fact that she

was a middle child among nine siblings. He concluded that his mother's remoteness was compounded when she gave birth to twin daughters when he was 3 years old. He and his therapist adopted the term that mother did not have enough to go around and that he was 'back-burnered' after their birth. His keen intelligence helped in that he retreated to his room as an avid and curious reader and achieved considerable academic recognition and success in school. Albeit his father was kind, he worked long hours in a foundry and was not actively involved with him in his growing-up years.

The following is a near-verbatim account of his emotional reactions in a therapy session following a weekend visit home to his elderly parents that seemed to repeat and amplify a lifelong sense of anhedonia, despair, and near-suicidal depressive feelings. His opening statement was, 'Man! I feel bad when I go home; it sucks the life out of me … I regress; it takes the life out of me. I feel irritable, strange. Observing myself I feel bad about my reactions – there's no reason.' (In a subsequent group therapy meeting, he summed up that weekend with his parents by saying he felt 'shitty'.) With a little prompting by his therapist, he conceded that this was much like feelings from his childhood wherein he would become quiet. Agreeing, he recalled how it was always very difficult to engage his parents, especially his mother. He used to wonder if they even noticed their disconnection. His therapist asked him to elaborate. Carl gave the example of how on this most recent visit, his mom kept irrelevantly referring to a Principal's Award in high school that he had received, for which he felt there was no great significance. He said he had tried to speak to her about the death of her two sisters, who had passed away over the past six months; he also learned for the first time that her father, his grandfather, had been hospitalized for a 'nervous breakdown'. In both instances, he described how she could hardly sustain the conversation and did not express any emotion. He said, 'Little or nothing was said or shared.' In this context, he shifted and recalled how when he was 12 or 13 years old, he experienced a lot of frustration, like there was something missing: 'I felt hopeless, a weight, like there was no point going on.' He wondered out loud that already at that age it explained the pull of alcohol on him. He elaborated a bit about his exchanges that weekend with his father. Carl said he felt again the old despair about the disconnect with his father, and how he had to deal then and now with the gaps in the conversation with him. Touchingly he shifted back to his mother and said, 'My mother has a story to tell but she won't tell it.' He agreed when his therapist corrected him and said, 'She can't.'

COMMENT

When Reading (2002) speaks of substituting inanimate connections for human ones, Carl's story typifies and gives meaning to how this occurs. His poignant recount and characterization of the weekend were painfully repeating and evoking in the present the long-standing distress and discomforting and insecure attachment that had haunted him throughout his growing-up years into the present. The case illustrates how useful and sensitizing it is to bear a client's attachment styles and proclivities in mind and their subtle re-enactment during the course of therapy. The therapist also has to maintain a reflective examination of the nature of their own responses to clients and how these can be optimized.

5.5 BRINGING IT TOGETHER: ADDICTION AS A DISORDER OF SELF-REGULATION

Clinical work with substance users reveals that the complex developmental, troubled self-states, and attachment issues involved in addictions pre-eminently lend themselves to the in-depth explorative and interactional aspects of psychodynamic psychotherapy.

Addicted individuals suffer, the suffering compels them to use, and they know not why. Drug-dependent behaviour is driven and notorious for the absence of self-reflection. The problem is that much of the behaviour derives from infancy and early development for which there are no memories, words, or mental representations (Lichtenberg, 1983; Gedo, 1986; Krystal, 1988; Khantzian, 1995). Dodes (1996) for this reason characterizes addictions as a compulsive disorder. Psychodynamic psychotherapy can be fundamentally useful and beneficial in accessing, identifying and therapeutically addressing these early predisposing and subsequent developmental factors, as well as the consequences, involved in addictive attachments and behaviours.

In our work, we have found it useful to conceptualize addiction as a self-regulation disorder. Guided by object-relation, self-psychology and attachment theory, a formulation of addiction as a self-regulation disorder allows for an understanding of how deficits and dysfunctions in regulating emotions, self-esteem, relationships and self-care are important, if not essential, to the development and maintenance of addictive disorders. As we have described, investigators adopting a developmental perspective remind psychotherapists how early life experiences are fundamentally important in subsequently influencing all these aspects of self-regulation in adult life and, when derailed, can contribute to and result in the self-regulation disturbances that govern so much of addictive behaviour.

As we have indicated, the addictively prone become powerfully and passionately attached to their drugs of choice and dangerous desires. This is so because the drugs work in the short term. The psychoactive properties of addictive drugs interact with the suffering and deficits in the regulation of affect, self-states, object relations and self-care in helping individuals to cope with these deficits. In the case of affects, addictively vulnerable individuals experience their emotions in the extreme, wherein they are intense and overwhelming or elusive or absent, thus feelings are unavailable to guide reactions and behaviour (Krystal & Raskin, 1970; McDougall, 1984; Krystal, 1988). Depending on the drug, it relieves or changes the confusion and distress of such extremes in feeling. Similarly, the pain accompanying self-other relationships of emptiness, dissociation and helplessness, or compensatory disavowal of needs, interpersonal cut-off and counter-dependence powerfully interact with drug effects to create, for the while, the sense that all is well. It is for these reasons that such reactions are incorrectly characterized as euphoria or pleasure. As Reading (2002) has indicated, the power of addiction resides in the fact that the addictive experience creates the illusion that substances can replace affectional bonds with addictive ones. It is worth noting in this respect, despite deficits in cognitive functions and memory associated with addiction, that drug-dependent individuals vividly remember how powerfully 'corrective' the ingestion of addictive drugs are, and why Reading observes that the drug experience becomes superordinate to all other interpersonal considerations and priorities.

It is for the above reason that the therapist best not be impassive, remote and insufficiently interactive. Therapists' energy, fine tuning and readiness to evoke and create words and emotions with patients can support, comfort and reassure, as the interactive and empathic aspects of psychotherapy create an anlage for patients to grow and develop in these underdeveloped aspects of personality organization. The climate of comfort and mutual respect afforded by this more contemporary psychotherapeutic approach also allows for a gentle challenge to interpersonal and psychic isolation and the characterologic defences that maintain it. Such an approach also allows the emergence, examination and resolution of disavowed, competing and ambivalent parts of self that produce so much internal and interpersonal distress, conflict and addictive responses. The comfort found in drugs is gradually replaced by the comfort initially stimulated in the therapeutic relationship, and subsequently, the comfort that can be experienced in one's relationship with self and others as internal intra-psychic and interpersonal barriers are therapeutically lifted and resolved.

5.6 REFLECTIVE PRACTICE

As noted, chronic substance misuse undermines reflective self-functions; as habits strengthen, alternatives recede and users immunize themselves, there is a corresponding loss of emotional range, cognitive flexibility and empathy for self and others. Here, however, we briefly touch upon the importance for the therapist in maintaining good reflective functions in the face of the difficult and discomforting feelings that the work can arouse. The traditional term in analytic tradition for this is the 'counter-transference', although we believe that this is a somewhat unwieldy term (indeed, we do not always know what the 'counter' aspect is; Weegmann, 2003). Suffice to note that in a disorder characterized by dysregulations of life and emotion, extreme internal worlds and irrationality, the worker can find it hard to contain and make sense of the responses which are aroused. After all, we witness chaotic worlds, crisis and drama, escalating situations and reversals (slips, relapses, demotivations) all the time. Misalignments occur easily, as we are baffled by the power of addictions to subvert progress, resulting in challenges to empathy, as illustrated in Case Study 5.3.

CASE STUDY 5.4   MILLIE

Millie is a single woman in her late forties, who I (EJK) have been following for about 18 months. She has been through no less than six detoxes and four rehab stints during that time. She has experienced severe medical and psychiatric complications as a consequence of the relapses. She is a remarkably bright individual and has succeeded in two professional careers but has languished professionally and vocationally for about the past decade. After several months working with her in individual and group psychotherapy, on a particular morning she was complaining how her mother just doesn't get it that her priorities are different than that of her mother. She gave the example of her 86-year-old mother's inclination to go to bed early, e.g. around 9 p.m. Millie described how mother might get up subsequently while Millie was still up watching TV and mother somewhat commandingly would refer to the time implying, 'Isn't this the time to be in bed?' What was striking about this was

(continued)

to witness Millie uncharacteristically bristle in describing this, bitterly complaining how still at the age of 49 years old, her mom was still trying to run her life.

Her mother is an impressive, regal lady. In the ninth decade of her life she still has a manner and a precise way of talking that make her convictions about how life should be imposing and difficult to take issue with, an aspect of Millie's relationship with her mom that has always been difficult. This occurs, whether it be how she times matters of when it's okay to go to bed, trying to get mother to understand the compelling disease nature of her alcoholism, or in sharing difficult personal developments and experiences that have caused her shame and guilt.

The example of the timing of when one should be in bed, albeit seemingly trivial, likely reflected a life-long theme of how Millie could feel misaligned and not understood by her mother. Kohut (1971) referred to 'telescoping of analogous experiences' where contemporary relationship issues and interactions reflect parallel examples from childhood for which there are not necessarily lasting memories, but which nevertheless mirror lifelong misalignments that are painfully recurrent and nagging and often beyond conscious awareness.

This dynamic was juxtaposed to how cruelly the addiction was treating Millie, her mother, and certain members of her family as they experienced the repeated cruel nightmarish emergency calls, admissions to hospital, and all the other multiple complications of the disease. What Millie shared in common with several other chronically relapsing patients with whom I was working was the cruelty of the relapses paralleling deep resentment going back to childhood of feeling chronically misaligned with their parent(s) – sometimes in violent, angry confrontations, at other times suffering in silence and feeling not heard or understood. Recently after an exasperating episode of attempting to get her to a rehab facility, which ultimately was successful, but trying and exhausting, I had a rare reaction, for me, of wanting to give up on Millie. Based on my response, and considering Millie's impatience with her mom and cousins in these efforts, and the impatience of the family, I came to the conclusion that whatever part empathic failures play in early development, there certainly is mutual empathic failure that develops as a consequence of the cruel and daunting consequences of addictive disorders. Perhaps the intersubjective experience of giving-up by me had in it an aspect of repetition in the treatment relationship involving painful perpetuation, and at the same time an attempt to resolve old relational/attachment issues. After her return from rehab, lasting five months, I shared how my sense of wanting to give up reflected some of her own feelings, and that of her family. She reacted receptively, considering thoughtfully out loud the consequences of the recurrent relapses for her, me and her mother. It is perhaps significant that interacting with her on the issue of empathic faltering for all of us, for the first time in 18 months there followed a period of no further relapses extending up to the present time (8 weeks).

5.7 INTERNAL RECOVERY

There is a paucity of convincing theories of how people actually get better. This is also true of psychodynamic approaches, where there is a corresponding lack of theory concerning the 'psychodynamics of recovery'. As experienced practitioners and theorists in the field, while acknowledging the enormous damage caused by addiction and the considerable deficits which make addiction more likely, as individuals seek to alleviate painful states of mind or restricted capacities, we are keenly interested in understanding more about those unpredictable powers of restoration which enable people to exit addictive careers and reconstruct broken lives. Indeed, we each have extensive experience in working with those in medium- and long-term recovery. But how is addictive vulnerability reversed, or at least lessened? How are psychological growth and integration promoted? How do individuals move forward, from attachment to inanimate containers to constructive human resources? How are more resilient 'self-structures' built? How does internal recovery come about? At this stage in the 'science' of recovery, it is perhaps too early to be sure of the answers, although with the benefit of clinical hindsight, much can be gleaned.

CASE STUDY 5.5   FAITH

Faith's out-of-control drinking and a devastating depression were precipitated when she was terminated from a highly placed executive position in a major health care corporation. A hypercritical, intimidating senior officer was instrumental in her removal from her position. Much of her success and ambition was driven and compensatory. She was raised by an immigrant mother who was insufficiently supportive and, like her boss, hypercritical of Faith, but this was further compounded by mother taking to her bedroom for years at a time by her own immobilizing depression. For most of her growing up years she says home was an unhappy place, given her mother's depression, her father's drinking, and her parents' constant fighting.

She was referred by her psychopharmacologist for individual and group psychotherapy to deal with her heavy drinking. Although she did not adopt abstinence, almost immediately she was successful in significantly cutting back the frequency and amount of her drinking. In her own words, she said she was 'self-medicating' her anxiety (in low to moderate doses)

and when the anxiety and depression mounted to unbearable levels, she would drink to obliterating levels (e.g. the entire bottle of wine) and go to bed.

From the start of treatment Faith quickly formed a positive attachment to her therapist and was openly expressive of her appreciation for the comfort and reassurance she was experiencing from the work with the therapist in her individual and group therapy. In a recent individual visit, even as she was wondering out loud why she was continuing to use alcohol, adding that she was no longer self-medicating, she spontaneously indicated that the antidepressant was relieving her sadness and despair. But she quickly added that her energy levels remained low and the alcohol energized her. She volunteered that she definitely felt better and that she was okay with the controlled drinking but was aware that it was a 'slippery slope' and realized she could get back to 'numbing' herself with alcohol. The therapist wondered out loud if she might think about what she might be numbing. She thought about how she used to get her 'adrenaline lift' from the kudos and recognition she obtained from her position, but then offered that she derived little comfort or satisfaction currently from her reading group, arts and crafts, or prettying up her home. She ended the session wondering about what else might give her a 'lift or pleasure'.

COMMENT

The progression from Faith's unthinking compulsive drinking to ameliorate her immense suffering to a relatively rapid development of a capacity to think and worry about her troubled state of being and her use of alcohol, was impressive. Her demeanour, especially early in treatment, was a melancholic and anxious one. It was notable to witness the comfort, support and clarification she drew from her individual and group therapy, as well as the opportunity to share her distress and gratitude in her treatment, interactions that were not likely or available in her family of origins. As much as her therapist was active in appreciating, validating and supporting her gifts and decency, it was also evident that she was drawing on her individual and group contacts to begin to feel better about, and within, herself. With the help of her therapist, she was fruitfully considering alternative ways to find comfort and self-acceptance beyond the external praise and admiration she derived from her work performance and career. Literally, a therapeutic process was being activated where she could begin to shift from deriving satisfaction from external accomplishments and admiration, to one where she was more and more appreciating that her comfort and better sense of self had to come from within. As they say in recovery, 'It's an inside job.' Put in terms of attachment theory, she was reversing the attachment to the inanimate (i.e. the alcohol) to the human ones afforded by her individual and group therapy. And, of course, as she got better, she was also reconnecting to her loving husband and three daughters from whom she had withdrawn as her alcohol use was progressively denying her these vital attachments.

5.8   CONCLUSION

Modern psychodynamic concepts for addressing the range of psychopathologies are equally and preeminently well suited for understanding and treating individuals suffering from addictive disorders. This is especially so when dealing with difficult and complicated cases that do not respond to traditional treatment. These contemporary approaches also help clinicians to understand and manage the troubling reactions and feeling that are stirred in treating their clients.

Substance-dependent individuals alternate in extreme and opposite states involving their emotions, sense of self and relational problems. These alternating and extreme states are further complicated by difficulties with managing their self-care concerning harm, threat and danger, especially those associated with addictions. In this chapter, we identify and explain how such patterns become enmeshed in and absorb the lives of addicted individuals, and how these modern psychodynamics paradigms allow the identification, exploration and resolution of these self-destructive and consuming processes. Such models and conceptualizations are critically necessary to counter misleading notions that addictions are driven by pleasure-seeking and human self-destructiveness. Such motives are tragically attributed to addicted individuals by society, and addicted individuals themselves, and too often stand in the way of an empathic understanding, more humane attitudes (clinically and at large), and effective treatments.

Clinicians need to remain attuned to the enormous suffering that is at the root of addictive disorders. Contemporary perspectives provided by object relationship, self-psychology and attachment theory provide complementary pathways to attune to the origins and nature of the suffering. They provide new and more enabling windows on addicted patients' experience, and to appreciate and empathically attune to their needs, and to free them of the compulsions and repetitions that drive their addictions. Such approaches also encourage therapists to depart from early impassive, strictly interpretive psychodynamic modes. They allow for, and encourage, more active and interactive ways to provide patients with instruction, clarification, support and empathic attunement to better appreciate how substances of misuse have interacted with their suffering to make them powerfully compelling, and to develop alternative paths to deal with their pain and confusion.

SUGGESTIONS FOR FURTHER READING

Flores, P. (2003). *Addiction as an attachment disorder*. Northvale, NJ: Jason Aronson.

Weegmann, M., & Cohen, R. (Eds.). (2002). *Psychodynamics of addiction*. Chichester: John Wiley & Sons, Ltd.

Weegman, M. & Khantzian, E. (2009). A question of substance: Psychodynamic reflections on addictive vulnerability and treatment. *Psychodynamic Practice, 15*, 365–380.

REFERENCES

Anderson, R. (1997). Booting the boot in: Violent defences against the depressive position. In D. Bell (Ed.), *Reason and passion: A celebration of the work of Hannah Segal* (pp. 75–88). London: Karnac Books.

Balint, M. (1968). *The basic fault*. London: Tavistock Publications.

Bowlby, J. (1973). *Attachment and loss*. vol. 2, *Separation, anxiety, anger*. New York: Basic Books.

Director, L. (2005). Encounters with omnipotence in the psychoanalysis of substance users. *Psychoanalytic Dialogues, 15*, 567–586. doi:10.1080/10481881509348851

Dodes, L. M. (1996). Compulsion and addiction. *Journal of American Psychoanalytical Association, 44*, 815–835.

Dodes, L. M. (2002). *The heart of addiction*. New York: HarperCollins.

English, C. (2009). The regulatory function of addiction: Maintaining internal cohesion by the drugging of parts of the personality. *Psychodynamic Practice, 15*, 341–349.

Flores, P. (2003). *Addiction as an attachment disorder*. Northvale, NJ: Jason Aronson.

Gedo, J. (1986). *Conceptual issues in psychoanalysis: Essays in history and method*. Hillsdale, NJ: The Analytic Press.

Hyatt-Williams, A. (1978). Depression, deviation and acting out in adolescence. *Journal of Adolescence, 1*, 309–317.

Khantzian, E. J. (1995). Group therapy for psychoactive substance use disorders. In G. Gabbard (Ed.), *Treatment of psychiatric disorders* (pp. 832–839). Washington, DC: American Psychiatric Press.

Khantzian, E. J. (2003). Understanding addictive vulnerability: An evolving psychodynamic perspective. *Neuro-Psychoanalysis, 5*, 5–21.

Khantzian, E. J., Mack, J. E., & Schatzberg, A. F. (1974). Heroin use as an attempt to cope: Clinical observations. *American Journal of Psychiatry, 131*, 160–164.

Kohut, H. (1971). *The analysis of the self.* New York: International Universities Press.

Kohut, H. (1977). *The restoration of the self.* New York: International Universities Press.

Krystal, H. (1988). *Integration and self-healing: Affect, trauma. alexithymia.* Hillsdale, NJ: The Analytic Press.

Krystal, H., & Raskin, H. A. (1970). *Drug dependence: Aspects of ego functions.* Detroit: Wayne State University Press.

Lichtenberg, J. D. (1983). *Psychoanalysis and infant research.* Hillsdale, NJ: The Analytic Press.

Lighdale, H., Mack, A., & Frances, R. (2011). Psychodynamics. In M. Gallanter, & H. Kleber (Eds.), *Psychotherapy for the treatment of substance misuse.* Arlington, VA: American Psychiatric Association.

McDougall, J. (1984). The 'disaffected' patient: reflections on affect pathology. *Psychoanalytic Quarterly, 53*, 386–409.

Reading, B. (2002). The application of Bowlby's attachment theory to the psychotherapy of addiction. In M. Weegmann, & R. Cohen (Eds.), *Psychodynamics of addiction* (pp. 13–30). Chichester: John Wiley & Sons. Ltd.

Reading, B. (2012). Addiction and attachment. Unpublished paper.

Segal, H. (1973). *Introduction to the work of Melanie Klein.* London: Hogarth Press.

Steiner, J. (1993). *Psychic retreats: Pathological organisations in psychotic, neurotic and borderline patients.* London: Routledge.

Sutherland, S. (1992; 2007). *Irrationality.* London: Pinter and Martin Ltd.

Weegmann, M. (2003). Work discussion groups for professionals. In B. Reading, & M. Weegmann (Eds.), *Group psychotherapy and addiction* (pp. 211–224). Chichester: John Wiley & Sons, Ltd.

Weegmann, M., & Cohen, R. (Eds.). (2002). *Psychodynamics of addiction.* Chichester: Johnn Wiley & Sons, Ltd.

Weegmann, M., & Khantzian, E. (2011). Envelopments: Immersion in and emergence from drug misuse. *American Journal of Psychotherapy, 65*(2), 163–177.

6 Mindfulness, Acceptance and Values in Substance Misuse Services

LIZ MCGRATH AND DOMINIC O'RYAN

 Camden and Islington NHS Foundation Trust, London, UK

CHAPTER OUTLINE

6.1   INTRODUCTION: WHAT ARE THE PRINCIPLES AND METHODS OF MINDFULNESS, ACCEPTANCE AND VALUES?

There has been a proliferation of interest in using mindfulness-based approaches in NHS settings over the past few years. Mindfulness-Based Cognitive Therapy (MBCT; Segal, Williams, & Teasdale, 2002) is recommended in the NICE Guidelines for the prevention of relapse in recurrent depression. Mindfulness is also an important element of approaches such as Dialectical Behaviour Therapy (DBT; Linehan, 1993), Mindfulness Based Relapse Prevention (MBRP; Bowen, Chawla, & Marlatt, 2010) and ACT is used for the treatment of various psychological problems including complex personality disorders and substance misuse. Together, such treatment approaches have been labelled 'contextual cognitive behaviour therapy' or 'contextual CBT' (Levin & Hayes, 2012). Contextual CBTs take a functional and contextual approach to the formulation and treatment of psychological problems. Accordingly, the types of interventions used within these models focus on how people relate to their thoughts, feelings and body sensations rather than the content of these experiences. Mindfulness and acceptance-based approaches use methods which encourage clients to develop a flexible, open, nonreactive, compassionate and non-judgemental way of relating to experience with a view to changing the function rather than the frequency or form of experiences. While there is a difference in emphasis in the various approaches, with MBCT and MBSR using more acceptance-based strategies, and ACT and DBT having more change-based strategies, all contextual CBTs encourage participants to get in touch with important personal values and develop values and congruent targets for behaviour change.

6.1.1   Mindfulness

It is common to hear people with substance misuse problems reporting that their drug or alcohol use happens without conscious attention or awareness. Contextual CBTs all focus on encouraging clients to develop a particular type of awareness of, and relationship to, everyday experience known as mindfulness. Mindfulness is an aspect of a number of ancient spiritual traditions including Buddhism. However, mindful awareness is not inherently religious. It has been described as a way of 'bringing one's complete attention to the present experience on a moment-to-moment basis' (Marlatt & Kristeller, 1999, p. 68) and as 'paying attention in a particular way: on purpose, in the present moment and non-judgementally' (Kabat-Zinn, 1994, p. 4). Mindfulness-based interventions include a number of methods for teaching mindful awareness. These include both formal and informal practices. In the formal practices, participants are encouraged to meditate for periods of a few minutes up to 40 minutes or so, directing their attention to their breath and other body sensations, thoughts and feelings. The informal practices involve participants paying a focused, curious attention to everyday activities such as washing, eating and walking.

In both the formal and informal practices, the instructions encourage participants to focus their attention on the activity – whether breathing, eating or walking – and to pay careful attention to what arises. They are invited to relate to all experience with the same kind of non-judgmental awareness, whether it is a negative thought, pleasant thought, comfortable or uncomfortable body sensation. In this way, participants learn to be with the present moment experience, regardless of whether it is pleasant, unpleasant or neutral. It is common for people trying to stop using substances to try to suppress cravings and urges. Paradoxically, this can lead to an increase in their frequency and intensity (Palfai, Colby, Monti & Rohsenow, 1997). Conversely, it has been shown that when people are able to accept their cravings as part of their experience, this is less likely to result in substance use, even if the subjective experience of craving is particularly strong (Ostafin & Marlatt, 2008).

Interestingly, the hypothesized mechanisms of action of mindfulness include exposure, relaxation and cognitive change, all which have been shown to be effective components of substance misuse treatment (Carroll, 1996; Breslin, Zack & McMain, 2002; Witkiewitz, Marlatt & Walker, 2005). Indeed, recent neurobiological studies indicate that mindfulness meditation leads to neurological changes associated with 'increased levels of alertness, relaxation, attentional control and reduced readiness for action' (Witkiewitz et al., 2005, p. 219). Hence, mindfulness may indeed help substance-misusing clients to become more attentive to their triggers for using, and choose other options.

6.1.2 Acceptance

There is a long theoretical and empirical history including self-report and prospective studies that support the hypothesis that substance misuse is often an attempt to escape from negative affect (Breslin et al., 2002). This 'non-acceptance' of inner experience, including thoughts, feelings and body sensations, known as 'experiential avoidance' in the ACT model, is associated with numerous psychological difficulties, including substance misuse (Chawla & Ostafin, 2007). Using substances can initially be a quick and effective method of avoiding pain and emotional distress. However, over time as tolerance develops and use increases, people who want to stop their use may then be faced with dealing with uncomfortable withdrawal symptoms in addition to having to face the underlying issues that the substance was originally an attempt to escape from.

In addition to using mindfulness-based exercises to encourage acceptance of present-moment experience, ACT also employs other strategies such as the use of metaphor. The 'quicksand' metaphor is often used to illustrate the concept of acceptance (Hayes et al., 1999). The key to survival in quicksand is to let go of fighting and to spread out to increase contact with the surface of the sand. In a similar way, clients in ACT are encouraged to stop fighting with their internal experiences and accept them for what they are. It is important to emphasize that in ACT, and other contextual CBTs, acceptance is not about resignation. Rather, it is about allowing our experience to be there, even if it is a difficult feeling such as anxiety, if it enables us to act on our values. Acceptance also encourages a recognition that painful experiences are part of the human condition and that attempts to avoid them ultimately lead to suffering.

6.1.3   Values

As previously mentioned, while important in all contextual CBTs, there is a particular and overt focus on values in ACT whereby values are:

> statements about what we want to be doing with our life: about what we want to stand for, and how we want to behave on an ongoing basis. They are leading principles that can guide and motivate us as we move through life.
>
> (Harris, 2009, p. 189)

ACT is a transdiagnostic model which proposes that various psychological difficulties are underpinned by the same mechanisms, one of which is a distance from values. Problems are thought to be caused or maintained by a lack of connection with important areas of life, and reconnecting with these is one of the therapeutic tools used in ACT.

One of the main underpinning principles of ACT is to increase psychological flexibility with a view to helping people build and live a 'rich, full and meaningful life' (Harris, 2009, p. 7). Hence, in ACT for substance misuse, the aim is clearly much broader than helping clients to stop using substances. ACT uses a wide range of values interventions, including conversations about hopes for the future, and exercises such as imagining what you would like people to be saying about you at your 80th birthday party. Participants who find it difficult to identify values may be encouraged to think about role models and people who inspire them with a view to recognizing the qualities they admire and would like for themselves. Values work in clients who have used substances for many years but often bring with them a range of painful emotions including loss, guilt and regret. Clinicians may need to help clients to accept these feelings. At the same time, contacting values can provide the foundation for meaningful change. The next step involves working with the client to translate these abstract values into more concrete goals and actions in order to build or re-build a life with meaning and purpose. As in other approaches, ACT emphasizes the importance of starting small. Of primary importance is that these small goals are clearly linked to the person's valued life direction.

6.2   HOW DOES ACT INTEGRATE WITH OTHER APPROACHES?

Mindfulness-based approaches in substance-misuse treatment are not fully recognized as an evidence-based interventions in their own right. The BPS/NTA Psychosocial toolkit (Pilling, Hesketh & Mitcheson, 2010) provides a useful summary and set of protocols for NICE-supported interventions for substance misuse (NICE, 2007) and is a useful companion to the American publication *Principles of Drug Addiction Treatment* (National Institute on Drug Abuse, 2012). Between them, they cite Motivational Interviewing (MI) and its variants, CBT, Contingency Management, network-/family-based interventions, and interventions aligned to the 12-Step Minnesota model as effective and evidence-based. It can be argued, then, that the use of ACT and associated interventions in substance misuse services may be a good example of what Kanter and colleagues (Kanter, Busch & Rusch, 2009) describe as a propensity for certain professions to engage in paradigm shifts ahead of the evidence.

In his review of the state of the art for ACT-based outcome studies, Öst (2008) concluded that methodological weaknesses undermine the pursuit of the evidence base for the effectiveness of ACT in terms of the conditions for which it was being tested. A comprehensive meta-analysis of ACT-based interventions reviewed 18 trials (Powers, Zum Vörde Sive Vörding & Emmelkamp, 2009). Unsurprisingly, ACT was found to be more effective than control conditions across a range of conditions, but it was not superior to established treatment protocols. In reviewing the emergent evidence, Smout, Hayes, Atkins, Klausen and Duguid (2012) concluded that ACT did seem to support significant improvements in addiction (among other conditions) and that the wise practitioner should consider it as part of their armoury, but that it was still evolving as an empirically supported intervention across a number of disorders.

For example, a more recent pilot study of acceptance and commitment therapy for methadone detoxification (Stotts et al., 2012) concluded that those clients who received an ACT-based intervention alongside the methadone reduction had reduced anxiety about the detox process, and it resulted in larger numbers completing the detox when compared to a treatment-as-usual drug-counselling protocol. Larger numbers and longer follow-up would be required for more significant conclusions to be drawn, but in a climate where services are encouraged to identify larger numbers of clients who might be suitable for short-term detox rather than long-term maintenance, ACT may reduce concerns in both the clients and staff groups.

However, ACT is explicitly a transdiagnostic intervention (Hayes, Strosahl & Wilson, 1999) that aims to meet 'the challenges of the human condition' (Hayes, Barnes-Holmes & Wilson, 2012). The publication of *DSM V* (American Psychiatric Association, 2013) seems to have had the paradoxical effect of further promoting the importance of transdiagnostic approaches to common mental health problems (see, e.g. Kinderman, Read, Moncrieff & Bentall, 2013). And beyond its transdiagnostic claims, ACT does not even seek to reduce symptoms. Rather, the aim of ACT is to help individuals develop a more psychologically flexible approach to their symptoms in order to promote values-based actions and the pursuit of a rich, full and meaningful life (Harris, 2009).

Nevertheless, mindfulness, acceptance and values-based interventions already have a rich pedigree within more established evidence-based substance misuse-specific treatments. In considering the state of the art for mindfulness and acceptance interventions for addictions, Wagner, Ingersoll and Rollnick (2012) describe Motivational

Interviewing (MI) as a first cousin to the 'third wave' behaviour therapies in its use of acceptance and values. An understanding of the client's values has always been at the heart of MI from its inception. The first edition of *Motivational Interviewing* (Miller & Rollnick, 1991) is clear about discussing the importance of developing the discrepancy between the client's current behaviour and their important personal goals and values, and the central role of acceptance is explicit. Although here they are inviting us to be accepting of the other, this is a prerequisite to the other becoming accepting of themselves. Alongside this, explicit values-eliciting activities in sessions are further developed in their third edition (Miller & Rollnick, 2012).

Reaching further across to the 'second wave', Greenberger and Padesky's (1995) core self-help manual, *Mind over Mood*, places a central role on the reader to develop an acceptance and mindful awareness of unhelpful thoughts, feelings and behaviours as an alternative to labelling them as dysfunctional or negative, and ahead of trying to reframe them. And even within any subsequent reframing, the core task, they suggest, is one of validating the thoughts, feelings and behaviours within the context of one's overall life experience; in much the same way the Self-in-Context attempts to do within ACT.

Variations on ACT techniques and ideas appear throughout Beck's specific diagnostic manual for addiction (Beck, Wright, Newman & Liese, 1993) and in Carroll's substance misuse manual (Carroll, 1998): functional analysis, urge-surfing, values-based action, control as the problem not the solution. However, it is in his key text *Cognitive Therapy and the Emotional Disorders* (Beck, 1976), which tops and tails a diagnostic review with the transdiagnostic underpinnings of CBT, that he is clearest on the importance of the principles and techniques that later emerge as the core components of ACT. Beck describes the central role of 'The Personal Domain' (p. 54) in unravelling the distinctive experience of events and relieving distress, by which he means the necessity of bringing into fuller awareness the values a person holds, in order to understand and change their appraisal systems and thus their experience of distress in the world. Furthermore, Beck reports the core technique of Experimentation, by which he means the skill of becoming an expert observer of the self, circumstances, contexts, behaviours, thoughts and outcomes. This has clear parallels with the broad ACT concepts of workability and psychological flexibility but also the more refined techniques of functional analysis and of self-in-context. Similarly, Beck's techniques of distancing and decentring have clear parallels with mindfulness and diffusion respectively.

It may be a contrivance to find a link between ACT and Contingency Management (Petry, 2000) beyond both having roots in traditional behaviour therapy and both serving to help clients establish patterns of sustainable behaviour. However, the Community Reinforcement Approach (CRAFT) of Meyers and colleagues (Meyers, Smith, Serna & Belon, 2013) combines contingency management strategies with network-focused strategies to support long-term behaviour change in substance misuse. Alongside Behavioural Couples Therapy (Fals-Stewart, Kashdan, O'Farrell & Birchler, 2002) and Social & Behavioural Network Therapy (Copello, Orford, Hodgson, Tober & Barrett, 2002), CRAFT moves away from blame and towards acceptance and forgiveness in pursuit of shared, explicit values and improved social and intimate relationships.

From another tradition, there are parallels between the components and principles of ACT and the 12 steps of the Minnesota model. For example, Wilson and colleagues (Wilson, Hayes & Byrd, 2000; Wilson & DuFrene, 2012) set out to describe the compatibilities between ACT and the 12-step treatment of addictions. Their view is that there is a significant degree of overlap in the philosophical and practical underpinnings of the approaches. Both advocate acceptance of the current condition and vulnerabilities, the development of an individual sense of spirituality and a wider context to living; and both require a long-term and ongoing commitment to behaviour change beyond a narrow problem definition and towards values-based activities in the service of establishing a richer, more meaningful life.

Thus, the growing evidence base for ACT as an intervention for substance misuse is further supported by the transdiagnostic intentions and principles of ACT and by its parallels with other more evidence-based interventions.

6.3   HOW DOES THE SERVICE USE THESE PRINCIPLES AND METHODS OF ACT?

In delivering ACT in the service, our intention was not to use ACT solely as a primary intervention. Rather, we hoped to infuse the therapeutic milieu with the concepts of acceptance and mindfulness throughout the client's recovery journey. To be clear, we will here describe ACT within three domains of practice: (1) directly with clients; (2) indirectly to clients through supervision and the Multidisciplinary Team; and (3) directly with staff.

Direct mindfulness, acceptance and values work with clients is delivered through individual or group interventions. In individual work with clients referred to the psychology team in the service for concurrent interventions for common mental health problems, mindfulness and values work is part of an array of techniques for most of the psychology team in broader formulations, usually informed by CBT or systemic thinking, as might be expected. Mindfulness and values-based approaches may also be part of the armoury of some of the key workers providing drug counselling (see below), who will be part of a stepped care approach to the overall difficulties of their client, as described most recently by Strang (2012).

Our groups have shifted in focus over time, from an initial Mindfulness Based Cognitive Therapy class, following the eight-week protocol (Segal et al., 2002), with adaptations for the mixed diagnostic client cohorts to a more fluid six- to eight-week ACT class, not following a set protocol, but instead taking a less rigid journey round the Hexaflex (Harris, 2009). Clients are recruited to the class through promotional flyers in the waiting areas of the different parts of the service and through their key workers. We have set only a few specific criteria for entry into the classes, the main one being a track record of engagement with treatment as shown by attendance at standard key working sessions, a commitment to attend straight and sober and a willingness to think differently about their difficulties. The natural tendency has been for clients further along their recovery journey to self-select for the classes, that is to say those clients who are stable on opiate substitute treatment or have stopped regular use of heroin, stimulants, alcohol or other drugs of choice. We aim to meet each client prior to the start, to give them a general overview of the model and to assess their expectations of the class.

The length of each session has varied, with some cycles of the class running with significantly longer sessions of two to two-and-a-half hours, including a break. Our experience has been that shorter sessions can be effective but the richness of the discussions in the class means that we can feel rushed to deliver all the material. Classes use a variety of techniques to teach the material, including class discussion, experiential exercises, personal reflection, poetry, stories and metaphor, PowerPoint and video clips. Class size has varied, with most classes showing some initial attrition but generally settling at around five clients.

Similarly, our relapse prevention groups have shifted in focus from a more traditional model based upon Wanigaratne, Wallace, Pullin, Keaney and Farmer (1990) to classes following Marlatt's most recent incarnation (Bowen et al., 2010) with mindfulness at its core. Even those groups and individual sessions that adhere more closely to previous structures tend to be infused with elements of mindfulness and acceptance. Finally, any client who has experience of mindfulness at any level, whether from their current treatment, previous treatment or their everyday lives, is also encouraged to attend the weekly mindfulness drop-in, which acts as a focus for their ongoing practice.

Ideas of mindfulness and values will influence the supervisory style of the psychologists in individual and group supervision to the teams, and thus key workers will be guided to think about the values of their clients as a guide to how they may conduct key working and structure their standard interventions. Group supervision sessions often incorporate brief experiential mindfulness exercises. Questions about clients' values and metacognitive processes will also be offered in the multidisciplinary team meetings, thus influencing the overall care plan for clients.

An additional development in the service has been the introduction of Resilience Training for staff. This three-session protocol, developed by Flaxman and colleagues (Flaxman, Bond & Livheim, 2013), is offered to staff groups of up to eight members, who are interested in learning about the utility of mindfulness and values teaching in their own lives and how such an approach can be useful to them outside of their client work. These classes have brought together staff across all the professions and grades of the service, with the only requirement being a commitment to attend all three sessions with an open mind. Examples of the experience of participants are shown below, and the effect of the training is also shown and discussed below. Alongside this, we offer regular MI training workshops and refresher training to larger groups of staff, with an emphasis on understanding the values of our clients.

Taken together, the resilience training, MI training, supervision, multidisciplinary team input, individual client work and group-work all combine to influence the overall culture of the service as one that both explicitly and implicitly promotes and encourages the use of mindfulness and the eliciting and development of clients' values in the service of supporting the clients' recovery.

6.4   HOW DO MINDFULNESS, ACCEPTANCE AND VALUES SUPPORT THE RESILIENCE OF STAFF IN THE FACE OF SEEMINGLY RELENTLESS RELAPSE AND OTHER BEHAVIOURS?

Although there has been a proliferation of interest in the benefits of mindfulness, acceptance and values-based approaches for clients, there has been relatively less attention paid to how these approaches may benefit clinicians (Sayrs, 2012). In both working with clients ourselves over many years, and in working with, and supervising, staff, the emotional toll that working in substance misuse services can generate is evident. Clinicians frequently work with clients who have experienced significant trauma, loss and rejection, and this can often be expressed as anger and blame. In addition, frequent relapses and disappointments can generate strong emotions in both clients and clinicians. It is an ongoing challenge to manage these emotions in the most therapeutic manner. How can we best respond to these challenges? In our practice, we have found great benefit from applying the same principles and methods to ourselves as to our clients. In our experience, the principles and practice of mindfulness, acceptance and values-based living impact on our lives and work in at least three important ways: (1) supporting the building and maintenance of the therapeutic alliance; (2) increasing openness and flexibility; and (3) building and maintaining personal strengths and resources.

6.4.1   Mindfulness, Acceptance, Values and the Therapeutic Alliance

Germer (2005) argues that 'when therapists are working with intense emotions such as shame, anger, fear and grief, it is essential that we maintain an open, compassionate and accepting attitude' (p. 7). ACT has been shown to help professional caregivers maintain their own equanimity in the face of significant human suffering (Berceli & Napoli, 2006). Moreover, Hayes et al. (2004) found that ACT reduced both burnout and negative attitudes towards clients in substance abuse counsellors.

Fulton (2005) also suggests that mindfulness meditation may be a means of helping therapists to develop the qualities necessary to build strong therapeutic alliances. Therapist qualities which underpin the therapeutic alliance include empathy, warmth, understanding and acceptance and a lack of blaming, ignoring and reject-ing (Lambert & Barley, 2002). Indeed, Bohart, Elliott, Greenberg and Watson (2002) propose that empathy may be even more influential in intervention-based treatment than relational-based therapy. As previously mentioned, mindfulness involves paying attention in the moment, and learning this skill can enable clinicians to stay present to whatever the client is saying and to be aware of their own emotional responses, however difficult they may be. Similarly, ACT also emphasizes the importance of accepting the whole reality of the present moment,

6.4.2   *Increasing Openness and Flexibility*

In addition to the ongoing need to build and maintain strong therapeutic relation-ships, the changing face of services and treatment expectations in UK substance mis-use services has necessitated some quite significant changes in priorities and prac-tice. In the 2010 drug strategy for England and Wales (HM Government, 2010), there was a change in focus from harm minimization, recruitment and retention to more of an emphasis on treatment completion and abstinence. Many staff who had been working in substance misuse services over a number of years felt that the work they had been doing to date was being undermined and devalued, making it difficult to embrace the new agenda. There was also concern that the new agenda was politically motivated rather than evidence-based and in the best interests of the clients. There is some evidence to suggest that ACT-based interventions could support staff in man-aging such change. For example, Varra, Hayes, Roget and Fisher (2008) found that an ACT intervention increased drug and alcohol counsellors' willingness to adopt a new type of pharmacotherapy.

6.4.3   *Building and Maintaining Personal Strengths and Resources*

Bond and Bruce (2000) showed that a workplace ACT programme led to improve-ments in employees' general mental health, innovation potential and levels of depres-sion. In a recent qualitative MSc study Pobereskin (2014, unpublished) interviewed a number of substance misuse staff working in our service in addition to staff working in other NHS services. All of the staff had recently participated in a work-based ACT course. Some interesting themes emerged from the interviews. She found that almost all participants described a sense of disconnection from themselves prior to the train-ing. This appeared to be caused by pressures from both in and outside of work. After the course, participants described a reconnection with their own goals and values and a deepened sense of living authentically.

It is often stated that clinicians working in substance misuse services experience high levels of burnout (Varra et al., 2008). When initially choosing to work in sub-stance misuse services, most clinicians have values-based reasons for doing so. How-ever, over time, those values can become more remote, and it seems that having the opportunity to get back in touch with them can be an important factor in building or maintaining personal resilience.

6.5   WHAT ARE THE EXPERIENCES OF STAFF WORKING WITH ACT?

Overall, the three-session workplace-based ACT course (Flaxman et al., 2013) has been received positively by the participants. Pobereskin (2014, unpublished) interviewed a number of the staff in our service after they had completed the ACT course. She asked them about their experience of the class, what they had taken away from the class and been able to apply, as well as what could have been done differently. Pobereskin and the participants have generously given us their permission to reproduce some of their comments here. We have also used quotes from participants who sent us feedback separately. Interestingly, in addition to themes related to the core ACT processes of mindfulness, acceptance and values, participants also talked about the benefit of doing the training in a group and the impact on the team.

6.5.1   *Mindfulness, Acceptance and Values*

Some staff talked about how the experience of practising mindfulness had enabled them to be more aware and accepting of their internal experiences and more able to make thoughtful choices about how to respond to them. Consistent with the ACT model, staff who had taken part in the three-session ACT course noticed an increase in self-acceptance having completed the course: 'I do get a bit anxious. I just have to accept this is who I am. It's helped me be a bit more hopeful and a bit more confident. Like, accepting that this is all that's going to happen.' Another noticed that, 'I'm able to do things and see people that I actually enjoy rather than having a sense of obligation. I just sort of feel a bit more able to say "Actually, no."'

One of the participants in the ACT class described her tendency of wanting to do things properly and 'unless I'm doing something properly, I'll just not do it'. However, by using some of the principles we had talked about in the ACT class of allowing your thoughts to 'come and go' and viewing them as 'thoughts and not facts', she was able to allow her perfectionistic thinking to be there and carry on with the task in hand. She described trying to do a homework task from the ACT class and noticing but ignoring her perfectionistic chatter in her head: 'I was just like, okay, here we go. I'm going to ignore this.'

Comments from staff who have participated in the ACT for staff class lend support to the idea that values are of fundamental importance and seem to be related to an increased sense of well-being and purpose. One participant stated:

> It helped me clarify that it's OK for values to conflict, and take priority at different times, something I'd struggled with for a while. I find it too easy to make abstract resolutions, or keep avoiding or putting off important things. I found the values goals action handout very helpful in setting meaningful goals I can actually keep to. I requested an electronic copy to keep updating, and to keep reminding me of my underlying values when I feel like giving up on my goals, particularly the value of helping others driving my career choice, despite the difficulties and challenges involved; from assessments and paperwork, to the emotional demands of working with distress.

Another commented that being in touch with her values 'means that there's something there to work towards that applies to everything you do in daily life'.

6.5.2   Impact on Client Work

In addition to the personal impact of using ACT, some participants commented on the impact it had on their client work. This appeared to relate both to their personal resilience and feelings about being at work as well as to how they related to clients. One participant commented:

> This training helps you think how you can put your strength into this. It gives more reason to it: more meaningful, more purposeful. I felt more at ease at work. It was a really busy week but I didn't feel as stressed out … I'm being more mindful at work and task-oriented, but it's more positive.

Another noted that taking some time to practise some mindful breathing in the morning helped her to 'disentangle [her] stuff and client's stuff'.

Another, who had begun working in a more ACT-based framework with her clients, noted the impact it seemed to be having on her client work;

> I co-facilitated a CBT-based relapse prevention group. One of the sessions was on goal setting, using a traditional SMART goal format. Clients seemed to find it really hard to think of goals, and seemed reluctant to do this, perhaps due to previous history of failure, often seen in SMS. We revised the session based on the ACT values and goals, and noticed how much more engaged clients were in the session. I think what was really powerful was the realization that they were living by several of their values already by engaging in treatment and recovery.

6.5.3   Team Impact

Interestingly, a number of the participants commented on the impact of doing the training as part of a team and how much they appreciated this. One participant commented:

> I think everyone should attend resilience training! I found it invaluable both professionally and personally. Professionally it allowed me to re-visit and clarify my understanding of ACT techniques and concepts. I feel it brought us closer together as team, enabling me to get to know colleagues I wouldn't be able to have much contact with otherwise. What I really appreciated was everyone being equal, there's no hierarchy, exaggerated by re-banding and redundancy in current NHS climate. Instead there was acknowledgement that struggle is part of being human, and even very senior psychologists have their 'demons in the boat' or 'passengers on the bus'.

Similarly, another reflected that 'We were a group of people who weren't afraid to share their experiences and be open and honest. Part of that very shared, experience … you were kind of given permission to have unhelpful thoughts in the first place.'

Some staff spoke about a desire for more of their colleagues to participate in the training and the potential impact they thought this would have upon the organisation. In particular, they identified the benefits of awareness and acceptance of other team members:

> I think if everyone in the team had this form of training, it would help them to understand another team member's situation, feelings and emotions. Those who've done the training are aware of feelings, emotions and mindfulness. And you can see it in their work. But people who haven't done it yet, you can feel the strain, the pressure.

6.5.4 Concerns

While the response to the training was generally positive, some concerns were raised about the potential motivation of organizations offering such courses. One participant who took part in the training raised concerns that the training could be used as a means of locating problems in her, rather than in the organization: 'Maybe the reason why I was struggling isn't anything to do with my level of resilience, but the fact that the organization in which I work is making unreasonable demands on any human being.' Although workplace-based ACT training has been shown to improve performance (Flaxman et al., 2013), in our training we are clear with our participants that we are offering this as something to enhance their well-being. Of course, these concerns could be addressed within the ACT framework by emphasizing the difference between acceptance and resignation as already discussed. That is, we were not inviting staff to be helplessly resigned to their current situations, but to acknowledge the experience that is already present as part of the process of moving forward in a valued direction.

It is also important to mention that the staff who participated in the course were a self-selecting group and many already had some experience of mindfulness or ACT. Staff who chose not to participate in the course gave a variety of reasons for making that decision. Some people had tried meditation before and didn't like it, others thought it would be an odd thing to do at work, fearing they would be 'exposed' in some way, and some staff did not feel able to commit to the demands of the between-session tasks.

6.6   WHAT ARE THE EXPERIENCES OF CLIENTS WORKING THIS WAY?

Some similar questions were asked of clients who had recently attended classes with us. Some of the feedback reflected the general group processes perhaps more than the specific content. For example, in thinking about the mixed cohort in each class (i.e. some people being abstinent from all substances, some still on reducing doses, while others may still be occasional users), equal numbers of people thought that the participants should be 'at the same stage' while others thought the mixed cohort was fine, so long as participants were respectful of the overarching rule of not attending affected by substances. Wherever participants were in their recovery, they generally experienced and appreciated a sense of the class 'coming together'.

Generally, clients appreciated the opportunities to practise skills that they had learnt in the class or with which they were already familiar. The structure and routine of the classes helped them implement techniques that they came to experience as 'beneficial to my mental health', The classroom was generally experienced as a 'time to take stock' and the skill of simple steps like focusing on the breath, being mindful of where we are at any time, what we are doing, listening to our body and responding accordingly were experienced as core skills of relapse prevention.

One client described the class as a 'turning point' for them. Experience of the ideas in their 1:1 therapy had piqued an interest in the idea that it was their way of thinking about the world that might lead to their 'downfall'. Subsequently, in the context of the supportive, lively discussions of the class, they fully embraced the notion that their ongoing efforts to 'control my world and my experience of it [were] actually more debilitating than just living it'. They experienced some frustrations in the teaching – for example, the 'constant banging on about passengers in the bus' (see http://www.youtube.com/watch?v=Z29ptSuoWRc for examples) but they also reported that they found that metaphor to be most useful in moving towards a place of acceptance. 'I've realized that this is how it is, this is my life; if I accept that, then I can go with the flow. Since then, life has worked out much better for me.'

Another client talked about joining the class because they knew that had to try something new: 'I've been trying the same things for 40 years.' Although their post-class evaluation was that they had not fully taken on board the concepts of the class, they described the central notion of taking stock, acceptance and committed action in a way that suggests they had wholly absorbed the ideas.

In spite of the use of poetry, metaphor and imagery contributing to one client's view of ACT as 'hocus-pocus', most participants valued their use in the class, even if this was sometimes experienced as repetitive, as they felt it helped summarize and condense the ideas into manageable and memorable pieces.

Naturally, this is a self-selecting cohort of clients who had chosen to offer feedback and there may be many quite different views of ACT from the client perspective. Nonetheless, this small sample gives a valid snapshot of clients' experience that maps well onto that of the staff and onto the overall model.

6.7 OUR EXPERIENCE OF ACT

This chapter reflects something of the personal journey for us as we developed our interest in mindfulness, acceptance and values and their place in our own lives and our work. Having discussed the experiences of staff and clients who have participated in classes, it would be remiss not to mention our own experiences.

Bennett-Levy (2006) makes a clear argument for the importance of self-practice in the acquisition of therapy skills in general and CBT in particular. Never more strongly does this seem to be the case than in Contextual CBT. Bennett-Levy (2006) describes a self-practice/self-reflection process based on a Declarative/Procedural/Reflective framework for understanding and enhancing learning. Declarative knowledge is what we know, for example, about things and events; procedural knowledge is about processes – how, why and when we apply what. However, it is the self-reflective process that enhances declarative knowledge and links it to procedural knowledge to create sophisticated and effective therapeutic interventions. Declarative knowledge and procedural knowledge could be taught and learned primarily (or at least functionally) through formal teaching, but reflection requires a different learning environment. Bennett-Levy seems to be arguing that reflection can be of two fundamental types – that which focuses on the therapist-client in all its dimensions, and that which focuses on the therapist themselves.

We came to mindfulness approaches at different times in our careers and with very different levels of dedication. However, we each now have a routine mindfulness practice, monthly peer supervision with a colleague specifically around ACT, and regularly attend workshops on mindfulness-based approaches. As a transdiagnostic approach that focuses on process over content, and since ACT argues that the processes are not merely universal but are in fact everyday occurrences, the perennial dilemma about self-disclosure in psychological therapies is considerably reduced; from an ACT perspective, 'we are all in the same boat' (Walser & Pistorello, 2004, p. 361). The use of the self in ACT is a powerful tool for teaching and for enhancing the therapeutic relationship. We set explicit behavioural goals for ourselves alongside the people in our classes and report back our successes or otherwise in carrying them out. In common with many groups, at the start we ask people to say a little of what brought them to the class, and each time we explain that the reason we are there is to share something that we have experienced as powerful and important in our own lives. Teaching ACT is a powerful tool for self-learning, too, as we often find ourselves reaching new insights into the model and ourselves (and each other!) through the groups we run, partly in the preparation phase but mostly in the class itself and in our reflections immediately after the class. Our overwhelming experience has been one of a sense of privilege that clients and staff alike have felt able to share their vulnerabilities in pursuit of their resilience.

SUGGESTIONS FOR FURTHER READING

Harris, R. (2009). *ACT made simple: An easy-to-read primer on acceptance and commitment therapy.* Oakland, CA: New Harbinger Publications.

Hayes, S. C., Strosahl, K., & Wilson, K. G. (1999). *Acceptance and commitment therapy: An experiential approach to behaviour change.* New York: The Guilford Press.

Segal, Z., Williams, J. M. G., & Teasdale, J. D. (2002). *Mindfulness-based cognitive therapy for depression: A new approach to preventing relapse.* London: The Guilford Press.

REFERENCES

American Psychiatric Association. (2013). *Diagnostic and statistical manual of mental disorders* (5th ed.). Arlington, VA: American Psychiatric Publishing.

Beck, A. (1976). *Cognitive therapy and the emotional disorders.* New York: International Universities Press.

Beck, A., Wright, F., Newman, C., & Liese, B. (1993). *Cognitive therapy of substance abuse*. New York: The Guildford Press.

Bennett-Levy, J. (2006). Therapist skills: A cognitive model of their acquisition and refinement. *Behavioural and Cognitive Psychotherapy, 34*, 57–78. doi:10.1017/S1352465805002420

Berceli, D., & Napoli, M. (2006). A proposal for a mindfulness-based trauma prevention program for social work professionals. *Complementary Health Practice Review, 11*, 153–165. doi:10.1177/1533210106297989

Bohart, A. C., Elliott, R., Greenberg, L. S., & Watson, J. C. (2002). Empathy. In J. C. Norcross (Ed.), *Psychotherapy relationships that work: Therapist contributions and responsiveness to patients* (pp. 89–108). New York: Oxford University Press.

Bond, F. W., & Bruce, D. (2000). Mediators of change in emotion-focussed and problem-focussed worksite stress management interventions. *Journal of Occupational Health Psychology, 5*, 156–163.

Bowen, S., Chawla, N., & Marlatt, G. A. (2010). *Mindfulness-based relapse prevention for addictive behaviours: A clinician's guide*. New York: The Guilford Press.

Breslin, F. C., Zack, M., & McMain, S. (2002). An information-processing analysis of mindfulness: Implications for relapse prevention in the treatment of substance abuse. *Clinical Psychology: Science and Practice, 9*, 275–299. doi:10.1093/clipsy.9.3.275

Carroll, K. M. (1996). Relapse prevention as a psychosocial treatment: A review of controlled clinical trials. *Experimental and Clinical Psychopharmacology, 4*, 46. doi:10.1037/1064-1297.4.1.46

Carroll, K. M. (1998). *A cognitive behavioural approach: Treating cocaine addiction*. Rockville, MD: National Institute of Health.

Chawla, N., & Ostafin, B. (2007). Experiential avoidance as a functional dimensional approach to psychopathology: An empirical review. *Journal of Clinical Psychology, 63*, 871–890. doi:10.1002/jclp.20400

Copello, A., Orford, J., Hodgson, R., Tober, G., & Barrett, C. (2002). Social behaviour and network therapy: Basic principles and early experiences. *Addictive Behaviors, 27*, 345–366. doi:10.1016/S0306-4603(01)00176-9

Fals-Stewart, W., Kashdan, T. B., O'Farrell, T. J., & Birchler, G. R. (2002). Behavioral couples therapy for drug-abusing patients: Effects on partner violence. *Journal of Substance Abuse Treatment, 22*, 87–96. doi:10.1016/S0740-5472(01)00218-5

Flaxman, P. E., Bond, F. W., & Livheim, F. (2013). *The mindful and effective employee. An acceptance and commitment therapy training manual for improving well-being and performance*. Oakla nd, CA: New Harbinger Publications.

Fulton, P. R. (2005). Mindfulness as clinical training. In C. K. Germer, R. D. Siegel, & P. R. Fulton (Eds.), *Mindfulness and psychotherapy* (pp. 55–72). New York: Guilford Press.

Germer, C. K. (2005). Mindfulness: What is it? What does it matter? In C. K. Germer, R. D. Siegel, & P. R. Fulton (Eds.), *Mindfulness and psychotherapy* (pp. 3–27). New York: The Guilford Press.

Greenberger, D., & Padesky, C. (1995). *Mind over mood: Change how you feel by changing the way you think*. New York: The Guilford Press.

Harris, R. (2009). *ACT made simple: An easy-to-read primer on acceptance and commitment therapy*. Oakland, CA: New Harbinger Publications.

Hayes, S., Barnes-Holmes, D., & Wilson, K. (2012). Contextual behavioral science: Creating a science more adequate to the challenge of the human condition. *Journal of Contextual Behavioral Science, 1*, 1–16. doi:10.1016/j.jcbs.2012.09.004

Hayes, S. C., Bissett, R., Roget, N., et al. (2004). The impact of acceptance and commitment training and multicultural training on the stigmatizing attitudes and professional burnout of substance abuse counselors. *Behavior Therapy, 35*, 821–835. doi:10.1016/S0005-7894(04)80022-4

Hayes, S. C., Strosahl, K., & Wilson, K. G. (1999). *Acceptance and commitment therapy: An experiential approach to behavior change*. New York: The Guilford Press.

HM Government. (2010). *Drug Strategy 2010: Reducing Demand, Restricting Supply, Building Recovery: Supporting People to Live a Drug Free Life.* London: HM Government.

Kabat-Zinn, J. (1994). *Wherever you go, there you are: Mindfulness meditation in everyday life.* New York: Hyperion.

Kanter, J., Busch, A., & Rusch, L. (2009). *Behavioral activation: Distinctive features.* Hove: Routledge.

Kinderman, P., Read, J., Moncrieff, J., & Bentall, R. P. (2013). Drop the language of disorder. *Evidence Based Mental Health,* 16, 2–3. doi:10.1136/eb-2012-100987

Lambert, M. J., & Barley, D. E. (2002). Research summary on the therapeutic relationship and psychotherapy outcome. In J. C. Norcross (Ed.), *Psychotherapy relationships that work: therapist contributions and responsiveness to patients* (pp. 17–32). Oxford: Oxford University Press.

Levin, M. E., & Hayes S. H. (2012) Contextual cognitive behavioral therapies for addictive problems. In S. H. Hayes, & M. E. Levin (Eds.), *Mindfulness and acceptance for addictive behaviors.* Oakland, CA: New Harbinger.

Linehan, M. M. (1993). *Skills training manual for treatment of borderline personality disorder.* New York: The Guilford Press.

Marlatt, G. A., & Kristeller, J. L. (1999). Mindfulness and meditation. In W. R. Miller (Ed.), *Integrating spirituality into treatment: Resources for practitioners* (pp. 67–84). Washington, DC: American Psychological Association.

Meyers, R. J., Smith, J. E., Serna, B., & Belon, K. E. (2013). Community reinforcement approaches: CRA and CRAFT. In P. Miller (Ed.), *Interventions for addiction: comprehensive addictive behaviors and disorders.* San Diego, CA: Academic Press.

Miller, W. R., & Rollnick, S. (1991). *Motivational interviewing: Preparing people for change.* New York: Guilford Press.

Miller, W. R., & Rollnick, S. (2012). *Motivational interviewing* (3rd ed.). New York: Guilford Press.

National Institute on Drug Abuse. (2012). *Principles of drug addiction treatment: A research-based guide* (3rd ed.). North Bethesda, MD: NIH. http://www.drugabuse.gov/publications/principles-drug-addiction-treatment-research-based-guide-third-edition

NICE. (2007). *Drug misuse: Psychosocial interventions.* London: National Institute for Health and Clinical Excellence.

Öst, L. (2008). Efficacy of the third wave of behavioral therapies: A systematic review and meta-analysis. *Behaviour Research and Therapy,* 46, 296–321. doi:10.1016/j.brat.2007.12.005

Ostafin, B. D., & Marlatt, G. A. (2008). Surfing the urge: Experiential acceptance moderates the relation between automatic alcohol motivation and hazardous drinking. *Journal of Social and Clinical Psychology,* 27, 404–418. doi:10.1521/jscp.2008.27.4.404

Palfai, T. P., Colby, S. M., Monti, P. M., & Rohsenow, D. J. (1997). Effects of suppressing the urge to drink on smoking topography: A preliminary study. *Psychology of Addictive Behaviors,* 11, 115. doi:10.1037/0893-164X.11.2.115

Petry, N. M. (2000). A comprehensive guide to the application of contingency management procedures in clinical settings. *Drug and Alcohol Dependence,* 58, 9–25. doi:10.1016/S0376-8716(99)00071-X

Pilling, S., Hesketh, K., & Mitcheson, L. (2010). *Routes to recovery: Psychosocial interventions for drug misuse.* London: National Treatment Agency for Substance Misuse.

Pobereskin, L. (2014). Workplace resilience training based upon Acceptance and Commitment Therapy (ACT). Unpublished MSc thesis. City University, London.

Powers, M. B., Zum Vörde Sive Vörding, M. B., & Emmelkamp, P. M. (2009). Acceptance and commitment therapy: A meta-analytic review. *Psychotherapy and Psychosomatics,* 78, 73–80. doi:10.1159/000190790

Sayrs, J. H. R. (2012). Mindfulness, acceptance and values-based interventions for addiction counselors: The benefits of practicing what we preach. In S. C. Hayes, & M. E. Levin (Eds.), *Mindfulness and acceptance for addictive behaviors.* Oakland, CA: New Harbinger Publications.

Segal, Z., Williams, J. M. G., & Teasdale, J. D. (2002). *Mindfulness-based cognitive therapy for depression: A new approach to preventing relapse.* London: The Guilford Press.

Smout, M. F., Hayes, L., Atkins, P. W., Klausen, J., & Duguid, J. E. (2012). The empirically supported status of acceptance and commitment therapy: An update. *Clinical Psychologist, 16*, 97–109. doi:10.1111/j.1742-9552.2012.00051.x

Stotts, A. L., Green, C., Masuda, A., et al. (2012). A stage I pilot study of acceptance and commitment therapy for methadone detoxification. *Drug and Alcohol Dependence, 125*, 215–222. doi:10.1016/j.drugalcdep.2012.02.015

Strang, J. (2012). *Medications in recovery: Re-orientating drug dependence treatment.* London: National Treatment Agency.

Varra, A. A., Hayes, S. C., Roget, N., & Fisher, G. (2008). A randomized control trial examining the effect of acceptance and commitment training on clinician willingness to use evidence-based pharmacotherapy. *Journal of Consulting and Clinical Psychology, 76*, 449. doi:10.1037/0022-006X.76.3.449

Wagner, C., Ingersoll, K., & Rollnick, S. (2012). Motivational interviewing: A cousin to contextual cognitive behavioural therapies. In S.Hayes, & M.Levin (Eds.), *Mindfulness and acceptance for addictive behaviors.* Oakland, CA: New Harbinger Publications.

Walser, R., & Pistorello, J. (2004). ACT in group formats. In S. Hayes, & K. Strosak (Eds.), *Practical guide to acceptance and commitment therapy.* New York: Springer.

Wanigaratne, S., Wallace, W., Pullin, J., Keaney, F., & Farmer, R. (1990). *Relapse prevention for addictive: A manual for therapists.* Oxford: Blackwell Science.

Wilson, K. G., & DuFrene, T. (2012). *The wisdom to know the difference: An acceptance and commitment therapy workbook for overcoming substance abuse.* Oakland, CA: New Harbinger.

Wilson, K. G., Hayes, S. C., & Byrd, M. (2000). Exploring compatibilities between Acceptance and Commitment Therapy and 12-Step treatment for substance abuse. *Journal of Rational-Emotive and Cognitive-Behavior Therapy, 18*, 209–234. doi:10.1023/A:1007835106007

Witkiewitz, K., Marlatt, G. A., & Walker, D. (2005). Mindfulness-based relapse prevention for alcohol and substance use disorders. *Journal of Cognitive Psychotherapy, 19*, 211–228. doi:10.1891/jcop.2005.19.3.211

PART 2

Clinical Applications of Addiction Psychology

7 The Role of Clinical Psychology within Alcohol Related Brain Damage

FRASER MORRISON[1] AND JENNY SVANBERG[2]

[1]NHS Lanarkshire Scotland UK
[2]Substance Misuse Department NHS Forth Valley Falkirk, Scotland, UK

CHAPTER OUTLINE

7.1   INTRODUCTION

Consuming large amounts of alcohol over a period of time can impair normal brain development (Tapert et al., 2001). Indeed, long-term alcohol misuse and dependence can result in brain damage, as in the case of Korsakoff's syndrome, a brain disorder caused by a lack of thiamine in the brain (Kopelman, 1995). The term 'Alcohol Related Brain Damage' (ARBD) describes a range of conditions that are associated with long-term alcohol misuse and associated vitamin deficiencies. With regards to specific cognitive deficits, alcohol dependence has an established association with deficits in a range of areas (Kolb & Whishaw, 1996). ARBD has been linked to immediate memory and learning problems, and difficulties with verbal memory tasks (Tracy & Bates, 1999). Within ARBD there are a range of psychosocial sequelae that have a detrimental impact on quality of life and outcome, including increased prevalence of mental health problems, impaired social relationships and poor socio-economic status. The role of an applied psychologist in this field includes assessment and treatment of cognitive difficulties in addition to the psychological sequelae of this form of acquired brain damage.

7.2   CLINICAL DEFINITION OF ALCOHOL RELATED BRAIN DAMAGE AND RELATED SYNDROMES

Alcohol Related Brain Damage is a term used to refer to a range of conditions associated with long-term alcohol misuse and vitamin deficiency, including Wernicke's encephalopathy, and Korsakoff's syndrome (Schmidt et al., 2005; Royal College of Psychiatrists, 2014). Existing diagnostic criteria provided by the *International Classification of Disorders* (ICD; World Health Organization, 1992) and the *Diagnostic and Statistical Manual* (DSM; APA 2013) do not offer a full description of the range of conditions that are described under this term. Furthermore, there can be confusion due to the term alcohol-related dementia which is often applied to individuals experiencing brain damage following long-term alcohol misuse. While it is the case that a cognitive decline does take place within this disorder when compared to pre-injury levels of functioning, it is clear that with abstinence from alcohol and improved nutrition, cognitive recovery can take place and the majority of disorders covered by the term ARBD are not neurodegenerative.

Alcohol can cause damage to the brain through a number of mechanisms, including:

- direct toxic effect on the brain;
- prevention of absorption of thiamine (vitamin B12) and other nutrients;
- poor nutrition and dehydration;
- liver disease (hepatic encephalopathy);
- changes to metabolism and blood supply to the brain;
- indirect damage caused by an increased risk of falls and accidents.

There are a number of characteristics commonly associated with ARBD. These can be considered in the form of a graded spectrum associated with alcohol use and vitamin deficiency. The early impact of significant alcohol use includes physical complications, such as compromised liver function, and associated cognitive deficits, including frontal and executive problems.

As dependence on alcohol develops, the chronic impact of associated deficits increases in severity to encompass complications of severe liver damage such as hepatic encephalopathy, substantive cognitive impairments such as executive dysfunction, memory impairment and associated confabulation, lack of insight and deficits in abstract thinking, and emotional disorder such as behavioural disinhibition. Chronic alcohol use in the context of poor nutrition may result in Wernicke's encephalopathy and the more chronic Korsakoff's syndrome, now commonly recognized as acute and chronic stages of the Wernicke-Korsakoff syndrome (Scalzo, Bowden & Hillbom, 2015).

ARBD can also be described in terms of the acute and sub-acute effects of alcohol intoxication and withdrawal, and further chronic disorders that develop following repeated cycles of this process in the context of poor nutrition or co-morbid physical health problems. Up to 25% of those presenting with ARBD may also have co-morbid difficulties relating to vascular or traumatic brain injury (Wilson et al., 2012).

Acute disorders associated with alcohol dependence are:

- acute withdrawal syndromes and delirium tremens;
- alcoholic hallucinosis;
- alcoholic blackouts;
- Wernicke's encephalopathy;
- hepatic encephalopathy; acute/chronic dysarthria or ataxia;
- seizures resulting from alcohol withdrawal, hypoglycaemia, or previous brain damage (e.g. epilepsy);
- peripheral neuropathy.

The chronic syndromes associated with alcohol dependence are:

- executive/frontal lobe dysfunction;
- Korsakoff's syndrome (alcohol-induced persisting amnesic disorder (*Diagnostic and Statistical Manual* (DSM-IV); APA, 1994);
- generalized cognitive deterioration associated with cortical atrophy.

7.3   EPIDEMIOLOGY OF ARBD AND RELATED SYNDROMES

The epidemiology of ARBD remains a largely underdeveloped area, and there is a lack of quality information on the prevalence of ARBD and the characteristics and needs of people with ARBD. A variety of prevalence estimates have been produced in terms of predicting rates of ARBD. A range of studies have used post-mortem examinations. The majority of these have focused on the Wernicke-Korsakoff syndrome and associated lesions. It has been estimated that prevalence in the general population in the United Kingdom is 0.5%, with the highest world rate of 2.8% found in Australia (Harper, 1998). Explanations for these findings have centred on increased rates of alcohol-related problems in these countries. Within an alcohol-dependent population, prevalence rates increase considerably to 12% (Wernicke-Korsakoff syndrome) and 26.8% (cerebellar atrophy) (Torvik, Lindboe & Rogde, 1982; Victor, Adams & Collins, 1989). Within specific neuropsychology services for ARBD and acquired brain injury, prevalence rates vary from 1.7% to 13% (Ferran et al., 1996).

Community estimates of ARBD rely on accessing medical notes and consequently an estimate of alcohol-related problems based on records in the notes, as opposed to a real-time measure of dependence. This is a considerable weakness of this method and consequently limits any findings. It may be that this methodology fails to fully represent actual rates of ARBD, given the apparent under-reporting by patients and the significant numbers of low socio-economic groups who often do not access standard healthcare systems and are concurrently more likely to experience ARBD. Cognitive impairment resulting from alcohol misuse has been documented among marginalized groups, including among Aboriginal communities in Australia (Cairney, Clough, Jaragba & Maruff, 2007), in areas such as the West of Scotland, which include high levels of poly-substance misuse, social deprivation, non-fatal overdose and repeated traumatic brain injuries, complicating the picture of ARBD (Bromley & Ormston, 2005).

There have been relatively few high-quality studies published recently examining the prevalence of ARBD in the United Kingdom, with much of the data centred on Scotland. Rates of 7–14.4 per 10,000 are suggested (Chiang, 2002), although several investigators have argued that ARBD is on the increase (e.g. McRae & Cox, 2003) and that these figures are likely to be a significant underestimation (Smith & Hillman, 1999). National trends in alcohol consumption also indicate that younger people are being exposed to more alcohol earlier in life with potential health implications (BMA Board of Science, 2008). Further, it has been noted that the current prevalence of ARBD is in a cohort whose alcohol consumption was half the current levels, thereby implying that alcohol-related impairments will increase further in coming years as the current cohort experiencing increased levels of consumption suffer increased rates of alcohol-related problems. Earlier studies suggest that the prevalence of ARBD is greater in areas of high socio-demographic deprivation (Chiang, 2002; Cox, Anderson & McCabe, 2004). Differences in gender and age have been noted with prevalence estimates significantly higher in men than in women (Chiang, 2002), and between the age of 50–60 years (McRae & Cox, 2003).

7.4 COGNITIVE FUNCTION IN ARBD

7.4.1 *Cognitive Deficits in ARBD*

Deficits in a number of areas of cognitive functioning have been reported, including problem-solving, verbal and non-verbal abstraction, and visual-motor coordination

(Parsons, 1998). Although there are clear links between alcohol dependence and cognitive impairment, the precise nature of these relationships can be difficult to categorize. Certain aspects of cognitive functioning can remain intact, such as language, whereas others, for example, planning, can be severely impaired. Several factors have been linked to level of cognitive deficits in alcohol dependence. These include quantity of alcohol intake (Giancola, 2007), duration of drinking problem (Hingson, Heeren & Winter, 2006), and age (Eckardt, Stapleton, Rawlings, Davis & Grodin, 1995). Cognitive deficits may arise through a number of direct and indirect causes, including toxic effects of alcohol or withdrawal, associated deficiency of vitamins, or via cirrhosis of the liver (Richardson et al., 1991). Severe chronic use of alcohol is known to induce neurotoxicity (Ratti et al., 1999) and may damage the brain.

ARBD is characterized by a range of deficits. Historically these have often been considered to be associated with each particular disorder. For example, Korsakoff's syndrome has commonly been reported as showing a disproportionate impairment in memory relative to other aspects of cognitive function (Kopelman, 1995). Further, memory deficits in terms of retrograde and anterograde amnesia are typically observed, accompanied by confabulation. However, it is now recognized that this chronic phase of the Wernicke-Korsakoff syndrome is characterized by a wide range of cognitive impairments of variable severity (Scalzo, Bowden & Hillbom, 2015).

A major feature of presentation is the dysexecutive syndrome (Ihara, Berrios & London, 2000) involving the frontal brain area. This term covers a range of functions including behavioural regulation, goal-setting inhibition and complex reasoning (Chen, Sultzer, Hinkin, Mahler & Cummings, 1998). Cognitive deficits in these areas can be affected with implications for impairment of social awareness (Uekermann & Daum, 2008) and increased risk behaviour (Bjork, Momenan, Smith & Hommer, 2008), and can therefore impact on engagement and outcome in treatment.

7.4.2   Neuropsychological Assessment in ARBD

Neuropsychological assessment is the applied science concerned with the behavioural expression of brain dysfunction (Lezak, 2004). The purpose of neuropsychological assessment is to offer insight into cognitive difficulties that may have an organic cause. In the field of ARBD, this is an essential area of assessment that the applied psychologist can perform.

For a review of specific tests, a number of texts are available, including Lezak (2004) and Spreen and Strauss (2006). In carrying out neuropsychological assessment with alcohol-using populations, it is often useful to focus assessment on a brief screen to capture overall functioning and guide further assessment, followed by a more comprehensive assessment particularly looking at memory and executive functioning impairments in order to guide treatment. There are a number of particular points to consider:

- If a referral comes from an acute setting, it will be important to assess the length of abstinence in order to obtain valid assessment results. Although 4–6 weeks abstinence is recommended, a cognitive screen, such as the ACE-III (Addenbrooke's Cognitive Examination; Hsieh, Schubert, Hoon, Mioshi

& Hodges, 2013) or the MoCA (Montreal Cognitive Assessment; Nasreddine et al, 2005), following initial detoxification can provide a baseline and suggest whether or not there may be a need for more comprehensive assessment.

- Premorbid functioning assessment can be complicated in the ARBD client group due to increased rates of socio-economic deprivation and reduced levels of literacy (Chiang, 2002). In order to supplement formal assessment, it is useful to obtain historical information from significant others, or thorough case note review.

- Memory assessment may cover different domains of memory, including: episodic memory (personally experienced events), semantic memory (meaning and general knowledge), working memory (manipulation of information), and broadly anterograde (new information) or retrograde (past events). In the early stages of ARBD, when executive functioning difficulties may be primary, memory retrieval may be disorganized, but memory encoding intact. In the profound memory impairment associated with Wernicke-Korsakoff syndrome, semantic memory and working memory may be intact, but episodic memory is impaired, with both anterograde and retrograde deficits, and a retrograde impairment that may stretch back for many years.

- Impairments in the executive functioning domain typically involve errors of planning, judgement, problem-solving, impulse control and abstract reasoning (Kipps & Hodges, 2005). A range of functions should be assessed using formal test batteries and clinical assessment. Executive functioning assessment using an ecologically valid psychometric tool such as the Behavioural Assessment of the Dysexecutive Syndrome (BADS; Wilson, Alderman, Burgess, Emslie & Evans, 1996) can be useful in order to inform recommendations for rehabilitation.

- Neuropsychological assessment may provide crucial information for care planning, particularly for those individuals who may be in the early stages of ARBD and may struggle to engage with traditional and motivation-focused treatment programmes.

- ARBD is associated with high rates of co-morbid physical and mental health problems. If the initial screen suggests impairments in other cognitive domains, it will be necessary to carry out a more comprehensive battery of assessments. Visuo-spatial impairments may sometimes be seen with ARBD, but language or other focal neurological impairments are suggestive of vascular or traumatic brain damage. Emotional distress and mental health problems may also impact on cognition, and should be assessed.

7.4.3   *Recovery of Cognitive Function in ARBD*

Following immediate presentation after detoxification from alcohol, a number of cognitive functions will undergo rapid recovery as the acute presentation resolves and improvements to physical health are witnessed (Bates, Bowden & Barry, 2002). Further, in the context of an alcohol-free environment, cognitive impairments can undergo spontaneous recovery in the absence of additional treatment, aside from abstinence. Follow-up studies examining brain changes using structural and functional MRI have demonstrated this form of recovery on an anatomical level (Bates et al., 2002).

There is evidence that some of the improvement may be related to general improvement in health, and a large degree of variance exists within the recovery of specific cognitive domains. For example, more complex cognitive functions such as executive function, including planning and abstract thinking, may take over one year to witness a significant improvement (Morrison, 2011). The prevalence of relapse within this clinical group means there is a sparse evidence of recovery within cognitive domains that is not influenced by the co-morbid variable of concurrent alcohol use.

In the field of ARBD it has been suggested that cognitive functioning can take between three and six weeks to fully recover following a period of increased alcohol consumption and the process of recovery levels off following three to six weeks of sobriety after inpatient detoxification (Ryan & Butters, 1986). This is an important issue clinically because, if a patient is tested prematurely, then test performance may be influenced by the residual effects of alcohol withdrawal and not reflect their 'true' level of cognitive functioning. After three to six weeks of abstinence, recovery appears to level off, with the most significant gains made during this period (Grant, Adam & Reed, 1986). These have also been identified to occur within the first two weeks of abstinence although the evidence base on this matter is inconsistent (Cocchi & Chiavarini, 1997). Further recovery of cognitive function can take longer, as is the case with other areas of acquired brain damage, with gradual improvements observed. In the range of neuropsychological functions affected by alcohol misuse, it has been established that different abilities are more susceptible to this cause (e.g. executive functioning). Thus it follows that different areas of functioning may also show variations in rates of cognitive recovery. For example, verbal learning deficits appear to resolve more rapidly than visuo-spatial skills (Parsons & Leber, 1982).

7.5 PSYCHOSOCIAL AND COGNITIVE REHABILITATION

7.5.1 Impact of Cognitive Deficits in ARBD and Rationale for Treatment

Given the documented cognitive deficits associated with prolonged alcohol dependence, it is clear these factors may interfere with the recovery of an individual from problem drinking. Significant cognitive deficits may make it unlikely that a treatment programme will be adhered to, or achieve optimal success. Recovery of neuropsychological function is therefore important for individuals who experience cognitive impairment in alcohol dependence if they are to progress in terms of meeting recovery goals with their addiction. Deficits in cognitive functioning can impair ability to function and consequently may increase the likelihood of relapse (McIntosh & Chick,

2006). For example, a deficit in executive functioning could result in an increase in disinhibited behaviour. In turn, this could lead to an increase in encounters with alcohol simply due to a lack of insight of the consequence of the behaviour or impulse control. Increases in cognitive functioning have been linked to improved treatment engagement and outcome (Bates et al., 2002).

If one is to successfully recover from alcohol dependence, then it is essential that psychosocial skills within an individual are well developed. Given that long-term behaviour change requires regular use of new coping skills, this can be assisted by improving cognitive functioning. The main aims of psychosocial treatments in alcohol dependence are to alter behaviour and develop skills to reduce the likelihood of relapse. These activities clearly require complex levels of cognitive skills and interactions.

The prevalence of alcohol-related changes in the brain is 1.5% of the general population and 30% of heavy drinkers (Cook, Hallwood & Thomson, 1998). Accompanied with the reported increases in ARBD cases (Ramayya & Jauhar, 1997), it is likely there are large numbers of individuals engaging unsuccessfully in treatment programmes due to these aforementioned deficits. Despite this, few treatment regimes account for the impact of cognitive impairment in alcohol dependence. Treatment approaches do not appear to account for the influence of cognitive dysfunction and could be greatly improved if this were to be included. For example, an individual with executive functioning deficits may benefit from the exclusion of abstract concepts and use of a concrete treatment strategy. The impact of specific instructions, such as goal setting, has been highlighted even in the early stages of detoxification from alcohol. Despite a range of cognitive deficits, goal-setting strategies have been shown to be effective in cognitive rehabilitation and therapy in alcohol dependence (Scheurich et al., 2004).

A range of approaches are used in terms of promoting recovery from cognitive dysfunction such as direct medical treatments (e.g. thiamine in the context of resolving severe neurological symptoms) and treatment of related medical conditions (e.g. liver damage or hepatic cirrhosis). The premise of these interventions is to prevent further brain damage, as is the case with the recommendation of abstinence from alcohol to promote natural spontaneous recovery. Following this initial stage of intervention and recovery, the consensus regarding further treatments for rehabilitation is taken from an emerging evidence base.

The aim of cognitive neuro-rehabilitation in alcohol dependence treatment approaches is to assist with improvement of neuropsychological functioning and recovery to allow patients to fully engage in treatment programmes, which will lead to improved psychosocial outcome.

Natural improvement can occur in ARBD, however, this is reliant on abstinence. Current estimates of relapse rates in alcohol dependence vary, however, it is suggested that 50% of individuals relapse within three months (Slattery et al., 2003). This does not account for the influence of cognitive impairment in the ARBD population. One can estimate that relapse rates in this group are likely to be considerably higher, attributable to the reduced coping skills due to brain injury. Neuro-rehabilitation can be used to assist in the years following a diagnosis of ARBD to improve efficacy of psycho-social interventions with the goal of reducing relapse and promoting natural cognitive recovery. Some individuals may require some form of legislative intervention as a result of impairment in their ability to protect themselves due to the limitations of their decision-making capacity. In terms of cognitive recovery rates within ARBD, Cox et al. (2004) suggest that 25% of patients with ARBD make a full recovery. A further 25% make a partial recovery, with another 25% making a minor recovery and the remainder showing no improvement at all. These findings were taken from clinical reports in the context of service provision. Within the context of Korsakoff's syndrome, recovery rates of 74% have been documented if abstinence is maintained over a 10-year period (Victor et al., 1971). There are examples of efficacy of specific neuro-rehabilitation approaches which will be commented on later.

Concurrent with increases in the incidence of ARBD, there are large numbers of individuals with alcohol dependence who also experience mental health problems. Up to 85% of users of alcohol services report experiencing mental health problems such as anxiety and depression (Department of Health, 2004). Surveys show that about a third of psychiatric patients also meet the criterion for alcohol dependence (Scottish Advisory Committee on Alcohol Misuse, 2002). Co-morbidity is also common among individuals with a primary diagnosis of alcohol dependence who experience psychiatric problems (Grant & Harford, 1995). For example, up to 50% of those with alcohol dependence have a concurrent diagnosis of personality disorder (Hasin et al., 2002). The types of mental health problems in those treated for alcohol dependence also include depression and anxiety, with strong associations between alcohol misuse and trauma, eating disorders and self-harm (Department of Health, 2004). Alcohol dependence is also associated with high rates of completed suicide (Raistrick, Heather & Godfrey, 2006).

Given the prevalence of mental health disorders in alcohol dependence, it is likely there are increasing numbers of individuals with ARBD experiencing similar psychiatric difficulties. This highlights the need for adaptation of existing psychosocial interventions for the ARBD client group to manage mental health problems.

7.5.2   *Adaptations to Alcohol Treatment Programmes*

Existing mechanisms of alcohol dependence treatment programmes have also been incorporated into neuro-rehabilitation for ARBD. It has been suggested that use of psychoeducation can be effective, and individuals can benefit from the disclosure of neuropsychological test results and information about alcohol's negative effect on cognition (Weinstein & Shaffer, 1993). It would appear that this may serve as motivational therapeutic tool in line with the standard approaches of Motivational Interviewing or Motivational Enhancement Therapy. Client motivation is central to any psychotherapeutic intervention in alcohol dependence (Miller & Rollnick, 2012). The aim of a motivational approach is to establish a working alliance with a client where you can begin discussing their substance misuse (Graham, 2004). Special emphasis should be placed on including elements of motivational interviewing in an adapted format when working with clients with ARBD (Morrison & Pestell, 2010).

Several different cognitive strategies can be used to help individuals with ARBD manage their symptoms of depression (Butler, Chapman, Forman & Beck, 2006). CBT can help individuals to modify their maladaptive cognitive and behavioural responses to physical symptoms. This has been demonstrated in a number of associated areas such as in managing depression in older adults (Laidlaw, Gallagher-Thompson, Thompson & Siskin-Dick, 2003) and is applicable to ARBD.

The structure of therapy may need to be adapted in traditional alcohol interventions for this client group. Each session ordinarily includes an agenda and review of previous goals (Butler et al., 2006). This structure and format of treatment may prove especially helpful to patients with problems initiating, organizing and monitoring goal-directed activities as a result of some of the specific cognitive difficulties that are associated with ARBD.

In addition to the structure of sessions, altering the length of therapeutic sessions may also be more beneficial. In particular, shorter sessions with breaks may be necessary, dependent on the type of cognitive impairment. One of the roles of the therapist is to facilitate the learning of the client. Thus, a well-informed assessment of their relative cognitive strengths and weaknesses is important in ARBD.

7.5.3   Cognitive Rehabilitation from Both ARBD and Brain Injury Settings

7.5.3.1   ARBD Settings

Research suggests that recovery of cognitive functioning can occur in ARBD with the aid of neuro-rehabilitation within specific domains of cognitive function. These include memory, with specific reference to elaborative processing, self-generation and cognitive remediation, including errorless learning, letter-fragment cueing, verbal prompting, and outcome reinforcement (Svanberg & Evans, 2013a).

There have been a number of studies that demonstrate repetition and practice on cognitive tasks can lead to improved functioning within that area of functioning. This has been shown more generally with use of training on simple cognitive skills required to perform complex tasks over repeated administrations (Goldman & Goldman, 1988). This study found a general improvement in functioning for individuals who had received cognitive training in comparison to the control group when performance on complex tasks was used as a performance measure. Cognitive training has also shown improvements in functioning in specific areas of cognitive tasks such as visuospatial functioning (Forsberg & Goldman, 1985). Limitations to this approach indicate that simple repetition or practice of cognitive tests or material will enhance test performance but does not generalize beyond the specific areas of task being measured, although it has been suggested that underlying skills are being developed in this process (Forsberg & Goldman, 1987). More recent evidence highlights that specific training in the concepts associated with a particular cognitive domain are more effective than general cognitive practice. A study on working memory found improvements among participants with ARBD who had received specific training when compared to a control group who were given simple repetition (Wetzig & Hardin, 1990).

In the area of cognitive remediation in ARBD, there are a limited number of studies that examine use of computer-assisted training programs. Fals-Stewart and Lam (2010) demonstrated the efficacy of specific computerized cognitive training in comparison to a muscle relaxation group, computer typing and no treatment group. Of those drug and alcohol abusers with cognitive deficit, 25% were specifically those with ARBD. Recovery of cognitive functioning was measured over two months and accompanied by improved psychosocial functioning. This was attributed to improved cognitive functioning (e.g. attention) allowing better engagement with the treatment regime offered. A study by Rupp and colleagues (2012) indicated that, in comparison with conventional alcohol dependence treatment, individuals who received supplemental cognitive remediation showed significant improvement in attention/executive function and memory domains (Rupp, Kemmler, Kurz, Hinterhuber & Fleischhacker, 2012). This was accompanied by increases in psychological well-being and reduced measures of relapse predictors (e.g. cravings). This group was not a homogeneous sample of clients with ARBD, however, given the history of significant alcohol dependence in all subjects, one could assume a relative degree of cognitive impairment among the group. This indicates that neuro-rehabilitation may be beneficial for individuals with milder cognitive difficulties in ARBD, as noted elsewhere (Bates et al., 2002).

Roehrich and Goldman (1993) have demonstrated the efficacy of self-help in the context of cognitive rehabilitation. A number of effective cognitive remediation tasks were collated into a self-guided workbook. This led to improved performance on neuropsychological assessment at six months, again linked to improvements in the acquisition of treatment programme content.

While a number of studies can demonstrate the efficacy of cognitive remediation in the context of a treatment programme, there are more limited accounts of longer-term follow-up studies. Price and colleagues (1988) followed up the outcomes of individuals after discharge from a cognitive remediation programme into standard community care. Approximately one third (27%) had maintained abstinence, while around half (54.1%) had returned to chaotic alcohol misuse (Price et al., 1988). Between 30% and 50% of individuals who present for alcohol treatment relapse within three months (Slattery et al., 2003), not accounting for cognitive deficits. This has been mirrored in other studies that indicate individuals with co-morbid alcohol dependence and cognitive impairment perform better in specialist services in comparison to standard care (Fals-Stewart, 1992). The trend in clinical services in the UK has been to aspire to place patients with ARBD in specialist nursing homes or rehabilitation facilities. This has been proven to be more effective in terms of psychosocial and cognitive functioning than if the individual was placed in a general setting (Ganzelves, Geus & Wester, 1994).

7.5.3.2   Brain Injury Settings

Within the area of memory rehabilitation a number of large reviews have made recommendations in terms of relevant treatment components. Training in the use of external compensations (including assistive technology) with direct application to functional activities is recommended as a practice guideline in subjects with moderate or severe memory impairment after traumatic brain injury (TBI) or stroke (Cicerone et al., 2005). Memory aids without electronic aid are possibly effective; specific learning strategies such as errorless learning are rated as probably effective; and electronic external memory devices are recommended as probably effective (Cappa et al., 2005). Similarly in the area of executive functioning, training of formal problem-solving strategies is recommended as a practice guideline with application to ecologically relevant situations (i.e. daily life) (Cicerone et al., 2005).

In severe acquired brain injury (ABI), there are a number of useful treatment components that can be adapted within ARBD services, in the context of supported accommodation for older homeless people. Common features of successful interventions include; management strategies that are highly individualized for each client, and comprehensive multidisciplinary approaches to assessment and treatment. Furthermore, within the service described, attention is given to offering individual support by increasing the staff-to-residents ratio and thereby allowing implementation of an individualized care approach (Rota-Bartelink & Lipmann, 2007).

7.5.4   Holistic Rehabilitation for ARBD

Cognitive rehabilitation techniques can be used to adapt evidence-based psychosocial interventions for treatment of people with cognitive impairments. In other areas of brain injury a number of existing psychosocial interventions have been adapted. These include; Coping skills training (Anson & Ponsford, 2006); Cognitive Behaviour Therapy (CBT) plus attention training following mild to moderate traumatic brain injury (TBI) (Tiersky et al., 2005); and CBT for emotional problems post TBI (Bradbury et al., 2008). These have largely developed from contemporary CBT interventions where it has been suggested that rehabilitation is likely to fail if we do not deal with the emotional issues (Prigatano, 1999).

In their description of ARBD services in the United Kingdom, Wilson et al. (2012) highlight the need for neuropsychological rehabilitation in this group. Five therapeutic phases of rehabilitation for ARBD are identified, including two stages of therapeutic rehabilitation which follow an initial stabilization and precede a recovery/relapse prevention period. Attention is given to individual care plans, as commented on within an Australian setting (Rota-Bartelink & Lipmann, 2007). An example of this is the agreement to supervised controlled drinking within the home environment, as opposed to implementing abstinence, which although it may have been less harmful for the client, could have resulted in attrition from treatment (Wilson et al., 2012).

A single case study analysed outcomes for a woman with Korsakoff's syndrome attending a 25-week neuropsychological programme. Gains were made in self-care, participation and a reduction of memory lapses, but no differentiation was made between aspects of the treatment programme and differential outcomes (Svanberg & Evans, 2013b).

7.5.5   Conclusion

In conclusion, the evidence base for the treatment of ARBD is currently developing. There are a number of studies that point to the efficacy of interventions in this client group, and over time the inclusion of more studies will help to improve this. The answer to the key question of whether one can work therapeutically with individuals who experience co-morbid mental health problems, alcohol dependence, and neuropsychological deficits as result of ARBD is complex. This group is often stigmatized and neglected due to the complex nature of their presenting difficulties, however, it is clear that existing therapeutic approaches can be modified to best fit their needs. Knowledge from associated areas with neuropsychological impairment, such as stroke, can be applied and lead to adaptations to conventional psychotherapeutic approaches. The resulting deficits from ARBD clearly present significant barriers to treatment, but can be overcome by modifying existing approaches with a degree of flexibility.

7.6   LEGAL FRAMEWORK: MENTAL CAPACITY

Given the prevalence of cognitive deficits within ARBD, the range of deficits an individual can experience has an important influence on their ability to make decisions in relation to daily activity. For example, an individual experiencing executive dysfunction secondary to ARBD may experience problems with abstract thinking and emotional regulation, which has clear implications for limited ability to engage in complex decision-making, such as personal care or financial management. Cognitive impairment may have an impact on the individual's awareness and understanding of their current circumstances in relationship to alcohol misuse and its potential damage. Furthermore, this may have an impact on the ability to understand and engage with therapeutic interventions. It is recommended that all cases in alcohol treatment services are given a full cognitive assessment, partly to screen for the aforementioned problems (NICE, 2011).

The long-term effects of alcohol can result in a range of disorders of alcohol related brain damage, which have direct implications for cognitive dysfunction. In particular, damage to the frontal lobes is commonly seen in ARBD (Ihara et al., 2000). This can result in executive dysfunction with behavioural difficulties including understanding concepts, multi-tasking, emotional regulation and reduced awareness of the consequences of decisions. The range of problems that executive dysfunction describes has obvious implications if one considers the issues that the term capacity covers. Indeed, it has been reported that evaluation of executive functions can be of particular importance in competency assessments in alcohol dependence since the relative preservation of language may lead to normal results on mental status testing and an over-estimation of the person's actual capacity (Hazelton, Sterns & Chisholm, 2003). Furthermore, the range of memory deficits (e.g. anterograde or episodic) present with ARBD has clear implications for making decisions and the ability to protect oneself in the environment. For example, an individual may not recall giving money to an associate when asked about it at a later date, thus making them vulnerable to exploitation.

A range of legislation exists in the United Kingdom that can be used to manage difficulties arising from cognitive impairment in ARBD (see, e.g. The Mental Capacity Act, 2005 (England and Wales), The Lord Chancellor, 2007; Mental Health (Care and Treatment) (Scotland) Act, 2003; Adult Support and Protection (Scotland) Act, 2007). Within all of the aforementioned legislation, reference is made to mental disorder being a barrier to ability to make clear and consistent decisions about complex issues. In this framework ARBD fulfils the legal criteria of mental disability. However, it should be noted that a person is not mentally disordered by reason only of dependence on, or use of, alcohol or drugs.

It is important to note that cognitive function in ARBD will fluctuate, as may capacity to make decisions. Consequently, regular re-assessments should be encouraged with a view to maximizing the individual's autonomy. The overarching principle underlying the various Acts is that any intervention in an individual's affairs should provide benefit to the individual, and should be the least restrictive option of those that are available which will meet the purpose of the intervention.

7.6.1   *Assessment of Capacity*

A range of guidance is available for each of the aforementioned Acts which is summarized here in terms of assessment. It is suggested the following areas are considered within assessment based on the Adults with Incapacity (Scotland) Act (2000); perception, understanding, logical thinking, memory, motivation, planning, reasoning, suggestibility, emotional disorder, thought disorder and communication problems. All of these are included in a comprehensive neuropsychological assessment. Further to this the following should also be borne in mind:

- make sure the capacity question is specific;
- consider evidence of impaired judgement prior to admission;
- differentiate between alcohol-related cognitive deficits and denial secondary to addiction;
- use vignettes to support exploration of the particular decision to be made to support those who may struggle to think abstractly (Moye et al., 2007).

7.7   RECOVERY

ARBD is not the same as having an intellectual disability or having a dementia, although there are some overlaps. It has been suggested that people affected by ARBD have needs more akin to adults of similar ages with acquired brain injury than to people with other dementias (Mental Welfare Commission for Scotland, 2010). A significant proportion of people with ARBD will make significant improvements with the right care and conditions. For example, the extent of recovery from Korsakoff's syndrome followed for up to 10 years ranged between 21% and 28% (Victor et al., 1971). These findings are confirmed by Smith and Hillman (1999), who suggested that in ARBD approximately 50% will make some form of significant recovery. This suggests that ARBD is distinct in terms of acquired brain injury in that the potential for recovery is clearly linked to the substance attributable to the disorder, namely alcohol. While it is clear that recovery is possible, this will only take place if the person with ARBD is given access to specialist rehabilitation interventions and support systems to manage their alcohol use in a manner most likely framed towards abstinence.

SUGGESTIONS FOR FURTHER READING

Graham, H. L. (2004). *Cognitive-behavioural Integrated Treatment (C-BIT): A treatment manual for substance misuse in people with severe mental health problems*. Chichester: John Wiley & Sons, Ltd.

Miller, W. R., & Rollnick, S. (2012). *Motivational interviewing: Preparing people for change*. New York: Guilford Press.

Svanberg J., Witall, A., Draper, B., & Bowden, S. (Eds.). (2015). *Alcohol and the adult brain*. London: Psychology Press.

REFERENCES

Adult Support and Protection (Scotland) Act. (2007). London: HMSO. http://www.legislation.gov.uk/asp/2007/10/contents

Adults with Incapacity (Scotland) Act. (2000). London: HMSO. http://www.legislation.gov.uk/asp/2000/4/contents

Anson, K., & Ponsford, J. (2006). Who benefits? Outcome following a coping skills group intervention for traumatically brain injured individuals. *Brain Injury, 20*, 1–13. doi:10.1080/02699050500309791

APA (American Psychiatric Association) (1994). *Diagnostic and statistical manual of mental Disorders* (4th ed.). Arlington, VA: American Psychiatric Publishing.

APA (American Psychiatric Association) (2013). *Diagnostic and statistical manual of mental disorders* (5th ed.). Arlington, VA: American Psychiatric Publishing.

Bates, M. E., Bowden, S. C., & Barry, D. (2002). Neurocognitive impairment associated with alcohol use disorders: Implications for treatment. *Experimental and Clinical Psychopharmacology, 10*, 193–212. doi:10.1037/1064-1297.10.3.193

Bjork, J., Momenan, R., Smith, A., & Hommer, D. (2008). Reduced posterior mesofrontal cortex activation by risky rewards in substance-dependent patients. *Drug and Aalcohol Dependence, 95*, 115–128. doi:10.1016/j.drugalcdep.2007.12.014.

BMA Board of Science. (2008). *Alcohol misuse: Tackling the UK epidemic*. London: British Medical Association.

Bradbury, C. L., Christensen, B. K., Lau, M. A., Ruttan, L. A., Arundine, A. L., & Green, R. E. (2008). The efficacy of cognitive behavior therapy in the treatment of emotional distress after acquired brain injury. *Archives of Physical Medical Rehabilitation, 89*, 61–68. doi:10.1016/j.apmr.2008.08.210

Bromley, C., & Ormston, R. (2005). *Part of the Scottish way of life? Attitudes towards drinking and smoking in Scotland: Findings from the 2004 Scottish Social Attitudes Survey*. Edinburgh: Scottish Executive.

Butler, A. C., Chapman, J. E., Forman, E. M., & Beck, A. T. (2006). The empirical status of cognitive-behavioral therapy: A review of meta-analyses. *Clinical Psychology Review, 26*, 17–31. doi:10.1016/j.cpr.2005.07.003

Cairney, S., Clough, A., Jaragba, M., & Maruff, P. (2007). Cognitive impairment in Aboriginal people with heavy episodic patterns of alcohol use. *Addiction, 102*, 909–915. doi:10.1111/j.1360-0443.2007.01840.x

Cappa, S. F., Benke, T., Clarke, S., Rossi, B., Stemmer, B., & van Heugten, C. M. (2005). EFNS guidelines on cognitive rehabilitation: Report of an EFNS task force. *European Journal of Neurology*, *12*, 665–680. doi:10.1111/j.1468-1331.2005.01330.x

Chen, S. T., Sultzer, D. L., Hinkin, C. H., Mahler, M. E., & Cummings, J. L. (1998). Executive dysfunction in Alzheimer's disease: Association with neuropsychiatric symptoms and functional impairment. *The Journal of Neuropsychiatry and Clinical Neuroscience*, *10*, 426–432.

Chiang, C. C. P. (2002). *Wernicke Korsakoff syndrome in Argyll and Clyde: A literature review, needs assessment and recommendation for the prevention, treatment and provision of Wernicke Korsakoff Syndrome*. Edinburgh: The Faculty of Public Health Medicine.

Cicerone, K. D., Dahlberg, C., Malec, J. F., Langenbahn, D. M., Felicettti, T., Kneipp, S., et al. (2005). Evidence-based cognitive rehabilitation: Updated review of the literature from 1998 through 2002. *Archive Physical Medical Rehabilitation*, *86*, 1681–1692.

Cocchi, R., & Chiavarini, M. (1997). Raven's coloured matrices in female alcoholics before and after detoxification: An investigation on 73 cases. *International Journal of Intellectual Impairment*, *11*, 45–49.

Cook, C., Hallwood, P., & Thomson, A. (1998). B Vitamin deficiency and neuropsychiatric syndromes in alcohol misuse. *Alcohol*, *33*, 317–336.

Cox, S., Anderson, I., & McCabe, L. (2004). *A fuller life: Report of the expert group on alcohol related brain damage*. Stirling: Dementia Services Development Centre, University of Stirling.

Department of Health. (2004). *National Treatment Agency for Substance Misuse: Co-morbidity of Substance Misuse and Mental Illness Collaborative Study (COSMIC)*. London: NTA.

Eckardt, M. J., Stapleton, J. M., Rawlings, R. R., Davis, E. Z., & Grodin, D. M. (1995). Neuropsychological functioning in detoxified alcoholics between 18 and 35 years of age. *American Journal of Psychiatry*, *152*, 45–52. doi:/10.1176/ajp.152.1.53

Fals-Stewart, W. (1992). Using the subtests of the Brain Age Quotient to screen for cognitive deficits among substance abusers. *Perceptual and Motor Skills*, *75*, 244–246. doi:10.2466/pms.1992.75.1.244

Fals-Stewart, W., & Lam, W. K. K. (2010). Computer-assisted cognitive rehabilitation for the treatment of patients with substance use disorders: A randomized clinical trial. *Experimental and Clinical Psychopharmacology*, *18*, 87–98. doi:10.1037/a0018058

Ferran, J., Wilson, K., Doran, M., Ghadiali, E., Johnson, F., Cooper, P., et al. (1996). The early onset dementias: A study of clinical and service need. *International Journal of Geriatric Psychiatry*, *11*, 863–869. doi:10.1002/(SICI)1099-1166(199610)11:10<863::AID-GPS394>3.0.CO;2-7

Forsberg, L. K., & Goldman, M. S. (1985). Experience-dependent recovery of visuospatial functioning in older alcoholic persons. *Journal of Abnormal Psychology*, *94*, 519–529. doi:10.1037//0021-843X.94.4.519

Forsberg, L. K., & Goldman, M. S. (1987). Experience-dependent recovery of cognitive deficits in alcoholics: Extended transfer of training. *Journal of Abnormal Psychology*, *96*, 345–353. doi:10.1037//0021-843X.96.4.345

Ganzelves, P. G. J., Geus, B. W. J., & Wester, A. J. (1994). Cognitive and behavioural aspects of Korsakoff's syndrome: The effect of special Korsakoff wards in a general hospital. *Tijdschrift voor Alcohol Drugs en Andere Psychotrope Stoffen*, *20*, 20–31.

Giancola, P. R. (2007). The underlying role of aggressivity in the relation between executive functioning and alcohol consumption. *Addictive Behaviors*, *32*, 765–783. doi:10.1016/j.addbeh.2006.06.015

Goldman, R., & Goldman, M. (1988). Experience-dependent cognitive recovery in alcoholics: A task component strategy. *Journal of Studies on Alcohol*, *49*, 142–148.

Graham, H. L. (2004). *Cognitive-Behavioural Integrated Treatment (C-BIT): A treatment manual for substance misuse in people with severe mental health problems*. Chichester: Wiley.

Grant, B. F., & Harford T. C. (1995). Comorbidity between DSM-IV alcohol use disorders and major depression: Results of a national survey. *Drug and Alcohol Dependence*, *39*, 197–206. doi:10.1016/0376-8716(95)01160-4

Grant, I., Adam, K. M., & Reed, R. (1986). Intermediate-duration (subacute) organic mental disorder of alcoholism. In I. Grant (Ed.), *Neuropsychiatric correlates of alcoholism* (pp. 37–60). Washington, DC: American Psychiatric Press.

Harper, C. (1998). The neuropathology of alcohol specific brain damage, or does alcohol damage the brain? *Journal of Neuropathology & Experimental Neurology, 57*, 101–110.

Hasin, D., Liu, X., Nunes, E., McCloud, S., Samet, S., & Endicott, J. (2002). Effects of major depression on remission and relapse of substance dependence. *Archives of General Psychiatry, 59*, 375–380. doi:10.1001/archpsyc.59.4.375

Hazelton, D., Sterns, G. L., & Chisholm, T. (2003). Decision-making capacity and alcohol abuse: Clinical and ethical considerations in personal care choices. *General Hospital Psychiatry, 25*, 130–135. doi:10.1016/S0163-8343(03)00005-7

Hingson, R. W., Heeren, T., & Winter, M. R. (2006). Age at drinking onset and alcohol dependence: Age at onset, duration, and severity. *Archives of Pediatrics & Adolescent Medicine, 160*, 739–746. doi:10.1001/archpedi.160.7.739

Hsieh, S., Schubert, S., Hoon, C., Mioshi, E., & Hodges J. R. (2013). Validation of the Addenbrooke's Cognitive Examination III in frontotemporal dementia and Alzheimer's disease. *Dementia and Geriatric Cognitive Disorders, 36*, 242–250. doi:10.1159/000351671.

Ihara, H., Berrios, G. E., & London, M. (2000). Group and case study of the dysexecutive syndrome in alcoholism without amnesia. *Journal of Neurology, Neurosurgery, and Psychiatry, 68*, 731–737. doi:10.1136/jnnp.68.6.731

Kipps, C., & Hodges, J. (2005). Cognitive assessment for clinicians. *Journal of Neurology, Neurosurgery and Psychiatry, 76*, 22–30.

Kolb, B., & Whishaw, I. (1996). *Fundamentals of human neuropsychology* (3rd ed.). New York: W. H. Freedom and Co.

Kopelman, M. D. (1995). The Korsakoff syndrome. *British Journal of Psychiatry, 166*, 154–173. doi:10.1192/bjp.166.2.154

Laidlaw, K., Gallagher-Thompson, D., Thompson, L. W., & Siskin-Dick, L. (2003). *Cognitive behavioural therapy with older people*. Chichester: John Wiley & Sons, Ltd.

Lezak, M. (2004). *Neuropsychological assessment*. New York: Oxford University Press.

Lord Chancellor, The. (2007). *The Mental Capacity Act* (England & Wales), 2005. London: HMSO. https://www.gov.uk/government/collections/mental-capacity-act-making-decisions

McIntosh, C., & Chick, J. (2006). Managing neurological problems in heavy drinkers. *Practitioner, 2*, 22–27.

McRae, R., & Cox, S. (2003). *Meeting the needs of people with alcohol related brain damage: A literature review on the existing and recommended service Provision and models of care*. Stirling: Dementia Services Development Centre, University of Stirling.

Mental Health (Care and Treatment) (Scotland) Act. (2003). London: HMSO. http://www.legislation.gov.uk/asp/2003/13/

Mental Welfare Commission for Scotland. (2010). Mr A Report. http://www.mwcscot.org.uk/media/51983/Mr_A.pdf

Miller, W. R., & Rollnick, S. (2012). *Motivational interviewing: Preparing people for change*. New York: Guilford Press.

Morrison, F. (2011). Neuropsychological impairment and relapse following inpatient detoxification in severe alcohol dependence. *International Journal of Mental Health & Addiction, 9*, 151–161. doi:10.1007/s11469-009-9261-x (First online 9 Dec. 2009)

Morrison, F., & Pestell, S. (2010). The application of cognitive behavioural therapy to individuals with comorbid depression and alcohol related brain damage. *Clinical Psychology Forum, 206*, 13–20.

Moye, J., Karel, M. J., Edelstein, B., Hicken, B., Armesto, A., & Gurrera, R. J. (2007). Assessment of capacity to consent to treatment: Challenges, the 'ACCT' approach, future directions. *Clinical Gerontology, 31*, 37–66. doi:10.1080/07317110802072140

Nasreddine, Z. S., Phillips, N. A., Bédirian, V., Charbonneau, S., Whitehead, V., Collin, I., et al. (2005). The Montreal Cognitive Assessment, MoCA: A brief screening tool for mild cognitive impairment. *Journal of the American Geriatrics Society, 53*, 695–699.

NICE (National Institute for Health and Care Excellence). (2011). *Alcohol dependence and harmful alcohol Use (CG115)*. London: NICE.

Parsons, O. A. (1998). Neurocognitive deficits in alcoholics and social drinkers: A continuum? *Alcoholism: Clinical and Experimental Research, 22*, 954–961. doi:10.1111/j.1530-0277.1988.tb03895.x

Parsons, O. A., & Leber, W. R. (1982). Alcohol, cognitive dysfunction and brain damage. In National Institute on Alcohol Abuse & Alcoholism, *Alcohol and health monograph no. 2: Biomedical processes and consequences of alcohol use*. Rockville, MD: US Department of Health & Human Services.

Price, J., Mitchell, S., Wiltshire, B., Graham, J., & Williams, G. (1988). A follow up study of patients with alcohol related brain damage in the community. *Australian Drug Alcohol Review, 7*, 83–7. doi:10.1080/09595238880000191

Prigatano, G. (1999). *Principles of neuropsychological rehabilitation*. Oxford: Oxford University Press.

Raistrick, D., Heather, N., & Godfrey, C. (2006). *Review of the effectiveness of treatment for alcohol problems*. London: National Treatment Agency for Substance Misuse.

Ramayya, A., & Jauhar, P. (1997). Increasing incidence of Korsakoff's psychosis in the East End of Glasgow. *Alcohol, 32*, 281–285.

Ratti, M. T., Soragna, D., Sibilla, L., Giardini, A., Albergati, A., Savoldi, F., et al. (1999). Cognitive impairment and cerebral atrophy in 'heavy drinkers'. *Progress in Neuro-Psychopharmacology and Biological Psychiatry, 23*, 243–258. doi:10.1016/S0278-5846(98)00103-1.

Richardson, E. D., Malloy, P. F., Longabaugh, R., Williams, J., Noel, N., & Beattie, M. C. (1991). Liver function tests and neuropsychological impairment in substance abusers. *Addictive Behaviors, 16*, 51–55. doi:10.1016/0306-4603(91)90039-K

Roehrich, L., & Goldman, M. S. (1993). Experience-dependent neuropsychological recovery and the treatment of alcoholism. *Journal of Consulting and Clinical Psychology, 61*, 812–821. doi:10.1037/0022-006X.61.5.812

Rota-Bartelink, A., & Lipmann, B. (2007). Supporting the long term residential needs of older homeless people with severe alcohol related brain injury in Australia: The Wicking Project. *Care Management Journals, 8*, 141–148. doi:10.1891/152109807781753763

Royal College of Psychiatrists. (2014). *Alcohol and brain damage in adults, with reference to high-risk groups*. College Report CR185. http://www.rcpsych.ac.uk/files/pdfversion/CR185.pdf

Rupp, C. I., Kemmler, G., Kurz, M., Hinterhuber, H., & Fleischhacker, W. W. (2012). Cognitive remediation therapy during treatment for alcohol dependence. *Journal of Studies on Alcohol and Drugs, 73*, 625–634. doi:http://dx.doi.org/10.15288/jsad.2012.73.625

Ryan, C., & Butters, N. (1986). The neuropsychology of alcoholism. In D. Wedding, A. Horton, & J. Webster (Eds.), *The neuropsychology handbook: behavioral and clinical perspectives* (pp. 376–409). New York: Springer.

Scalzo, S., Bowden, S., & Hillbom, M. (2015). Wernicke-Korsakoff Syndrome. In J. Svanberg, A. Withall, B. Draper, & S. Bowden (Eds.), *Alcohol and the adult Brain*. Hove: Psychology Press.

Scheurich, A., Muller, M. J., Szegedi, A., et al. (2004). Neuropsychological status of alcohol-dependent patients: Increased performance through goal-setting instructions. *Alcohol and Alcoholism, 39*, 119–125. doi:10.1093/alcalc/agh026

Schmidt, K. S., Jallo, J. L., Ferri, C., et al. (2005). The neuropsychological profile of alcohol related dementia suggests cortical and subcortical pathology. *Dementia and Geriatric Cognitive Disorders, 20*, 286–291. doi:10.1159/000088306

Scottish Advisory Committee on Alcohol Misuse. (2002). *Plan for action on alcohol problems*. Edinburgh: Scottish Executive.

Slattery, J., Chick, J., Cochrane, M, et al. (2003). *Prevention of relapse in alcohol dependence health technology assessment report3*. Glasgow: Health Technology Board for Scotland.

Smith, I., & Hillman, A. (1999) Management of alcohol Korsakoff syndrome. *Advances in Psychiatric Treatment, 5,* 271–278. doi:10.1192/apt.5.4.271

Spreen, O., & Strauss, E. A. (2006). *Compendium of neuropsychological tests.* New York: Oxford University Press.

Svanberg, J., & Evans, J. J. (2013a). Neuropsychological rehabilitation in Alcohol Related Brain Damage: A systematic review. *Alcohol, 48,* 704–711. doi:10.1093/alcalc/agt131

Svanberg, J., & Evans, J. J. (2013b). Impact of SenseCam on memory, identity and mood in Korsakoff's syndrome: A single case experimental design study. *Neuropsychological Rehabilitation. E publication.* doi:10.1080/09602011.2013.814573

Tapert, S. F., Brown, G. G., Kindermann, S. S., Cheung, E. H., Frank, L. R., & Brown, S. A. (2001). fMRI measurement of brain dysfunction in alcohol-dependent young women. *Alcoholism: Clinical & Experimental Research, 25,* 236–245. doi:10.1111/j.1530-0277.2001.tb02204.x

Tiersky, L. A., Anselmi, V., Johnston, M. V., et al. (2005). A trial of neuropsychologic rehabilitation in mild-spectrum traumatic brain injury. *Archives of Physical Medical Rehabilitation, 86,* 1565–1574. doi:10.1016/j.apmr.2005.03.013

Torvik, A., Lindboe, C. F., & Rogde, S. (1982). Brain lesions in alcoholics. A neuropathological study with clinical correlations. *Journal of Neurological Sciences, 56,* 233–248. doi:10.1016/0022-510X(82)90145-9

Tracy, J. I., & Bates, M. E. (1999). The selective effects of alcohol on automatic and effortful memory processes. *Neuropsychology, 13,* 282–290. doi:10.1037//0894-4105.13.2.282

Uekermann, J., & Daum, I. (2008). Social cognition in alcoholism: A link to prefrontal cortex dysfunction? *Addiction, 103,* 726–735. doi:10.1111/j.1360-0443.2008.02157.x

Victor, M., Adams, R. D., & Collins, G. H. (Eds.). (1971). *The Wernicke-Korsakoff syndrome and related neurological disorders due to alcoholism and malnutrition* (1st ed.). Philadelphia, PA: FA Davis.

Victor, M., Adams, R. D., & Collins, G. H. (Eds.). (1989). *The Wernicke-Korsakoff syndrome and related neurological disorders due to alcoholism and malnutrition* (2nd ed.). Philadelphia, PA: FA Davis.

Weinstein, C. S., & Shaffer, H. J. (1993). Neurocognitive aspects of substance abuse treatment: A psychotherapist's primer. *Psychotherapy, 30,* 317–333. doi:10.1037/0033-3204.30.2.317

Wetzig, D. L., & Hardin, S. I. (1990). Neurocognitive deficits of alcoholism: An intervention. *Journal of Clinical Psychology, 46,* 219–229. doi:10.1002/1097-4679(199003)46:2<219::AID-JCLP2270460216>3.0.CO;2-M

Wilson, B. A., Alderman, N., Burgess, P. W., Emslie, H., & Evans, J. J. (1996). *Behavioural assessment of the dysexecutive syndrome.* Bury St Edmunds: Harcourt Assessment.

Wilson, K., Halsey, A., Macpherson, H., et al. (2012). The psycho-social rehabilitation of patients with alcohol related brain damage in the community. *Alcohol and Alcoholism, 47,* 304–311. doi:http://dx.doi.org/10.1093/alcalc/agr167 304-311

World Health Organization. (1992). *ICD-10 classification of mental and behavioural disorders: Clinical descriptions and diagnostic guidelines.* Geneva: World Health Organization.

8 Trauma and Addiction

DAVID CURRAN

Queens University Belfast, Northern Ireland, UK

CHAPTER OUTLINE

8.1 PSYCHOLOGICAL TRAUMA AND PTSD

Individuals who develop substance misuse problems will often experience other forms of psychopathology, with the majority in many samples meeting diagnostic criteria for other mental health problems (Axis I and Axis II) and reporting higher rates of self-harm and suicide attempts (Regier et al., 1990; Darke, 2013). Whether proximal or distal in nature, psychological trauma has been recognized as a common co-occurring problem experienced by many individuals presenting with Substance Use Disorders (SUD) (Shora, Stone & Fletcher, 2009). Additionally, Carruth (2006) has suggested that psychological trauma can be a significant 'complicating factor' for individuals seeking to recover from SUD.

Psychological trauma can be viewed as the emotional consequence of being exposed to an extremely stressful or life-threatening situation. Such experiences are perceived by the individual as being intense and overwhelming (Terr, 1992), with the impact of the trauma exceeding the resources they have for dealing with the event. Such events can be experienced or witnessed. The nature of human experience focused on in trauma research is wide and varied; some authors focus on adverse childhood experiences (e.g. physical, emotional, sexual abuse), others on the experience of life-threatening illness, road traffic accidents, combat-related stress, and natural disasters.

Clear criteria exist for diagnosing trauma disorders such as Post Traumatic Stress Disorder (PTSD) and Acute Stress Disorder. PTSD is perhaps the best recognized, and is characterized by three categories of symptoms: (1) re-experiencing; (2) hyper-arousal; and (3) persistent avoidance/emotional numbing (Carr, 1999). However, for many clients, the nature of their trauma exposure and its psychological sequelae mean they pose a challenge to existing diagnostic criteria. For example, when clients have been exposed to multiple adverse experiences in childhood, the impact on their psychological development can be profound and can take many forms.

Estimates of lifetime prevalence of trauma exposure and PTSD vary greatly in the literature, with levels of PTSD reported to be highest in post-conflict societies (up to 37.4%; De Jong et al., 2001; Ferry et al., 2013). It is thought that in the course of their life most people will be exposed to at least one traumatic event, with most people managing to come to terms with the experience. For a minority the consequences of the trauma do not abate but rather become more distressing and troubling over time. In a study conducted in the Netherlands using a representative adult population (aged 18–80 years), the estimated lifetime prevalence of any potential trauma was found to be 80.7%, with the lifetime prevalence of PTSD in the same group was found to be 7.4% (De Vries & Olff, 2009). The high level of lifetime exposure to any potential trauma was consistent with research from other countries. The lifetime prevalence of PTSD reported was consistent with that found in the United States but would be higher than in many other European countries (De Vries & Olff, 2009). The presence of other co-morbid mental health problems, such as substance abuse/dependence, Generalized Anxiety Disorder, and Major Depressive disorder, has been noted to be commonplace in individuals with a diagnosis of PTSD (Kessler, Sonnega, Bromet, Hughes & Nelson, 1995).

What one person perceives to be traumatic, another may not. Certain personal characteristics (e.g. intelligence, neuroticism, high self-esteem, positive attachment experiences, good family or social support) appear to provide a protective function, buffering an individual from the development of PTSD once trauma has been experienced (McNally, 2009). Emerging research evidence would suggest that when PTSD is present, other psychological constructs such as 'distress tolerance' play a role in determining PTSD symptom severity (Potter, Vujanovic, Marshall-Berenz, Bernstein & Bonn-Miller, 2011). Individuals with low distress tolerance are more likely to engage in behaviours which help them reduce their exposure to aversive experiences.

McNally (2009) has noted the dose-response principle with regard to PTSD. The suggestion being that there will be an increasing likelihood of the development of PTSD depending on the actual severity of the stressor encountered. There is also evidence that psychological changes caused by early trauma exposure play an important mediating role (e.g. shame as a result of sexual abuse). It has been noted that exposure to trauma at an earlier point in an individual's life can sensitize them and leave them prone to the development of PTSD when exposed to trauma at a later point (Breslau, Chilcoat, Kessler & Davies, 1999). Evidence from longitudinal studies would question whether this is the case. Breslau, Peterson and Schultz (2008) found that PTSD needed to have been experienced in response to an earlier trauma for it to be predictive of subsequent PTSD. Likewise, Koenen et al. (2008) found most individuals in their sample who developed PTSD had experienced mental health problems at an earlier point in their life.

The term Complex Trauma (or complex PTSD) has been developed to capture the impact of trauma experienced over prolonged time periods (frequently with an early onset), or as the result of exposure to repeated traumatic events (Herman, 1992; Van der Kolk, 2005). In addition to the core defining features of PTSD highlighted above, individuals with complex PTSD will typically display difficulties in a range of other domains, including; problems with self-concept (e.g. low self-esteem, excessive shame), dissociation, difficulty with affect regulation, problems in terms of interpersonal functioning (e.g. lack of empathy), compromised cognitive functioning (e.g. planning, judgement, self-monitoring), and difficulties in terms of impulse control (Cook et al., 2005). There is also growing evidence that some of these features of Complex PTSD can be related to the adverse impact of early exposure to trauma on the developing brain (Gaskill & Perry, 2011). In their Expert Clinician Survey on best practice in the treatment of complex PTSD, Cloitre et al. (2011) found that the majority of such symptoms were reported to be present. In particular, emotion regulation difficulties, difficulties in interpersonal functioning, and disturbed belief systems were endorsed at least as frequently as the core clinical features of PTSD (re-experiencing, hyperarousal, and avoidance).

As previously noted, there is a great deal of individual difference in terms of the human capacity to respond to trauma exposure. Recognizing the presence of psychological trauma is important as it has the potential to impact on the process of therapy, and can exert a negative influence on treatment outcome. For clinicians working in the area of substance misuse, recognizing and assessing the client experience of trauma, incorporating this into psychological formulation, and addressing both areas concurrently are essential for successful long-term therapeutic progress. Being able to monitor and evaluate client outcomes and effectiveness of clinical interventions across relevant domains over time is essential.

8.2   THE RELATIONSHIP BETWEEN ADDICTION AND PSYCHOLOGICAL TRAUMA

In an addiction setting an individual may not meet formal diagnostic criteria for a trauma disorder, but may still experience difficulties related to their trauma history. Likewise, individuals presenting to mental health services may also be struggling with substance misuse at subclinical levels. In both scenarios it is likely that any treatment endeavour will be compromised by a failure to identify and assist with the co-existing problem.

McGovern et al. (2009) note it is estimated that up to half of people entering addiction treatment will have a lifetime diagnosis of PTSD, with this an ongoing problem for many. This is consistent with research elsewhere which estimates that among substance misuse clients, 11–41% will meet diagnostic criteria for current PTSD, with a much higher percentage reporting lifetime trauma experience (Van Dam, Vedel, Ehring & Emmelkamp, 2012; Van Dam, Ehring, Vedel & Emmelkamp, 2013).

Histories of childhood abuse have repeatedly been found in research in clinical populations (Darke, 2013). Childhood sexual abuse (CSA) in particular has been linked to the early onset of substance use and the subsequent development of problematic use of substances in adulthood (Sartor et al., 2013). However, it is worthy of note that when an individual experiences CSA, they will often also encounter pervasive family pathology (e.g. domestic violence, parental mental health or substance misuse problems, and other forms of abuse/neglect), which may also exert an adverse impact on development (Sartor et al., 2013). In a twin study, Sartor et al. (2013) controlled for other familial influences and were able to demonstrate that CSA was a clear risk factor for early onset of tobacco, cannabis and in particular alcohol use among their sample of adolescent females. Such findings would be in keeping with self-medication theories with regard to addiction (see below).

Research with individuals who have a formal diagnosis of PTSD has suggested that around half of men (52%) and approaching one third of women will develop a substance misuse problem, with alcohol-related difficulties the most commonly encountered (Kessler et al., 1995). While there is variability in the prevalence rates for SUD–PTSD co-morbidity reported by different studies, the consistent message is that these difficulties frequently co-exist. This is likely to impact on symptom severity for both conditions, and have clinical implications. Therefore for many clients, in addiction (or mental health) settings, any proposed intervention will have to be adapted to account for the presence of trauma-based difficulties.

Multiple studies have sought to explore the relationship between PTSD and substance use. Researchers interested in such relationships will often look to temporal sequencing to provide insights and enhance understanding with regard to the presence of two or more co-occurring problems, the basic premise being that the presence of one problem results in the increased likelihood of an individual experiencing the other problem. However, it is important to note that causality cannot be automatically inferred because one condition predates another (Abraham & Fava, 1999). Other possible explanations would suggest that any relationship is correlational in nature and the result of an underlying vulnerability (e.g. genetic risk, physical/sexual abuse in childhood) (Chilcoat & Breslau, 1998). Chilcoat and Breslau (1998) conducted a prospective, longitudinal study which specifically sought to explore potential causal pathways as suggested by three of the dominant theories with regard to trauma and addiction: (1) the high-risk hypothesis; (2) the self-medication hypothesis; and (3) the susceptibility hypothesis.

The high-risk hypothesis proposes a causal relationship whereby substance abuse can lead to the individual participating in, or carrying out, 'high-risk' behaviours which ultimately increase the risk of exposure to trauma and the likelihood of subsequently developing PTSD (Hien, Cohen & Campbell, 2005). The self-medication hypothesis is based largely on clinical observations and suggests a reverse relationship. It proposes that substance misuse fulfils an important function in that it relieves traumatic memories and other painful symptoms of PTSD (Khantzian, 1985; Stewart, 1996). Prolonged attempts to self-medicate can, however, result in substance dependence as associations between substance misuse, trauma reminders and PTSD symptoms become established over time (Baker, Piper, McCarthy, Majeskie & Fiore, 2004). Based on this model, PTSD must predate the onset of substance misuse. The susceptibility hypothesis proposes that misusing substances leaves an individual more susceptible to developing PTSD following exposure to a traumatic event. A possible mechanism of action here might be the failure to develop adequate coping skills for managing psychological distress, as a result of an early onset substance misuse history. Another proposed hypothesis is that PTSD and SUD are the result of an unknown 'third variable' (e.g. genetic factors, temperament, poor coping skills) which increase the risk of the development of various forms of pathology following trauma exposure (Van Dam et al., 2013). For example, it has been noted that the cumulative effects of childhood adversity could impact negatively on neurobiology, neuroendocrinology and brain development, resulting in later development of psychopathology (McEwen & Wingfield, 2003; Nolte, Guiney, Fonagy, Mayes & Luyten, 2011; Luyten, Van Houdenhove, Lemma, Target & Fonagy, 2012).

There are varying amounts of evidence for all the aforementioned hypotheses, and all are plausible explanations for the relationship between psychological trauma and substance misuse. It is also possibly artificial to view them as separate as at times they may act in combination. For example, Hien et al. (2005) have noted that childhood trauma (and the associated psychological distress) could lead to later substance abuse (self-medication hypothesis), and also to further trauma exposure in adulthood (i.e. revictimization).

Results from the Chilcoat and Breslau (1998) study provided support for the self-medication hypothesis in particular. Self-medication theories, such as that proposed by Edward Khantzian (1985; 2012), which emphasize the role of psychological distress, and the use of substances to reduce negative affect, remain popular and continue to generate research interest (Darke, 2013; Sartor et al., 2013). There is evidence to support this model from large-scale studies conducted with non-clinical samples (Kessler et al., 1995; Mills, Teesson, Ross & Peters, 2006). Mills et al. (2006) found that for two-thirds of those in their study meeting criteria for PTSD and SUD, the traumatic event predated the development of the alcohol/drug problem.

Self-medication theories are not without their critics. A number of issues have been identified which are problematic for those seeking to demonstrate a causal role for childhood adversity in the development of SUD, for example, the risk of recall bias in individuals with substance misuse/mental health problems, and their attribution of causality to such experiences. Breslau (2013) has noted that individuals with mental health problems are more likely to recall negative life events (Kessler, 1997). Furthermore, Breslau has reviewed evidence which suggests that it is not the trauma history but rather a diagnosis of PTSD which is predictive of subsequent SUD. This would point to the significance of predisposition, and other 'third variables' which independently exert an influence on the development of different forms of psychopathology. Dupont and Gold (2007) express concern that viewing substance misuse as simply a form of self-medication could lead to substance misuse being seen as simply a symptom of a primary mental health problem. They suggest that when a co-morbidity is present, each condition should be treated as a 'separate and serious illness', and question whether it is possible that treating an underlying condition (PTSD) could automatically result in SUD recovery. They also highlight how, for some individuals, addressing their substance misuse can lead to a reduction in psychological distress.

Not all individuals with a substance misuse problem will have experienced lifetime trauma or meet diagnostic criteria for PTSD. There is evidence that not all of those who have experienced psychological trauma will require an intervention to address such difficulties, and some may see a reduction in psychological distress as a result of recovery in terms of substance misuse. Nevertheless high rates of substance misuse and psychological trauma are evident in clinical populations, and for many this remains a barrier to treatment success.

8.3   ASSESSMENT

At the assessment interview, therapists working in SUD settings can be reluctant to explore or enquire about traumatic experiences. Sometimes this is because there is a view that the problematic use of substances should be the primary focus of work undertaken. Additionally there can be concern that they either lack the clinical skills to manage such disclosures, or that focusing on such issues can hinder progress in relation to treatment for SUD. Worse still, there can be concerns that focusing on trauma experiences can potentially destabilize the client and lead to a deterioration in their psychological well-being. For this reason it is thought the level of PTSD/trauma is often under-recognized and under-reported in clinical settings (Curran, McLaughlin & Kelly, 2016). It has been demonstrated that a systematic approach to screening and assessing for such issues can lead to a four times higher detection rate (Van Dam et al., 2012).

8.3.1   *The Clinical Interview*

The assessment process should facilitate the development of a formulation, or shared understanding, of the presenting problems. In turn, the formulation developed should inform any proposed intervention. The presence of a trauma history may not always be immediately apparent, or readily disclosed. When trauma has taken place at an earlier stage in development, or was part of day-to-day experience, it may not be recognized by the client as something significant, or important, to share with the therapist. For some clients, the clinical interview may be the first time they have disclosed or shared their trauma history. Therapists should be cognizant of this, prioritizing client safety and containment of distress. During the assessment process it is important to ascertain available sources of social support.

A comprehensive assessment will include a detailed developmental history, and a timeline which charts significant or traumatic life events. During the assessment the therapist should note any 'hot cognitions' and associated emotions as these may subsequently become a focus in terms of intervention. When trauma exposure is identified, the clinician should be mindful of the key features of different forms of trauma, for example, the three symptoms clusters (re-experiencing, avoidance, and hyperarousal) associated with a diagnosis of PTSD, and, if present, how they impact on the daily life and functioning of the individual. This should be accompanied by a thorough history of alcohol and drug use, including changes in pattern of use over time. Of particular interest will be any points in time when the client perceives substance use to have moved from being recreational, or social, to a more problematic, or dependent, pattern of use. This may provide the clinician with insights into the relationship between substance misuse and trauma exposure. Normalization of their difficulties and psychoeducation are important in the early stages of contact with the client. Details of any previous episodes of treatment, or therapy, and any benefit derived will also help to inform intervention.

8.3.2   *Self-Report Measures*

It is helpful to supplement the clinical interview with standardized assessment tools, or self-report measures. Such instruments are a useful and objective method for gauging level of symptomology. They also help to provide a baseline, and can be useful to repeat periodically throughout the course of treatment to monitor progress. The client themselves can be encouraged to self-monitor and complete such measures over time. As well as assisting the clinician in gauging the efficacy of the intervention, it can be rewarding for the client to be able to chart their own progress.

With regard to establishing the presence and severity of PTSD, structured and semi-structured interviews, such as the Structured Clinical Interview for DSM-IV

(SCID) (First, Spitzer, Gibbon & Williams, 1996) have been recognized as the 'gold standard'. It is lengthy and clinician-administered. There are a number of other popular measures such as the Impact of Events Scale (IES; Horowitz, Wilner & Alvarez, 1979), the Post-traumatic Diagnostic Scale (PDS; Foa, Cashman, Jaycox & Perry, 1997), and the Trauma Screening Questionnaire (TSQ; Brewin et al., 2002). These measures can be completed by the client and have a good reliability and validity (Brewin, 2005).

To assess for trauma exposure, whether during childhood or across the lifespan, measures such as the Childhood Trauma Questionnaire (Bernstein & Fink, 1998) and the Trauma History Questionnaire (Green, 1996) can be helpful.

8.4 TREATMENT OF CO-EXISTING TRAUMA AND SUBSTANCE USE DISORDERS

Co-morbidity has repeatedly been found to impact negatively on treatment outcomes in individuals with substance misuse problems (Bradizza, Stasiewicz & Paas, 2006). When any form of mental health condition is present, this will add a layer of complexity to any proposed intervention, and will result in the need for a treatment package that is individually tailored to meet the client's needs. There is consistent evidence that individuals with co-morbid substance use and mental health problems are found more frequently in long-term treatment, display higher rates of relapse, have more treatment episodes, demonstrate poorer treatment outcomes and have higher treatment costs than those without a co-morbid problems (Regier et al., 1990; Bradizza et al., 2006; Ouimette, Read, Wade & Tirone, 2010).

Specifically with regard to PTSD, in their review of the literature, Bradizza et al. (2006) found that for individuals in treatment for substance misuse problems, those with PTSD relapsed faster, with severity of PTSD re-experiencing symptomatology a significant predictor. In an early longitudinal study, Ouimette, Ahrens, Moos and Finney (1997) sought to explore the impact of co-occurring PTSD on outcome at a one-year follow-up in a population of individuals seeking treatment for substance dependence. Results revealed that individuals with co-morbid PTSD and substance misuse problems, had more readmissions into treatment programmes for either condition, and more commonly reported other psychological or social problems (e.g. were more often unemployed and more often described experiencing greater emotional distress). In a similar study, Najavits, Weiss, Shaw and Muenz (1998) explored response to substance misuse treatment in individuals presenting to treatment with or without PTSD. Those with co-morbid PTSD were found to be less compliant with treatments, and displayed a higher level of complexity in terms of other physical and psychological health-related problems. Even when there is evidence of progress in relation to substance misuse, ongoing difficulties in other domains (e.g. mental health, psychosocial functioning) can compromise progress and leave an individual vulnerable to relapse (McGovern et al., 2009). In their review, van Dam et al. (2012) note that for clients with PTSD, an intervention which focuses exclusively on SUD can lead to an exacerbation of PTSD symptoms, and result in higher treatment attrition rates.

Clients can often feel trapped in a cycle with regard to dual problems of addiction and trauma. Evidence such as that cited above, which clearly indicates poorer treatment outcomes among individuals with co-morbid substance use disorder and PTSD, has led researchers and clinicians to seek to establish interventions that better meet the need of this client group. Clients cannot alter the life events which they have been exposed to at some point in the past, however, they can change their perception of the event and how it impacts on them in the present. Historically, providers of addiction services have been somewhat wary of seeking to address co-morbid difficulties such as PTSD. This reticence is in part explained by fears that offering a trauma-focused psychological intervention could lead to re-experiencing symptoms (i.e. nightmares, flashbacks) and ultimately contribute to relapse (McGovern et al., 2009). However, proponents of self-medication theories in relation to addiction (Khantzian, 2012) would suggest that distressing affect in relation to the trauma experience is a primary motivator in relation to substance misuse. Therefore, any treatment endeavour which does not adequately address such underlying issues, or counteract the need for the 'emotional numbing' provided by the substance, is likely to fail.

There are several key components to any form of trauma-focused psychological intervention as recommended by agencies such as the National Institute for Clinical Excellence (NICE, 2005). The first step will usually involve psychoeducation and 'skills training', during which the client will be encouraged to develop techniques which will provide some symptom relief, such as assertiveness training, stress management, relaxation and breathing techniques. The next step will involve exposure work. Typically, those suffering from trauma will expend much energy in trying to avoid thoughts and feelings associated with their experience. Exposure, perhaps in a graduated fashion, will help the client confront these thoughts and feelings and help develop a more coherent narrative in relation to their trauma experience. Finally, the use of cognitive techniques will usually complement exposure work. Cognitive interventions will allow for the exploration of thoughts, memories and appraisals associated with the trauma which may be helping to perpetuate the problem. With complex PTSD, there may be additional treatment foci such as assisting the client with issues such as low self-esteem, excessive shame/guilt, dissociation, affect regulation, and interpersonal functioning.

The majority of the treatment packages which have been developed for use with this population, and which have been formally evaluated in the literature, are predominantly cognitive-behavioural in nature. However, other therapeutic modalities may also be of benefit, particularly with complex PTSD presentations. For example, there is evidence that approaches such as experiential and emotion-focused therapy, Dialectical Behaviour Therapy (DBT), and psychoanalytic therapy (Courtois & Ford, 2009; Shedler, 2010; Woodford, 2012) can also be effective in cases of more complex co-morbid disorders.

8.4.1   *Sequential Versus Parallel Treatment*

When seeking to address co-morbidity in SUD populations, a sequential approach to treatment has often been popular. This would involve focusing initially on the substance misuse, and either attaining controlled use, avoiding problematic use or achieving abstinence. Alongside this, a stance of 'watchful waiting' can be adopted in relation to other mental health issues, such as trauma. Should these problems not resolve after substance misuse has been addressed, only then would they merit some form of intervention.

Early research efforts aimed at improving treatment outcomes in individuals with co-morbid PTSD/substance misuse focused on sequential treatment, with substance stabilization a primary aim before any potential exploration of trauma experience and PTSD symptoms. Ouimette, Moos and Brown (2003) argued that sequencing treatment in this way enabled the client to achieve control and maintenance of substance dependence, and in so doing led to improvements in ability to self-regulate difficult emotions associated with a PTSD diagnosis. It has been further argued that as problematic substance use and withdrawal have been associated with intensification of PTSD symptoms (Stewart, 1996), delaying trauma work until substance use is stabilized allows for observation for changes in co-occurring PTSD symptoms (Ouimette, Moos, & Finney, 2003). NICE (2005) guidance on the treatment of co-morbid disorders offers some support for this approach, suggesting that treatment of the drug or alcohol problem should be prioritized when 'alcohol or drug use may significantly interfere with effective treatment' of PTSD.

However, others have questioned the utility of seeking to address the SUD first (or in isolation), suggesting that such an approach 'underestimates the realities of the close and often mutually reinforcing relationships between trauma and substance use' (Finkelstein et al., 2004). Parallel or integrated approaches to treatment involve both the substance use problem and the PTSD being treated by the same practitioner at the same time. Mueser, Noordsy, Drake and Fox (2003), in exploring the need for closer integration between mental health and substance misuse services, have argued that attempting to address the addiction without simultaneously attending to the co-existing problem can be counterproductive. This approach to treatment is potentially problematic, especially when individuals are self-medicating to cope with other co-existing psychological difficulties. Services are often not designed to offer more integrated 'parallel treatment', rather, mental health and addiction services often operate within their own discrete silos with strict inclusion and exclusion criteria governing access. This can preclude service users from accessing the help they require.

8.4.2   *Trauma-Focused Versus Non-Trauma-Focused Interventions*

In recent years a number of standardized treatment packages have been developed with the specific intention of offering a more holistic psychological intervention to those presenting with co-morbid PTSD and substance misuse problems. In their review,

Van Dam et al. (2012) identified 17 studies which had sought to evaluate the effectiveness of 10 different treatment protocols. These included: Seeking Safety (SS; Najavits et al., 1998), Substance Dependence PTSD Therapy (SDPT; Triffleman, Carroll & Kellogg, 1999), Concurrent Treatment of PTSD and Cocaine Dependence (CTPCD; Back, Dansky, Carroll, Foa & Brady, 2001; Brady, Dansky, Back, Foa & Carroll, 2001), Transcend (Donovan, Padin-Rivera & Kowaliw, 2001), SS plus Exposure Therapy-Revised (Najavits, Schmitz, Gotthardt & Weiss, 2005), and CBT for PTSD in SUD treatment (McGovern et al., 2009). Typically, such interventions draw largely on cognitive behavioural principles but vary somewhat in terms of format, structure and emphasis (e.g. cognitive restructuring versus exposure for PTSD, PTSD treatment being trauma-focused versus non-trauma-focused). Trauma-focused interventions place an emphasis on the client re-visiting and re-processing the original trauma experience. Non-trauma-focused interventions typically aim to enhance coping skills.

Based on their analysis, Van Dam et al. (2012) noted that almost a third (four out of ten) of the identified treatment packages, including SS, delivered a PTSD intervention which was non-trauma-focused in nature. Seeking Safety (Najavits et al., 1998) is the most researched, and combines CBT for SUD with a PTSD intervention which focuses on the development of self-control and interpersonal and communication skills alongside cognitive restructuring. CBT for PTSD in SUD (McGovern et al., 2009) and SDPT (Triffleman et al., 1999) also adopt a largely cognitive behavioural approach and emphasize the development of coping skills. The Transcend programme (Donovan et al., 2012) is informed by a broader range of theoretical perspectives, and includes the sharing of trauma experiences within a group work context. However, Van Dam et al. (2012) note that, as this is not a central focus for the intervention, it therefore cannot be defined as imaginal exposure.

Most of the recognized treatment packages which have been developed have been trauma-focused in nature. SS plus Exposure Therapy-Revised (Najavits et al., 2005) is essentially the seeking safety intervention with exposure therapy as an additional treatment component. Coffey, Stasiewicz, Hughes and Brimo (2006) also devised a treatment package which incorporated imaginal exposure for PTSD. Concurrent Treatment of PTSD and Cocaine Dependence (CTPCD; Back et al., 2001) combined CBT for SUD with exposure therapy (imaginal and in-vivo) for PTSD. In recent years, CTPCD (Back et al., 2001) and Exposure Therapy-Revised (Najavits et al., 2005) have been superseded by Concurrent Treatment of PTSD and Substance Use Disorders Using Prolonged Exposure (COPE; Mills et al., 2012) and Creating Change (Najavits & Hien, 2013), respectively. Exploration of the efficacy of such approaches remains at an early stage with both interventions highlighted above subject to ongoing treatment trials (Van Dam et al., 2012).

Van Dam et al. (2012) note that all the treatment packages they reviewed demonstrated effectiveness in terms of impact on PTSD symptomatology. Specifically with regard to non-trauma-focused interventions. there was evidence of improvement in PTSD symptoms in both RCTs and uncontrolled studies, however, there was no evidence that such interventions were superior to treatment for SUD only. A more limited number of studies to date have reported on trauma-focused interventions, but these do report promising findings. Of note, many of the intervention studies reviewed have involved populations which would traditionally be excluded from randomized control studies (e.g. recent interpersonal difficulties, homelessness, history of incarceration) (Najavits & Hien, 2013).

While there is growing interest in this area, there continues to be a limited evidence base to draw on and a need for more methodologically robust studies. Issues such as treatment attrition and long-term follow-up/outcome in particular need to be attended to more closely. There is a suggestion that the extent to which a client is able to tolerate an exposure-based approach and complete treatment is important, and this would be consistent with PTSD research more generally (Bisson et al., 2007; van Dam et al., 2012).

The use of phased approaches to the treatment of PTSD has been recommended as a way of increasing the efficacy of the interventions, particularly when there may be a concern around a client's potential for dissociation (Cloitre, Petkova, Wang & Lu, 2012).

8.5 CLINICAL IMPLICATIONS

8.5.1 *Attending to the Therapeutic Relationship*

As with other client groups, when seeking to engage clients who present with co-occurring addiction and trauma in psychotherapy, attending to what is taking place within the therapeutic relationship is an important aspect of the work. Herman (1992) identified the importance of establishing a strong therapeutic alliance and equipping the clients with skills for managing difficult affect prior to any trauma-focused work. Establishing a 'secure base' will enable the client to safely explore: their current/previous patterns of relating to significant figures in their lives; their relationship with the therapist; and efforts to establish a different pattern of relating to others into the future (Potter-Efron, 2006).

When clients have had a problematic early history in terms of relationships, this can result in difficulties in terms of interpersonal functioning, and a poor understanding of the social rules with regard to the formation and maintenance of 'normal' healthy relationships. As a result, there is the potential for challenges and 'boundary violations' in the therapy relationship. Thus, the clinician should be mindful of this, and the transference and countertransference issues that emerge during the therapeutic encounter (Najavits, 2006).

8.5.2 *Identifying Treatment Goals*

The process of assessment should lead to a shared understanding, or formulation, in relation to the client's difficulties. This in turn should aid the process of identifying treatment goals, and should help manage both therapist and client expectations in terms of what is likely to be achieved through therapy and the timescales involved. For clients with co-existing trauma and SUD, establishing goals around substance misuse can be particularly problematic. Insisting the client achieve abstinence prior to commencement of trauma work may be both unrealistic and counterproductive. At worst, it could result in disengagement from treatment, a reduced sense of self-efficacy, and increased feelings of hopelessness (Litt, 2013). The client may have had repeated experiences of treatment failure in the past, especially if treatment has been offered sequentially. Further 'failed' treatment episodes can have implications in terms of confidence and self-esteem, and can leave the client feeling demoralized. This in turn can have an impact on subsequent efforts to return to, and engage in, therapy.

When treatment goals are not carefully agreed, there is also a risk that the client may 'act out' in a variety of ways (e.g. blaming others, being non-compliant/oppositional), which can be interpreted as unconscious efforts to avoid painful emotions being encountered in therapy. When a client is ambivalent about, or unwilling to, address their substance misuse, therapy still has the potential to be of benefit through equipping them with a greater understanding of their difficulties, and aiding the development of skills to manage psychological distress more adaptively. Over time this may lead to increased confidence and a willingness to reduce reliance on substances (Litt, 2013).

8.5.3 Treatment Retention

The current evidence base would indicate that many of the dual-pronged interventions previously discussed have a more lasting impact on PTSD symptomatology than SUD. Najavits and Hien (2013) have suggested that this is consistent with the idea that SUD tends to be a condition that is chronic and relapsing in nature. The duration of many of the interventions offered would also indicate that treatment is unlikely to be short-term in nature. It is perhaps the case that, for many clients, multiple treatment episodes may be normative, and that recovery is unlikely to follow a smooth trajectory. Indeed, for some clients, there may be a need for longer-term or ongoing support in order to maintain treatment gains (Najavits & Hien, 2013).

As previously noted, some authors have raised concerns with regard to attrition rates when delivering treatment packages aimed at addressing co-morbid substance misuse and PTSD (McGovern et al., 2009; Van Dam et al., 2012). As well as being a significant limitation when reviewing treatment outcomes with regard to such interventions, this raises concerns with regard to risk and patient safety. This has led to suggestions that the format and focus of PTSD treatment are particularly important in this population, and Van Dam et al. (2012) have suggested that when devising treatment protocols, it is important to be mindful of ways in which client retention in treatment can be optimized. McGovern et al. (2009) noted that treatment attrition is less problematic when a cognitive restructuring approach, rather than exposure-based approach, is adopted in relation to PTSD (Marks, Lovell, Noshirvani, Livanou & Thrasher, 1998). Research continues to explore how best to adapt treatment for use with this population (Najavits & Hien, 2013). In general, expert opinion would indicate that a phased approach to treatment with an initial focus on safety and the development of self-regulation skills is best (Cloitre et al., 2011). Additionally, when a complex PTSD is present, it is generally considered that interventions are likely to be most beneficial when they are multimodal, titrated, and target the most disabling symptoms first.

8.5.4   Exploring Trauma

Exposure is an important element of a standard PTSD intervention. As has been noted, in a phased approach to treatment, initially therapy will focus, for example, on enhancing emotion regulation skills, anxiety management, or other strategies for managing and reducing psychological distress. Equipped with such skills, the client will be better able to manage the re-processing of the original trauma associated with the next phase of treatment.

Formal PTSD interventions will inevitably require the client to access and process trauma memories. A number of approaches (reviewed in NICE, 2005; e.g. Eye Movement Desensitization and Reprocessing (EMDR), CBT, Prolonged Exposure) can be helpful in seeking to integrate these trauma memories into existing cognitive architecture. For many clients, emotions associated with their trauma will have been historically difficult for them to express, and they can often have become disconnected from these emotions. Therapists should be aware of the risk of iatrogenic harm when clients are encouraged to 'open up' or share trauma experiences too early in the therapeutic process (Litt, 2013). For psychotherapists operating from within different therapeutic modalities, a common aim will be helping the client to identify and express such emotions, or access 'near conscious' thoughts, and this will be an important element of the work undertaken. However, for many clients, this is potentially overwhelming, and many individuals may be placed at higher risk of relapse in response to such emotions being evoked. Again, a sense of safety within the therapy relationship is fundamental, and for some clients it can take a considerable period in recovery from an SUD before they feel able to address underlying trauma issues (Davis, 2006).

Clients presenting with co-existing difficulties have often been viewed as a 'vulnerable population', and for that reason more formal trauma-focused interventions have been used sparingly. As noted elsewhere in this chapter, increasing attention is being paid to how trauma-focused interventions can be adapted to make them more suitable for use with such populations. Nevertheless, this type of work is likely to be counter-indicated when clients: are experiencing significant life stressors presently; continuing to experience episodes of trauma; have limited sources of social support available; or have other significant physical health problems (Litt, 2013).

8.5.5   Emotional Reactivity

The potential for dissociation is one of a number of other potential challenges faced by individuals who present for treatment with addiction and trauma-based difficulties (particularly developmental trauma) (Najavits, 2006). Dissociation can be viewed as an alteration in an individual's consciousness which results in feeling removed from/ unable to attend to events that are taking place around them. The experience of dissociation is not uncommon, particularly in individuals with more complex PTSD presentations (Van der Kolk, Roth, Pelcovitz, Sunday & Spinazzola, 2005). Dissociative experiences are thought to operate on a continuum, and are often seen as a coping mechanism, or a way of managing stress, especially when an individual is exposed to a reminder of the original trauma which evokes similar feelings of threat. A tendency towards dissociation (or in extreme cases Dissociative Identity Disorder) can result in phenomena such as 'splitting' where clients can flip between different self-states. In such circumstances, clinicians need to be aware of the risks associated with, and the 'intense reactivity' to, intra-psychic or extra-psychic cues that can be experienced by many (Najavits, 2006). Both can result in potentially harmful behaviour. Clinicians interested in engaging in trauma-focused work should always ensure that they avail themselves of appropriate training and supervision in relation to their work.

8.5.6   *Training*

There is increasing recognition that because conditions so commonly co-occur, clinicians in both mental health and addictions should have adequate training so they feel competent and confident to conduct a comprehensive assessment, to identify when, and to what extent, such difficulties are present (Crome & Bloor, 2007). It is perhaps unrealistic that clinicians in both settings are trained to a level whereby they have the knowledge and skills required to treat all presenting issues they might encounter. However, for clinicians working in an addiction setting, they should have an appreciation of common mental health issues and how they can interact with a substance misuse problem. This can be supported by training, regular supervision, and a team ethos which accepts the need for more integrated treatment pathways.

More specifically, with regard to trauma, clinicians should have an understanding of the potential impact of lifetime trauma exposure, the various trauma-related disorders, and how they are defined (e.g. Acute Stress Disorder; PTSD; Complex PTSD; Dissociative Identity Disorder). Experience of trauma should be incorporated into their assessment protocol, and they should be able to produce a case formulation that is informed by such factors. Within an addiction service there is a need for a range of knowledge and skills when it comes to working with SUD and trauma (Carruth & Burke, 2006). All clinicians should be alert to the presence of co-existing trauma and be able to assess and screen for such difficulties. A further subgroup of clinicians should, under appropriate supervision, be capable of delivering protocolized treatments which aim to address the potential manifestations of trauma. A number of treatments have been mentioned previously in this chapter (e.g. Seeking Safety; Najavits et al., 1998) which focus on psychoeducation and helping the client develop a range of coping skills without the need for in-depth exploration of trauma memories. Finally, services should also have a smaller group of clinicians who are 'trauma-competent' (Najavits, 2006), and who possess the training and skills to be able to adapt treatment protocols, or utilize different therapeutic modalities, when they encounter complex presentations. Such individuals should also be available to provide supervision and consultation to other team members so as to ensure that practice remains safe and effective (Copello & Tobin, 2007).

8.6   CONCLUSION

Co-morbid presentations of SUD and psychological trauma are commonly found in different clinical populations. Even at subclinical or threshold levels, clinicians should be aware of the potential for a detrimental impact of narrowly focused interventions. Particularly for clinicians working in SUD settings, assessment protocols should routinely alert them to the presence of different forms of psychological trauma. Services should be resourced to work with different levels and intensity of trauma, and supervision and consultation should be available to support good practice.

SUGGESTIONS FOR FURTHER READING

Breslau, N. (2013). The role of trauma in drug use disorders. *Addiction*, 108, 669–670. doi:10.1111/add.12025

Carruth, B. (2006). *Psychological trauma and addiction treatment*. Binghamton, NY: The Haworth Press, Inc.

Courtois, C., & Ford, J. (Eds.). (2009). *Treating complex traumatic stress disorders: An evidence-based guide*. New York: Guilford Press.

Litt, L. (2013). Clinical decision making in the treatment of complex PTSD and substance misuse. *Journal of Clinical Psychology*, 69, 534–542. doi:10.1002/jclp.21989

Najavits, L. M., & Hien, D. (2013). Helping vulnerable populations: A comprehensive review of the treatment outcome literature on Substance Use Disorder and PTSD. *Journal of Clinical Psychology*, 69, 433–479. doi:10.1002/jclp.21980

REFERENCES

Abraham, H. D., & Fava, M. (1999). Order of onset of substance abuse and depression in a sample of depressed outpatients. *Comprehensive Psychiatry*, 40, 44–50. doi:doi.org/10.1016/S0010-440X(99)90076-7

Back, S. E., Dansky, B. S., Carroll, K. M., Foa, E. B., & Brady, K. T. (2001). Exposure therapy in the treatment of PTSD among cocaine-dependent individuals: Description of procedures. *Journal of Substance Abuse Treatment*, 21, 35–46. doi:doi.org/10.1016/S0740-5472(01)00181-7

Baker, T. B., Piper, M. E., McCarthy, D. E., Majeskie, M. R., & Fiore, M. C. (2004). Addiction motivation reformulated: An affective processing model of negative reinforcement. *Psychological Review*, 111, 33–51. doi:10.1037/0033-295X.111.1.33

Bernstein, D., & Fink, L. (1998). *Childhood trauma questionnaire: A retrospective self-report*. San Antonio, TX: The Psychological Corporation.

Bisson, J. I., Ehlers, A., Matthews, R., Pilling, S., Richards, D., & Turner, S. (2007). Psychological treatments for chronic post-traumatic stress disorder: Systematic review and meta-analysis. *The British Journal of Psychiatry*, 190, 97–104. doi:10.1192/bjp.bp.106.021402

Bradizza, C. M., Stasiewicz, P. R., & Paas, N. D. (2006). Relapse to alcohol and drug use among individuals diagnosed with co-occurring mental health and substance use disorders: A review. *Clinical Psychological Review*, 26, 162–178. doi:doi.org/10.1016/j.cpr.2005.11.005

Brady, K. T., Dansky, B. S., Back, S. E, , Foa, E. B., & Carroll, K. M. (2001). Exposure therapy in the treatment of PTSD among cocaine-dependent individuals: Preliminary findings. *Journal of Substance Abuse Treatment*, 21, 47–54. doi:doi.org/10.1016/S0740-5472(01)00182-9

Breslau, N. (2013). The role of trauma in drug use disorders. *Addiction*, 108, 669–670. doi:10.1111/add.12025

Breslau, N., Chilcoat, H. D., Kessler, R. C., & Davis G. C. (1999). Previous exposure to trauma and PTSD effects of subsequent trauma: Results from the Detroit Area Survey of Trauma. *American Journal of Psychiatry*, 156, 902–907.

Breslau, N., Peterson, E. L., & Schultz, L.R. (2008). A second look at prior trauma and the Post Traumatic Stress Disorder effects of subsequent trauma: A prospective epidemiological study. *Archives of General Psychiatry*, 65, 431–437. doi:10.1001/archpsyc.65.4.431

Brewin, C. R. (2005). Systematic review of screening instruments for adults at risk of PTSD. *Journal of Traumatic Stress*, 18, 53–62. doi:10.1002/jts.20007

Brewin, C. R., Rose, S., Andrews, B., et al. (2002). Brief screening instrument for post-traumatic stress disorder. *The British Journal of Psychiatry*, 181, 158–162. doi:10.1192/bjp.181.2.158

Carr, A. (1999). *The handbook of child and adolescent clinical psychology: A contextual approach*. London: Routledge.

Carruth, B. (2006). *Psychological trauma and addiction treatment*. Binghamton, NY: The Haworth Press, Inc.

Carruth, B., & Burke, P. A. (2006). Psychological trauma and addiction treatment. *Journal of Chemical Dependency Treatment*, 8, 1–14. doi:10.1300/J034v08n02_01

Chilcoat, H. D., & Breslau, N. (1998). Investigations of causal pathways between PTSD and drug use disorders. *Addictive Behaviors*, 23, 827–840. doi:10.1016/S0306-4603(98)00069-0

Cloitre, M., Courtois, C. A., Charuvastra, A., Carapezza, R., Stolbach, B. C., & Green, B. L. (2011). Treatment of complex PTSD: Results of the ISTSS expert clinician survey on best practices. *Journal of Traumatic Stress*, 24, 615–627. doi:10.1002/jts.20697

Cloitre, M., Petkova, E., Wang, J., & Lu, F. (2012). An examination of the influence of a sequential treatment on the course and impact of dissociation among women with PTSD related child abuse. *Depression and Anxiety*, 29, 709–717. doi:10.1002/da.21920

Coffey, S. F., Stasiewicz, P. R., Hughes, P. M., & Brimo, M. L. (2006). Trauma-focused imaginal exposure for individuals with comorbid posttraumatic stress disorder and alcohol dependence: Revealing mechanisms of alcohol craving in a cue reactivity paradigm. *Psychology of Addictive Behaviors*, 20, 425–435. doi:10.1037/0893-164X.20.4.425

Cook, A., Spinazzola, J., Ford, J., Lanktree, C., Blaustein, M., Cloitre, M., et al. (2005). Complex trauma in children and adolescents. *Psychiatric Annals*, 35, 390–398.

Copello, A., & Tobin, D. (2007). Clinical team supervision for practitioners treating co-existing mental health and drug and alcohol problems. In A. Baker, & R. Velleman (Eds.), *Clinical handbook of co-existing mental health and drug and alcohol problems* (pp. 371–387). Hove: Routledge.

Courtois, C., & Ford, J. (Eds.). (2009). *Treating complex traumatic stress disorders: An evidence-based guide*. New York: Guilford Press.

Crome, I., & Bloor, R. (2007). Training in co-existing mental health and drug and alcohol problems. In A. Baker, & R. Velleman (Eds.), *Clinical handbook of co-existing mental health and drug and alcohol problems* (pp. 351–370). Hove: Routledge.

Curran, D., McLaughlin, E., & Kelly, M. (2016) Psychological trauma in an addictions population: a case note and self-report comparison. *Clinical Psychology Forum, 278*, 18–21.

Darke, S. (2013). Commentary on Sartor et al. (2013): Trauma and drug use—more evidence for self-medication? *Addiction, 108*, 1001. doi:10.1111/add.12154

Davis, B. (2006). Psychodynamic psychotherapies and the treatment of co-occurring psychological trauma and addiction. *Journal of Chemical Dependency Treatment, 8*, 41–69. doi:10.1300/J034v08n02_03

De Jong, J. T., Komproe, I. H., Van Ommeren, M., et al. (2001). Lifetime events and posttraumatic stress disorder in 4 post-conflict settings. *Journal of the American Medical Association, 286*, 555–562. doi:10.1001/jama.286.5.555.

De Vries, G., & Olff, M. (2009). The lifetime prevalence of traumatic events and Post Traumatic Stress Disorder in the Netherlands. *Journal of Traumatic Stress, 22*, 259–267. doi:10.1002/jts.20429

Donovan, B., Padin-Rivera, E., & Kowaliw, S. (2001). 'Transcend': Initial outcomes from a posttraumatic stress disorder/substance abuse treatment program. *Journal of Traumatic Stress, 14*, 757–772.

DuPont, R. L., & Gold, M. S. (2007). Comorbidity and 'self-medication'. *Journal of Addictive Disorders, 26*, 13–23. doi:10.1300/J069v26S01_03

Ferry, F., Bunting, B., Murphy, S., O'Neill, S., Stein, D., & Koenen, K. (2013). Traumatic events and their relative PTSD burden in Northern Ireland: A consideration of the impact of the 'Troubles'. *Social Psychiatry and Psychiatric Epidemiology, 49*, 435–446. doi:10.1007/s00127-013-0757-0

Finkelstein, N., VanDeMark, N., Fallot, R., Brown, V., Cadiz, S., & Heckman, J. (2004). *Enhancing substance abuse recovery through integrated trauma treatment*. Sarasota, FL: National Trauma Consortium.

First, M. B., Spitzer, R. L., Gibbon, M., & Williams, J. B. W. (1996). *Structured clinical Interview for DSM-IV Axis I disorders*. New York: New York State Psychiatric Institute.

Foa, E. B., Cashman, L., Jaycox, L., & Perry, K. (1997). The validation of a self-report measure of posttraumatic stress disorder: The Posttraumatic Diagnostic Scale. *Psychological Assessment, 9*, 445–451. doi:10.1037/1040-3590.9.4.445

Gaskill, R. L., & Perry, B. D. (2011). Child sexual abuse, traumatic experiences and their impact on the developing brain. In P. Goodyear-Brown (Ed.), *Handbook of child sexual abuse: Identification, assessment, and treatment*. Hoboken, NJ: John Wiley & Sons, Inc.

Green, B. L. (1996). Trauma history questionnaire. In B. H. Stamm (Ed.), *Measurement of stress, trauma, and adaptation* (pp. 366–369). Lutherville, MD: Sidran Press.

Herman, J. L. (1992). *Trauma and recovery: The aftermath of violence – from domestic abuse to political terror*. New York: Basic Books.

Hien, D., Cohen, L., & Campbell, A. (2005). Is traumatic stress a vulnerability factor for women with substance use disorders? *Clinical Psychology Review, 25*, 813–823. doi:10.1016/j.cpr.2005.05.006

Horowitz, M. J., Wilner, N. R., & Alvarez, W. (1979). Impact of Events Scale. A measure of subjective stress. *Psychosomatic Medicine, 41*, 209–218.

Kessler, R. C. (1997). The effects of stressful life events on depression. *Annual Reviews of Psychology, 48*, 191–214. doi: 10.1146

Kessler, R. C., Sonnega, A., Bromet, E., Hughes, M., & Nelson, C. B. (1995). Posttraumatic stress disorder in the National Comorbidity Survey. *Archives of General Psychiatry, 52*, 1048–1060.

Khantzian, E. J. (1985). The self-medication hypothesis of addictive disorders: Focus on heroin and cocaine dependence. *American Journal of Psychiatry, 142*, 1259–1264.

Khantzian, E. J. (2012). Reflections on treating addictive disorders: A psychodynamic perspective. *The American Journal on Addictions, 21*, 274–279. doi:10.1111/j.1521-0391.2012.00234.x

Koenen, K. C., Fu, Q. J., Ertel, K., Lyons M. J., Eisen S. A., True W. R., et al. (2008). Common genetic liability to major depression and posttraumatic stress disorder in men. *Journal of Affective Disorders, 105*, 109–115. doi:10.1016/j.jad.2007.04.021

Litt, L. (2013). Clinical decision making in the treatment of complex PTSD and substance misuse. *Journal of Clinical Psychology, 69*, 534–542. doi:10.1002/jclp.21989

Luyten, P., Van Houdenhove, B., Lemma, A., Target, M., & Fonagy, P. (2012). A mentalization-based approach to the understanding and treatment of functional somatic disorders. *Psychoanalytic Psychotherapy, 26*, 121–140. doi:10.1080/ 02668734.2012.678061

Marks, I., Lovell, K., Noshirvani, H., Livanou, M., & Thrasher, S. (1998). Treatment of posttraumatic stress disorder by exposure and/or cognitive restructuring: A controlled study. *Archives of General Psychiatry, 55*, 317–325. doi:10.1001/archpsyc.55.4.317

McEwen, B. S., & Wingfield, J. C. (2003). The concept of allostasis in biology and biomedicine. *Hormone & Behavior, 43*, 2–15. doi:doi.org/10.1016/S0018-506X(02)00024-7

McGovern, M. P., Lambert-Harris, C., Acquilano, S., Xie, H., Alterman, A. I., & Weiss, R. D. (2009). A cognitive behavioral therapy for co-occurring substance use and posttraumatic stress disorders. *Addictive Behaviour, 34*, 892–897. doi:doi.org/10.1016/j.addbeh.2009.03.009

McNally, R. J. (2009). Can we fix PTSD in DSM-V? *Depression and Anxiety, 26*, 597–600. doi:http://dx.doi.org/10.1002/da.20586

Mills, K. L., Teesson, M., Ross, J., & Peters, L. (2006). Trauma, PTSD and Substance Use Disorders: Findings from the Australian National Survey of mental health and well-being. *The American Journal of Psychiatry, 163*, 652–658. doi:10.1176/appi.ajp.163.4.652

Mills, K. L., Teesson, M., Back, S. E., Brady, K. T., Baker, A. L., Hopwood, S., et al. (2012). Integrated exposure-based therapy for co-occurring Posttraumatic Stress Disorder and substance dependence: A randomized controlled trial. *Journal of the American Medical Association, 308*, 690–699. doi:10.1001/jama.2012.9071

Mueser, K. M., Noordsy, D. L., Drake, R. E., & Fox, L. (2003). *Integrated treatment for dual disorders: Aa guide to effective practice*. New York: Guilford Press.

Najavits, L. M. (2006). Managing trauma reactions in intensive addiction treatment environments. *Journal of Chemical Dependency Treatment, 8*, 153–161. doi:10.1300/J034v08n02_08

Najavits, L. M., & Hien, D. (2013). Helping vulnerable populations: A comprehensive review of the treatment outcome literature on Substance Use Disorder and PTSD. *Journal of Clinical Psychology, 69*, 433–479. doi:10.1002/jclp.21980

Najavits, L. M., Schmitz, M., Gotthardt, S., & Weiss R. D. (2005). Seeking Safety plus Exposure Therapy: An outcome study on dual diagnosis in men. *Journal of Psychoactive Drugs, 37*, 425–435. doi:10.1080/02791072.2005.10399816

Najavits, L. M., Weiss, R. D., Shaw, S. R., & Muenz, L. R. (1998). 'Seeking Safety': Outcome of a new cognitive-behavioral psychotherapy for women with posttraumatic stress disorder and substance dependence. *Journal of Traumatic Stress, 11*, 437–456. doi:10.1023/A:1024496427434

NICE (National Institute for Clinical Excellence). (2005). *Post-Traumatic Stress Disorder (PTSD): The management of PTSD in adults and children in primary and secondary care*. London: NICE. https://www.nice.org.uk/guidance/cg26

Nolte, T., Guiney, J., Fonagy, P., Mayes, L. C., & Luyten, P. (2011). Interpersonal stress regulation and the development of anxiety disorders: An attachment-based developmental framework. *Frontiers in Behavioral Neuroscience, 5*, 55. doi:10.3389/fnbeh.2011.00055

Ouimette, P., Ahrens, C., Moos, R. H., & Finney, J. W. (1997). Posttraumatic stress disorder in substance abuse patients: Relationship to 1-year posttreatment outcomes. *Psychology of Addictive Behaviors, 11*, 34–47. doi:10.1037/0893-164X.11.1.34

Ouimette, P., Moos, R. H., & Brown, P. J. (2003). Substance use disorder-posttraumatic stress disorder comorbidity: A survey of treatments and proposed practice guidelines. In P. Ouimette, & P. J. Brown (Eds.), *Trauma and substance abuse: Causes, consequences, and treatment of comorbid disorders* (pp. 91–110). Washington , DC: American Psychological Association. doi:10.1037/10460-005

Ouimette, P., Moos, R. H., & Finney, J. W. (2003). PTSD treatment and 5-year remission among patients with substance use and posttraumatic stress disorders. *Journal of Consulting and Clinical Psychology*, *71*, 410–414. doi:10.1037/0022-006X.71.2.410

Ouimette, P., Read, J. P., Wade, M., & Tirone, V. (2010). Modelling associations between post-traumatic stress symptoms and substance use. *Addictive Behaviors*, *35*, 64–67. doi:10.1016/j.addbeh.2009.08.009

Potter, C. M., Vujanovic, A. A., Marshall-Berenz, E. C., Bernstein, A., & Bonn-Miller, M. O. (2011). Posttraumatic stress and marijuana use coping motives: The mediating role of distress tolerance. *Journal of Anxiety Disorders*, *25*, 437–443. doi:10.1016/j.janxdis.2010.11.007

Potter-Efron, R. (2006). Attachment, trauma and addiction. *Journal of Chemical Dependency Treatment*, *8*, 71–87. doi:10.1300/J034v08n02_04

Regier, D. A., Farmer, M. E., Rae, D. S., et al. (1990). Comorbidity of mental disorders with alcohol and other drug abuse: Results from the Epidemiological Catchment Area (ECA). *Journal of the American Medical Association*, *264*, 2511–2518. doi:10.1001/jama.1990.03450190043026

Sartor, C. E., Waldron, M., Duncan, A. E., et al. (2013). Childhood sexual abuse and early substance use in adolescent girls: The role of familial influences. *Addiction*, *108*, 993–1000. doi:10.1111/add.12115

Shedler, J. (2010). The efficacy of psychodynamic psychotherapy. *American Psychologist*, *65*, 98–109. doi:10.1037/a0018378

Shora, S., Stone, E., & Fletcher, K. (2009). Substance use disorders and psychological trauma. *Psychiatric Bulletin*, *33*, 257–260. doi:10.1192/pb.bp.108.019554

Stewart, S. H. (1996). Alcohol abuse in individuals exposed to trauma: A critical review. *Psychological Bulletin*, *120*, 83–112. doi:10.1037/0033-2909.120.1.83

Terr, L. (1992). *Too scared to cry: Psychic trauma in childhood*. New York: Basic Books.

Triffleman, E., Carroll, K., & Kellogg, S. (1999). Substance dependence posttraumatic stress disorder therapy: An integrated cognitive-behavioral approach. *Journal of Substance Abuse Treatment*, *17*, 3–14. doi:10.1016/S0740-5472(98)00067-1

Van Dam, D., Ehring, T., Vedel, E., & Emmelkamp, P. M. G. (2013). Trauma-focused treatment for posttraumatic stress disorder combined with CBT for severe substance use disorder: A randomized controlled trial. *BMC Psychiatry*, *13*, 172. doi:10.1186/1471-244X-13-172

Van Dam, D., Vedel, E., Ehring, T., & Emmelkamp, P. M. G. (2012). Psychological treatments for concurrent posttraumatic stress disorder and substance use disorder: A systematic review. *Clinical Psychology Review*, *32*, 202–214. doi:10.1016/j.cpr.2012.01.004

Van der Kolk, B. A. (2005). Developmental trauma disorder: Towards a rational diagnosis for chronically traumatized children. *Psychiatric Annals*, *33*, 401–408.

Van der Kolk, B. A., Roth, S., Pelcovitz, D., Sunday, S., & Spinazzola, J. (2005). Disorders of extreme stress: The empirical foundation of a complex adaptation to trauma. *Journal of Traumatic Stress*, *18*, 389–399. doi:10.1002/jts.20047

Woodford, M. S. (2012). *Men, addiction & intimacy*. New York: Routledge.

9 Narrative Identity and Change: Addiction and Recovery

MARTIN WEEGMANN

NHS and Independent Practice, London, UK

CHAPTER OUTLINE

9.1 NARRATIVE THEORY

When the philosopher MacIntyre (1984) said that human beings, 'are story telling animals', he expressed an assumption at the heart of narrative theory, and when the writer and poet Oscar Wilde (1891) observed, 'life imitates art', he drew attention to the aesthetic 'shaping' of how we express our lives. To tell a story involves the notion of narrative (in Latin, 'to recount' and 'to know'), in which events, or experiences, are linked in time, centred around actors, or protagonists, and structured according to plot. Since the 1970s there has been a veritable 'narrative turn' in a whole range of social science disciplines, including psychology. Centred around the construction of meaning, narrative theory advocates, 'the need to focus attention on human existence as it is lived, experienced and interpreted by each human individual' (Crossley, 2000, p. 45). Sarbin's (1986) book was a manifesto to narrative psychology, describing as it does the many ways in which people talk to and recount their experiences in 'story-like' forms; in other words, human beings are continually engaged in implicit day-to-day story-telling and hearing. Similarly, developmental psychologists have focused on the 'proto-conversations' between mothers and babies, even micro-stories expressed in playful, melodic forms and which constitute 'dynamic narrative envelopes' of sound and meaning offered by the caregiver (Stern, 1985; Trevarthen, 2010); later in child development we see the formation of a rudimentary narrative identity for the child of, 'who I am'. Considerable research has accrued concerning the ways in which people construct stories across the life cycle about personal events, critical periods and memories to create a veritable 'life story' that provides the person with a sense of coherence and purpose to, and 'reasons for', their lives (Linde, 1993; McAdams, 1993). In many ways, then, we carry, and continually edit, an implicit life story as we 'go along', stories coming into play 'after the event' as a way of accounting for what we have done, or events and obstacles encountered. In other words, stories are building blocks for identity, providing familiar ways of portraying ourselves, expressive of dominant themes in our lives and are intimately connected to the culture in which we live. Pithily, Bauer, McAdams and Pals (2008, p. 81) say, 'Narrative identity refers to the internal, dynamic life story that an individual constructs to make sense of his or her life.'

9.2 NARRATIVE THERAPY

Michael White and David Epston's *Narrative Means to Therapeutic Ends* (1990) was foundational in introducing a narrative approach to psychotherapy and has inspired many practitioners, family therapists in particular. The approach was novel in concentrating on client strengths and in seeing clients and therapists as partners, with narrative therapy seen as a collaborative, ongoing conversation (i.e. 'co-constructed'), in which the therapist helps the client to articulate the implicit 'story' behind their sufferings and self-accounts and which, through so doing, becomes open in principle to revision (Polkinghorne, 2004).[1] Long before, however, psychoanalysis began when attention shifted from the visible symptoms of suffering people, to a practice of extended listening to the inner story of that suffering, the unconscious story. Implied stories (e.g. 'I am always the victim', 'It is always down to me to be the strong one', 'My dad is heroic') can constitute liabilities and assets, i.e. may keep people stuck or trapped and/or may be sources of comfort and strength. Either way, their familiarity counts. But stories are often multi-layered ('multistory') and can frequently be contradictory, reflecting quite different aspects of a person's experience. Narrative approaches suggest that it is important to characterize accounts of suffering not so much in standard diagnosis, although this can play a role, but in narrative terms (Roberts, 2000). To list some possible examples: (1) stuck, or unresolved stories (as in repetitious patterns, self-defeating disorders etc.); (2) narrative disruption (as in unexpected grief); (3) shattered narrative (as in PTSD); (4) untold, shame-filled story (as in violence and abuse); (5) chaotic or incoherent narrative (as in Alzheimer's), and so on. A primary psychological challenge, following negative experiences, is to try to make sense out of them, as rendering such experiences meaningful helps make them more manageable. One area of importance is that of 'post-traumatic growth' whereby an individual negotiating a major threat to their integrity may, sometimes, develop a new, hopeful perspective on the self and world (Meichenbaum, 2006). According to White and Epston (1990), by enabling the development of richer ('thicker') narratives to client experience, the hold of unproductive, negative and repetitive ('thin') narratives upon the client is loosened; clients become more articulate and better able to envision alternative, more flexible, accounts of themselves. Narrative therapists thus attend closely to how their clients talk, the 'position' in language in which they place themselves, their distinguishing expressions and figures of speech. 'Externalisation' is a key technique, 'that encourages persons to objectify and, at times, to personify the problems that they experience as oppressive' (White & Epston, 1990, p. 38). In this way, a person is helped to make an all-important shift, from seeing themselves as the problem, to seeing themselves as a person with a problem. To assist a person to tell and re-tell their story, highlighting subtle differences, and to envisage alternative, more productive, accounts of themselves is part of the therapeutic process of 're-authoring'.

In the rest of the chapter, we do the following: (1) explore the relevance of narrative understanding to addiction; (2) look at ways of generating client narrative and related techniques of intervention; and (3) examine social resources that enable narratives of recovery.

9.3 NARRATIVE THEORY AND ADDICTION

Clients describe suffering, disorder and illness in a range of ways, including the use of everyday metaphors and analogies. There is a lived, cultural and discursive aspect to both physical and mental disorders that is powerfully influential over and beyond its 'literal' aspects. Some illnesses have had a particularly significant cultural component; consider leprosy in the Middle Ages, or deformities before the advent of modern medicine and remediation; illnesses like TB, cancer and HIV still do have enormous cultural connotations (Sontag, 1979). What of substance misuse?

Throughout history, addiction was a disorder inescapably bound up with wider cultural dimensions, which in modern parlance we might characterize as 'stigma', some of which remains potent in social discourse. Whether regarded as penchant, excess, sin, disease, deviance or defiance, substance misuse is overlain by such wide moral and symbolic meanings. These are linked to how a given society, or time, views unruly appetites and desires, judges appropriate indulgence, and sets up norms regarding who and what is, or is not, considered normal. Marlatt and Fromme (1988) link addiction to classical myths and stories, such as those of Bacchus, Pandora and Icarus. The cultural load applies to the substances themselves, with drugs seen as magic, elixirs, cures, demons, poisons, charms, etc. and to their users, seen variously as inebriates, habitual drunkards, junkies, fiends, anti-social or vulnerable individuals, depending on the era and culture. Either way, as Zieger (2008, p 10) puts it, 'Addiction, with its incoherent subjects, chronic repetitions ... presents its own distinct blur in the side of rational Enlightenment modernity and progress.'

Clients with substance issue problems experience a serious 'biographical disruption' of their lives (Bury, 1982). And, as their problems accrue, it becomes increasingly difficult to be able to characterize their life in healthy and productive ways; in fact, quite the opposite. Erikson's (1963) classic 'life-stages' approach concerns the growing, formation, maintenance and passing on of viable and accomplished identity. Good early experiences promote, in Erikson's view, an enduring legacy of hope, or in the terminology of the theory used in this chapter, of narrative optimism. The problem is that when drug or alcohol dependence sets in, it unpicks normal sources of identity and seriously reduces horizons. As a person is caught in a cycle of decline, in some form another, hope in a better alternative recedes. The person is caught with all the dilemmas and difficulties of what sociologists call 'spoiled identity' (Goffman, 1963). One client, looking back over his life, said with dim realization, 'I'm getting nowhere, and very fast. Everything I had is gone and anything I was given is wasted. What the hell have I got to show for the last 20 years?'

The narrative approach to addiction awaits fuller development, although with respect to recovery from addiction, there are good examples of its use, particularly in research. The pioneer of motivational interviewing, William Miller (Miller & Rose, 2009) has considered 'language markers' that characterize so-called 'change talk' in sessions, and how this can have both preparatory (i.e. preparing to change) and mobilizing (i.e. concrete steps and behavioural change) features. Diamond's (2002) book, however, remains a model for narrative understanding of addiction recovery. He regards therapy as a process of 'narrating the unconscious' and of externalizing the problem so that a client can see more clearly what they are 'up against'.[2] He refers to the loss and bereavements of addiction, and places great store on the use of 'letter writing'.

9.4   CLIENT TALK

Listening carefully, in narrative terms, to how clients describe their lifestyles and addictions, one notices many interesting, evocative communications: e.g. 'I'm going round and round in circles', 'This roller-coaster life will have me dead before long',

'I'm fighting demons', 'I'm an escapist and it's my way of running away', 'Drink is my best friend, or rather, it was ...', and so on. Marlatt and Fromme (1988), and Shinebourne and Smith (2010) provide other interesting examples of addiction metaphors and analogies. People use other tropes besides metaphor, such as metonymy (one thing standing for another), such as 'brown' for heroin, 'the bottle' for alcoholic drinks, 'scripts' for prescribed substitute medication, and so on; their coinage in particular discursive contexts, such as the street or clinic, is that 'everyone knows' what they mean. 'Struggle' and 'conflict' metaphors are particularly common, as clients tell us how they are 'torn', behave 'just like Jekyll and Hyde', 'holding on for dear life', and so on. In narratives such as these, the person presents a multiple self (Shinebourne & Smith, 2009). When talking of their histories, clients seldom offer a bare chronology of their substance misuse, but present a vivid account that includes a picture of who they are, accounts of what they have done, and various outcomes of their using, the 'story so far', if you like. Thematically, overall accounts of addiction usually take the form of a story of decline, although if the person does not see any problems associated with their using, they may relay a self-justifying story of glamour and bravado (which could be typified as 'romance' and 'war' stories), or present a normalized version of their activities, for instance, 'It's what everyone's doing, isn't it?'.

Narrative approaches make full note of these distinctive, idiosyncratic communications and forms which are the basis on which the therapist starts their work of reflection and paraphrasing. They are invaluable windows into how clients see and live out their reality, and often all it takes is for the therapist to pluck an expression, or repeat a key phrase, and the client is enabled to further elaborate the meaning of their activities.

In the following illustrations, the importance of attending precisely to both client language and context is emphasized.

CASE STUDY 9.1   TONY'S RECORD

In a ward round, Tony said, 'My criminal record is very long- and that tells its own story.'

COMMENT

In narrative terms, Tony was using language condensation. He does not feel the need to explain his criminal history, as 'it tells its own story'. Perhaps the audience, in this context, the doctors, nurses, etc., are meant to understand something like, 'I don't need to elaborate *that* here.' Depending on tone and emphasis, the same statement to a counsellor might be heard as a cry for help (e.g. this man has been through a great deal, has seen and caused trouble, and might elicit the response, 'Why don't you tell me some more about that?'), while the same statement to his peers, might have an entirely different connotation, for example, 'stay clear of me'. His phrase could imply a status (e.g. 'hard man'), with his implied personal story resonating with cultural plots suggestive of toughness, street credibility, and so on.

CASE STUDY 9.2   SARAH'S SLIP

Sarah had a slip to heroin after a lengthy period of abstinence. She was angry with herself, 'There I was, going straight, doing the right things, crystal clear and all of a sudden I'd let the bloody monster back in. Fortunately, I got him out quick … I'll have to keep my eyes open …'

COMMENT

Sarah's brief account is rich in metaphor. In fact, what she says resembles a very short story, with a 'before' (when she is 'going straight', itself a common metaphor of abstinence) and an 'after', an outcome, which she describes imaginatively (the monster, male as it happens, like a stalking or opportunistic figure) and a self-declared consequence for the future, also expressed in metaphor (she needs to keep her 'eyes open').

Professionals do not always use objective, lifeless language, they too have preferred metaphors, which are, at bottom, ways of connecting with their clients. One nurse was fond of using metaphors and analogies of 'fog', such as 'coming out of a fog', 'clearing the mind', being in the 'midst of using', and so on. A psychiatrist frequently used 'battle' imagery in talking about his clients' struggles with addiction, as in 'mounting guard against relapse' and 'beating addiction'. and so on.

As an example, although the scientific psychology of relapse prevention seems objective, replete with its diagrams and analysis of (re-)lapse factors, it, too, uses imaginative, semi-literary metaphors, intended to engage the client, such as in conceiving relapse as a 'journey', with slips indicating 'minor turns' of course, or relapse as the outcome of a succession of decisions made at various 'junctions'. In fact, 'journey metaphors' are common not only in relapse prevention therapy but also in accounts of recovery (Weegmann, 2005). Not only that, but relapse prevention actively encourages creative metaphors as an aid to coping, such as the image of 'fighting a craving' or 'urge surfing'. In this way, relapse prevention, as any other practice, requires deft use of language every bit as much as its scientific models. It is important for professionals to be aware of their preferences, not to assume that these will work in the same way with all clients, and be willing to change, or adapt, metaphors so as to better engage with our clients' worlds.

9.5   GENERATING NARRATIVE

The following narrative techniques can be used to help a person with addiction to better elaborate their relationship to substances, to help them assess where they are and, hopefully, to build recovery, however early or provisional that might be.

9.5.1　Letters

Clients can be invited to compose 'Dear Drugs' (or 'Dear Alcohol' or 'Dear Using Life-style') letters, as if writing to a person. They should have the time and privacy to do this (e.g. a quiet time at home, an allocated part of a session) and it can be explained thus, 'This might be a useful way of getting your thoughts and feelings down in black and white about your relationship to drugs, etc. You might find it quite a revelation, like a self-check. All you have to do it to write whatever comes to your head follow-ing the words, "Dear drugs ...", and you can sign off in your own way.' This is an extension of ideas borrowed from Diamond's (2002) book, where he gives powerful examples of 'goodbye letters' to drugs. Depending on the setting and stage of addic-tion, it can be useful to leave the question of what *type* of letter it should be an open one. Although this does not pretend to be a scientific typology, the possible types of letter might include, 'goodbye' letters (common, in the author's experience), 'love-like' letters (reflecting attachment to, and the idealization of, using) and 'bereavement-like' letters (reflecting ambivalence and anticipated loss of the substance). Depending on the context, such materials lend further openings into the ongoing motivational, psy-chodynamic or other therapies deployed. Finally, a therapist can write a letter verbatim on behalf of the client if there are literacy issues. Once generated, such letters serve as creative documents and are excellent resources for further conversation, reflection and re-visiting. Not only this, but the author has also experimented with the use of 'Dear recovery' letters as an important counter-balance to the emphasis on the substances.

Once elicited, therapeutic dialogue can ensue, encouraging further expansion from the client and also challenges, such as 'OK, if addiction is this demon, how might you reduce its powers?', or 'If you and your friend alcohol are having such troubles, has the time come for a separation?'

Elsewhere (Weegmann, 2005), I have discussed the use of letter writing *to* clients as a way of providing formulations in an accessible manner.

9.5.2　Chapters

A useful way of helping clients break down their using history into manageable, story-like components is to suggest that for each phase of their use they offer a caption or chapter heading, as though it were part of a book still being written. This is inspired by the work of Dan McAdams (1993) on narratives of the life story and identity. Most clients take to the idea, with visual diagrams a helpful extra.

CASE STUDY 9.3　EPISODES IN TERRY'S DRUG STORY

Terry began using heroin (non-de-pendently) around 18, within a motorbike fraternity. He was the archetypal rebel, but lacked any 'cause' other than drug taking, he said with the benefit of hind-sight. Asked to describe this as an 'opening chapter' in his drug story, he chose 'Motorcycle diaries' as his title. Within two years he had become dependent on heroin, itself a source of injured pride (he believed that he could control it while others could not), which he entitled 'Getting in deep', and later there were breaks in drug use, which he called 'Reprieves'. Narrative therapists are keenly interested in exceptions to the standard story, or 'unique outcomes', which is why the examination of drug-free periods, brief or extended, is important, yet often overlooked (by both the client and the professional). So in the case of a 'reprieve', curiosity can be actively expressed about what enabled such a change in pattern.

In addition to the idea of 'past chapters', the present and the future dimension are also important, so one might ask, 'If you were to give "nowadays" a chapter heading, what would that be?' or 'What do you want the next chapter in your life to look like?' Terry, now in mid-life, spoke of 'Light at the end of the tunnel' as well as, 'Uncertain times ahead'.

9.5.3   Evocative Questions

To help 'bring out' implicit narrative assumptions and to kindle emergent stories of change, narrative therapists seek to raise evocative questions, i.e. questions that aim to elicit deeply meaningful schemas and which consolidate important realizations. Some examples are questions like, 'Can you describe an important turning point that persuaded you that things had to change?', or, 'If you were to put it in a sentence or two, what sort of person you are trying to be now, what would you say?' It can be helpful to dwell upon responses, often repeating them, as a way of amplifying the importance of such self-statements. McAdams (1993), in his detailed exploration of life stories, offers a whole range of other questions and lines of inquiry. It is inspiring, and often surprising, to witness how articulate people in recovery can be, once freed from old habits and patterns, including old ways of seeing and talking about themselves.

9.5.4   Poems, Books, Stories

Narrative therapy can draw on any existing discursive resources (e.g. myths) that might be of assistance. Using poems and other bibliographic resources can encourage creativity and offer general or universal models through which a person can identify patterns and thus glimpse a way forward. This can soften self-blame. Robert Frost's (1920) poem, 'The Road Not Taken', is a well-known example of a poem that signifies choice, inviting clients to consider paths that they have not used. Interestingly, it was not written with addiction in mind whatsoever, but has become associated with it subsequently. Copies can be given to clients, or they can be encouraged to express their difficulties in their own prose and poems.

Myths are valuable for the cultural stories they contain. One client was intrigued by the Greek myth of Sisyphus, the figure condemned to push a boulder up a mountain, only to have it roll back down every time. She found it a compelling metaphor for the misspent energy devoted to addiction, 'I always ended up on the floor, time and time again.' In general, books or films are a neglected resource, yet can speak vividly to people. Another client loved football and found reading *Addicted* by Tony Adams (1998) most revealing of his own patterns. The tradition of confessional books on people suffering from addiction goes back to the Romantic period, and some clients will be helped by such bibliographic resources.

Narrative therapy is consistent with other psychosocial approaches to addiction. For those still using drugs, it can help in building the confidence that addiction can be faced and alleviated, increasing self-efficacy. Motivation is strengthened through engagement in some of the imaginative exercises described, which encourage addicted clients to clarify stories about who they are as well as who they might become. They have a particular strength, however, when people move into some form of recovery, to which we now turn.

9.6   NARRATIVES OF RECOVERY

Although optimistic in tone, narrative therapy is not naïve. Addictive habits and patterns are by nature compelling, and individuals experience negative consequences repeatedly before being in a position, or state of mind, to make commitments to change. Narrative therapy helps those who are still addicted by enabling reflection, engendering different ways of seeing the problem and thus offering 'bridges' to alternative ways of managing oneself. When an individual begins to change and the stranglehold of the drug is broken, narrative approaches come into their own as a resource for figuring a way forward and constructing a meaningful life; 'In the transition from addiction to recovery, each client must find ways to draw life meaning and purpose … to forge new prescriptions for daily living, and generate hope for the future' (White, Laudet, & Becker, 2006, p. 18). Clients need convincing 'narratives of recovery' that help them see themselves in a new way and to give a meaningful account of their struggles and achievements; like having a map, such narratives help with navigation but do not guarantee a problem-free journey. As we shall see, people benefit from a whole variety of such 'maps' as they fashion alternatives to addiction.

9.7   VARIETIES OF RECOVERY STORY

When people exit from addictive careers, they construct ways of accounting for their former activities and 'condition' so that they can move on. Former lives are re-evaluated and so too are 'former selves' (i.e. a story of 'how I was then' versus 'how I am now'). Given the vast biographical disruption caused by addiction, people in recovery face a considerable task of re-writing ('re-authoring') a sense of who they are. Some time ago Biernacki (1986) deployed a narrative approach to highlight the role that 'identity work' plays in resolving drug addiction, while more recently others have looked in further detail at the construction of a 'non-addict' identity, whereby previous behaviour and current lifestyle are reevaluated (McIntosh & McKeganey, 2000). This section focuses on social sources of narrative, as distinct from the individual story.

When asked to describe recovery, some clients are brief, as if giving headlines, for example, 'I was an unreliable drunk, quite useless', 'I'm over it and I'm giving something back', or 'I used to play the victim, blame others'. Others describe or become able to articulate elaborated narratives of reconstruction, often as a result of the benefit of growing recovery time, which may be supported by collective stores of narrative, such as those provided by, for example, a church group, a post-rehabilitation network, or fellowship groups. In other words, personal stories of recovery are not solely created in the minds of individuals, but invariably resonate with, and draw on, cultural resources. Unsurprisingly, most accounts of addiction recovery emphasize a process of descent and ascent, decline and renewal, in some form or another, just as metaphors of 'up' and 'down' (e.g. 'I'm low in mood') are common in language (Lakoff & Johnson, 1980). Beyond this generality, however, there is an enormous variety in the forms which recovery narratives take. For reasons of space the following examples of types of narrative are highly condensed.

Chapter 14 in this volume considers the 'narrative capital' of Alcoholics Anonymous (AA), and other such fellowships, an area which has attracted considerable research. As is argued in that chapter, AA was one of the first mutual-help groups to explicitly value the importance of story (telling, sharing and hearing), recognizing that a story can indeed help 'set one free'. One can suggest that AA narrative structures and 'speech acts' are not only readily available and long-standing, but that they also offer practical wisdom and a coherence or consistency that is not easily found elsewhere (Cain, 1991; O'Halloran, 2008). A product of its time, in many ways AA has also stood the test of time.

AA inspired other 12 Step fellowships. In a comparable mix of culture and individual story, reported Al Anon narratives (i.e. for those living with and supporting alcoholics) of the 1950s, when the membership was almost exclusively female, reflect the values of that time and are different in emphasis to those of later eras, which were influenced by feminism, equality rights and increased societal acknowledgement of 'family secrets' such as violence. Later still, Adult Children of Alcoholics groups generated hybrid narratives that are an interesting blend of 12 Step story forms, survivor literature and humanistic psychotherapy discourses (Rice, 1996).

Long before the advent of AA and the other fellowship groups, temperance societies proliferated in America and throughout much of Europe from the 1840s onwards. If one puts aside contemporary condescension towards such movements, a great deal can be learned from them, not least for their meteoric rise and mobilizing power.

A growing body of temperance narratives helped 'habitual drunkards' to become 'reformed inebriates', living free of the 'enslavement' of drink and finding redemption, as communicated in lectures, testimonials and pamphlets; with values akin to the Protestant ethic, 'moral suasion' was their guiding method, intent as they were on sobriety and betterment. The movements varied considerably in their styles, and in terms of social class, religiosity, secularism, and so on. Crowley's (1999) collection of temperance narratives of the famous Washingtonian Movement, the first proper mutual aid society for drinkers,[3] is a remarkable one, creating as it did solidarity, testimony, models of change and therapeutic rituals, of which the 'pledge' was central. Crowley notes that women folk had an important, even elevated status, in such discourses as redeeming figures of stability, constancy and household. This was during a period in which female alcoholics, as distinct from family members, were even less visible, although some temperance societies did emerge for such women.

Berridge's (2013) ongoing contribution to the study of English temperance details the shift from moderation to abstinence, and describes such groups as early examples of 'pressure groups' with their combination of individual recovery and political agitation. As she states, 'Temperance was a powerful influence – amongst others – in helping to form a mass culture not founded of hard drinking' (2013, p. 44).

It is impossible, and no doubt premature, to provide a complete typology of recovery stories, although attempts have been made to describe more common forms. From a perspective of exit from addiction and abstinence, researchers have suggested specific recovery story types, such as, 'personal growth story', 'love story', 'mastery story', 'conversion story', 'AA story' 'story strength and will-power' (e.g. Hänninen & Koski-Jännes, 1999; Blomqvist, 2002). There are also 'resolved' and 'unresolved' stories, depending on the success, or otherwise, of recovery (Koski-Jännes, 2002). As for the 'conversions', or 'spiritual stories', Miller and C' de Baca (2001) refer to instances of sudden, benevolent and lasting change which can occur, and which they label 'quantum change', although for others such shifts in value and outlook occur over a long period of time. Most often, however, identities of change in this field are constructed around the state of abstinence, and it is interesting to speculate on the relative absence of developed 'stories of (e.g. alcohol) moderation' in our culture. An exception perhaps are the accounts witnessed in Moderation Management, a US self-help network aimed at controlled drinking for less severely dependent drinkers (Klaw & Humphreys, 2000).

Different services and rehabilitation services are governed by differing philosophies, and each will have an impact on how their respective clients might tend to talk about themselves, the vocabularies they use, and the framing of their recoveries. Some programmes formally incorporate the idea of presenting one's 'life story' to one's fellows as a requirement. It interesting to speculate on the question on how clients 'learn' the narratives that they then use as their 'own'. Different philosophies and cultures will have different narrative appeal to clients, although it is difficult to predict 'what works best for whom' in advance. The strength (flexibility?) and durability of narratives are critical, as individuals consolidate change. As Hänninen and Koski-Jännes (2004, p. 244) say, 'If the narrative anticipation of recovery passes the test of reality, the full recovery story results; if not, a new cycle begins.'

9.8   CONCLUSION

Narrative approaches for those in recovery aim to help clients broaden descriptions of themselves and their lives. In turn, they allow people to have different visions of themselves, hopefully addressing unmet needs. They help create viable alternative identities, as a 'person in recovery', a 'non-user', an 'ordinary person', and so on. Using a journey metaphor might be seen as a way back, of recovery, or as well as finding new territory of discovery. One client, after two years of psychotherapy, said, 'Now I feel excited to be me and to be always discovering things. It is a whole world apart from the using and abusing and all that crap that I did in the past – to me and to others around me.'

A variety of techniques and clinical sensitivities have been illustrated, whose purpose is to enable clients to change how they understand and describe themselves. The narrative approach to addiction and recovery is intimately concerned with the generation of meaning, language and the personal and cultural stories that our clients bring with them into our rooms. Some might call it something like 'meaning-based' medicine (Kleinman, 1988). Narrative approaches hone in on the client's implicit, unique story, including their metaphors and detailed descriptions, helping clients to expand upon, and revise, long-held, dominant narratives so that they can fashion alternatives.

When people's lives fall apart and are riddled with disruption and chaos, it is important that they begin a process of rebuilding, in which they can make sense of these awful experiences and fashion credible, new accounts of who they are and who they can be. Narrative therapy is a resource that can enable such movement.

ACKNOWLEDGEMENTS

This chapter is a much expanded version of a paper originally published by Weegmann (2010).

NOTES

1) Polkinghorne's (2004) chapter provides a useful summary of the various strands that influenced the development of narrative therapy. In it, he explains that narrative theory is premised on: (1) client strengths (there is a complementarity to 'solution-focused' approaches as described by Geel, in Chapter 13 in this volume); (2) clients and therapists as partners (a view now shared with most psychological approaches); (3) a constructivist approach to meaning; and (4) emphasis on the narrative and story form of meaning.

2) Diamond is particularly innovative in bringing about an integration of the narrative and psychodynamic, combined with an appreciation of the role of mutual-help fellowships (see the interview with him; Bacigalupe, 2004).

3) White's (2000) review of Crowley's (1999) book on the Washingtonians is a useful summary of a movement which, starting in the 1840s, had run out of steam three or four years later, but not without first mobilizing hundreds of thousands of men.

SUGGESTIONS FOR FURTHER READING

Diamond, J. (2002). *Narrative means to sober ends: Treating addiction and its aftermath.* New York: Guilford Press.

White, M., & Epston, D. (1990). *Narrative means to therapeutic ends.* New York: Norton.

REFERENCES

Adams, T. (1998). *Addicted*. London: HarperCollins.

Bacigalupe, G. (2004). Theories are personal: An interview with Jonathan Diamond. *Journal of Systemic Therapies, 23*, 80–90. doi:10.1521/jsyt.23.4.80.57834

Bauer, J., McAdams, D., & Pals, J. (2008). Narrative identity and eudaimonic well-being. *Journal of Happiness Studies, 9*, 81–104. doi:10.1007/s10902-006-9021-6

Berridge, V. (2013). *Demons: Our changing attitudes to alcohol, tobacco and drugs*. Oxford: Oxford University Press.

Biernacki, P. (1986). *Pathways from heroin addiction recovery without treatment*. Philadelphia, PA: Temple University Press.

Blomqvist, J. (2002). Recovery with and without treatment: A comparison of resolutions of alcohol and drug problems. *Addiction Research and Theory, 10*, 119–158. doi:10.1080/16066350290017248

Bury, M. (1982). Chronic illness as biographical disruption. *Sociology of Health and Illness, 4*, 167–182. doi:10.1111/1467-9566.ep11339939

Cain, C. (1991). Personal stories: Identity acquisition and self-understanding in Alcoholics Anonymous. *Ethos, 19*, 201–253.

Crossley, M. (2000). *Introducing Narrative psychology: Self, trauma and the construction of meaning*. Buckingham: Open University Press.

Crowley, J. (Ed.). (1999). *Drunkard's progress: Narratives of addiction, despair, and recovery*. Baltimore, MD: The Johns Hopkins University Press.

Diamond, J. (2002). *Narrative means to sober ends: treating addiction and its aftermath*. New York: Guilford Press.

Erikson, E. (1963). *Childhood and society* (2nd ed.). New York: W.W. Norton.

Frost, R. (1920). The road not taken. In *Mountain interval*. New York: Henry Holt & Company.

Goffman, E. (1963). *Stigma: Notes on the management of spoiled identity*. New York: Simon & Schuster.

Hänninen, V., & Koski-Jännes, A. (1999). Narratives of recovery from addictive behaviours. *Addiction, 94*, 1837–1848. doi:10.1046/j.1360-0443.1999.941218379.x

Hänninen, V., & Koski-Jännes, A. (2004). Stories of attempts to recover from addiction. In P. Rosenqvist, A. Koski-Jännes, & L.Ojesjo (Eds.), *Addiction and the Life Course* (pp. 231–246). Helsinki: NAD.

Klaw, E., & Humphreys, K. (2000). Life stories of Moderation Management mutual help groups. *Contemporary Drug Problems, 27*, 779–803. doi:10.1177/009145090002700404

Kleinman, A. (1988). *The illness narratives: Suffering, healing and the human condition*. New York: Basic Books.

Koski-Jännes, A. (2002). Social and identity projects in the recovery from addictive behaviours. *Addiction Research and Theory, 10*, 183–202. doi:10.1080/16066350290017266

Lakoff, G., & Johnson, M. (1980). *Metaphors we live by*. Chicago: University of Chicago Press.

Linde, C. (1993). *Life stories: The creation of coherence*. Oxford: Oxford University Press.

MacIntyre, A. (1984). *After virtue: Sa study in moral theory*. Notre Dame, IN: University of Notre Dame Press.

Marlatt, A., & Fromme, K. (1988). Metaphors for addiction. In S.Peele (Ed.), *Visions of addiction: Major contemporary perspectives on addiction & alcoholism*. Lanham, MD: Lexington Books.

McAdams, D. (1993). *The stories we live by: Personal myths and the making of the self*. New York: Guildford Press.

McIntosh, J., & McKeganey, N. (2000). Addicts' narratives of recovery from drug use: Constructing a non-addict identity. *Social Science and Medicine, 50*, 1501–1510.

Meichenbaum, D. (2006). Resilience and post-traumatic growth: A constructive narrative perspective. In L. Calhoun, & R. Tedeschi (Eds.), *Handbook of post-traumatic growth; research and practice*. Mahwah, NJ: Lawrence Erlbaum.

Miller, W., & C' de Baca, C. (2001). *Quantum change: When epiphanies and sudden insights transform ordinary lives*. New York: Guilford Press.

Miller, W., & Rose, G. (2009). Toward a theory of Motivational Interviewing. *American Psychologist*, *64*, 527–537.

O'Halloran, S. (2008). *Talking oneself sober: the discourse of Alcoholics Anonymous*. Amherst, NY: Cambria Press.

Polkinghorne, D. E. (2004). Narrative therapy and postmodernism. In L. Angus, & J. McLeod (Eds.), *The handbook of narrative and psychotherapy: practice, theory & research*. Thousand Oaks, CA: Sage Publications.

Rice, J. S. (1996). *A disease of one's own: Psychotherapy, addiction, and the emergence of co-dependency*. New Brunswick, NJ: Transaction Publishers.

Roberts, G. (2000). Narrative and severe mental illness: What place do stories have in an evidence-based world? *Advances in Psychiatric Treatment*, *6*, 432–441. doi:10.1192/apt.6.6.432

Sarbin, T. (1986). *Narrative psychology: The storied nature of human conduct*. New York: Praeger.

Shinebourne, P., & Smith, J. (2009). Alcohol and the self: An interpretative phenomenological analysis of the experience of addiction and its impact on the sense of self and identity. *Addiction Research and Theory*, *17*, 152–167. doi:10.1080/16066350802245650

Shinebourne, P., & Smith, J. (2010). The communicative power of metaphors: An analysis and interpretation of metaphors in accounts of the experience of addiction. *Psychology and Psychotherapy: Theory, Research, Practice*, *83*, 59–73. doi:10.1348/147608309X468077

Sontag, S. (1979). *Illness as metaphor*. London: Allen Lane.

Stern, D. (1985). *The interpersonal world of the infant: A view from psychoanalysis and developmental psychology*. New York: Basic Books.

Trevarthen, C. (2010). What is it like to be a person who knows nothing? Defining the active intersubjective mind of a newborn human being. *Infant and Child Development*, *20*, 119–135. doi:10.1002/icd.689

Weegmann, M. (2005). The road to recovery: Journeys and relapse risk maps. *Drugs & Alcohol Today*, *5*, 42–45. doi:10.1108/17459265200500047

Weegmann, M. (2010). Just a story? Narrative approaches to addiction and recovery. *Drugs and Alcohol Today*, *10*, 29–36. doi:10.5042/daat.2010.0468

White, M., & Epston, D. (1990). *Narrative means to therapeutic ends*. New York: Norton.

White, W. (2000). Book review: *Drunkard's progress: Narratives of addiction, despair and recovery*, by John Crowley. http://www.williamwhitepapers.com/

White, W., Laudet, A.B., & Becker, J.B. (2006). Life meaning and purpose in addiction recovery. *Addiction Professional*, *4*(4), 18–23.

Wilde, O. (1891). The decay of lying: An observation. In *Intentions*. New York: Yurita Press.

Zieger, S. (2008). *Inventing the addict: Ddrugs, race and sexuality in 19th century British and American literature*. Cambridge, MA: University of Massachusetts Press.

10 Addiction and Mental Health

ADAM HUXLEY

Change Grow Live, London, UK

CHAPTER OUTLINE

10.1 INTRODUCTION

During their lifetime, approximately 50% of people with a mental health problem will use substances at some point and experience difficulties as a result of this use (Weaver et al., 2003). There have been numerous national health initiatives that have attempted to identify the treatment needs of this population and ensure that treatment providers are equipped to meet their needs (Department of Health, 2002). The concept of elucidating 'dual diagnosis' or 'co-occurring disorders' seems quite a challenge when there continues to be a considerable variation in the terms used to describe a heterogeneous cohort of individuals who experience mental health problems and who engage in the misuse of substances. People with mental health problems use substances for many different reasons; understanding the context in which these difficulties co-exist is crucial for treatment services aimed at reducing harmful behaviours associated with both disorders. Substance misuse is a broad term encompassing the hazardous use of any psychotropic substance, including alcohol, legal and illegal drugs. Such use is usually regarded as 'problematic' if there is evidence of dependence and a negative influence on the course and treatment of the mental health problem (Margolese, Malchy, Negrete, Tempier & Gill, 2004). The nature of the relationship is also less clear, with some authors arguing that terms 'dual diagnosis' or 'co-occurring' do little to explain the multiple physical, social and psychological needs of this population (Barker, 1998).

Existing literature suggests that living with a mental health problem and using substances is more likely to lead to longer-term negative outcomes (Najt, Fusar-Poli & Brambilla, 2011). When they occur together, the adverse impact on the individual's life is amplified considerably. This chapter will review the evidence for the association between experiencing a mental health problem and using substances. For the purposes of clarity, the term 'substance misuse' in this chapter refers to alcohol, illicit substances and the over-use of prescribed medicines. There is a growing evidence base that novel psychoactive substances or NPS, such as Mephedrone, are beginning to have a deleterious effect on users' mental health (Royal College of Psychiatrists, 2014). The longer-term impact of NPS would merit greater attention in future editions. Mental health problems encompass a wide range of diagnostic terms, including psychosis, personality and mood disorders. For the purpose of this chapter, we will only focus on adults diagnosed with severe and enduring mental health problems, such as psychotic disorders, who use substances problematically. The extent of alcohol misuse among this cohort is significant and warrants separate consideration. Epidemiological surveys suggest excessive alcohol use occurs among people with depression and anxiety disorders. Grant et al. (2004) found that 32.8% of clients who sought treatment for alcohol use disorders were found to have co-morbid depression, and 33.4% were found to have a co-morbid anxiety disorder. Degenhardt, Hall and Lynskey (2001) have shown in the United States and Australia that alcohol-dependent individuals are three to four times more likely to have a co-occurring anxiety or affective disorder when compared to the general population. This chapter will not cover young people, although services are identifying co-occurring disorders as an area of focus. Studies of adolescents in substance use treatment programmes also show the majority have co-occurring mental disorders (e.g. Chan, Dennis & Funk, 2008).

10.2 ASSOCIATION BETWEEN SUBSTANCE MISUSE AND PSYCHOSIS

The association between experiencing a mental health problem and the use of substances has been well established (Mueser, Drake & Wallach, 1998). The evidence for this association is not just statistically, socially, and clinically significant, but is of particular importance to healthcare treatment providers. There is evidence that substance misuse occurs across a wide range of mental health problems such as personality disorders and psychosis (see e.g. Merikangas et al., 1996; Trull, Sher, Minks-Brown, Durbin & Burr, 2000). Studies have shown that clients with schizophrenia and antisocial personality disorder (ASPD) are more likely to have co-morbid substance use disorder than clients without such disorders (Caton et al., 1994). First, it might be clinically meaningful to differentiate between association and causation in the sense that if a variable frequently occurs in a particular disorder, it does not mean that that this variable is the sole cause of the disorder. In other words, not all people who use substances will go on and develop a mental health problem, and vice versa. Temporal precedence is not usually established in most prevalence studies.

There are, however, a number of theories that attempt to explain the nature of this relationship. One such theory is that an underlying common cause is responsible for the expression of both disorders, such as a genetic commonality (Kendler, Prescott, Myers & Neale, 2003). For instance, a study by Chambers, Krystal and Self (2001) suggests that people with schizophrenia have a vulnerability to engage in substance misuse due to the neuropathology of schizophrenia and the neural circuitry reinforcing substance misuse. They suggest that abnormalities in the hippocampal formation and frontal cortex support substance use; moreover, the dysregulated neural integration of dopamine and glutamate signalling in the nucleus accumbens, resulting from frontal cortical and hippocampal dysfunction, promotes drug-using behaviour. Due to a lack of integration of signalling, the individual experiences neural and motivational changes that would be expected of someone with long-term drug use but without necessarily having used drugs previously. Kalivas and Volkow (2005) further argue that cellular alterations in prefrontal glutamatergic innervation of the accumbens sustain the drive to seek out rewards from drug use by reducing the importance of natural rewards, reducing a sense of cognitive control (choice), and enhancing glutamatergic drive when presented with stimuli associated with drug use.

A second pathway is where a psychiatric disorder is considered a precipitant to a substance-use disorder. The 'self-medication hypothesis' (as described, e.g. by Gregg, Barrowclough & Haddock, 2007) argues that people with a mental health problem may use substances in order to manage the distressing effects of their problems. These authors hypothesize that substances become an effective symptom management strategy to alleviate dysphoria, or to alleviate the side effects of antipsychotic medication, or as a preferred alternative to antipsychotic medication, or to achieve improvements in anxiety, energy and social skills. As part of this process, people make selections on the type of substance they might want to use in order to manage particular types of distress, for example, using an opiate to manage voices, or using alcohol to manage social anxiety. People who experience stigma as a result of their mental health problems may also attempt to create a social identity among a non-mentally ill, but substance-misusing, peer group, or find themselves drifting into using substances due to a number of vulnerability factors, such as poverty, poor housing, or engagement in the sex industry (Baigent, Holme & Hafner, 1995).

A third pathway refers to a suggested causal model operating in the opposite direction. This pathway, known as the 'toxicity hypothesis', argues that substance use leads to the development of mental health problems. A significant number of studies have supported this hypothesis by showing a positive association between higher cannabis use and earlier onset of psychosis (see, e.g. Kuepper et al., 2010). Nevertheless, the use of cannabis by people at high genetic risk of schizophrenia has also been associated with brain abnormalities and later risk of psychosis (Welch et al., 2011). Moreover, existing evidence suggests that cannabis, and in particular the effects of delta-9-tetrahydrocannabinol (Δ-9-THC), are key risk factors for relapse and readmission among people with psychosis, although a more recent meta-analysis did not indicate a clear effect in established psychosis (Barrowclough, Emsley, Eisner, Beardmore & Wykes, 2013). Although this alone cannot account for cannabis being the sole risk factor associated with the onset of mental health difficulties, Arseneault, Cannon, Witton and Murray (2004) argue that cannabis use is a component cause among many others (including availability and accessibility), forming part of a number of causal variables that result in psychosis.

There is also some evidence that other types of substances are associated with later onset psychosis. Rössler, Hengartner, Angst and Ajdacic-Gross (2012) examined data from a 30-year period on the effects of poly-drug use over the onset of symptoms of psychosis. They found that schizotypal signs were predominantly associated with regular cannabis use in adolescence, suggesting that a significant portion of the occurrence of subclinical psychosis symptoms in adulthood could be attributed to excessive drug use during adolescence. This finding supports the finding from an earlier meta-analysis of 11 longitudinal studies that concluded that cannabis use is associated with increased risk of long-lasting psychosis (Moore et al., 2007), although simply reducing the amount of cannabis does not seem to lead to symptomatic improvement (Barrowclough et al., 2013).

While early intervention studies suggest that the first contact with mental health service is often precipitated by substance use, there is limited good quality research to determine the causal role of substances in later psychosis. The onset of both disorders may occur at similar times, both have deleterious effects on functioning and overall well-being, and therefore establishing temporal precedence remains difficult. Barrowclough et al. (2007) suggest that multiple risk factors can maintain substance use in people with psychosis. They suggest that particular events might trigger substance-related thoughts which leave the person vulnerable to use. As people with psychosis have impaired abilities to cope, they may be more vulnerable to developing problems with substances. Research consistently shows people use drugs and alcohol with psychosis for many of the same reasons as those reported by the general population. However, these reasons may be considerably amplified for people with mental health difficulties who experience multiple disadvantages and typically have reduced coping skills (MacAulay & Cohen, 2013). Lobann et al. (2010) showed that factors influencing use among individuals with a recent onset psychosis were attributions regarding the function and benefits of (initial and ongoing) drug-taking behaviour, changes in life goals, and maladaptive beliefs about the links between mental health and drug use.

10.3   PREVALENCE AND EPIDEMIOLOGY

There are a number of mediating factors between having a mental health problem and using substances. Research suggests that the prevalence of substance misuse among people with psychosis is higher than the general population. In the UK general population, 15% of adults drink double the recommended daily limits on at least one occasion per week (National Statistics, 2015a), while 2.2% of adults are frequent drug users (National Statistics, 2015b). The Epidemiological Catchment Area (ECA) study (Regier et al., 1990) of 20,291 individuals across five countries, found that 47% of subjects with a diagnosis of schizophrenia and 56.1% of those with a diagnosis of bi-polar disorder had some form of substance use disorder. There also appears to be a consistent pattern of substance misuse in people with psychosis internationally, with alcohol usage being the most common legal substance (Weaver et al., 2003) and cannabis being the most common illicit substance (Koskinen, Löhönen, Koponen, Isohanni & Miettunen, 2009). The European Schizophrenia Cohort study data (Carrà et al., 2012) also looked at 1,208 clients aged 18–64 with a diagnosis of schizophrenia across nine centres. They found that lifetime rates for co-morbid dependence on any substance were highest in the United Kingdom (35%), followed by 21% in Germany and 19% in France. Dependence on alcohol and on other psychoactive substances showed similar variations; in the United Kingdom 26%, Germany 18%, and in France 14%.

The extent of substance misuse among people with mental health problems seems to be context-specific. The COSMIC study (Weaver et al., 2003), which at the time of writing is the most recent study of this kind, identified that 44% of community mental health team clients reported past-year problematic drug use, while 75% of them reported harmful alcohol use. Ninety-five per cent of clients attending drug services and 85% of alcohol services' clients had a past-year psychiatric disorder. More recent studies have continued to replicate these patterns and have reported as high as 82% of admissions to a psychiatric unit have used substances previously in inner-urban settings (Fløvig, Vaaler & Morken, 2009). A review by Carrà and Johnson (2009) indicated that the demographic patterns of substance misuse among people with psychosis are largely similar to those seen in the general population, where demographic correlates of use include being male, unmarried, aged under 50, residing in urban areas and having a familial history. Taken together, the above findings suggest that social and personal risk factors should also not be understated. Negative affective states, low self-esteem, impaired social skills, poverty, social exclusion and incomplete education have been identified as risk factors for substance misuse in the general population (Koskinen, Löhönen, Koponen, Isohanni & Miettunen, 2010). Many people with psychosis experience such risk factors which may arise either as a direct result of symptoms, or as a longer-term consequence of living with a severe mental illness.

10.4   OUTCOMES ASSOCIATED WITH CO-OCCURRING DISORDERS

Service users who present with co-occurring disorders demonstrate reduced functioning across a variety of domains; they are reported to have longer and more frequent hospitalizations, more severe symptomatology (including disorders of mood and reality distortion) and violent incidents (Cuffel, Shumway, Choujian & Macdonald, 1994), greater treatment non-compliance, reduced self-efficacy and increased suicidal behaviours (Morojele, Saban & Seedat, 2012). Co-morbidity is highly predictive of negative treatment outcomes, such as poor physical health and decreased life expectancy (Schmidt, Hesse & Lykke, 2011). People with schizophrenia who use substances are also at increased risk of social exclusion and problems with housing, homelessness and psychosocial instability (Green, Drake, Brunette & Noordsy, 2007). There is some evidence that use among this cohort leads to longer-term cognitive impairment which has a negative impact on functional outcomes, such as the ability to benefit from psychological treatment and engage in self-directed behaviour change (McCleery, Addington & Addington, 2006). However, a systematic review by Donoghue and Doody (2012) suggests caution with interpreting such findings as they found substance users performed significantly better than non-users in attention, psychomotor speed and verbal memory.

10.5   TREATMENT APPROACH AND EFFECTIVENESS

In terms of therapeutic interventions, people who present with co-occurring disorders may have decreased motivation to change, difficulty in engaging in treatment, higher dropout rates, limited or maladaptive coping strategies and typically make slower treatment gains (Mueser, Drake, Sigmon & Brunette, 2005; Barrowclough, Haddock, Fitzsimmons & Johnson, 2006). In addition, these service users often have deficits in interpersonal skills and problem-solving abilities (Drake, Mueser, Brunette & McHugo, 2004) which, if present, would be considered to be protective factors for successful management of one's difficulties.

Noordsy, McQuade and Mueser (2003) describe a well-established assessment and intervention process that includes comprehensive assessment, behavioural functional analysis and treatment planning. Treatment approaches consider a range of contextual, environmental, personal and situational factors that become important in understanding the origin and maintenance of both disorders. Good treatment efficacy of a range of psychosocial interventions has been shown for substance misusers without mental health problems, and it follows that these same interventions should be effective for people with co-occurring disorders as the psychological processes regarding the onset and maintenance of substance misuse are largely the same (Barrowclough et al., 2006). The majority of routinely offered interventions can be categorized into three comprehensive models of care for people with co-occurring psychosis and substance misuse.

The 'sequential model' implies that the individual receives treatment for the separate disorders one after the other. The 'parallel model' delivers separate interventions from separate treatment providers (which obviously relies on the presence of good inter-services liaison). There is evidence of effectiveness for a number of approaches that aim to help people make changes in their substance misuse that have been applied to people with mental health problems. Commonly used approaches include motivational interviewing (Miller & Rollnick, 2012), the involvement of families and social networks (Copello, Williamson, Orford & Day, 2006; Mueser et al., 2013; see also Copello & Walsh, Chapter 3 in this volume) and cognitive behavioural therapy (CBT) incorporating individualized formulation and appropriate models of relapse prevention (e.g. Marlatt & Donovan, 2005; see also Hill & Harris, Chapter 15 in this volume). In addition, clients can receive ongoing support from self-help groups such as Alcoholics and Narcotics Anonymous (see Weegmann, Chapter 14 in this volume).

On the other hand, 'integrated interventions' occur simultaneously, from the same service provider who has competence in both treatments (Green et al., 2007), reducing the opportunity to drop out of treatment by minimizing the burden to attend separate treatment facilities. When working with people who present with co-occurring disorders, early engagement in the treatment process is seen as a key task that requires a flexible and motivational approach which is dependent on the context of the clinical setting (e.g. community or in-patient) and grounded in a recovery approach. The UK Drug Policy Commission Consensus Group (2008) defines recovery as 'a process from problematic substance misuse characterized by voluntary sustained control over substance use which maximizes health and well-being and participation in the rights, roles and responsibilities of society'. Cruce, Öjehagen and Nordström (2012) found that clients' participation and motivation in their care were increased if they experienced care conveying meaningfulness and empowerment.

10.6   EVIDENCE FOR EFFECTIVENESS

There have been successful attempts with integrated interventions such as cognitive-behavioural integrated treatment (C-BIT) (Graham et al., 2006) based on the premise that certain thinking styles and thoughts are central in the development and maintenance of the problem (e.g. 'cannabis is the only thing that stops my voices, so I need to smoke cannabis to have any control over them'). C-BIT stresses a collaborative approach as a way of engaging clients in treatment in order to target substance use and its interaction with mental health difficulties through a stepped care approach. The core components of C-BIT include motivation to change, behaviour change, management of mood, lifestyle balance and relapse management.

The results of trials assessing the effectiveness of delivering integrated psychosocial interventions for co-occurring disorders are encouraging yet equivocal (Mueser et al., 2005; Horsfall, Cleary, Hunt & Walter, 2009; Dixon et al., 2010). The aim of such interventions is to reduce distress associated with symptoms of the mental health problem and help people make positive reductions or abstain from substance misuse. The NICE Guidelines (2011) provide little direct evidence of effectiveness for most psychological interventions for people with psychosis and co-existing substance misuse, partially due to complex methodological issues such as small, heterogeneous samples, high attrition rates, unclear diagnostic categories, short follow-up periods and unclear description of treatment components (Horsfall et al., 2009).

Drake et al. (2004) reviewed 26 controlled studies of psychosocial interventions published over 10 years (1994–2003) and found that the cumulative evidence supported integrating treatments into a single intervention, targeting both substance misuse and mental health. Drake, O'Neal and Wallach (2008) found data from 45 controlled studies that suggests contingency management, residential dual diagnosis treatment and group counselling result in consistent positive treatment outcomes. In a randomized controlled trial (RCT) of a group psychological intervention for psychosis with co-morbid cannabis dependence, Madigan et al. (2013) found that group psychological interventions improved subjective quality of life, but did not reduce use of cannabis, or result in improvement in clinical outcomes such as global functioning and attitudes to treatment. Hunt, Siegfried, Morley, Sitharthan and Cleary (2013) reported on 32 RCTs and found no compelling evidence to support any one psychosocial treatment over another for reducing substance use, or improving the mental state in people with serious mental illnesses.

Barrowclough et al. (2001) demonstrated the effectiveness of a programme of care integrated with motivational interviewing, CBT, and family intervention over routine psychiatric care alone for clients with co-occurring disorders. More recently, Barrowclough et al.'s (2010) RCT of 327 participants examining the effectiveness of integrated MI and CBT in addition to standard care found MI and CBT did not improve outcome of treatment on clinical outcomes such as relapses, psychotic symptoms, functioning, and self-harm, but did reduce the amount of substances used for at least one year after completion of therapy, and had a statistically significant effect on readiness to change use at 12 months. Haddock et al.'s (2003) study involved 29 sessions of CBT and MI over 9 months, with 12- and 18-month follow-up, and demonstrated significant improvements in negative symptoms and general function, but no significant difference on the number of days of non-drug use. Baker et al. (2006) conducted an RCT of a 10-session intervention of motivational interviewing and CBT in a community sample of people with a psychotic disorder who had hazardous alcohol, cannabis and/or amphetamine use during the preceding month. They found motivational interviewing or CBT intervention was associated with modest health improvements but with no improvement on substance use at 12 months. A systematic review of treatment studies of co-morbid alcohol misuse and severe depression or anxiety carried out by Baker, Thornton, Hiles, Hides and Lubman (2012) showed that MI and CBT interventions were overall associated with significant reductions in alcohol consumption and depressive or anxiety symptoms. Despite the general trend for advocating for integrated interventions, Boden and Moos (2013) argue that non-integrated treatments may be beneficial for people with co-occurring disorders. They followed 236 male clients receiving 12-step facilitation or a cognitive-behavioural-oriented intervention and found improvement in symptoms, satisfaction and proximal outcomes in both groups. RCTs of brief interventions for substance misuse among people with severe mental disorders were reviewed by Kavanagh and Mueser (2007), who concluded that such interventions have limited impact on substance use, and that extended cognitive-behaviour therapy tended to have better outcomes, albeit with decay of gains over time.

Finally, Kay-Lambkin, Baker, Lewin and Carr (2009) showed there is some evidence for novel approaches such as computer-based treatments. They looked at intensive MI/CBT targeting both depression and substance use simultaneously and found equivalent results to a 'live' intervention at 12 months. Other psychological approaches such as acceptance and commitment therapy (ACT) are also being developed (Richardson, 2013) but evidence is so far limited and warrants further investigation. Further research that controls for the methodological flaws of previous trials will help clinicians determine which interventions are most effective for this client group.

10.7   CONCLUSION

Despite the clear evidence of the numerous harms associated with using substances for people with mental health problems, the motivation to make reductions or abstain from use remains low among this population (Baker et al., 2002). Psychological therapies such as CBT and MI are often used as stand-alone therapies in non-intensive, one-on-one treatments. A lack of dedicated integrated treatment resources may present barriers to effective engagement in treatment services, and the lack of clear guidance on what works by way of treatment approaches hinders consistent engagement in treatment and research into transparent treatment outcomes and effectiveness (Abou-Saleh & Crome, 2012). Moreover, the quality of psychosocial treatments varies so greatly that it is difficult to determine what, which type and how much of it is needed (Veilleux, Colvin, Anderson, York & Heinz, 2010). Study methodologies, participant characteristics and outcome measures vary across studies, which makes reviewing treatment effectiveness problematic. Understanding the dynamic relationship between experiencing a mental health problem and using substances is a key task for treatment providers. Providing a framework for clients to identify the factors that have influenced the development and maintenance of their difficulties, and to consider the impact of their substance misuse on their mental health (and vice versa), could help to promote self-management of their difficulties through self-regulation, adaptive coping and relapse prevention plans. Pharmacological intervention should be considered as an adjunct treatment. The delivery of specific interventions at discrete stages can retain clients in treatment, providing integrated interventions without the need to access numerous services, and can promote collaboration.

The nature of the association between having a mental health problem and misusing substances is a complex one. Greater consideration should be given to flexible delivery of integrated treatments. Addiction could be seen as a multiply determined disorder that requires flexible models and integrated models of care (Orford, 2008). Establishing a more robust evidence base for treatment effectiveness through more randomized trials that account for 'real-world' interventions will allow clinicians to match clients to the most appropriate intervention techniques, allowing consideration for populations that are currently underserved or slipping through mainstream treatment services such as homeless populations, older adults and the emerging population of people with mental health problems who are also using novel psychoactive substances.

SUGGESTIONS FOR FURTHER READING

Graham, H. L. (2004). *Cognitive-behavioural integrated treatment (C-BIT): A treatment manual for substance misuse in people with severe mental health problems.* Chichester: John Wiley & Sons, Ltd.

Graham, H. L., Copello, A., Birchwood, M. J., & Mueser, K. T. (Eds.). (2006) *Substance misuse in psychosis: Approaches to treatment and service delivery.* Chichester: John Wiley & Sons, Ltd.

Weaver, T., Madden, P., Charles, V., et al. (2003). Comorbidity of substance misuse and mental illness in community mental health and substance misuse services. *The British Journal of Psychiatry, 183,* 304–313. doi:dx.doi.org/10.1192/bjp.183.4.304

REFERENCES

Abou-Saleh, M., & Crome, I. (2012). National Institute for Health and Clinical Excellence (NICE) guideline: Psychosis with coexisting substance misuse. *Addiction, 107,* 1–3. doi:10.1111/j.1360-0443.2011.03542.x

Arseneault, L., Cannon, M., Witton, J., & Murray, R. M. (2004). Causal association between cannabis and psychosis: Examination of the evidence. *The British Journal of Psychiatry, 184,* 110–117. doi:10.1192/bjp.184.2.110

Baigent, M., Holme, G., & Hafner, R. J. (1995). Self reports of the interaction between substance abuse and schizophrenia. *Australasian Psychiatry, 29,* 69–74.

Baker, A., Lewin, T., Reichler, H., Clancy, R., Carr, V., Garrett, R., et al. (2002). Motivational interviewing among psychiatric in-patients with substance use disorders. *Acta Psychiatrica Scandinavica, 106,* 233–240. doi:10.1034/j.1600-0447.2002.01118.x

Baker, A., Bucci, S., Lewin, T. J., Kay-Lambkin, F., Constable, P. M., & Carr, V. J. (2006). Cognitive-behavioural therapy for substance use disorders in people with psychotic disorders randomised controlled trial. *The British Journal of Psychiatry, 188,* 439–448. doi:10.1192/bjp.188.5.439

Baker, A., Thornton, L. K., Hiles, S., Hides, L., & Lubman, D. I. (2012). Psychological interventions for alcohol misuse among people with co-occurring depression or anxiety disorders: A systematic review. *Journal of Affective Disorders, 139,* 217–229. doi:10.1016/j.jad.2011.08.004

Barker, I. (1998). Mental illness and substance misuse. *Mental Health Review, 3,* 6–13.

Barrowclough, C., Emsley, R., Eisner, E., Beardmore, R., & Wykes, T. (2013). Does change in cannabis use in established psychosis affect clinical outcome? *Schizophrenia Bulletin*, *39*, 339–348. doi:10.1136/bmj.c6325

Barrowclough, C., Haddock, G., Fitzsimmons, M., & Johnson, R. (2006). Treatment development for psychosis and co-occurring substance misuse: A descriptive review. *Journal of Mental Health*, *15*, 619–632. doi:10.1080/09638230600998920

Barrowclough, C., Haddock, G., Lowens, I., Allott, R., Earnshaw, P., Fitzsimmons, M., & Nothard, S. (2007). Psychosis and drug and alcohol problems. In A. Baker, & R. Velleman (Eds.), *Clinical handbook of co-existing mental health and drug and alcohol problems* (pp. 241–265). London: Routledge.

Barrowclough, C., Haddock, G., Tarrier, N., Lewis, S. W., Moring, J., O'Brien, R., et al. (2001). Randomized controlled trial of motivational interviewing, cognitive behavior therapy, and family intervention for patients with comorbid schizophrenia and substance use disorders. *American Journal of Psychiatry*, *158*, 1706–1713. doi:10.1176/appi.ajp.158.10.1706

Barrowclough, C., Haddock, G., Wykes, T., Beardmore, R., Conrod, P., Craig, T., et al. (2010). Integrated motivational interviewing and cognitive behavioural therapy for people with psychosis and comorbid substance misuse: Randomised controlled trial. *British Medical Journal*, *341*. doi:10.1136/bmj.c6325

Boden, M. T., & Moos, R. (2013). Predictors of substance use disorder treatment outcomes among patients with psychotic disorders. *Schizophrenia Research*, *146*, 28–33. doi:10.1016/j.schres.2013.02.003

Carrà, G., & Johnson, S. (2009). Variations in rates of comorbid substance use in psychosis between mental health settings and geographical areas in the UK. *Social Psychiatry and Psychiatric Epidemiology*, *44*, 429–447. doi:10.1007/s00127-008-0458-2

Carrà, G., Johnson, S., Bebbington, P., Angermeyer, M. C., Heider, D., Brugha, T., et al. (2012). The lifetime and past-year prevalence of dual diagnosis in people with schizophrenia across Europe: Findings from the European Schizophrenia Cohort (EuroSC). *European Archives of Psychiatry and Clinical Neuroscience*, *262*, 607–616. doi:10.1007/s00406-012-0305-z

Caton, C. L., Patrick, E., Shrout, P. F., Eagle, L. A., Opler, A. F., & Boanerges, D. (1994). Risk factors for homelessness among schizophrenic men: A case-control study. *American Journal of Public Health*, *84*, 265–270. doi:10.1017/S0033291700027835

Chambers, A. R., Krystal, J. H., & Self, D. W. (2001). A neurobiological basis for substance abuse comorbidity in schizophrenia. *Biological Psychiatry*, *50*, 71–83. doi:10.1016/S0006-3223(01)01134-9

Chan, Y., Dennis, M. L., & Funk, R. R. (2008). Prevalence and comorbidity of major internalizing and externalizing problems among adolescents and adults presenting to substance abuse treatment. *Journal of Substance Abuse Treatment*, *34*, 114–124. doi:10.1016/j.jsat.2006.12.031

Cruce, G., Öjehagen, A., & Nordström, M. (2012). Recovery-promoting care as experienced by persons with severe mental illness and substance misuse. *International Journal of Mental Health and Addiction*, *10*, 660–669. doi:10.1007/s11469-011-9363-0

Copello, A., Williamson, E., Orford, J., & Day, E. (2006). Implementing and evaluating Social Behaviour and Network Therapy in drug treatment practice in the UK: A feasibility study. *Addictive Behaviors*, *31*, 802–810. doi:10.1016/j.addbeh.2005.06.005

Cuffel, B. J., Shumway, M., Choujian, T. L., & Macdonald, T. (1994). A longitudinal study of substance use and community violence in schizophrenia. *Journal of Nervous and Mental Disease*, *182*, 704–708. doi:10.1097/00005053-199412000-00005

Degenhardt, L., Hall, W., & Lynskey, M. (2001). Alcohol, cannabis and tobacco use among Australians: A comparison of their associations with other drug use and use disorders, affective and anxiety disorders, and psychosis. *Addiction*, *96*, 1603–1614. doi:10.1046/j.1360-0443.2001.961116037.x

Department of Health. (2002). *Mental health policy implementation guide: Dual diagnosis good practice guide*. London: Department of Health.

Dixon, L. B., Dickerson, F., Bellack, A. S., Bennett, M., Dickinson, D., Goldberg, R. W., et al. (2010). The 2009 schizophrenia PORT psychosocial treatment recommendations and summary statements. *Schizophrenia Bulletin, 36*, 48–70. doi:10.1093/schbul/sbp115

Donoghue, K., & Doody, G. A. (2012). Effect of illegal substance use on cognitive function in individuals with a psychotic disorder: A review and meta-analysis. *Neuropsychology, 26*, 785. doi:10.1037/a0029685

Drake, R. E., Mueser, K. T., Brunette, M. F., & McHugo, G. J. (2004). A review of treatments for people with severe mental illnesses and co-occurring substance use disorders. *Psychiatric Rehabilitation Journal, 27*, 360. doi:10.2975/27.2004.360.374

Drake, R. E., O'Neal, E. L., & Wallach, M. A. (2008). A systematic review of psychosocial research on psychosocial interventions for people with co-occurring severe mental and substance use disorders. *Journal of Substance Abuse Treatment, 34*, 123–138. doi:10.1016/j.jsat.2007.01.011

Fløvig, J. C., Vaaler, A. E., & Morken, G. (2009). Substance use at admission to an acute psychiatric department. *Nordic Journal of Psychiatry, 63*, 113–119. doi:10.1080/08039480802294787

Graham, H. L., Copello, A., Birchwood, M., Orford, J., McGovern, D., Mueser, K. T., et al. (2006). A preliminary evaluation of integrated treatment for co-existing substance use and severe mental health problems: Impact on teams and service users. *Journal of Mental Health, 15*, 577–591. doi:10.1080/09638230600902633

Grant, B. F., Stinson, F. S., Dawson, D. A., Chou, S. P., Dufour, M C., Compton, W., et al. (2004). Prevalence and co-occurrence of substance use disorders and independent mood and anxiety disorders: Results from the National Epidemiologic Survey on Alcohol and Related Conditions. *Archives of General Psychiatry, 61*, 807. doi:10.1001/archpsyc.61.8.807

Green, A., Drake, R., Brunette, M., & Noordsy, D. (2007). Schizophrenia and co-occurring substance use disorder. *American Journal of Psychiatry, 164*, 402–408. doi:10.1176/appi.ajp.164.3.402

Gregg, L., Barrowclough, C., & Haddock, G. (2007). Reasons for increased substance use in psychosis. *Clinical Psychology Review, 27*, 494–510. doi:10.1016/j.cpr.2006.09.004

Haddock, G., Barrowclough, C., Tarrier, N., Moring, J., O'Brien, R., Schofield, N., et al. (2003). Cognitive-behavioural therapy and motivational intervention for schizophrenia and substance misuse: 18-month outcomes of a randomised controlled trial. *The British Journal of Psychiatry, 183*, 418–426. doi:10.1192/bjp.183.5.418

Horsfall, J., Cleary, M., Hunt, G. E., & Walter, G. (2009). Psychosocial treatments for people with co-occurring severe mental illnesses and substance use disorders (dual diagnosis): A review of empirical evidence. *Harvard Review of Psychiatry, 17*, 24–34. doi:10.1080/10673220902724599

Hunt, G. E., Siegfried, N., Morley, K., Sitharthan, T., & Cleary, M. (2013). Psychosocial interventions for people with both severe mental illness and substance misuse. *Cochrane Database of Systematic Reviews, 10*. doi:10.1002/14651858.CD001088.pub3

Kalivas, P. W., & Volkow, N. D. (2005). The neural basis of addiction: A pathology of motivation and choice. *American Journal of Psychiatry, 162*, 1403–1413. doi:10.1176/appi.ajp.162.8.1403

Kavanagh, D. J., & Mueser, K. T. (2007). Current evidence on integrated treatment for serious mental disorder and substance misuse. *Journal of Norwegian Psychological Association, 44*, 618–637.

Kay-Lambkin, F. J., Baker, A. L., Lewin, T. J., & Carr, V. J. (2009). Computer-based psychological treatment for comorbid depression and problematic alcohol and/or cannabis use: A randomized controlled trial of clinical efficacy. *Addiction, 104*, 378–388. doi:10.1111/j.1360-0443.2008.02444.x

Kendler, K. S., Prescott, C. A., Myers, J., & Neale, M. C. (2003). The structure of genetic and environmental risk factors for common psychiatric and substance use disorders in men and women. *Archives of General Psychiatry, 60*, 929. doi:10.1001/archpsyc.60.9.929

Koskinen, J., Löhönen, J., Koponen, H., Isohanni, M., & Miettunen, J. (2009). Prevalence of alcohol use disorders in schizophrenia: A systematic review and meta-analysis. *Acta Psychiatrica Scandinavica, 120*, 85–96. doi:10.1111/j.1600-0447.2009.01385.x

170   ADDICTION: PSYCHOLOGY & TREATMENT

Koskinen, J., Löhönen, J., Koponen, H., Isohanni, M., & Miettunen, J. (2010). Rate of cannabis use disorders in clinical samples of patients with schizophrenia: A meta-analysis. *Schizophrenia Bulletin, 36*, 1115–1130. doi:10.1093/schbul/sbp031

Kuepper, R., Morrison, P. D., van Os, J., Murray, R. M., Kenis, G., & Henquet, C. (2010). Does dopamine mediate the psychosis-inducing effects of cannabis? A review and integration of findings across disciplines. *Schizophrenia Research, 121*, 107–117. doi:http://dx.doi.org/10.1016/j.schres.2010.05.031

Lobban, F., Barrowclough, C., Jeffery, S., Bucci, S., Taylor, K., Mallinson, S., et al. (2010). Understanding factors influencing substance use in people with recent onset psychosis: A qualitative study. *Social Science & Medicine, 70*, 1141–1147. doi:10.1016/j.socscimed.2009.12.026

MacAulay, R., & Cohen. A. S. (2013). Affecting coping: Does neurocognition predict approach and avoidant coping strategies within schizophrenia spectrum disorders? *Psychiatry Research, 209*, 136–141. doi:10.1016/j.psychres.2013.04.004

Madigan, K., Brennan, D., Lawlor, E., Kinsella, A., Russel, V., et al. (2013). A multi-center, randomized controlled trial of a group psychological intervention for psychosis with comorbid cannabis dependence over the early course of illness. *Schizophrenia Research, 143*, 138–142. doi:10.1016/j.schres.2012.10.018

Margolese, H. C., Malchy, L., Negrete, J. C., Tempier, R., & Gill, K. (2004). Drug and alcohol use among patients with schizophrenia and related psychoses: Levels and consequences. *Schizophrenia Research, 67*, 157–166. doi:10.1016/S0920-9964(02)00523-6

Marlatt, G. A., & Donovan, D. M. (Eds.). (2005). *Relapse prevention: Maintenance strategies in the treatment of addictive behaviors* (2nd ed.). New York: Guilford Press.

McCleery, A., Addington, J., & Addington, D. (2006). Substance misuse and cognitive functioning in early psychosis: A 2 year follow-up. *Schizophrenia Research, 88*, 187–191. doi:10.1016/j.schres.2006.06.040

Merikangas, K. R., Angst, J., Eaton, W., Canino, G., Rubio-Stipec, M., Wacker, H., et al. (1996). Comorbidity and boundaries of affective disorders with anxiety disorders and substance misuse: Results of an international task force. *The British Journal of Psychiatry Supplement, 30*, 58–67.

Miller, W. R., & Rollnick, S. (2012). *Motivational interviewing: Preparing people for change*. New York: Guilford Press.

Moore, T. H. M., Zammit, S., Lingford-Hughes, A., Barnes, T. R. E., Jones, P. B., Burke, M., & Lewis, G. (2007). Cannabis use and risk of psychotic or affective mental health outcomes: A systematic review. *The Lancet, 370*, 319–328. doi:10.1016/S0140-6736(07)61162-3

Morojele, N. K., Saban, A., & Seedat, S. (2012). Clinical presentations and diagnostic issues in dual diagnosis disorders. *Current Opinion in Psychiatry, 25*, 181–186. doi:10.1097/YCO.0b013e328351a429

Mueser, K. T., Drake, R. E., Sigmon, S. C., & Brunette, M. F. (2005). Psychosocial interventions for adults with severe mental illnesses and co-occurring substance use disorders: A review of specific interventions. *Journal of Dual Diagnosis, 1*, 57–82. doi:10.1300/J374v01n02_05

Mueser, K. T., Drake, R. E., & Wallach, M A. (1998). Dual diagnosis: A review of etiological theories. *Addictive Behaviors, 23*(6), 717–734.

Mueser, K. T., Glynn, S. M., Cather, C., Xie, H., Zarate, R., Fox Smith, L., et al. (2013). A randomized controlled trial of family intervention for co-occurring substance use and severe psychiatric disorders. *Schizophrenia Bulletin, 39*, 658–672. doi:10.1093/schbul/sbr203

Najt, P., Fusar-Poli, P., & Brambilla, P. (2011). Co-occurring mental and substance abuse disorders: A review on the potential predictors and clinical outcomes. *Psychiatry Research, 186*, 159–164. doi:10.1016/j.psychres.2010.07.042

National Statistics. (2015a). *Adult drinking habits in Great Britain*. Newport: ONS.

National Statistics. (2015b). *Drug misuse: Findings from the 2014/15 crime survey for England and Wales*. Newport: ONS.

NICE (National Institute for Health and Care Excellence) (2011). *Psychosis with coexisting substance misuse: Assessment and management in adults and young people.* CG120. http://www.nice.org.uk/nicemedia/live/13414/53729/53729.pdf

Noordsy, D. L., McQuade, D. V., & Mueser, K.T. (2003). Assessment considerations. In H. L. Graham, A. Copello, M. J. Birchwood, & K. T Mueser (Eds.), *Substance misuse in psychosis: Approaches to treatment and service delivery* (pp. 159–181). Chichester: John Wiley & Sons, Ltd.

Orford, J. (2008). [Commentary] Joining the queue of dissenters. *Addiction, 103,* 706–707. doi:10.1111/j.1360-0443.2007.02128.x

Regier, D. A., Farmer, M. E., Rae, D. S., Locke, B. Z., Keith, S. J., Judd, L. L., & Goodwin, F. K. (1990). Comorbidity of mental disorders with alcohol and other drug abuse. *Journal of the American Medical Association, 264,* 2511–2518. doi:dx.doi.org/10.1001/jama.1990.03450190043026

Richardson, T. H. (2013). Substance misuse in depression and bipolar disorder: A review of psychological interventions and considerations for clinical practice. *Mental Health and Substance Use, 6,* 76–93. doi:dx.doi.org/10.1080/17523281.2012.680485

Rössler, W., Hengartner, M. P., Angst, J., & Ajdacic-Gross, V. (2012). Linking substance use with symptoms of subclinical psychosis in a community cohort over 30 years. *Addiction, 107,* 1174–1184. doi:dx.doi.org/10.1111/j.1360-0443.2011.03760.x

Royal College of Psychiatrists. (2014). *One new drug a week: Why novel psychoactive substances and club drugs need a different response from UK treatment providers.* London: Faculty of Addictions Psychiatry, Royal College of Psychiatrists.

Schmidt, L. M., Hesse, M., & Lykke, J. (2011). The impact of substance use disorders on the course of schizophrenia: A 15-year follow-up study: Dual diagnosis over 15 years. *Schizophrenia Research, 130,* 228–233. doi:dx.doi.org/10.1016/j.schres.2011.04.011

Trull, T. J., Sher, K. J., Minks-Brown, C., Durbin, J., & Burr, R. (2000). Borderline personality disorder and substance use disorders: A review and integration. *Clinical Psychology Review, 20,* 235–253. doi:dx.doi.org/10.1016/S0272-7358(99)00028-8

UK Drug Policy Commission Consensus Group. (2008). *A vision of recovery.* London: UK Drug Policy Commission.

Veilleux, J. C., Colvin, P. J., Anderson, J., York, C., & Heinz, A. J. (2010). A review of opioid dependence treatment: Pharmacological and psychosocial interventions to treat opioid addiction. *Clinical Psychology Review, 30,* 155–166. doi:dx.doi.org/10.1016/j.cpr.2009.10.006

Weaver, T., Madden, P., Charles, V., Stimson, G., Renton, A., Tyrer, P., et al. (2003). Comorbidity of substance misuse and mental illness in community mental health and substance misuse services. *The British Journal of Psychiatry, 183,* 304–313. doi:dx.doi.org/10.1192/bjp.183.4.304

Welch, K. A., McIntosh, A. M., Job, D. E., Whalley, H. C., Moorhead, T. W., Hall, J., et al. (2011). The impact of substance use on brain structure in people at high risk of developing schizophrenia. *Schizophrenia Bulletin, 37,* 1066–1076. doi:dx.doi.org/10.1093/schbul/sbq013

11 Substance Misuse in Older Adults

SARAH WADD[1] AND TONY RAO[2]

[1]Substance Misuse and Ageing Research Team (SMART), University of Bedfordshire, Luton, UK
[2]Psychiatry Department, South London and Maudsley NHS Foundation Trust, London, UK

CHAPTER OUTLINE

11.1   INTRODUCTION

Older adults are a culturally and socially diverse population that range from the healthy, employed and active to the frail, incapacitated and institutionalized. However, multiple biological, psychological and social changes that accompany the ageing process mean that older adults have needs that require special consideration in terms of substance misuse. This chapter describes the extent and nature of substance misuse in older adults, and how practice can be adapted to meet their needs.

11.2   DEFINITION OF OLDER ADULT

There is no standard definition for 'older adult' in the research literature, but the cut-off is generally 40–50 years for illicit drug misuse, and 50–65 years for other substance misuse. This cut-off is relatively low for two reasons. First, there is a belief that some people with chronic substance misuse problems age prematurely, therefore their needs may be similar to people aged 65 and over, even in middle age. Second, using lower cut-off points means that more people with substance misuse problems fall into the 'older' age category, providing sufficient numbers to justify substance misuse programmes, or services, specifically for this age group.

However, there are also a number of disadvantages to using low age cut-offs. They create even more heterogeneity in what is already a diverse group; most substance users do not age prematurely, and the majority of people in their forties and fifties do not consider themselves to be an 'older person'. Here we use 65 and over as the cut-off, unless stated otherwise.

11.3   ALCOHOL

11.3.1   Extent and Nature of Alcohol Use and Misuse

A number of large nationwide surveys in Great Britain collect information on alcohol use and misuse in people living in private households. These surveys enable drinking behaviour in older adults to be compared with that of younger adults, and as they are repeated on a regular basis, the data can be examined for trends. Table 11.1 shows some of the most relevant findings from the General Lifestyle Survey (GLS; Office for National Statistics, 2013), the Psychiatric Morbidity Survey (PMS; NHS Information Centre, 2009) and the Opinions Survey (Lader & Steel, 2009).

The data from these surveys suggests that older adults drink less than younger adults and are less likely to misuse alcohol. Surveys in other countries have reported similar findings (Hajema, Knibbe, & Drop, 1997; Ramstedt & Hope, 2005; Grant et al., 2006; Hallgren, Hogberg & Andreasson, 2009). This is likely to be due to a combination of factors. For example, physical changes associated with ageing tend to reduce

Table 11.1 *Data on alcohol use and misuse in older adults from household surveys in Great Britain*

Behaviour	Prevalence/ amount in older adults (65+)	Compared to younger adults (16–64)	Trends for 65+ age group	Survey
Had alcoholic drink in past week	63% of men and 42% of women	Less likely, although older men more likely to have drunk in past week than men aged 16–24	Small reduction in men (3%) and women (1%) since 2005	GLS 2011
Average weekly alcohol consumption	12.5 units for men and 4.6 units for women	Lower than for any other age group for men and women	Small reduction in men (0.9 units) and women (0.5 units) since 2005	GLS 2010
Exceeding the recommended weekly drink limits	20% of men and 9% of women	Lower than for any other age group for men and women	1% reduction for both men and women since 2005	GLS 2010
Alcohol dependence	3.0% of men and 0.6% of women aged 65–74; 0.5% of men and 0% of women aged 75+[1]	Lower than for any other age group for both men and women.	Earlier data not comparable.	PMS 2007
Binge drinking in past week	6% of men and 2% of women	Lower than for any other age group	No change for men or women since 2005	GLS 2011
Drinking every day in past week	17% of men and 9% of women	Higher than for any other age group	Data not available	GLS 2011
Drank at home on heaviest drinking day in past week	55% of men and 64% of women	Higher than for any other age group	Data not available	Opinions 2009
Drank alone on heaviest drinking day in past week	16% of men and 20% of women	Higher than for any other age group	Data not available	Opinions 2009

Note: [1] Figures should be treated with caution due to small sample size.

the amount that people can comfortably consume, therefore they generally drink less as they get older (an ageing effect); the present generation of older adults have always drunk less and they have carried that level of drinking into old age (a cohort effect); and, the earlier death of heavier drinkers leaves behind lighter drinking survivors, who generally continue this lighter drinking as they age (Poikolainen, 1995; Fillmore et al., 1998; Leino et al., 1998).

The surveys also provide important information about the way that older adults use alcohol. Older adults are more likely to drink alcohol on a daily basis, perhaps because they have more time to spare than younger adults, or because they have fewer work or family responsibilities. This is a concern, because daily use can induce tolerance and may be a sign that an older person is using alcohol to cope with negative emotional states. One study found that older adults often report feeling depressed, bored or lonely prior to consuming their first drink of the day (Schonfeld & Dupree, 1991). Older adults are also more likely to drink at home alone, and this means that alcohol problems are less likely to be noticed by friends or family, individuals have to set their own boundaries for acceptable levels of consumption, and drinks poured at home are often much larger than those measured in pubs.

11.3.2   *Onset of Alcohol Misuse*

Some older adults develop an alcohol problem for the first time in later life (Adams, Garry, Rhyne, Hunt & Goodwin, 1990; Liberto, Oslin & Ruskin, 1992; Johnson, Gruenewald, Treno & Taff, 1998; Moore, Endo & Carter, 2003; Moos, Brennan, Schutte & Moos, 2005). Known as 'late-onset' problem drinkers, this group make up approximately one-third of older adults with alcohol problems (Dufour & Fuller, 1995; Mellor et al., 1996). 'Early-onset' problem drinkers comprise the remaining two-thirds, and are individuals who develop an alcohol problem earlier in life and have continued problem drinking in old age. The late onset age cut-off is not standard in the literature, varying between 40 and 65 years.

A number of differences between early and late onset problem drinkers have been identified (see Table 11.2). These differences are important for two main reasons. First, they show that late-onset problem drinkers have fewer alcohol-related problems than early-onset drinkers, therefore professionals frequently overlook their drinking because they appear too healthy or 'normal' to raise suspicion (Nemes et al., 2007). Second, they show that early-onset drinkers have a longer history of misuse, higher levels of consumption, higher frequency of alcohol-related problems and depleted social resources, suggesting that they may require both more intense and longer periods of treatment.

11.3.3   *Circumstances that Can Lead to Increased Alcohol Use and Misuse*

Studies have found that some older adults increase their drinking, or develop alcohol problems, in response to losses, life changes and transitions that are associated with the ageing process (Rosin & Glatt, 1971; Zimberg, 1974; Ekerdt, deLabry, Glynn & Davis, 1989; Brennan, Moos & Mertens, 1994; Brennan & Moos, 1996; Goldstein, Pataki & Webb, 1996; Kirchner, et al., 2007; St. John, Montgomery & Tyas, 2009; Moos, Brennan, Schutte & Moos, 2010). These include loss of a loved one through bereavement, loss of friends and social status, loss of occupation, loss of independence, more time and opportunity to drink, loneliness and boredom, chronic pain, caregiving responsibilities and altered financial circumstances. The extent to which these

Table 11.2 *Comparison of characteristics and early and late onset problem drinkers*

Characteristic	Early onset	Late onset	Reference
Alcohol consumption	Higher	Lower	(Brennan & Moos, 1991; Schonfeld, et al., 1987; Wetterling, Veltrup, John & Driessen, 2003)
Alcohol-related problems	More	Fewer and less severe	(Brennan & Moos, 1991; Liberto & Oslin, 1995; Wetterling et al., 2003)
Alcohol dependence	More likely	Less likely	(Brennan & Moos, 1991; Wetterling et al., 2003)
Binge drinking	More likely	Less likely	(Watson et al., 1997; Wetterling et al., 2003)
Social resources	Fewer	More	(Brennan & Moos, 1991; Liberto & Oslin, 1995)
Psychiatric comorbidity	More likely	Less likely	(Atkinson, Turner, Kofoed & Tolson, 1985; Liberto & Oslin, 1995; Wetterling et al., 2003)
Family history of alcohol problems	More likely	Less likely	(Atkinson, Tolson & Turner, 1990; Atkinson et al., 1985; Liberto & Oslin, 1995; Wetterling et al., 2003)
Life satisfaction	Poorer	Greater	(Schonfeld et al., 1987)
Treatment prognosis	Poorer	Better	(Atkinson et al., 1990; Wetterling et al., 2003)

stressors influence late-life drinking appears to depend on a variety of factors including their severity (Schonfeld & Dupree, 1991), social resources and coping responses (Brennan & Moos, 1996).

11.4   ILLICIT DRUG USE

11.4.1   *Extent and Nature of Illicit Drug Use*

In contrast to alcohol, there is a paucity of data on illicit drug use in older adults from nationwide surveys in the UK. The main source of data for younger adults is the British Crime Survey, but this survey excludes people aged 60 and over as an 'economy measure, reflecting their very low prevalence rates for the use of prohibited drugs' (Home Office, 2013).

The Scottish Crime and Justice Survey has no upper age cut-off, and in 2010–2011, of the 3,793 people aged 60 and over who gave information about illicit drug use, only 3.7% reported ever having used illicit drugs, 0.2% had used them in the last year and 0.1% had used them in the last month (The Scottish Government, 2012). There is some data on illicit drug use among older adults in England from the 2007 Psychiatric Morbidity Survey (NHS Information Centre, 2009), however, estimates of prevalence derived from this dataset should be treated with caution due to the small sample size of older adults. Our analysis of this data found that of the 1,978 people aged 65 and over, 7 people (0.4%) had used cannabis in the past year, 5 (0.3%) had used magic mushrooms, and 1 person had used crack (0.05%).

The European Monitoring Centre for Drugs and Drug Addiction (EMCDDA) carried out an analysis of data on previous year cannabis use among Europeans aged 45–54 and found that England and Wales had levels of use in this population which were above the European average (EMCDDA, 2010). In the United States, 2007–2009 data from the National Survey on Drug Use and Health found that 2.3% of those aged 60 and over had misused medications or used illicit drugs in the past year and 1.1% had used cannabis (Substance Abuse and Mental Health Services Administration, 2011).

There is evidence that the prevalence of illicit drug use is increasing in older age groups in Europe. An analysis of Psychiatric Morbidity Survey data from 1993, 2000 and 2007 found that the lifetime use of cannabis, amphetamine, cocaine and LSD in 50–64-year-olds in England has increased significantly since 1993 (Fahmy, Hatch, Hotopf & Stewart, 2012). Other European countries, including France, Germany and Spain, also report increasing prevalence of past year cannabis use in older age groups (EMCDDA, 2010).

Older drug users have high levels of physical and mental morbidity and hepatitis C infection (Hser et al., 2004; Roe, Beynon, Pickering & Duffy, 2010), poor quality of life (Roe et al., 2010), high levels of loneliness, stress and fear of victimization (Levy & Anderson, 2005; Beynon, Roe, Duffy & Pickering, 2009), and they often experience injecting-related vein damage that can lead to riskier injecting practices (Beynon et al., 2009).

11.4.2   *Onset of Illicit Drug Use*

While it is thought that the majority of drug problems in older adults have an early onset (Simoni-Wastila & Yang, 2006), there are occasional reports of late-onset problematic drug use in the literature (Nambudiri & Young, 1991; Kouimtsidis & Padhi, 2007; Sterk & Elifson, 2008; Beynon et al., 2009; Boeri, Roe et al., 2010), and our analysis of data from the 2007 Psychiatric Morbidity Survey found that 8/35 (23%) of people aged 50 and over who had ever used cannabis, said that they first used the drug after the age of 40.

11.4.3   *Circumstances that Can Lead to Late-Onset Drug Use*

The few cases of late-onset illicit drug use in the literature were attributed to stressful life events such as divorce or bereavement, close personal relationships with a drug user (Roe et al., 2010), or a reduction in motivations for controlling use such as raising of children or work responsibilities (Boeri et al., 2008). Kouimtsidis and Padhi (2007) describe a case of a man who had contact with several out-patient and in-patient psychiatric and specialist addiction teams in England. He had no history of alcohol or other substance misuse until he was introduced to cocaine by a sex worker at the age of 68 years with the aim of enhancing his sexual performance. The use of cocaine escalated to daily use, and at the age of 70 he started using crack and very rapidly became dependent.

11.5   MEDICATION MISUSE

11.5.1   *Extent and Nature of Medication Misuse*

The two main classes of prescription drugs subject to misuse are benzodiazepines (primarily used for the treatment of anxiety and sleep disorders) and opioid analgesics. Therapeutic dose dependence is the largest category of people dependent on benzodiazepines (Simoni-Wastila & Yang, 2006) and these drugs can result in physiologic dependency in as little as two months (Woods & Winger, 1995). Older adults are at an increased risk of benzodiazepine dependence, and are more sensitive to the adverse effects such as memory problems, daytime sedation, impaired motor coordination, and increased risk of motor vehicle accidents and falls (Madhusoodanan & Bogunovic, 2004). Adverse effects on cognition can be mistaken for the effects of old age. Withdrawal from benzodiazepines can be life-threatening.

Opioid analgesics can produce a sense of euphoria and well-being and have the potential to produce physical and psychological dependency. Some drugs containing low doses of opioids such as codeine are available without a prescription (over-the-counter medication). The risk of addiction to opioid analgesics is low in individuals without a previous history of substance misuse (Fishbain, Cole, Lewis, Rosomoff & Rosomoff, 2008). Although withdrawal from these drugs is uncomfortable, it is not potentially life-threatening, or particularly dangerous compared with benzodiazepine withdrawal (Simoni-Wastila & Yang, 2006).

Older adults receive the highest proportion of the prescription medication dispensed in the United Kingdom (Royal College of Psychiatrists, 2011), therefore they may have greater exposure to medications with potential for misuse. One estimate suggests that up to 40% of people in care homes are prescribed benzodiazepines (Reav, 2009). There is very little national level data on medication misuse among older adults in the United Kingdom. The 2007 Adult Psychiatric Morbidity Survey found that 9 of 1,978 (0.5%) people aged 65 and over had used tranquillizers in the last 12 months and of these, three people were showing signs of dependence (NHS Information Centre, 2009). However, tranquillizers include non-addictive antipsychotics as well as benzodiazepines. Data from England's National Drug Monitoring System in 2009–2010 found that 16% (32,510) of people in drug treatment services reported medication misuse, but data was not reported by age group (National Treatment Agency of Substance Misuse, 2011). There is very little information on the prevalence of medication misuse in older adults from other countries. One study in the United States estimated that 11% of women aged 60 years and over misuse psychoactive prescription medications each year (National Center on Addiction and Substance Abuse, 1998), while another found that 1.4% of community-living adults aged 50 and over reported misusing prescription analgesics during the previous year (Blazer & Wu, 2009).

Medication misuse by older adults is usually unintentional, and the term 'involuntary addiction' is used by some to describe the type of drug dependence which has occurred through medications taken initially to treat a medical condition (and often under medical supervision) but on which the patient has subsequently become dependent (Reav, 2009).

11.5.2   Onset of Medication Misuse

While no data are available on the age at which older adults who misuse medication first developed the problem, the fact that many will have first started using these drugs later in life suggests that a large proportion of these cases are late onset.

11.5.3   Risk Factors for Medication Misuse in Older Adults

Risks factors for medication misuse in older adults are thought to include female sex, social isolation, poor health and chronic illness, polypharmacy, previous history of substance misuse and a previous history of psychiatric illness (Simoni-Wastila & Yang, 2006).

11.6   ASSESSMENT OF OLDER PEOPLE WITH SUBSTANCE MISUSE

The guidance offered below is taken from the author's (TR) clinical practice, supported by evidence-based practice and guidelines (including NICE, 2010, 2011) on managing alcohol problems.

11.6.1   Principles of Assessment

The assessment of older people with substance misuse should incorporate a range of knowledge, skills and attitudes acquired from both addiction and older people's mental health services. Older people have immense life experience and have often encountered both improvements and setbacks in their lives from substance misuse. Past experiences need to be acknowledged and acted upon, as they will contribute to both assessment and treatment. The approach taken should be non-judgemental, with individual choice and maintenance of dignity being paramount.

More attention is required in regulating the flow of the assessment according to need, with special consideration for comfort. The assessor should be aware of other considerations such as sensory impairment, clouding of consciousness, problems with understanding and communication, as well as underlying cognitive impairment.

More often than not, presentations are atypical, compounded by the likelihood of under-reporting as a consequence of denial, stigma, lack of awareness or memory impairment. It is for this reason that any additional information from other sources can contribute considerably to the assessment process. The final care plan will differ from younger people in that it will have a greater emphasis on physical co-comorbidity and functional status, as well as on the influence of loss events and changes in social support such as retirement, bereavement and social isolation. It is helpful to build up a clinical picture over more than one assessment.

11.6.2   Systematic Assessment

The comprehensive assessment of an older person with substance misuse needs to include the following areas:

- covering substances individually (i.e. alcohol / nicotine / over-the-counter / prescribed / illicit), including preferred substance;
- age at first use, weekend, weekly and daily use; age at any dependence syndrome;
- maximum use (age and duration); pattern (quantity / frequency) over day / week; route of administration;
- cost / 'funding';
- treatment (age, service uses, intervention, outcome); abstinence / relapse and link to stability / life events;
- past and family history of mental health;
- occupational and psychosexual history;
- medical history (especially known complications from substance and effects and chronic pain);
- forensic history (especially public order, acquisitive offences and drink driving);
- risk of falls, social / cultural isolation, financial and other elder abuse;
- activities of daily living, statutory / voluntary / private care;
- social support from informal carers and friends (including family conflict and caring roles);
- social pressures from debt, substance-using 'carers', open drug dealing.

Collateral information is invaluable and includes a number of possible sources such as: relatives, friends and informal carers (taking account of information sharing and confidentiality); General Practitioners; hospital discharge summaries; home carer reports; day centre reports; reports from housing officers / wardens of supported housing; criminal justice agencies; and results from previous investigations (including cognitive testing and neuroimaging).

11.6.3   Identifying Substance Misuse

Identifying substance misuse requires the ability to detect the acute and chronic effects of substances; these include intoxication, overdose, withdrawal and dependence. In older people, attention to physical co-morbidity is essential. Physical disorders such as hypertension, diabetes mellitus and disorders are more common in older than younger people and substances may exacerbate the consequences of these disorders. A high degree of vigilance over interactions with prescribed and over-the-counter medication should be observed.

Many barriers exist in the detection of substance misuse. For example, ageism may result in overlooking presentations with sleep and appetite disturbance and attributing these to 'growing old'. Older people may also under-report their substance misuse as a consequence of stigma and shame. Signs of substance misuse such as lack of energy and changes in mood may be misattributed to depression or physical illness.

A higher threshold for detection may occur from stereotyping, such as overlooking substance misuse in older women. Older people may experience alcohol-related problems at low levels of alcohol use due to physiological changes associated with ageing, physical disorders, functional impairment or interactions with medications.

It is crucial that clinicians are particularly vigilant when circumstances that can lead to substance misuse (described previously) are identified. When taking a history, it is common for service users to have multiple interacting problems; these also frequently present atypically, such as behavioural problems rather than typical withdrawal symptoms. Problems more commonly encountered in older people are instability and falls, incontinence, cognitive impairment and problems associated with poor nutrition. Assessments are also more challenging than in younger people, due to the greater length of time required and care taken to examine sight, hearing, and language deficits.

CASE STUDY 11.1   MR BE

Mr BE, a 77-year-old widowed construction worker, was referred to a community old age psychiatry team by his General Practitioner (GP) following concerns over anxiety and increased preoccupation with his own health and finances. He had attended his GP practice on six occasions over the previous three months, complaining of feeling 'not quite right'. A diagnosis of depressive disorder was made by the community team and he was followed up in his own home. There was little response to antidepressant treatment and he was admitted on three separate occasions for in-patient assessment over the next 18 months, during which his mood improved within a few days of admission and no clear physical precipitants or associations were found. There were also no abnormalities on a routine blood screen. At a home visit following his third admission, a chance enquiry was made about alcohol intake and he then reported that he had been drinking at least one bottle of whisky per week since his wife died 5 years previously. A brief intervention was delivered, and further visits used a motivational interviewing framework to assess readiness to change drinking behaviour. BE was discharged 6 months later, at which point he had been abstinent for 3 months. No further referrals were made to the community mental health team.

11.6.4 Screening and Identification

Screening tools for substance misuse can be incorporated into any general approach to the assessment of health and well-being, but those used for identifying substance misuse in older people are currently restricted to alcohol misuse, as there are no validated instruments for detecting other substance misuse in an older population. The CAGE questionnaire (Ewing, 1984) screens for the core features of alcohol dependence, but is relatively insensitive to harmful/hazardous drinking. The most widely used age-specific screening tool, the Short Michigan Alcoholism Screening Test – Geriatric version (SMAST-G; Blow, Gillespie, Barry, Mudd & Hill, 1998) has been validated for use in older hospital in-patients. It asks questions related to problems more commonly seen in older people such as, 'drinking after a significant loss' or 'to take your mind off your problems'.

The 10-question Alcohol Use Disorders Identification Test (AUDIT; Saunders, Aasland, Babor & Grant, 1993) is the best evaluated alcohol screening tool available. The tool focuses on the early signs of increasing and high-risk drinking. Modifications of the AUDIT have also been validated in older populations. These include the AUDIT-5, a five-item version of the full AUDIT (Piccinelli et al., 1997) and the AUDIT-C, which asks only the three alcohol consumption questions of the full AUDIT (Bush, Kivlahan, McDonnell, Fihn & Bradley, 1998). It should be noted that older people may show a lower threshold for identifying alcohol misuse. For example, lowering the threshold to ≥5 (instead of 8) for the AUDIT and ≥4 (instead of 5) for the AUDIT-C improves the sensitivity in detecting hazardous drinking (Aalto, Alho, Halme & Seppä, 2011). Given a lack of specific screening tools for alcohol problems in older people, such tools need to be combined with quantity/ frequency measures and a comprehensive assessment that covers use, misuse and dependence.

11.6.5 Mental State Examination

The commonest presentations of substance misuse in older people are delirium (acute confusional state), mood disorders (depression and anxiety), cognitive impairment and psychotic symptoms. Delirium is commonly associated with intoxication or withdrawal of substances, and its recognition in acute hospital settings is especially important, given the association with high morbidity and mortality and potential treatability.

Those at risk before, or in, the earliest stages of withdrawal require appropriate detoxification plans and nutritional support. In the case of alcohol withdrawal, Wernicke's encephalopathy may be missed and may also present with signs of delirium, so prompt detection and treatment with high dose thiamine are essential. Low mood and anxiety may accompany the misuse of a range of substances, particularly alcohol, sedatives and hypnotics. It is not uncommon to find an atypical presentation of symptoms suggestive of a mood disorder. These include being 'masked' by cognitive impairment or 'somatized' by presenting as physical symptoms such as lack of energy.

Accompanying physical problems may make the detection of depression and anxiety more difficult, particularly some biological symptoms of depression, such as lack of energy, which are also associated with many physical disorders, such as arthritis. The detection of mood disorders then relies on cognitive and behavioural symptoms, such as poor concentration, pessimism, suicidal ideation and irritability. The assessment of alcohol misuse is particularly important in older people at risk of suicide, where alcohol misuse often accompanies the worsening of depressive symptoms and lowers impulse control in the suicidal act itself.

Cognitive impairment associated with alcohol misuse may present with alcohol-related brain injury (see Morrison & Svanburg, Chapter 7 in this volume), such as is seen with amnestic disorders confined to memory impairment, or with alcohol-related dementia, where there is a global loss of cognitive function that involves language and visuospatial problems. In either case, screening cognitive function using a tool covering a range of cognitive domains such as the mini-mental state examination (MMSE; Folstein, Folstein & McHugh, 1975) is required.

However, the MMSE does not assess frontal lobe function, which is known to be more sensitive than other brain areas to the initial effects of alcohol toxicity (Zahr, Kaufman, & Harper, 2011). If a more comprehensive assessment of cognitive function is required, the Addenbrooke's Cognitive Examination offers such a screen (Mioshi, Dawson, Mitchell, Arnold, & Hodges, 2006).

Psychotic symptoms can be associated with the acute effects of a variety of substances such as cannabinoids, stimulants and hallucinogens. Withdrawal states accompanying alcohol or sedatives/hypnotics are also commonly associated with transient psychotic symptoms.

11.6.6 *Physical Examination*

There are particular areas in the physical examination that need to be covered to ensure a comprehensive assessment. These include general frailty, self-care, gait and balance, tar staining of the fingers and hair, signs of chronic liver disease, signs of injected drug misuse, poor nutrition (e.g. gum disease), breathing problems from tobacco and cannabis misuse, high blood pressure from smoking or alcohol misuse, and effects of substances on the nervous system, such as cerebellar syndrome and peripheral neuropathy.

Functional status should cover both personal and instrumental (domestic) activities of daily living (ADLs), complemented by an account of a typical day. Most assessment scales cover a variety of set functions, such as in the Barthel Index (Mahoney, 1965).

11.6.7 *Referral to Other Services*

It is common for older people with substance misuse to be assessed and treated in both parallel and sequential patterns within services. The appropriate referral to other services is central to improving the quality of care, patient experience, reducing harm and improving health and social outcomes. Within such a model of integrated care, it is essential that there is a lead service with a defined care coordinator or equivalent. A wide range of services need to work together, these include: geriatrics, old age psychiatry, addictions, psychology, primary and social care.

11.7 PSYCHOSOCIAL INTERVENTIONS

There are a number of psychosocial interventions that can benefit both those older people with whom there is the potential for opportunistic assessment and brief advice, or else those who have substance dependence. This latter group often also have complex needs and should be offered specialist treatment in an addiction services.

Empirical data on which interventions work best with older people are limited, but it is generally acknowledged that empirically supported treatments in adults can be successfully applied to the treatment of older people (Kalapatapu, Paris, & Neugroschl, 2010).

11.7.1 Brief Advice

Brief advice can be effective for hazardous drinkers. It has been shown to reduce the mean amount of alcohol consumed and the number of episodes of binge drinking per week (Fleming et al., 2000). It can take many forms, such as, brief feedback about drinking based on the AUDIT score, or in an information leaflet. It may also be extended into the FRAMES structure (Miller, 1996). The FRAMES structure adopts a systematic approach that also draws upon internal resources and comprises the following features:

- personalized **F**eedback on risk and harm;
- emphasis on personal **R**esponsibility for change;
- **A**dvice to the patient to make a change in drinking behaviour;
- a **M**enu of alternative strategies for making a change;
- an **E**mpathic and non-judgemental approach;
- an attempt to increase **S**elf-efficacy or confidence in being able to change behaviour.

11.7.2 Motivational Interviewing

Motivational interviewing (MI) is a person-centred counselling style for addressing the common problem of ambivalence about change, based on existing techniques, such as active listening, summarizing and reflection (Miller & Rollnick, 2013; and see also Dutheil & Galis, Chapter 16 in this volume).

MI differs from previous approaches that were based on confronting denial and breaking down resistance through confronting, challenging and persuading. The

MI approach takes into account the presence of denial and ambivalence to changing drinking behaviour using the development of insight through the affirmation of positive changes. The key to MI is a motivational shift that leads to behavioural change.

11.7.3 Supporting Families and Carers

When faced with alcohol problems in a family member, other family members typically take a long time to identify a problem and to seek the help that they need (AdFam, 2013; and see Copello and Walsh, Chapter 3 in this volume).

There remains limited support available to the families of older alcohol users as well as a general lack of awareness of how to support them in dealing with age-specific problems, such as financial insecurity, retirement, lack of social integration and activities, bereavement, social isolation and depression in older people. These risks are compounded by a loss of mobility and poor physical health.

Families may have difficulties in identifying exactly how much older people drink (as mentioned previously). However, there is much that families can do to improve the quality of life in an older person, particularly as there is evidence that the concerns of family members and friends are the most common factor motivating older people to seek treatment for alcohol problems (Finlayson, Hurt, Davis & Morse, 1988), and that obtaining help from family members and friends has been shown to lower the likelihood of alcohol-related problems in older drinkers (Moos, Schutte, Brennan & Moos, 2004).

Families can also help with harm reduction in improving diet, being vigilant over possible drug interactions and supporting advice from practitioners on sensible drinking.

11.8 LEGAL AND ETHICAL CONSIDERATIONS

11.8.1 Mental Capacity

In the UK, the Mental Capacity Act 2005 (Lord Chancellor, 2007) states that a person lacks capacity in relation to a matter if he/she is unable to make a decision for himself in relation to a matter because of an impairment of, or a disturbance in the functioning of, the mind or brain. Also implicit in this definition is the fact that such capacity may change over time.

The complexity of problems associated with substance use in older people means that there are particular risks around capacity, particularly when there is conflict between capacity and the role of practitioner in encouraging the older person to give up substance misuse (Hazelton, Sterns & Chisholm, 2003). This is especially relevant, given that one of the core features of dependence syndromes is the persistence of substance misuse in spite of being aware of the harm from the substance being taken. Using the core feature of harm awareness, an assessment of mental capacity in substance misuse may therefore help to distinguish unwise decisions from a lack of mental capacity *per se*.

11.8.2   Elder Abuse

Elder abuse is defined by the World Health Organization (2002) as, 'a single or repeated act or lack of appropriate action occurring within any relationship where there is an expectation of trust, which causes harm or distress to an older person or violates their human and civil rights'. Substance abuse is more likely to occur in the perpetrators of the abuse compared with the person suffering abuse (Anetzberger, 2005). In those perpetrators with a health problem, heavy consumption of alcohol or drug substances is not uncommon (O'Keefe et al., 2007), this may even extend to care settings, where theft from care staff to fund substance misuse may occur (Griffore et al., 2009). Victims who are female, have a neurological or mental disorder, and abuse drugs or alcohol are at highest risk of elder abuse (Friedman, Avila, Tanouye & Joseph, 2011).

11.8.3   Mental Health Act

The 1983 Mental Health Act (amended 2007) applies to England and Wales. It states that dependence on alcohol and drugs is not considered, under the Act, to be a disorder or disability of the mind. In other words, people of any age cannot be detained under the Act on the basis of substance dependence alone. However, detention may be applicable if a person with substance dependence has a co-existing mental disorder. In the case of older people, this may typically be depression or alcohol-related brain injury.

A similar approach has been adopted by the Mental Health (Care and Treatment) Act 2003 in Scotland and the Mental Health Act (2001) in Ireland. However, it may still be appropriate to consider the Mental Capacity Act as the least restrictive framework under which to act in the patient's best interest.

11.9   USING AND EVALUATING HEALTH AND SOCIAL OUTCOMES

Outcome measures for substance misuse must be psychometrically sound (valid, reliable and sensitive to change), practical, cover both alcohol and drug use and be multi-dimensional, also assessing different domains of alcohol and drug use, and include physical and emotional functioning. Only one scale covers all of these areas, this being the Health of the National Outcome Scale (HoNOS; Wing et al., 1998) which is commonly used across a variety of mental health settings. It includes a single item on 'problem drinking and drug taking', in which the interviewer is asked to rate the severity of alcohol or drug misuse in the 12 days prior to admission on a five-point scale, ranging from 0–4.

Although HoNOS recording is mandatory in some mental health Trusts, completion of the drug and alcohol item remains patchy (Bell et al., 2013). The other outcomes instrument with potential utility is the Outcomes Star, a tool for supporting and measuring change. The original Outcomes Star was developed in the United Kingdom for the homelessness sector (Burns, Graham & McKeith, 2006), with more recent versions including separate Stars for drug and alcohol use (developed by Triangle Consulting Social Enterprise Limited with NORCAS (Norfolk Community Alcohol and Drug Services)) and older people (developed by Triangle Consulting Social Enterprise Limited with service providers and commissioners from Camden, Westminster, Brent and Hammersmith and Fulham Borough Councils).

This has ten outcome areas; drug use, alcohol use, physical health, meaningful use of time, community engagement, emotional health, accommodation, money, offending and family & relationships. The underlying model of change covers the areas of being stuck, accepting help, believing, learning and self-reliance. For the older people's Outcomes Star, the areas covered are staying as well as you can (physical and mental health), keeping in touch (use of time and social networks), feeling positive (motivation and managing change), being treated with dignity (choice and control), looking after yourself (self-care and mobility), staying safe (safety), and managing money (economic well-being). The model of change focuses on re-enablement, as well as maximizing independence and well-being.

There remains considerable scope for assessing the potential utility of combining the original Outcomes Star with that for drug and alcohol in older people.

11.10   CONCLUSION

While older adults are a diverse population, the biological, psychological and social changes associated with ageing mean that they have shared needs that require special consideration in terms of substance misuse. Evidence suggests that substance misuse may be less common in older adults, but age-related physiological changes mean that they are particularly susceptible to substance misuse-related harm. Substance misuse may occur for the first time in old age, often due to stresses associated with ageing, such as bereavement and loneliness.

Under-reporting is common and collateral information is important. During assessment, there should be an emphasis on physical functioning and functional status, as well as age-related factors that may have led to, or compounded the substance misuse. It is generally acknowledged that psychosocial interventions that are used with younger adults can also be used with older adults, but they may need adapting to meet their age-related needs.

SUGGESTIONS FOR FURTHER READING

Royal College of Psychiatrists. (2011). *Our invisible addicts*. London: Royal College of Psychiatrists. http://www.rcpsych.ac.uk/usefulresources/publications/collegereports/cr/cr165.aspx

Wadd, S., & Galvani, S. (2014). The forgotten people: Drug problems in later life. Luton: Tilda Goldberg Centre for Social Work and Social Care, University of Bedfordshire. Available at: http://www.biglotteryfund.org.uk/-/media/Files/Research%20Documents/Older%20People/the_forgotten_people.pdf

Wadd, S., Lapworth, K., Sullivan, M., Forrester, D., & Galvani, S. (2011). Working with older drinkers. Luton: Tilda Goldberg Centre for Social Work and Social Care, University of Bedfordshire. http://alcoholresearchuk.org/downloads/finalReports/FinalReport_0085

REFERENCES

Aalto, M., Alho, H., Halme, J. T., & Seppä, K. (2011). The alcohol use disorders identification test (AUDIT) and its derivatives in screening for heavy drinking among the elderly. *International Journal of Geriatric Psychiatry*, 26, 881–885. doi:10.1002/gps.2498

Adams, W. L., Garry, P. J., Rhyne, R., Hunt, W. C., & Goodwin, J. S. (1990). Alcohol intake in the healthy elderly: Changes with age in a cross-sectional and longitudinal study. *Journal of the American Geriatric Society*, 38, 211–216. doi:10.1111/j.1532-5415.1990.tb03493.x

AdFam. (2013). Keeping it in the family. *Families Up Front*, 10, 6–7. Available at: http://www.adfam.org.uk/cms/fuf/doc/Adfam_Families_UpFront_Issue_10.pdf

Anetzberger, G. J. (2005). The reality of elder abuse. *Clinical Gerontologist*, 28, 1–25. doi:10.1300/J018v28n01_01

Atkinson, R. M., Tolson, R. L., & Turner, J. A. (1990). Late versus early onset problem drinking in older men. *Alcoholism: Clinical and Experimental Research*, 14, 574–579. doi:10.1111/j.1530-0277.1990.tb01203.x

Atkinson, R. M., Turner, J. A., Kofoed, L. L., & Tolson, R. L. (1985). Early versus late onset alcoholism in older persons: Preliminary findings. *Alcoholism: Clinical and Experimental Research*, 9, 513–515. doi:10.1111/j.1530-0277.1985.tb05594.x

Bell, J., Kilic, C., Prabakaran, R., Wang, Y. Y., Wilson, R., Broadbent, M., & Curtis, V. (2013). Use of electronic health records in identifying drug and alcohol misuse among psychiatric in-patients. *The Psychiatrist*, 37, 15–20. doi:10.1192/pb.bp.111.038240

Beynon, C. M., Roe, B., Duffy, P., & Pickering, L. (2009). Self-reported health status, and health service contact, of illicit drug users aged 50 and over: A qualitative interview study in Merseyside, United Kingdom. *BMC Geriatrics*, 9, 45. doi:10.1186/1471-2318-9-45

Blazer, D. G., & Wu, L. (2009). Nonprescription use of pain relievers by middle-aged and elderly community-living adults: National Survey on Drug Use and Health. *Journal of the American Geriatrics Society*, 57, 1252–1257. doi:10.1111/j.1532-5415.2009.02306.x

Blow, F. C., Gillespie, B. W., Barry, K. L., Mudd, S. A., & Hill, E. M. (1998). Brief screening for alcohol problems in elderly populations using the Short Michigan Alcoholism Screening Test-Geriatric Version (SMAST-G). *Alcoholism: Clinical and Experimental Research*, 22, 54.

Boeri, M. W., Sterk, C. E., & Elifson, K. W. (2008). Reconceptualizing early and late onset: A life course analysis of older heroin users. *Gerontologist*, 48, 637–645. doi:10.1093/geront/48.5.637

Brennan, P. L., & Moos, R. H. (1991). Functioning, life context, and help-seeking among late-onset problem drinkers: Comparisons with nonproblem and early-onset problem drinkers. *British Journal of Addiction*, 86, 1139–1150. doi:10.1111/j.1360-0443.1991.tb01882.x

Brennan, P. L., & Moos, R. H. (1996). Late-life problem drinking: Personal and environmental risk factors for 4-year functioning outcomes and treatment seeking. *Journal of Substance Abuse, 8,* 167–180. doi:10.1016/S0899-3289(96)90227-8

Brennan, P. L., Moos, R. H., & Mertens, J. R. (1994). Personal and environmental risk factors as predictors of alcohol use, depression, and treatment-seeking: A longitudinal analysis of late-life problem drinkers. *Journal of Substance Abuse, 6,* 191–208. doi:10.1016/S0899-3289(94)90217-8

Burns, S., Graham, K., & MacKeith, J. (2006). *The outcomes star.* London: Triangle Consulting and the London Housing Foundation.

Bush, K., Kivlahan, D. R., McDonell, M. B., Fihn, S. D., & Bradley, K. A. (1998). The AUDIT alcohol consumption questions (AUDIT-C): An effective brief screening test for problem drinking. *Archives of Internal Medicine, 158,* 1789. doi:10.1001/archinte.158.16.1789

Dufour, M., & Fuller, R. K. (1995). Alcohol in the elderly. *Annual Review of Medicine, 46,* 123–132. doi:10.1146/annurev.med.46.1.123

Ekerdt, D. J., deLabry, L. O., Glynn, R. J., & Davis, R. (1989). Change in drinking behaviours with retirement: Findings from the normative ageing study. *Journal of Studies on Alcohol, 50,* 347–353.

EMCDDA (European Monitoring Centre for Drugs and Drug Addiction). (2010). *Treatment and care of older drug users.* Lisbon: European Monitoring Centre for Drugs and Drug Addiction.

Ewing, J. A. (1984). Detecting alcoholism: The CAGE questionnaire. *JAMA: The Journal of the American Medical Association, 252,* 1905–1907. doi:10.1001/jama.1984.03350140051025

Fahmy, V., Hatch, S. L., Hotopf, M., & Stewart, R. (2012). Prevalences of illicit drug use in people aged 50 years and over from two surveys. *Age and Ageing, 41,* 556. doi:10.1093/ageing/afs020

Fillmore, K. M., Golding, J. M., Graves, K. L., Kniep, S., Leino, E. V., Romelsjo, A., et al. (1998). Alcohol consumption and mortality III: Studies of female populations. *Addiction, 93,* 219–229. doi:10.1046/j.1360-0443.1998.9322196.x

Finlayson, R., Hurt, R., Davis, L., & Morse, R. (1988). Alcoholism in elderly persons: A study of the psychiatric and psychosocial features of 216 inpatients. *Mayo Clinic Proceedings, 63,* 761–768.

Fishbain, D. A., Cole, B., Lewis, J., Rosomoff, H. L., & Rosomoff, R. S. (2008). What percentage of chronic nonmalignant pain patients exposed to chronic opioid analgesic therapy develop abuse/addiction and/or aberrant drug-related behaviors? A structured evidence-based review. *Pain Medicine, 9,* 444–459. doi:10.1111/j.1526-4637.2007.00370.x

Fleming, M. F., Mundt, M. P., French, M. T., Manwell, L. B., Stauffacher, E. A., & Barry, K. L. (2000). Benefit-cost analysis of brief physician advice with problem drinkers in primary care settings. *Medical Care, 38,* 7–18. doi:10.1097/00005650-200001000-00003

Folstein, M. F., Folstein, S. E., & McHugh, P. R. (1975). 'Mini-mental state': A practical method for grading the cognitive state of patients for the clinician. *Journal of Psychiatric Research, 12,* 189–198. doi:10.1016/0022-3956(75)90026-6

Friedman, L. S., Avila, S., Tanouye, K., & Joseph, K. (2011). A case-control study of severe physical abuse of older adults. *Journal of the American Geriatrics Society, 59,* 417–422. doi:10.1111/j.1532-5415.2010.03313.x

Goldstein, M. Z., Pataki, A., & Webb, M. T. (1996). Alcoholism among elderly persons. *Psychiatric Services (Washington, D.C.), 47,* 941–943.

Grant, B. F., Dawson, D. A., Stinson, F. S., Chou, S. P., Dufour, M. C., & Pickering, R. P. (2006). The 12-month prevalence and trends in DSM-IV alcohol abuse and dependence: United States, 1991–1992 and 2001–2002. *Drug and Alcohol Dependence, 74,* 223–234. doi:10.1016/j.drugalcdep.2004.02.004

Griffore, R. J., Barboza, G. E., Mastin, T., Oehmke, J., Schiamberg, L. B., & Ann Post, L. (2009). Family members' reports of abuse in Michigan nursing homes. *Journal of Elder Abuse & Neglect, 21,* 105–114. doi:10.1080/08946560902779910

Hajema, K. J., Knibbe, R. A., & Drop, M. J. (1997). Changes in alcohol consumption in a general population in The Netherlands: A 9-year follow-up study. *Addiction, 92,* 49–60. doi:10.1111/j.1360-0443.1997.tb03637.x

Hallgren, M., Hogberg, P., & Andreasson, S. (2009). Alcohol consumption among elderly European Union citizens: Health effects, consumption trends and related issues. Paper presented at the Expert Conference on Alcohol & Health, 21–22 September 2009, Stockholm, Sweden. https://www.researchgate.net/publication/234057043_Alcohol_consumption_among_elderly_European_Union_citizens_Health_effects_consumption_trends_and_related_issues

Hazelton, L. D., Sterns, G. L., & Chisholm, T. (2003). Decision-making capacity and alcohol abuse: Clinical and ethical considerations in personal care choices. *General Hospital Psychiatry, 25*, 130–135. doi:10.1016/S0163-8343(03)00005-7

Home Office. (2013). *User guide to drug misuse: Findings from the crime Survey for England and Wales.* London: Home Office.

Hser, Y. I., Gelberg, L., Hoffman, V., Grella, C. E., McCarthy, W., & Anglini, M. D. (2004). Health conditions among aging narcotics addicts: Medical examination results. *Journal of Behavioural Medicine, 27*, 622. doi:10.1007/s10865-004-0005-x

Johnson, F. W., Gruenewald, P. J, Treno, A. J., & Taff, G. A. (1998). Drinking over the life course within gender and ethnic groups: A hyperparametric analysis. *Journal of Studies on Alcohol and Drugs, 59*, 568–580. doi:10.15288/jsa.1998.59.568

Kalapatapu, R. K., Paris, P., & Neugroschl, J. A. (2010). Alcohol use disorders in geriatrics. *The International Journal of Psychiatry in Medicine, 40*, 321–337. doi:10.2190/PM.40.3.g

Kirchner, J. E., Zubritsky, C., Cody, M., Coakley, E., Hongtu, C., Ware, J. H., et al. (2007). Alcohol consumption among older adults in primary care. *Journal of General Internal Medicine, 22*, 92–97. doi:10.1007/s11606-006-0017-z

Kouimtsidis, C., & Padhi, A. (2007). A case of late-onset dependence on cocaine and crack. *Addiction, 102*, 666–667. doi:10.1111/j.1360-0443.2007.01757.x

Lader, D., & Steel, M. (2009). *Drinking: Adults' Behaviour and Knowledge in 2009.* Newport: Office for National Statistics.

Leino, E. V., Romelsjo, A., Shoemaker, C., Ager, C. R., Allebeck, P., Ferrer, H. P., et al. (1998). Alcohol consumption and mortality II: Studies of male populations. *Addiction, 93*, 205–218. doi:10.1046/j.1360-0443.1998.9322055.x

Levy, J. A., & Anderson, T. (2005). The drug career of the older injector. *Addiction Research and Theory, 13*, 245–258. doi:10.1080/16066350500053

Liberto, J. G., & Oslin, D. W. (1995). Early versus late onset of alcoholism in the elderly. *Substance Use and Misuse, 30*, 1799–1818. doi:10.3109/10826089509071056

Liberto, J. G., Oslin, D. W., & Ruskin, P. E. (1992). Alcoholism in older persons: A review of the literature. *Hospital & Community Psychiatry, 43*, 975–984. doi:10.1176/ps.43.10.975

Lord Chancellor. (2007). The Mental Capacity Act, 2005. https://www.gov.uk/government/collections/mental-capacity-act-making-decisions

Madhusoodanan, S., & Bogunovic, O. J. (2004). Safety of benzodiazepines in the geriatric population. *Expert Opinion on Drug Safety, 3*, 485–493. doi:10.1517/14740338.3.5.485

Mahoney, F. I. (1965). Functional evaluation: The Barthel Index. *Maryland State Medical Journal, 14*, 61–65.

Mellor, M. J., Garcia, A., Kenny, E., Lazerus, J., Conway, J. M., Rivers, L., & Viswanathan, N. (1996). Alcohol and aging. *Journal of Gerontological Social Work, 25*, 71–89. doi:10.1300/J083V25N01_06

Mental Health (Care and Treatment) (Scotland) Act, 2003. http://www.legislation.gov.uk/asp/2003/13/

Mental Health Act 1983, amended 2007. www.legislation.gov.uk/ukpga/2007/12/…/ukpgaen_20070012_en.pdf

Mental Health Act, Ireland 2001. Available at: Mental Health Act, 2001, Irish Statute Book www.irishstatutebook.ie/2001/en/act/pub/0025/

Miller, W. R. (1996). Motivational interviewing: Research, practice, and puzzles. *Addictive Behaviors, 21*, 835–842. doi:10.1016/0306-4603(96)00044-5

Miller, W. R., & Rollnick, S. (2013). *Motivational interviewing: Preparing people for change*. New York: Guilford Press.

Mioshi, E., Dawson, K., Mitchell, J., Arnold, R., & Hodges, J. R. (2006). The Addenbrooke's Cognitive Examination Revised (ACE-R): A brief cognitive test battery for dementia screening. *International Journal of Geriatric Psychiatry*, 21, 1078–1085. doi:10.1002/gps.1610

Moore, A. A., Endo, J. O., & Carter, M. K. (2003). Is there a relationship between excessive drinking and functional impairment in older persons? *Journal of the American Geriatric Society*, 51, 44–49. doi:10.1111/j.1465-3362.2010.00271.x

Moos, R. H., Brennan, P. L., Schutte, K. K., & Moos, B. S. (2005). Older adults' health and changes in late-life drinking patterns. *Aging and Mental Health*, 9, 49–59. doi:10.1080/13607860412331323818

Moos, R. H., Brennan, P. L., Schutte, K. K., & Moos, B. S. (2010). Older adults' health and late-life drinking patterns: A 20-year perspective. *Aging & Mental Health*, 14, 33–43. doi:10.1080/13607860902918264

Moos, R. H., Schutte, K., Brennan, P., & Moos, B. S. (2004). Ten-year patterns of alcohol consumption and drinking problems among older women and men. *Addiction*, 99, 829–838. doi:10.1111/j.1360-0443.2004.00760.x

Nambudiri, D. E., & Young, R. C. (1991). A case of late-onset crack dependence and subsequent psychosis in the elderly. *Journal of Substance Abuse Treatment*, 8, 253–255. doi:10.1016/0740-5472(91)90047-E

National Center on Addiction and Substance Abuse. (1998). *Under the rug: Substance abuse and the mature woman*. New York: Columbia University Press.

National Treatment Agency of Substance Misuse. (2011). *Addiction to medicine*. London: National Treatment Agency. http://www.nta.nhs.uk/uploads/addictiontomedicinesmay2011a.pdf

Nemes, S., Weil, J., Zeiler, C., Munly, K., Holtz, K., & Hoffman, J. (2007). Alcohol and substance abuse among older adults. In R. Yoshida (Ed.), *Trends in alcohol abuse and alcoholism research*. New York: Nova Science Publishers Inc.

NHS Information Centre. (2009). *Adult psychiatric morbidity in England 2007: Results of a household survey*. London: Health & Social Care Information Centre. http://www.hscic.gov.uk/pubs/psychiatricmorbidity07

NICE (National Institute for Health and Care Excellence). (2010). *Alcohol-use disorders: Diagnosis and clinical management of alcohol-related physical complications*. CG100. https://www.nice.org.uk/guidance/cg100

NICE (National Institute for Health and Care Excellence). (2011). *Alcohol-use disorders: Diagnosis, assessment and management of harmful drinking and alcohol dependence*. CG115. https://www.nice.org.uk/guidance/cg115

Office for National Statistics. (2013). *Drinking: General Lifestyle Survey overview: A report on the 2011 GLS*. London: Office for National Statistics.

O'Keefe, M., Hills, A., Doyle, M., McCreadie, C., Scholes, S., Constantine, R., et al. (2007). *UK study of abuse and neglect of older people: Prevalence survey report*. London: National Centre for Social Research.

Piccinelli, M., Tessari, E., Bortolomasi, M., Piasere, O., Semenzin, M., Garzotto, N., & Tansella, M. (1997). Efficacy of the alcohol use disorders identification test as a screening tool for hazardous alcohol intake and related disorders in primary care: A validity study. *British Medical Journal*, 314, 420. doi:10.1136/bmj.314.7078.420

Poikolainen, K. (1995). Alcohol and mortality: A review. *Journal of Clinical Epidemiology*, 48, 455–465. doi:10.1016/0895-4356(94)00174-O

Ramstedt, M., & Hope, A. (2005). The Irish drinking habits of 2002: Drinking and drinking-related harm in a European comparative perspective. *Journal of Substance Use*, 10, 273–283. doi:10.1080/14659890412331319443

Reav, G. (2009). *An inquiry into physical dependence and addiction to prescription and over-the-counter medication.* London: All-Party Parliamentary Drugs Misuse Group. http://seroxatusergroup.org.uk/parliamentary-drugs-misuse-OTC.pdf

Roe, B., Beynon, C., Pickering, L., & Duffy, P. (2010). Experiences of drug use and ageing: Health, quality of life, relationship and service implications. *Journal of Advanced Nursing, 66,* 1968–1979. doi:10.1111/j.1365-2648.2010.05378.x

Rosin, A. J., & Glatt, M. M. (1971). Alcohol excess in the elderly. *Quarterly Journal of Studies on Alcohol, 32,* 53–59.

Royal College of Psychiatrists. (2011). *Our invisible addicts.* London: Royal College of Psychiatrists. http://www.rcpsych.ac.uk/usefulresources/publications/collegereports/cr/cr165.aspx

Saunders, J. B., Aasland, O. G., Babor, T. F., & Grant, M. (1993). Development of the alcohol use disorders identification test (AUDIT): WHO collaborative project on early detection of persons with harmful alcohol consumption II. *Addiction, 88,* 791–804. doi:10.1111/j.1360-0443.1993.tb02093.x

Schonfeld, L., & Dupree, L. W. (1991). Antecedents of drinking for early- and late-onset elderly alcohol abusers. *Journal of Studies on Alcohol and Drugs, 52,* 587–592. doi:http://dx.doi.org/10.15288/jsa.1991.52.587

Schonfeld, L., et al. (1987). Alcohol abuse and the elderly: Comparison of early & late-life onset. Paper presented at the 95th Annual Convention of the American Psychological Association, New York, August 28–September 1, 1987. http://eric.ed.gov/?id=ED287135

Simoni-Wastila, L., & Yang, H. K. (2006). Psychoactive drug abuse in older adults. *American Journal of Geriatric Pharmacotherapy, 4,* 380–394. doi:10.1016/j.amjopharm.2006.10.002

St. John, P. D., Montgomery, P. R., & Tyas, S. L. (2009). Alcohol misuse, gender and depressive symptoms in community-dwelling seniors. *International Journal of Geriatric Psychiatry, 24,* 369–375. doi:10.1002/gps.2131

Substance Abuse and Mental Health Services Administration. (2011). *National survey on drug use and health report: Illicit drug use amongst older adults.* London: Substance Abuse and Mental Health Services Administration.

The Scottish Government. (2012). *2010/11 Scottish crime and justice survey: Drug use.* Edinburgh: The Scottish Government. http://www.gov.scot/Publications/2012/03/2775

Watson, C. G., Hancock, M., Gearhart, L. P., Malovrh, P., Mendez, C., & Raden, M. (1997). A comparison of the symptoms associated with early and late onset alcohol dependence. *The Journal of Nervous and Mental Disease, 185,* 509. doi:10.1097/00005053-199708000-00005

Wetterling, T., Veltrup, C., John, U., & Driessen, M. (2003). Late onset alcoholism. *European Psychiatry, 18,* 112–118. doi:10.1016/S0924-9338(03)00025-7

Wing, J. K., Beevor, A. S., Curtis, R. H., Park, S. B., Hadden, S., & Burns, A. (1998). Health of the Nation Outcome Scales (HoNOS): Research and development. *The British Journal of Psychiatry, 172,* 11–18. doi:10.1192/bjp.172.1.11

Woods, J. H., & Winger, G. (1995). Current benzodiazepine issues. *Psychopharmacology, 118,* 107–115. doi:10.1007/BF02245824

World Health Organization (WHO). (2002). *Missing voices: Views of older persons on elder abuse.* Geneva: World Health Organization.

Zahr, N. M., Kaufman, K. L., & Harper, C. G. (2011). Clinical and pathological features of alcohol-related brain damage. *Nature Reviews Neurology, 7,* 284–294. doi:10.1038/nrneurol.2011.42

Zimberg, S. (1974). Two types of problem drinkers: Both can be managed. *Geriatrics, 29,* 135–136.

12 Issues Arising in Hepatitis C Work: The Role of the Clinical Psychologist

JO M. NICHOLSON

Sheffield Teaching Hospitals, Sheffield, UK

CHAPTER OUTLINE

12.1   INTRODUCTION

This chapter is intended to provide psychologists with an introduction to the issues that arise in working with people with Hepatitis C infection. It is acknowledged that the focus and conceptualization of the psychology role presented here are influenced by the setting in which the author works (an acute treatment hospital). While an attempt has been made to provide salient information for all psychologists, the location of the author's work means there is an emphasis on issues arising primarily in this setting. However, the research, arguments and approach should still provide a useful dialogue to highlight the issues that can arise, regardless of service setting.

12.2   HEPATITIS C BACKGROUND: THE VIRUS AND TREATMENT

Hepatitis C Virus (HCV) is a blood-borne virus which primarily affects the liver. Chronic infection is estimated to affect 215,000 people in the UK (Public Health England, 2013a). HCV infection can lead to scarring of the liver, and ultimately cirrhosis. In addition, national data indicates that rates of admissions and deaths from HCV-related end-stage liver disease and hepatocellular carcinoma are rising (Public Health England, 2013a).

The majority of HCV infection is concentrated in marginalized groups, with injecting drug use being the major risk factor for HCV infection in the UK. The prevalence of HCV infection for people who inject drugs (PWID) has recently been surveyed at 49% England, 34% Northern Ireland, 33% Wales and 53% Scotland (Public Health England, 2013b). There is currently no vaccine for HCV, but effective curative treatments are available.

Significant change in treatment options in the last year have seen the introduction of the first direct-acting antiviral (DAA) of the class protease inhibitors (PI) (see USA Food and Drug Administration, 2014). These new treatments have brought parity of curative response rate between the different HCV genotypes. Genotype refers to the classification of the virus based on genetic material in the RNA (ribonucleic acid) strands. Different genotypes have different treatment response rates.

Most of the UK infection is genotype 1 (G1) and genotype 3 (G3) with a smaller but significant number having genotype 2 (G2). The standard treatment is 16–24 weeks of Pegylated Interferon and Ribavirin for G2 and G3, and 48 weeks for G1. Standard treatment curative response rates are up to 80% for G2 and G3, and 40% for G1. The newly licensed DAAs are effective for G1 and are prescribed in addition to the existing regime of Pegylated Interferon and Ribavirin with complex dosing schedules (referred to as 'triple therapy'). Resistance to PI caused by mutation of the virus can develop easily with triple therapy if adherence is not maintained, but adding a PI has the potential to shorten treatment for G1 to 24–28 weeks and increases curative response rates to up to 80%. Clinical factors such as fibrosis score, Body Mass Index

(BMI), presence of cirrhosis, co-infection with Human Immunodeficiency Virus (HIV), and demographic factors such as ethnicity and gender, influence response for most treatment regimes (see NICE, 2004).

While effective curative treatment exists, enabling patient cohorts to access treatment presents significant challenges that will become apparent over the course of the chapter. It is relevant at this point to consider that the majority of treatment for HCV continues to be provided within acute hospital settings. Typically treatment is provided in either an Infectious Diseases or a Hepatology Department. There are some good practice examples of community-based treatment initiatives in the United Kingdom, but these do not necessarily overcome the barriers to access.

12.3   SOCIAL AND CLINICAL CHARACTERISTICS OF THE HCV PATIENT POPULATION

The majority of patients that present to a HCV treatment service have complex social and psychological vulnerabilities. Around 90% of the patient cohort in a HCV treatment setting will either be current drug users, or have a history of intravenous drug use. There are also significant numbers from ethnic minority immigrant groups whose mode of transmission is frequently contaminated blood products or medical devices. This means the majority of those infected are from socially disadvantaged and excluded populations.

Disadvantage is compounded by high levels of psychiatric co-morbidity in the PWID population. This impacts on access rates not only to physical health care but also substance misuse services. A study by Weaver et al. (2003) examined co-morbidity rates across UK community mental health teams and substance misuse services. They found the high rates of psychiatric co-morbidity in substance misuse services (75% of drug service and 85% of alcohol service). Importantly, they observed that most co-morbid patients appeared ineligible for cross-referral between services and that high proportions of patients were not identified and received no specialist intervention for the co-morbid problem. The implication is that many HCV-infected patients presenting in treatment settings will have elevated levels of mental health needs, and many will not have been assessed or treated for these specific needs.

A number of research studies demonstrate that prevalence rates for depression are significantly elevated within the HCV population, with rates of between 24% and 70% (Lee, Jamal, Regenstein & Perrillo, 1997; Weissenborn et al., 2004; Lang et al., 2006). Furthermore, there is some evidence suggesting that HCV affects the central nervous system (CNS) both directly and indirectly. For example, there is evidence for reduced dopamine, serotonin transporter binding (Weissenborn et al., 2006), alterations in electroencephalogram (EEG) activity of HCV-infected patients (Montagnese et al., 2005), and with a general inflammatory process in the CNS similar to HIV(Forton, Allsop, Foster, Thomas & Taylor-Robinson, 2001; Cacciarelli, Martinez, Gish,

Villanueva & Krams, 1996). There is evidence of a significant (negative) impact on quality of life in HCV patients, merely through diagnosis of infection (Rodger, Jolley, Thompson, Lanigan & Crofts, 1999), and quality of life is reduced regardless of presence of cirrhosis (Foster, 2009) that improves after curative treatment (Ware, Bayliss, Mannocchia & Davis, 1999).

The longer people are infected, the greater the impact on mental well-being and coping. Rates of depression are associated with duration since initial HCV diagnosis (Kraus, Schäfer, Csef, Scheurlen & Faller, 2000) and with greater fatigue (Weissenborn et al., 2004). Coping behaviours are also shown to change over time. For those infected for more than 5 years, when compared to those infected for less than 5 years, there is reduced problem-solving behaviour, distraction, self-revalorization, more 'depressive coping' and cognitive avoidance dissimulation (Kraus et al., 2000). According to these authors, patients who are not offered treatment as an option have a greater risk of depression than those on a treatment pathway.

12.4   HCV TREATMENT CHALLENGES

There are multiple treatment challenges for HCV treatment that are relevant to consider. The standard treatment with Pegylated Interferon and Ribavirin has a range of adverse side-effects including physical symptoms (i.e. anaemia, neutropaenia, fatigue, rash and flu-like symptoms) and psychiatric symptoms (i.e. depression, suicidal agitation, psychosis). Both physical and psychiatric side-effects are chiefly transient to the treatment episode with full recovery at treatment cessation. Pegylated Interferon is the key agonist for psychiatric side-effects, with the mechanism hypothesized as having pro-inflammatory cytokine effects that have known associations with depression and anxiety. This can lead to discontinuation, or dose reduction, of Pegylated Interferon which in turn can compromise therapeutic response rates (see NICE, 2004; 2010).

The NICE Guidance for treatment of HCV is heavily medically focused (NICE 2004; 2010). This is despite acknowledgement of the complex psycho-social needs of the HCV population presenting significant challenges in administration of medical procedures. NICE guidance (2004) states that a 'severe psychiatric condition' is a contraindication for Ribavirin (which runs contrary to the evidence that Pegylated Interferon is the known psychoactive agent). It also fails to define the term 'severe psychiatric condition', or to specify management strategies for arising psychiatric problems.

In the author's experience, many acute medical services do not treat currently injecting drug users, and are generally reticent to treat those with other active illicit drug use. Similarly, patients who have high levels of alcohol use are not seen as good treatment candidates, often due to adherence issues, but also to the potential futility of prevention of liver disease. It should be noted that Pegylated Interferon and Ribavirin have few drug-drug interactions and this would include interactions with most illicit drugs.

The majority of the side-effects for the new direct-acting antiviral drugs are physical. However, they have high drug-drug interactions, making concurrent illicit drug use extremely problematic and potentially very dangerous due to risk of potentiating toxicity.

12.5   PEGYLATED INTERFERON-RELATED ADVERSE PSYCHIATRIC SIDE-EFFECTS

The association between Pegylated Interferon treatment and neuropsychiatric side-effects (i.e. depression, anxiety, agitation, sleep disturbance, cognitive deficit) is well documented (see NICE, 2004; 2010). However, interpreting the evidence regarding incidence rates presents many challenges. The majority of studies suffer from significant methodological issues. The following overview of research presents key papers and evidence that are pertinent to psychologists working in the area.

Most studies investigating the incidence of psychological side-effects do not consider the severity of the presenting symptoms. This latter point is important because severity and new presentations of psychiatric symptoms carry the highest risk for treatment discontinuation and risk to the individual patient. For instance, most authors fail to differentiate between depression and low mood, or to include cut-offs for identification of clinical depression. The most robust studies, which use clinician-administered interview, find an incidence of depression during Interferon treatment of between 15% and 17% (Lee et al., 1997; Raison et al., 2007).

Most studies focus on the incidence of depression, even though some studies suggest anxiety occurs with equal frequency. Only a small number of studies report incidence rates for psychosis, irritability and suicidal behaviour, although these are also known adverse side-effects of Pegylated Interferon treatment. An Italian study by Fattovich, Giustina, Favarato and Ruol (1996), with a sample of over 900 HCV patients, found reports of new presentations of psychosis in 0.9%, and suicide attempts by 0.02%.

In the past, concerns about psychiatric side-effects have acted as a barrier to treatment access for people with a history of mental health problems. The implicit assumption was that this patient group would have a higher risk of adverse psychiatric side-effects. However, emerging consensus indicates that individual risk is extremely difficult to predict. Raison, Demetrashvili, Capuron and Miller (2005) argue that past history of substance abuse, gender, age, HCV genotype and prior history of depression are *not* reliably associated with depression during treatment. But this statement is not universally shared (see, e.g. Schaefer & Schulz, 2008). The strongest evidence suggests that the best predictive factor for increased risk of adverse psychiatric side-effects is presence of depressive symptoms at the time of treatment initiation. This includes 'sub-syndromal' depressive symptoms and is regardless of prior history of formal clinical diagnosis (Raison et al., 2005).

There is additional evidence we can use to build a coherent picture of needs and potential points for psychological intervention while in treatment. There is a relatively predictable timeline for onset of common psychiatric side-effects (Constant et al., 2005; Dan et al., 2006), generally within three months of treatment initiation. Most patients who develop depression show symptoms within the first four to eight weeks. Furthermore, duration of treatment elevates rates of depression, and depression can intensify over time.

Early identification and management of psychiatric side-effects are extremely important. Pegylated Interferon-related depression and anxiety symptoms can usually be managed quickly and effectively with anti-depressant or anxiolytic medications. These medications reduce symptom levels very quickly, suggesting a different mechanism of action than typical depressive presentations. In the author's experience, talking therapies act as an additional support to help the person maintain motivation, adhere to treatment and promote positive coping. It is only in the absence of timely support, or in the face of severe psychiatric reactions, that dose reduction or discontinuation of HCV treatment needs to be considered.

There is significant literature that explores prophylactic use of antidepressants in 'at risk' patients (see, e.g. Al-Omari, Cowan, Turner & Cooper, 2013; Ehret & Sobieraj, 2014). In the United States, prophylactic use has also been extended to whole treatment cohorts and this is promoted as a management strategy. It is not possible within the constraints of this chapter to cover this literature adequately. However, the research findings in this area are varied, there are ethical issues of prescribing medications that are not indicated by clinical presentation, and there are common methodological flaws across studies.

12.6   HCV-INFECTED MENTAL HEALTH POPULATIONS

Data from the United States and Australia show that psychiatric populations have increased prevalence rates of HCV, with inpatient rates estimated at between 3.2% and 6.7% (Cividini et al., 1997; Gunewarde, Lampe, & Ilchef, 2010). Despite this increased prevalence, as already outlined, concerns about psychiatric side-effects have commonly acted as a barrier for patients with known psychiatric diagnosis. Due to the side-effects profile, most patients with known psychiatric problems have been excluded from Pegylated Interferon trials, and there is a lack of robust data about the effects of Pegylated Interferon on patients with pre-existing mental health problems. However, since the majority of patients with HCV have complex psychosocial needs, including high rates of psychiatric co-morbidity, exclusion on this basis is not a workable model for practice.

Although severe psychiatric condition is a contraindication for treatment, there are consensus statements recommending treatment on at least a case-by-case basis through comprehensive integrated programmes of care (see, e.g. National Institute of Health: Consensus Statement on Management of Hepatitis C, 2002, from the United States). Sylvestre et al. (2004) conclude that patients with co-morbid psychiatric illness can complete Pegylated Interferon treatment as long as careful monitoring and timely intervention are provided. They recommend that interventions for psychiatric conditions are integrated to treatment algorithms, but comment that few programmes are designed to manage such co-morbidity.

Evidence that may reduce concerns about elevated risk, and support the need for better treatment access for patients with psychiatric disorders, is growing. A number of studies demonstrate that patients with known psychiatric disorder can be effectively treated without significant detriment to adherence, curative response rates, or increased prevalence of psychiatric side-effects (Schaefer et al., 2003; Knott et al., 2006; Schaefer, 2009).

A few key studies examine the impact of different models of mental health provision for patient outcomes in HCV treatment. Knott et al. (2006) found that integrated psychiatric care led to improved treatment access rates and increased adherence for patients with pre-existing psychiatric problems. This study found that patients with parallel mental health care (including addiction services) had better treatment adherence rates than patients with no co-morbid needs. They also found that patients accessing the integrated co-located psychiatric nurse specialist were more likely to access and complete treatment compared to patients accessing external mental health provision. Patients receiving any mental health support had improved rate of HCV treatment access and adherence compared to patients refusing psychiatric referral.

Conversely, Guillemard et al. (2009) found that systematic psychiatric consultation had no significant impact on frequency and intensity of depression, treatment discontinuation, use of antidepressants and end-of-treatment curative rates. However, it can be argued that this supports the need for integrated provision, as case identification alone has a low impact for case management and improved outcomes. A recent randomized controlled trial by Garcia-Retortillo et al. (2011) found that patients in a multidisciplinary support programme showed higher treatment adherence and sustained virological response than those in a conventional treatment programme. The multi-disciplinary programme included standard patient education, open and flexible visit scheduling, continued psychiatric evaluation and active medication provided by hepatologists, nurses, pharmacists, psychologists and health care assistants in comparison to a conventional programme. They found the multidisciplinary support programme was more effective with lower costs. Costs were measured as cost of drugs and health professionals, as well as the long-term complications of the disease.

It is worth stating, for those working within an acute hospital setting, that contact with the treatment clinic may be the only regular coherent health care provision the patient accesses. In the author's experience, many patients accessing hospital-based treatment services, who have a history of mental health problems, have an essential mistrust of 'helping services' and have often worked very hard to distance themselves from that aspect of their history. They are frequently highly antagonistic about discussion of mental health problems, and may seek to minimize prior problems and associated risks. This places high levels of demand within HCV services for sensitive engagement and assessment of mental health needs, and requires an integrated provision of mental health support and case management to facilitate HCV treatment access. Without integrated mental health provision those people with either a history of, or current, mental health problems are likely to face unnecessary delays or insurmountable barriers to HCV treatment.

Despite this evidence and experience, few UK or international services treating people with HCV have integrated mental health provision. The standard of care is typically through Liaison Psychiatry services or informal links to mental health providers (i.e. in the absence of an agreed care pathway and contracting). A reliance on mental health services to provide opinion on psychological risks pre-treatment, or assessment/treatment of adverse psychiatric side-effects during treatment is not viable, as patients are unlikely to meet the thresholds for care, or for rapid response within these services. Liaison Psychiatry services may provide more flexibility and faster response times for one-off assessments, but are often not configured to provide an ongoing care package.

12.7   SO WHAT IS THE ROLE OF THE PSYCHOLOGIST?

In every professional's mind, the main issue for patients with HCV should be making a clear, collaborative decision about treatment access. Regardless of setting, treatment access is key, due to the risk of infecting others as well as the risk to health and mortality for the individual. This does not mean every patient can be safely treated at a given time point, but that every patient should be aware that curative treatments do exist, and they should be involved in decisions about whether these treatments are right for them. The main role of the psychologist working with patients with HCV infection is to use their skill set to maximize treatment access, reduce the likelihood of treatment drop out, provide assertive management of adverse side-effects, increase adherence, and thereby maximize the chances for curative response.

In considering the description of the needs of the HCV population, and the complex challenge of treatment itself, it can be seen that, within HCV provision, there is a demand for specialist mental health skills and knowledge. However, the challenge is not just in the arena of mental health. There are significant challenges that require knowledge and skills in addiction, health behaviour change and adjustment issues. The skill set of the psychologist is arguably best matched to meeting the full range of patient needs. The role of the psychologist can be conceptualized across four levels of care as outlined in Table 12.1.

Table 12.1 *Four levels of psychological care for HCV patients*

Level	Staff group	Role of psychologist
1	All staff – basic psychological skills	• Support all staff, including clerical and reception, to have basic understanding and knowledge of mental health problems and communication challenges with HCV population, to maximize compassionate care and promote positive engagement from the first point of contact
2	Health and social care staff – enhanced psychological skills	• Support medical and nursing team to implement and maintain robust NICE-compliant monitoring of mental health at appropriate intervals through the treatment pathway • Deliver training packages to key staff that promote use of effective psychological strategies to optimize adherence • Develop strategies to aid nursing and medical communication with patients who present severe relationship challenges • Ensure psychological provision is compliant with best practice, within competencies and with adequate supervisory and clinical support • Enable staff to understand and develop coherent HCV treatment strategies for patients who are seen as having 'severe psychiatric condition' contraindication

Level	Staff group	Role of psychologist
3	Specialist psychological practitioners, i.e. counselling and specific psychological interventions delivered to an explicit theoretical framework	• Understand that many patients have sub-clinical mental health problems that would not ordinarily require a formal intervention, but in the context of HCV treatment necessitate a lower threshold for assessment, monitoring and intervention • Liaise with psychological therapies agencies, drug and alcohol workers to promote access to, and develop understanding of, HCV treatment challenges, and achieve agreements for joint working and information sharing • Provide specialist assessment of mental state to assist the decision-making of GP, nurse practitioner and medical staff in the prescribing of antidepressant medication
4	Highly specialist mental health	• Provide assessments of capacity • Provide assessments of cognition in relation to adherence with complex drug regimes • Engage hard-to-reach and difficult-to-treat sub-populations • Provide rapid access for specialist assessment and intervention due to mental health co-morbidity prior to HCV treatment start • Provide tailored psycho-education • Provide specialist assessment, intervention and management advice for patients who develop de novo psychological side-effects during HCV treatment • Providing assessments which can discern 'ordinary crisis' from psychiatric presentations that are predominately due to HCV treatment side-effects, and provide appropriate management plans according to formulation • Liaise with community and other specialist mental health services to promote access and develop understanding of HCV treatment challenges, and achieve agreements for joint working and information sharing • Develop enhanced care HCV treatment plans for high-risk patients that provide clearly delineated thresholds of concern, and contingencies and responsibilities for management, to be shared across services, the patient and carer/family members • Provide interventions for complex grief and adjustment reactions

Psychological provision also supports practitioners working at levels 1–3, ensuring appropriate training and supervision support needs are met, and that best practice in psychological care is adhered to. The psychologist also plays a key role in creating positive links with the complex stepped-care structures of mental health and drug and alcohol services to facilitate patient access.

This conceptualization is not an exhaustive list, but provides examples of the range of work a psychologist may undertake in supporting HCV patients either directly, or indirectly.

CASE STUDY 12.1   AN EXAMPLE OF AN HCV PSYCHOLOGICAL STEPPED-CARE MODEL

In the Sheffield area in the United Kingdom, HCV treatment is provided within both Infectious Diseases and the Hepatology departments. The psychological resource is integrated to both departments. The treatment services have a full multidisciplinary team (MDT) – comprising specialist nurses, nurse consultant, clinical psychologist, dietician, social worker and specialist medical staff – who work collaboratively to meet patients' needs. Within the acute trust hospital, the criteria access for Liaison Psychiatry services crisis response are prioritized for inpatients. Patients being treated on an outpatient basis with crisis mental health presentations would need to be referred through mainstream duty teams in the mental health care trust.

The structuring of psychological input for HCV patients has been progressive and developmental. Familiarity of medically trained staff with psychological issues is variable; this is not the 'core business' of the specialist nurses, or medical staff. Staff also have different skills sets with which to increase their knowledge of mental health. Psychological leadership, through the development of protocols, provision of training and supervision, can help all staff understand that emotional well-being and identification of mental ill health have benefits across the whole pathway and are everyone's business. The following sections provide an overview of some of the work undertaken by the psychologist within such a service.

12.7.1   Promoting Treatment Access for People with 'Severe Psychiatric Condition'

Leadership for psychological care initially focused on ensuring that consensus was built across the team in understanding that a contraindication for 'severe psychiatric condition' should be treated no differently in terms of approach than a contraindicated other medical problem. For contraindicated physical health problems, doctors and nurses would feel confident to seek opinion and advice on treatment risks and management strategies. They would share a common language that made them feel comfortable in reaching a clear team decision about treatment.

This means part of the psychologist's role is to 'translate' psychological and psychiatric terms, assisting staff to view mental health problems as just another illness process. This is a pragmatic approach to promote equity of access to physical health care. The debates of psychology regarding whether mental health problems should be equated to 'illness' is a level of complexity that is not facilitative in the setting. The known inequality in mortality rates for those people with a mental health diagnosis is a reality that can be grasped and cannot be overlooked in debates for philosophical territory.

Through progressive dialogue, the team has built confidence to assertively treat people with severe mental illness. This has been achieved through developing a coherent understanding of what 'severe psychiatric conditions' as a contraindication for treatment mean. In mental health services this term does not have common usage but may equate to 'severe mental illness' – a term commonly used to refer to psychiatric disorders such as psychosis and bi-polar spectrum illness. This is a problematic definition, as it leads people to assume that conditions such as depression and anxiety are not as serious in presentation. However, common mental health disorders, such as depression and anxiety, can present in severe, debilitating and chronic forms that are resistant to treatment.

Staff have been assisted to understand that the term 'severe psychiatric conditions' needs to be used with caution and with the following proviso understandings. 'Severe psychiatric condition' is best used to describe those patients with high levels of symptomatic distress aor disability acquired through mental ill health, regardless of diagnosis. It should not be assumed that specific diagnosis automatically correlates to particular levels of severity. Instead, staff are encouraged to understand that severity is highly individual to patient presentations and these will vary across time (i.e. a person can have long periods of wellness but still have a chronic underlying depressive process). This provides a more fluid and realistic understanding of what constitutes a 'severe psychiatric condition' and potential suitability for treatment.

12.7.2 Systematic Identification of Mental Health Problems

The Clinical Psychologist has worked with the MDT to develop a protocol, based on best practice evidence, that aims to enable more equitable access for those with severe mental health problems, while maintaining good adherence to treatment regimes and managing risk. The protocol is integrated into a systematic assessment undertaken by key medical and nursing staff in the department at first point of contact. Initial screening of new patients includes routine questions about history of psychiatric diagnosis, presence of current symptoms and perceived severity, history of admission to psychiatric service, as well as current or recent risk behaviour that is secondary to mental health problems.

Patients with significant psychiatric needs are then referred in a timely manner to the psychology resource for further assessment of needs relating to treatment access. At first point of contact, use of clozapine is also used as an early identification of a 'psychiatric subgroup'. This is due to its overlapping toxicity not only with Interferon but also with PI and all drugs causing neutropaenia, which, if severe, can result in indefinite cessation of clozapine therapy. Staff also have access to NICE-compliant protocols for assessment and management of common mood disorder that is supported by training, supervision and consultation.

Like most services, there is routine monitoring of patients on treatment with self-report psychiatric screening tools. This enables staff to quickly identify changes in mental state for all patients, regardless of prior history. Prioritizing a rapid response to on-treatment psychiatric side-effects aims to maximize effective management strategies that promote adherence, and, if possible, prevent early discontinuation. This is important as the clinical and research community holds good consensus for the strong and rapid emergence of adverse psychiatric side-effects which, in the absence of responsive support services, means discontinuation is a risk.

12.7.3   *Intensive Case Management Approach*

The outcome for the majority of patients seen for pre-treatment assessment by the psychologist is to offer advice to nursing staff on the tailoring of psycho-education, tips for adherence, direction and the threshold for monitoring and reporting of problems. For some patients, the formal direct screen of mental state is booked with the psychologist as part of their commitment to clinic follow-up while on treatment. For a small number of patients referred, there are those who need intensive input due to such issues as limited capacity to consent or current high levels of residual symptoms of mental ill health or chronic patterns of risk behaviour. These patients may, or may not, have ongoing drug and alcohol problems which are part of their risk profile.

This latter group are provided with additional preparation and support sessions prior to HCV treatment start and intensive monitoring across treatment. The aim of the preparation sessions is to provide a documented plan that forms the basis for gaining the informed consent of the patient, carers, mental health and other providers, and the HCV service itself. Essentially, this forms a partnership contract among patients, mental health services and the medical team that enables treatment to proceed (Gallucci & Smolinski, 2001).

The case management plan provides a clear statement of prior, or existing, risk behaviours, setting a baseline by which to measure change. The plan identifies key 'relapse' behaviours or symptoms that would indicate a need for increased monitoring or intervention and review of HCV continuation. The plan clearly contracts assigned responsibilities between the different partners, including the patients themselves. It sets thresholds for discontinuation, and explores the patient's wishes should they be subject to psychiatric hospitalization during treatment (which may not be attendant to psychiatric side-effects).

For patients who have a history of hypomanic symptoms, there is clear instruction for the HCV prescribing professionals not to initiate an antidepressant without specialist psychiatric advice. As some patients have significant prior histories but do not have current contact with mental health services, there is clear agreement about thresholds for concern and clarity about duty of care for referral to such services, should the need arise. Such patients would often fit a diagnosis along a personality disorder spectrum, and have ongoing risk behaviour, but fall short of thresholds for referral to the community mental health team (CMHT), or have been 'rejected' due to lack of available positive therapeutic interventions. The plan also identifies positive attributes, such as motivation and determination (frequently high in this group), and coping strategies and positive strengths the patient may bring to treatment.

The intensive case management approach is not used solely with the severe psychiatric subgroup, but may be adapted for use with people with high levels of offending behaviour. 'Joined-up' working with the probation service can often be useful to maximize continuation of HCV treatment should the person re-offend. This enables early identification of the person's location in the criminal justice system and liaison with appropriate medical staff in that site.

12.7.4 *Promoting Resilience*

Thus far, this chapter can be seen to focus on an approach that identifies problems and barriers to HCV treatment. It can therefore be seen to be 'problem-saturated'. This can have a systemic impact, encouraging a view of patients as problems, and often resonates with the patient's/person's view of themselves as a problem. The psychology and social work staff have worked jointly to promote a critical dialogue within the Infectious Diseases team that counters this. Work has been undertaken to encourage debate about the strengths, capacity and skills that people infected with HCV arrive with, to promote a view of positive resilience in HCV patients.

A resilience approach (e.g. Treloar & Hopwood, 2008) in a HCV clinic promotes a critical view of language as shaping and forming our relationships and expectations of the people we meet. It identifies how the language we choose is extremely important in setting up constructs about the identity, skills and abilities of the person we are working with. Put more simply, the resilience approach acknowledges that how we talk about people changes the way we view them and how they view themselves. The simple metaphor for all staff draws upon the shared, common observation that despite the old adage 'sticks and stones may break your bones, but words can never hurt you' – words do hurt and have a lasting impact upon people's emotional well-being and can damage it. The increased awareness of the impact of bullying in public consciousness is facilitative in building this understanding.

Staff are encouraged to think about how the language we use can lead us to ignore or neglect aspects of the person that may be critical to treatment factors, such as adherence and coping with side-effects. The resilience approach encourages a view of the complicated life stories that accompany the person to the clinic as stories of depth and richness. Most people attending HCV services have already undertaken a significant journey of change and recovery. This includes those people whose route of transmission is not intravenous drug use, because we all have a life story that includes challenge, loss and trauma.

Resilience is understood within the clinic to be the degree to which we can 'bounce back' from challenging experiences. Treloar and Hopwood (2008) identified that clinical management of HCV that directly assesses factors such as social support networks and cognitive strategies may actually contribute to resilience and help adaptive coping in the long term with treatment.

For patients, who do not have significant mental health needs, there is integrated psychosocial assessment within the preparation phase of HCV treatment access. As well as meeting with the nursing team (who lead treatment delivery) for two preparation appointments, patients meet with either the psychologist or social worker and complete a 'resilience interview'. The semi-structured interview explores humour, optimism, the ability to link events across the life-span, liking oneself, hope, determination, moral code, social connections, and motivation and determination. Tebes, Irish, Puglisi Vasquez and Perkins (2004) have identified factors such as these in helping some people to transform their understanding of even very traumatic experiences into positive growth.

In the author's experience, people with HCV often struggle to see themselves and their achievements in a positive light, frequently using very negative language to describe themselves. They will often deny or minimize achievement. We use the resilience interview to identify personal and social resources that may be facilitative and to promote a sense of 'can do'. The interview can help reframe negative self-scripts into positive stories of survival and coping that reduce discrepancies and expectations of failure. Acknowledging such skills is critical to the treatment process, particularly in terms of ability to cope with the side-effects and maximize adherence. Shifting the perspective to include assessment of resilience allows our services to draw on the person's own strengths and better tailor support packages. The resilience interview is summarized for both the patient and the service as a report, listing coping strengths and helpful motivational self statements.

12.8 PSYCHOLOGICAL STEPPED-CARE MODEL IN HCV TREATMENT

This integration of early identification, intensive case management of psychiatric subgroup, rapid crisis management and the resilience approach provides a fully coherent 'stepped-care' model. The psychological provision is designed to ensure those with the highest levels of need receive the most input, and facilitative links with external agencies and services are well used and maintained. The role of the psychologist remains clearly consistent with the broader service aims: to promote treatment access, increase service engagement, increase adherence, reduce dropout and assertively manage risk issues. The model of psychological care for patients attending the HCV treatment service is described in Table 12.2.

Table 12.2 *Psychological stepped-care model in HCV treatment*

Treatment pathway stage	Psychology assessment/intervention
Pre-treatment Patients referred at earliest identified point in assessment pathway, if fulfilling any one of the following criteria: • contraindicated 'severe mental illness' for Pegylated Interferon, including prior diagnosis of schizophrenia, bi-polar, or psychotic spectrum disorder • current psychiatric symptoms at moderate/severe level (including common mental health disorders such as anxiety and depression) • unstable mental health symptoms (e.g. high levels of residual symptoms despite medication, or psychosocial intervention) • history of admission to psychiatric inpatient services • Clozapine (Clopixol) maintained patient • current/recent risk behaviour secondary to mental health	*Psychiatric subgroup* Full assessment of mental health history and current problems tailored to inform HCV treatment decisions and design of appropriate support package: • low intensity intervention: psychological preparation for treatment (<6 sessions) • low intensity intervention: planned screening during treatment (>2 sessions) • high intensity intervention: case management (intensive monitoring + shared care arrangements)
Treatment preparation All patients, other than 'psychiatric subgroup'	*Non-psychiatric group* • Conduct low-intensity psychosocial screening, 'resilience interview' (in collaboration with social worker) • Provide resilience report, shared with patient identifying coping strategies, potential trouble black spots for treatment, and contingencies for management
In treatment Issues of management for complex patients that present significant challenge to skill set of referring professional including: • suspicion of Pegylated Interferon-induced depression, or other mental health problems • significant change in scores on screening tools used by specialist nurses as part of integrated monitoring of mood. Raise in Generalised Anxiety Disorder (GAD-7; Spitzer, Kroenke, Williams & Löwe, 2006) or Patient Health Questionnaire (PHQ-9; Kroenke, Spitzer & Williams, 2001) to moderate/severe, severe score	Identification of on-treatment psychiatric side-effects: • medium-intensity intervention; psychological intervention or review of psychotropic medication effectiveness • high-intensity intervention: crisis management (intensive monitoring + shared care arrangements)

(Continued)

Table 12.2 *(Continued)*

Treatment pathway stage	Psychology assessment/intervention
• high index of suspicion regarding adherence • significant deterioration in coping • change in risk profile (new risk behaviours and/or significant elevation of baseline risk behaviours)	
Post treatment Prolonged psychiatric disturbance despite discontinuation of Pegylated Interferon that was not present at baseline Discontinuation or failed treatment with poor adjustment	Remain as point of access for mental health support: • monitor recovery (patients with significant on-treatment psychiatric side-effects) • monitor discontinuation of psychotropic medication (patient choice – GP may supervise)

12.9   FUTURE CHALLENGE

It is anticipated that the HCV treatment landscape will change rapidly in coming years due to research and the development of progressively more effective direct-acting antiviral drugs. For a variety of clinical and financial reasons, however, Pegylated Interferon and Ribavirin are likely to remain the components of treatment over the next decade. The development of improved medication regimes does not overcome the basic barriers to access experienced by this population. Innovation in treatment setting and methods of engagement will be a big priority in the next ten years. At the baseline, the complex vulnerabilities of the population remain, regardless of treatment regime.

Therefore, the focus of the role of the psychologist may alter but does not substantially change. Core business remains to assist in maximizing access and engagement, promoting adherence and reducing risk of early treatment discontinuation. New treatments bring new challenges such as risks of drug resistance, and therefore issues of adherence have a new level of significance not previously encountered. Currently, we are developing training and support programmes for our nursing staff to equip them with motivational interviewing skills (Miller & Rollnick, 2013) to maximize adherence to medication regimes.

12.10   CONCLUSION

There is broad scope for psychology practitioners to have a significantly positive impact upon the design of pathways and the direct care of patients with HCV infection. Persuasive arguments need to be built to support the recruitment of staff for an integrated multidisciplinary team approach incorporating psychological support for

HCV-infected patients. The evidence base clearly delineates how this support needs to be structured; the model described above is a synthesis of evidence and best practice. Further initiatives and evidence are needed to explore the effectiveness of the psychological provision in promoting engagement, access and adherence in the new treatment landscape.

In the treatment of chronic illness, the need for services to promote the psychosocial well-being of patients is increasingly recognized. There are advantages to services, and to patients, in adopting a broader biopsychosocial approach; it reduces patient distress, increases the quality of life, improves the equity of service for harder to reach patient groups, and enhances treatment adherence (Rustgi, 2009; Mental Health Confederation, 2012). There is already a small evidence base that demonstrates cost effectiveness for integrated mental health specialists in HCV services. However, there is need for improved information about which aspects of delivery are most cost-effective. This author would argue that there are additional benefits in having psychologists as team members as they contribute a broader knowledge of health and health behaviours. The skills of the psychologist as a scientist practitioner enables an adaptive, knowledgeable, intelligent response to changes in HCV patient need, treatment landscape and pathway design.

SUGGESTIONS FOR FURTHER READING

Raison, C. L., Demetrashvili, M., Capuron, L., & Miller, A. H. (2005). Neuropsychiatric adverse effects of Interferon-[alpha]: Recognition and management. *CNS Drugs*, 19, 105–123. doi:10.2165/00023210-200519020-00002

Raison, C. L., Woolwine, B. J., Demetrashvili, M. F., Borisov, A. S., Weinreib, R., Staab, J. P., et al. (2007). Paroxetine for prevention of depressive symptoms induced by interferon-alpha and ribavirin for hepatitis C. *Alimentary Pharmacology & Therapeutics*, 25, 1163–1174. doi:10.1111/j.1365-2036.2007.03316.x

Schaefer, M. (2009). Strategies for preventing, diagnosing, and managing depression in patients receiving HCV therapy. Clinical Care Options – Hepatitis C. Presentation. www.clinicaloptions.com/hep

Schaefer, M., Schmidt, F., Folwaczny, C., Lorenz, R., Martin, G., Schindlbeck, N., et al. (2003). Adherence and mental side-effects during hepatitis C treatment with interferon alfa and Ribavirin in psychiatric risk groups. *Hepatology*, 37, 443–451. doi:10.1053/jhep.2003.50031

Schaefer, M., & Schulz, J. (2008). Clinical data and best practices for managing depression in HCV-infected patients with PegInterferon and Ribavirin. PostGraduate Institute for Medicine/Clinical Care Options – Hepatitis C. Report. www.clinicaloptions.com/hep

REFERENCES

Al-Omari, A., Cowan, J., Turner, L., & Cooper, C. (2013). Antidepressant prophylaxis reduces depression risk but does not improve sustained virological response in Hepatitis C patients receiving interferon without depression at baseline: A systematic review and meta-analysis. *Canadian Journal of Gastroenterology*, 27, 575–581.

Cacciarelli, T. V., Martinez, O. M., Gish, R. G., Villanueva, J. C., & Krams, S. M. (1996). Immunoregulatory cytokines in chronic Hepatitis C virus infection: Pre- and posttreatment with Pegylated Interferon alfa. *Hepatology, 24*, 6–9. doi:10.1002/hep.510240102

Cividini, A., Pistorio, A., Regazzetti, A., Cerino, A., Tinelli, C., Mancuso, A., et al. (1997). Hepatitis C virus infection among institutionalised psychiatric patients: A regression analysis of indicators of risk. *Journal of Hepatology, 27*, 455–463.

Constant, A., Castera, L., Quintard, B., Bernard, P., Ledinghen, V., Couzigou, P., et al. (2005). Psychosocial factors associated with perceived disease severity in patients with chronic Hepatitis C: Relationship with information sources and attentional coping styles. *Psychosomatics, 46*, 25–33. doi:http://dx.doi.org/10.1176/appi.psy.46.1.25

Dan, A. A., Martin, L. M., Crone, C., Ong, J. P., Farmer, D. W., Wise, T., et al. (2006). Depression, anaemia and health related quality of life in chronic Hepatitis C. *Journal of Hepatology, 44*, 491–498. doi:10.1016/j.jhep.2005.11.046

Ehret, M., & Sobieraj, D. M. (2014). Prevention of interferon-alpha-associated depression with antidepressant medications in patients with Hepatitis C virus: A systematic review and meta-analysis. *International Journal of Clinical Practice, 68*, 255–261. doi:10.1111/ijcp.12268

Fattovich, G., Giustina, G., Favarato, S., & Ruol, A. (1996). A survey of adverse events in 11,241 patients with chronic viral hepatitis treated with alfa Pegylated Interferon. *Journal of Hepatology, 24*, 38–47.

Forton, D. M., Allsop, J. M., Foster, G. R., Thomas, H. C., & Taylor-Robinson, S. D. (2001). Evidence for a cerebral effect of the Hepatitis C virus. *Lancet, 358*, 38–39. doi:http://dx.doi.org/10.1016/S0140-6736(00)05270-3

Foster, G. (2009). Quality of life considerations for patients with chronic Hepatitis C. *Journal of Viral Hepatitis, 16*, 605–611. doi:10.111/j.1365-2893.2009.01154x

Gallucci, G., & Smolinski, J. (2001). Treatment contacts for patients with Hepatitis C, psychiatric illness and substance abuse. *Psychosomatics, 42*, 353–358. doi:10.1176/appi.psy.42.4.353

Garcia-Retortillo, M., Cirera, I., Marquez, C., Canete, N., Carrio, J. A., Castellvi, P., et al. (2011). Multidisciplinary program bested traditional method in HCV treatment. Paper presented at 62nd Annual Meeting of the American Association for the Study of Liver Diseases; November 3–8; San Francisco. http:www.natap.org/AASLD/AASLD_97.htm.

Guillemard, C., Cognard, C., Bretagne, A. L., Elfadel, S., Even, C., Beaujard, E., et al. (2009). Systematic psychiatric intervention in chronic Hepatitis C patients treated by Peg-Pegylated Interferon A2B and Ribavirin: Randomized multicentre prospective study. *Journal of Hepatology, 50*, S222.

Gunewarde, R., Lampe, L., & Ilchef, R. (2010). Prevalence of hepatitis C in two inpatient psychiatric populations. *Australasian Psychiatry, 18*, 330–334. doi:10.3109/10398561003763273

Knott, A., Dieperink, E., Willenbring, M. L., Heit, S., Durfee, J. M., Wingert, M., et al. (2006). Integrated psychiatric/medical care in a chronic Hepatitis C clinic: Effect on antiviral treatment evaluation and outcomes. *American Journal of Gastroenterology, 101*, 2254–2262. doi:10.1111/j.1572-0241.2006.00731.x

Kraus, M. R., Schäfer, A., Csef, H., Scheurlen, M., & Faller, H. (2000). Emotional state, coping styles, and somatic variables in patients with chronic Hepatitis C. *Psychosomatics, 41*, 377–384. doi:http://dx.doi.org/10.1176/appi.psy.41.5.377

Kroenke, K., Spitzer, R. L., & Williams, J. B. (2001). The PHQ-9: Validity of a brief depression severity measure. *Journal of General Internal Medicine, 16*, 606.

Lang, C. A., Conrad, S., Garrett, L., Battistutta, D., Cooksley, G. E., Dunne, M. P., et al. (2006). Symptom prevalence and clustering of symptoms in people living with chronic Hepatitis C infection. *Journal of Pain and Symptom Management, 31*, 335–344. doi:10.1016/j.jpainsymman.2005.08.016

Lee, D. H., Jamal, H., Regenstein, F. G., & Perrillo, R. P. (1997). Morbidity of chronic Hepatitis C as seen in a tertiary care medical center. *Digestive Diseases and Sciences, 42*, 186–191. doi:10.1023/A:1018818012378

Mental Health Confederation. (2012). Investing in emotional and psychological wellbeing for patients with long-term conditions. London: NHS Confederation. http://www.nhsconfed.org/Publications/Documents/Investing%20in%20emotional%20and%20psychological%20well-being%20for%20patients%20with%20long-tern%20conditions%2018%20April%20final%20for%20website.pdf

Miller, W. R., & Rollnick, S. (2013). *Motivational interviewing: Helping people change*. New York: Guilford Press.

Montagnese, S., Gordon, H. M., Jackson, C., Smith, J., Tognella, P., Jethwa, N., et al. (2005). Disruption of smooth pursuit eye movements in cirrhosis: Relationship to hepatic encephalopathy and its treatment. *Hepatology, 42*, 772–781. doi:10.1002/hep.20855

National Institute of Health. (2002). Consensus statement on management of Hepatitis C. *NIH Consensus and State-of-Science Statements, 19*, 1–46.

NICE (National Institute for Health and Care Excellence). (2004). *Interferon Alfa (Pegylated and non-Pegylated) and Ribavirin for the treatment of chronic Hepatitis C. NICE technology appraisal guidance (TA 75)*. London: NICE.

NICE (National Institute for Health and Care Excellence). (2010). *Peginterferon Alfa and Ribavirin for the treatment of chronic Hepatitis C. NICE technology appraisal guidance (TA 200)*. London: NICE.

Public Health England (PHE). (2013a). *Hepatitis C in the UK: 2013 report*. London: Public Health England.

Public Health England (PHE). (2013b). *Hepatitis C: Guidance, data and analysis*. London: Public Health England.

Raison, C. L., Demetrashvili, M., Capuron, L., & Miller, A. H. (2005). Neuropsychiatric adverse effects of Interferon-[alpha]: Recognition and management. *CNS Drugs, 19*, 105–123. doi:10.2165/00023210-200519020-00002

Raison, C. L., Woolwine, B. J., Demetrashvili, M. F., Borisov, A. S., Weinreib, R., Staab, J. P., et al. (2007). Paroxetine for prevention of depressive symptoms induced by interferon-alpha and Ribavirin for Hepatitis C. *Alimentary Pharmacology & Therapeutics, 25*, 1163–1174. doi:10.1111/j.1365-2036.2007.03316.x

Rodger, A. J., Jolley, D., Thompson, S. C., Lanigan, A., & Crofts, N. (1999). The impact of diagnosis of Hepatitis C virus on quality of life. *Hepatology, 30*, 1299–1301. doi:10.1002/hep.510300504

Rustgi, V. (2009). *HCV advanced practice curriculum: The importance of patient quality of life*. http://www.clinicaloptions.com/Hepatitis/Treatment%20Updates/HCV%20Curriculum%202009.aspx

Schaefer, M. (2009). Strategies for preventing, diagnosing, and managing depression in patients receiving HCV therapy. Clinical Care Options – Hepatitis C. Presentation. www.clinicaloptions.com/hep

Schaefer, M., Schmidt, F., Folwaczny, C., Lorenz, R., Martin, G., Schindlbeck, N., et al. (2003). Adherence and mental side-effects during Hepatitis C treatment with interferon alfa and Ribavirin in psychiatric risk groups. *Hepatology, 37*, 443–451. doi:10.1053/jhep.2003.50031

Schaefer, M., & Schulz, J. (2008). Clinical data and best practices for managing depression in HCV-infected patients with PegInterferon and Ribavirin. PostGraduate Institute for Medicine/Clinical Care Options – Hepatitis C. Report. www.clinicaloptions.com/hep

Spitzer, R. L., Kroenke, K., Williams, J. B. W., & Löwe, B. (2006). A brief measure for assessing generalized anxiety disorder: The GAD-7. *Archives of Internal Medicine, 166*, 1092–1097. doi:10.1001/archinte.166.10.1092

Sylvestre, D. L., Loftis, J. M., Hauser, P., Genser, S., Cesari, H., et al. (2004) Co-occurring Hepatitis C, substance use and psychiatric illness. *Journal of Urban Health, 81*, 719. doi:10.1093/jurban/jth153

Tebes, J. K., Irish, J. T., Puglisi Vasquez, M. J., & Perkins, D. V. (2004). Cognitive transformation as a marker of resilience. *Substance Use and Misuse, 39*, 769–788. doi:10.1081/JA-120034015

Treloar, C., & Hopwood, M. (2008). 'Look, I'm fit, I'm positive and I'll be all right, thank you very much': Coping with Hepatitis C treatment and unrealistic optimism. *Psychology, Health & Medicine, 13,* 360–366. doi:10.1080/13548500701477532

USA Food and Drug Administration. (2014). *Drug development guidelines for Hepatitis C virus.* http://www.fda.gov/drugs/newsevents/ucm385395.htm

Ware, J. E., Bayliss, M. S., Mannocchia, M., & Davis, G. L. (1999) Health-related quality of life in chronic hepatitis C: Impact of disease and treatment response. *Hepatology, 30,* 550–555. doi:10.1002/hep.510300203

Weaver, T., Madden, V., Charles, G., Stimson, G., Renton, A., Tyrere, P., et al. (2003). Comorbidity of substance misuse and mental illness in community mental health and substance misuse services. *British Journal of Psychiatry, 183,* 304–313. doi:10.1192/02-623

Weissenborn, K., Ennen, J. C., Bokemeyer, M., Ahl, B., Wurster, U., Tillmann, H., et al. (2006). Monoaminergic neurotransmission is altered in Hepatitis C virus infected patients with chronic fatigue and cognitive impairment. *Gut, 55,* 1624–1630. doi:10.1136/gut.2005.080267

Weissenborn, K., Krause, J., Schüler, A., Ennen, J. C., Ahl, B., Hecker, H., et al. (2004). Hepatitis C virus infection affects the brain: Evidence by psychometric studies and magnetic resonance spectroscopy. *Journal of Hepatology, 41,* 845–851. doi:10.1016/j.jhep.2004.07.022

13 The Psychology and Treatment of Gambling Disorders

ANDRÉ GEEL[1], REBECCA FISHER[2], AND ASKA MATSUNAGA[3]

[1]Addictions Service, Central and North West London NHS Foundation Trust, London, UK
[2]Camden and Islington NHS Foundation Trust, London, UK
[3]Central and North-West London NHS Foundation Trust, London, UK

CHAPTER OUTLINE

13.1 INTRODUCTION

Gambling is not a problem for most people. So how does it become a problem? When does that problem require treatment? What is the psychology behind all of this? The idea of gambling being problematic for some probably began with the advent of gambling itself and games of chance involving money or wager of some kind. When people began losing items of value, did they then begin to question the utility, fun and enjoyment of this activity? And when they lost more than they could afford, and continued to do so in spite of the negative consequences, gambling became 'problem gambling'.

The term 'problem gambling' appeared to be first used along with the establishment of Gamblers Anonymous around 1957, a self-help fellowship to assist people 'addicted' to this behaviour (Hodgins, Stea & Grant, 2011). Seen by some as a compulsion and the failure of will in the face of temptation, the best treatment was that of a support group, or fellowship, to strengthen and support the will not to engage in, or be tempted by, that pastime. The approach, very similar to that of Alcoholics Anonymous, was to avoid and distance oneself from gambling. The approach, highly effective for many, did not need to look beyond its own assumptions in order to be successful. Thus, it was up to others to look beyond to see what else might be going on (to motivate, describe and explain this manifestation), and possibly to suggest additional ways to alleviate the suffering caused by its excess.

The profile of problem gambling was raised in the 1980s with its inclusion in the Third Edition of the *Diagnostic and Statistical Manual of Mental Disorders* (American Psychiatric Association, 1980) as an Impulse Control Disorder, which then brought it under the psychiatric spotlight as a mental disorder. Labelling it 'pathological gambling', and defining it as a mental health problem in this way, by association, implied there was a treatment for it. Cognitive and behavioural therapy has, so far, appeared to provide the most convincing and credible evidence base to date (Toneatto & Ladouceur, 2003; Rickwood, Blaszczynski, Delfabbro, Dowling & Heading, 2010).

13.2 DEFINITION

The definition of 'problem gambling' (PG) is problematic in itself, with the terms 'problem' and 'pathological' gambling used interchangeably in the field (Hodgins et al., 2011). According to the *Diagnostic and Statistical Manual of Mental Disorders – Fourth Edition* classification, five or more criteria must be met for gambling behaviour to be rated as 'pathological', whereas for 'problem' gambling, it is just three (DSM IV; American Psychiatric Association, 2000). In contrast, the other major diagnostic reference – that of the World Health Organization's *International Classification of Disorders*, 10th Revision (ICD-10; WHO, 2010) – only pathological gambling is described and is loosely equated to 'compulsive gambling', and no other description for 'problem gambling' is offered.

The *Diagnostic and Statistical Manual of Mental Disorders* Fifth Edition (DSM-V; American Psychiatric Association, 2013) modified the definition once again, and changed the name to 'gambling disorder'. For practical purposes we will tend to refer still to DSM-IV, as all the research quoted herein, when it does refer to DSM, relates mainly to that definition.

The most significant changes from DSM-IV to DSM-V are the dropping of 'illegal acts' to finance the gambling habit as one of the criteria; having a minimum of four (instead of five) of those criteria present to confirm the disorder; and for those criteria to be present in the last 12 months (DSM-IV did not specify such a time limit). Gambling disorder is now classified under the section 'Substance-Related and Addictive Disorders', having moved from the 'Impulse-Control Disorders Not Elsewhere Classified' of DSM-IV.

As already discussed, there is a lack of precision in the nomenclature which presents researchers and clinicians with considerable challenges in defining the 'condition' (and this is further exacerbated by many authors not specifying the criterion they have used).

For the purposes of this chapter, the term 'problem gambling' will be used as an overarching term to evaluate the risk of developing a gambling addiction, or to gamble at what is a self-reported, or other reported, 'problematic' level. DSM-IV and ICD-10 refer to 'pathological gambling' and 'compulsive gambling', while DSM-V uses the term 'gambling disorder'. All three definitions include:

- the presence of a preoccupation with gambling and increased frequency and salience of gambling in the person's life;
- needing to gamble with increasing amounts of money;
- carrying on gambling despite losses and significant problems caused by the gambling;
- repeated failed attempts to control or abstain from gambling;
- suffering irritability and mood disorders when attempting to stop gambling;
- gambling as a way of escaping problems.

The features of problem gambling often include attempting to hide the extent of gambling, committing deceitful, or even illicit, acts in order to continue to gamble, jeopardizing or losing jobs, relationships, etc. and relying on others to relieve desperate financial or other problems caused by gambling.

13.3 PREVALENCE

This process of labelling some forms of gambling as pathological served to raise its awareness in the public domain and led to questions about its prevalence in the general community. One of the first studies of this kind in the United Kingdom was conducted in 2007 (Wardle et al., 2007), with the second prevalence study in 2010 (Wardle et al., 2010). According to the authors, the UK prevalence of problem gambling (using the DSM-IV criteria) has increased from 0.6% in 1999 and 2007 to 0.9% in 2010 (approximately 451,000 adults aged 16 or over). This prevalence rate is similar to other European countries, particularly Norway and Switzerland (Carbonneau, Vitaro, Wanner & Tremblay, 2011), but notably lower than America and Hong Kong where rates of 3.5 and 5.3 are reported (Currie, Miller, Hodgins & Wang, 2009).

Although the British Gambling Prevalence Survey (BGPS) has been discontinued, data on problem gambling has continued to be collected via the Health Survey for England (Craig & Mindell, 2012), which reports a 65% prevalence rate of gambling in the population and a 0.4%–0.5% incidence of problem gambling.

13.4   DEMOGRAPHIC RISK FACTORS

The multiple risk factors and co-morbidity associated with problem gambling (PG) suggest it is not a homogeneous 'illness', nor is it found in a homogeneous population, a conclusion made by numerous authors who advocate an alternative model, proposing PG as a heterogeneous disorder with subtypes that share characteristics (Moreyra, Ibáñez, Saiz-Ruiz, Nissenson & Blanco, 2000; Kalyoncu, Pektaş & Mirsal, 2003). The inclusive conceptualization of problem gambling developed by Blazczynski and Nower (2002) in their 'Pathways Model' provides one such useful framework in which to explore the risk factors for developing PG.

13.4.1   The Pathways Model of Problem Gambling

In order to introduce a logical structure to this debate we will use Blaszcynski and Nower's (2002) 'Pathways Model of Problem Gambling' as a framework for the discussion, and as a way of organizing the varied research material on the topic.

This model proposes three types, or groups, of problem gambler:

- the Behavioural Conditioned (characterized, e.g. by various environmental factors, having a 'big' win, the social context of the gambling and having a family history of gambling);
- the Emotionally Vulnerable (characterized, e.g. by mood disorders such as depression and anxiety);
- the Antisocial Impulsivist (including elements of a personality disorder such as might be found in anti-social personality disorder and borderline personality disorder).

13.4.2   The 'Behavioural Conditioned' Group

The Behavioural Conditioned are those problem gamblers who have been 'conditioned' (as in behavioural psychology or behaviourism) via their environment (pro- or gambling-positive), a big (and often early) win, social gambling (where friends, colleagues and family are engaged), and a family history of gambling or problem gambling, to be problematic, pathological or excessive gamblers.

13.4.2.1   Age

Research has consistently demonstrated that a younger age is a risk factor for developing problem gambling (Johansson, Grant, Kim, Odlaug & Gunnar Götestam, 2009) specifically for those under 30 (Bondolfi, Osiek & Ferrero, 2000; Volberg, Abbott, Rönnberg & Munck, 2001; Clarke et al., 2006) with higher incidence rates in those aged 16–24 years (Wardle et al., 2010). This is an important factor for government health policy and psychological intervention, considering adult problem gamblers report gambling at a significantly younger age than those without problems (Productivity Commission, 1999; Abbott, McKenna & Giles, 2000). Moreover, Burge, Pietrzak and Petry (2006) found that those who started gambling in pre- or early adolescence (mean age 10.5 yrs) reported increased family, social, substance abuse and psychiatric problems as assessed by the Addiction Severity Index (ASI; McLellan, Luborsky, O'Brien & Woody, 1980) in comparison with those who start gambling later in life (mean age 23 yrs). Yet few adolescents, in this key developmental stage, seek help for gambling difficulties (Wilber & Potenza, 2006).

Countering this evidence, however, is research by Winters, Stinchfield, Botzet and Anderson (2002) who found that as age increased through adolescent years, so did risk of gambling, but that the rate of problem gambling remained stable over time and across age ranges. In fact, the older adult population (65 years and above) has been found to be the group demonstrating the highest growth rate in participation of gambling (Morgan Research, 2000; Desai, Maciejewski, Dausey, Caldarone & Potenza, 2004).

13.4.2.2   Gender

A strong gender bias is found in the PG literature with males more likely to be problem gamblers than females (Govoni, Rupcich & Frisch, 1996; Winters, Bengston, Door & Stinchfield, 1998; Bondolfi et al., 2000; Volberg et al., 2001; Winters et al., 2002; Chalmers & Willoughby, 2006; Clarke et al., 2006; Johansson et al., 2009; Shead, Derevensky & Gupta, 2010; Wardle et al., 2010) with comparative rates demonstrating significant differences between the two sexes across the literature, albeit inconsistent in size, for example, 1.5% of men versus 0.3% of women (Wardle et al., 2010) and 11.8% of male versus 4.8% female problem gamblers (Govoni et al., 1996).

This appears to be borne out by unpublished, anecdotal accounts from some of the treatment services in the United Kingdom who report that referrals are predominantly men. These accounts also suggest that it might be due to women being less willing to admit to such a problem, and instead using internet gambling for privacy and avoidance of any discomfort (Gainsbury et al., 2013). If problem gambling is more related to impulse control disorders, as both ICD-10 and DSM-IV suggest, then the gender bias might partially be explained as men tend to present with a higher incidence of such disorders. Another hypothesis is that there are gender differences in risk assessment with women tending to take fewer risks than men. Since gambling is perceived as risky behaviour with an uncertain outcome, women may tend to avoid participating (Harris, Jenkins & Glaser, 2006).

13.4.2.3   Socioeconomic Status and Occupation

One is more likely to gamble if from a disadvantaged neighbourhood (Welte, Wieczorek, Barnes & Tidwell, 2006) and the British Gambling Prevalence Survey (Wardle et al., 2010) found that those with no money, or who had severe financial difficulties, were significantly more at risk of developing PG. Perhaps going some way to explain this is the correlation found between an excess of provision of gambling 'opportunity' (e.g. non-casino gaming machines) with areas classified as being 'highly deprived' (e.g. Wheeler, Rigby & Huriwai, 2006), where individuals are more likely to be struggling financially and looking for ways to ease their financial burden. In this case, it has been argued that their anxiety or worry is a consequence of gambling, not the cause (Blaszczynski & Nower, 2002).

Linked to this concept are the associated risk factors of unemployment and job type that are linked to problem gambling. Martínez-Pina et al. (1991) found that problem gamblers were more likely than control participants to lack work, with unemployment subsequently and consistently being found to be a risk factor for PG (Feigelman, Kleinman, Lesieur, Millman & Lesser, 1995; Hall Carriero, Takushi, Montoya, Preston, & Gorelick, 2000; Clarke et al., 2006; Wardle et al., 2010). Indeed, individuals living on social welfare have demonstrated similar associations (Rönnberg et al., 1999; Volberg et al., 2001). A possible antecedent to this occupational situation is that lower academic achievement has been associated with more PG in adolescents (Winters et al., 2002; Shead et al., 2010), college students (Winters et al., 1998) and adults (Scherrer et al., 2007; Yip et al., 2011), which may impact on the individuals' ability to find suitable employment.

13.4.2.4   Criminality

General criminality and an increasing amount of arrests have been associated with problem gambling (McConaghy, 1980; Feigelman et al., 1995; Hall et al., 2000; Welte, Barnes, Wieczorek, Tidwell & Parker, 2004). It has been hypothesized that perhaps crime is committed by individuals in efforts to pay debts (Ashley & Boehlke, 2012) after a study by Nower (2003) found that 21%–85% of problem gamblers had committed crimes ranging from fraud, theft and embezzlement to robbery, assault and blackmail. Anecdotal evidence from treatment services in the United Kingdom, and the authors' clinical experiences, suggest a significant proportion of problem and pathological gamblers have engaged in criminal behaviour to fund their gambling habits after they had developed a gambling problem.

Arguably there could exist a potential circular causality in this argument when considering the pathways model of problem gambling, where criminal behaviour might precede or occur simultaneously in the context of the 'Antisocial Impulsivist' group, whereas with the 'Behaviourally Conditioned' and 'Emotionally Vulnerable' groups, criminal behaviour would most likely be a 'last resort' to recover gambling losses.

13.4.2.5   Ethnicity

Non-Caucasian ethnicities have been associated as having a higher risk of problem gambling (Abbott & Volberg, 1996; Welte et al., 2006). For example, those with Asian/Asian British and Black/Black British ethnicity were over-represented in problem gamblers compared to those with White ethnicity (2.8%, 1.5% and 0.8% respectively, Wardle et al., 2010) replicating findings of Welte et al. (2004) who found an over-representation of African American, Asian and Hispanic ethnicity among problem gamblers.

13.4.2.6   Parental Gambling

The perceived presence of problem gambling in a family member has been associated with self-perceived gambling problems (Cronce, Corbin, Steinberg & Potenza, 2007) and actual defined parental problem gambling or regularity of gambling has been correlated to subsequent problem gambling in their offspring (Winters et al., 2002; Wardle et al., 2010). Interestingly, Clarke and Clarkson (2009) also found that the amount parents had gambled (as well as the belief that their parents had gambled too much) were significantly related to problem gambling in older adults.

13.4.3   The 'Emotionally Vulnerable' Group

The Emotionally Vulnerable group gamble to an excessive or pathological extent in order to compensate, distract, alleviate (or 'self-medicate') for another, pre-existing emotional problem usually depression, anxiety or posttraumatic stress disorder (PTSD). Indeed, suppression and reactive coping styles have been found in problem gamblers as well as lower scores on reflective coping styles (Getty, Watson & Frisch, 2000).

13.4.3.1   Depression and Anxiety

Depression and anxiety have been associated with greater likelihood of PG (Blaszczynski, 1995; Ibáñez et al., 2001; Scherrer et al., 2007; Shead et al., 2010; Yip et al., 2011) both in treatment and at follow-up (Smith, Kitchenham & Bowden-Jones, 2011). Dussault, Brendgen, Vitaro, Wanner and Tremblay (2011) conducted a longitudinal study of over 1,000 males to explore the directionality of the links between depression and problem gambling. The authors found that impulsivity at age 14 predicted depression and problem gambling by age 17, and that this in turn increased depressive symptoms between the ages of 17 to 23. Also of note, however, is that depressive symptoms at 17 also predicted an increase in problem gambling in early adulthood, highlighting a mutual, and potentially complex, relationship between problem gambling and depression and one for further exploration. Higher anxiety levels have been found in those with PG (Coman, Burrows & Evans, 1997; Ibáñez et al., 2001; Shead et al., 2010), as well as higher intensity of obsessive compulsive disorder (OCD) symptoms (Frost, Meagher & Riskind, 2001; Johansson et al., 2009).

13.4.3.2 Post Traumatic Stress Disorder (PTSD)

Ledgerwood and Petry (2006) found 34% of individuals seeking treatment for PG had high levels of PTSD (assessed through self-report measures) appearing to corroborate earlier findings where people with PG were found to have experienced major traumatic life events (Taber, McCormick & Ramirez, 1987; Kausch, Rugle & Rowland, 2006). Indeed, the overall occurrence of PTSD in PG has been estimated to be from 12.5%–29% (Ledgerwood & Petry, 2006). This has highlighted a pattern of worse functioning and higher pathology in PG with PTSD compared to those without (Najavits, Meyer, Johnson & Korn, 2011).

13.4.3.3 Substance Misuse

Higher alcohol use has been associated with gambling (Feigelman et al., 1995; Ladouceur, Boudreault, Jacques & Vitaro, 1999), and dependence on alcohol has been identified as a risk factor for problem gambling (Welte et al., 2006). An association between substance use and PG has been found in adolescence (Winters et al., 2002; Delfabbro, Lahn & Grabosky, 2006; Shead et al., 2010) and substance abuse disorders in adults (Welte et al., 2004; Hodgins, Tiihonen & Ross, 2005; Petry, Weinstock, Ledgerwood & Morasco, 2005; Yip et al., 2011) with drug dependence associated with past year PG (Scherrer et al., 2007) and methadone treatment correlated to higher gambling rates, too (Feigelman et al., 1995).

13.4.4 The 'Antisocial Impulsivist' Group

The Antisocial Impulsivist group is that group who have a pre-existing borderline or anti-social personality disorder, and gambling happens to be one form (or sometimes many other forms) of impulsive behaviour. Indeed, higher incidence of personality disorders have been found in problem gamblers (Ibáñez et al., 2001; Petry et al., 2005), particularly anti-social personality disorder (McConaghy, 1980; Slutske et al., 2001; Scherrer et al., 2007). This second finding being consistent with such a group's disregard for risk-taking in the context of showing less regard and respect for the social values around money and the requirement to repay debts.

13.4.4.1 Impulsivity

Greater rated PG severity has been associated with higher rates of impulsivity (Vitaro, Arsenault & Tremblay, 1997; Shead et al., 2010). Indeed, Shenassa, Paradis, Dolan, Wilhelm and Buka (2012) conducted a 30-year prospective community-based study and found that those individuals who were exhibiting impulsive behaviours at age 7 were 3.09 times (95% CI: 1.40–6.82) more likely to report problem gambling in later years. Further to this, Grall-Bronnec et al. (2011) found that in problem gambling, high impulsivity levels or a history of anxiety disorders were a co-morbid risk factor with ADHD. Furthermore, Dussault et al. (2011) also found that impulsivity at age 14 predicted depressive symptoms and gambling problems at age 17. Evidence has, however, been found to the contrary, where no relationship was found between impulsivity and gambling in a sample of male adolescents aged between 16 and 18 years (Gerdner & Svensson, 2003). There is also the suggestion that there might be a neurological component in this impulsive group (Shaffer & Korn, 2002).

13.4.4.2 Neuropsychology

Neuropsychological findings are steadily growing in the research on a better understanding of gambling behaviours, and have been acknowledged widely as 'a promising area' for further investigation (Rickwood et al., 2010). Transmitter activity and localization of function are two areas of research that have received the greatest attention in relation to gambling.

Dopaminergic, serotonergic, noradrenergic, and opioidergic pathways have been linked to gambling on various levels, but dopaminergic pathways have predominantly received most attention, followed closely by serotonergic pathways. Dopamine is known for its associations with learning motivation, including rewards, and alterations to this pathway underlie the seeking of rewards, which in turn release dopamine to the system. Dopaminergic mesolimbic pathways, in coordination with diminished function in the ventromedial and ventrolateral prefrontal cortex, as well as the ventral striatum, are thought to be involved in PG by blunting the response to rewards and losses, providing a possible mechanism for facilitating uninhibited gambling behaviour (Hodgins et al., 2011). In addition, antagonists of dopamine have been found to enhance gambling motivations. In support of this, prior research has found PGs to have decreased levels of dopamine in their cerebrospinal fluid in comparison to control subjects (Johansson et al., 2009). Although several transmitters have been studied in relation to PG, the complex interaction of neurotransmitters renders results that are often difficult to interpret, and sometimes there is a failure to recruit human subjects or control comparisons, and therefore this field continues to require further comprehensive research.

Cognitive control and impulse regulation are critically dependent on intact prefrontal cortex functioning, and in particular the inferior frontal cortex, anterior cingulate and dorsolateral prefrontal cortex. In an fMRI study by van Holst, van Holstein, van den Brink, Veltman and Goudriaan (2012), inhibition during cue reactivity of problem gamblers and healthy controls was compared; it was found that gamblers rely on compensatory brain activity to achieve similar performance to healthy controls when exposed to neutral cues. However, when gamblers were exposed to gambling-related cues they maintained fewer behavioural errors and lower brain function in the core areas mentioned above. Therefore, cognitive function for PGs is not disrupted by motivational processes, but can require a significantly increased effort when in non-gambling-related scenarios. In turn, this supports the notion and growing evidence from neurobiological, neuropsychological, and clinical studies (Shaffer & Korn, 2002) that impulsivity is linked to PG, as problem gamblers fail to use core regions required for impulse regulation.

Finally, much research has drawn on the neuropsychological links between PG and dependent substance misuse. Abnormalities in the cortico-meso-limbic brain structures have suggested a common molecular pathway in both groups, and pharmacological studies have also shed light on a common performance deficit. Naltrexone is an opioid antagonist which has been shown to be effective in blocking the reinforcing effects of gambling (Holden, 2001; Shah, Potenza & Eisen, 2004). It is important to note, however, that caution must be exercised with such neuropsychological research as associations may be a 'consequence of repeated exposure' to arousal, stimuli, and behaviours (Rickwood et al., 2010).

13.4.5 Conclusion

As stated above, on a note of caution, the literature investigating psychiatric co-morbidity and PG should be considered with the caveat of association rather than causation. There may well be multiple interactions of a variety of variables placing an individual at higher risk of PG, making causality very difficult to determine (Ashley & Boehlke, 2012). Indeed, when analysed separately, risk factors may well correlate to PG, but when combined in simultaneous prediction models, many effects can be nullified, suggesting a careful consideration of the literature is needed. Indeed, Jackson, Dowling, Thomas, Bond and Patton (2008) noted this very point in their study, where the number of risk factors for gambling in adolescence significantly reduced when entered into simultaneous prediction.

Problem gambling is a relatively newly identified disorder which has aspects of a pure behavioural addiction, co-morbidity with existing mental disorders and neurological aspects, and is a complex, multifaceted and emerging field. While the causal connections between problem gambling and co-morbid disorders and conditions have not been established, we should be mindful that the definition and aetiology so far are embryonic, so to begin to view it from a bio-psycho-social perspective seems to be a usefully broad position to take.

Pathological gambling is one of the few disorders that seems to sit more comfortably and convincingly within a behavioural explanation of its aetiology and cause at present. Currently the most pragmatic, effective and evidence-based way of treating the problem (and getting good results) is the behavioural and cognitive-behavioural approach, but this does not explain the aetiology of the problem. Variables such as co-morbidity and neuropathology are very likely linked to this behaviour and need to be incorporated in the explanation of the condition in the future.

13.5 TREATMENT OF GAMBLING DISORDERS

13.5.1 Cognitive-Behavioural Interventions

Hodgins et al. (2011), in their review of research on gambling disorders, state that although they did not evaluate which specific types of treatments were more effective than others, most studies of treatment outcomes that were included in their meta-analysis were done within the behavioural, cognitive and cognitive-behavioural formats. Rickwood et al. (2010) partly support this view, confirming that cognitive-behavioural therapies have been cautiously recommended as 'best practice' for the psychological treatment of problem gambling, and go on to confirm that there is a substantial literature evaluating a range of cognitive and behavioural procedures. These have included stimulus control, systematic desensitization, behavioural counselling, cue exposure, imaginal desensitization, as well as cognitive restructuring, alternative activity planning, problem-solving training, financial planning and limit setting, social skills and communication training, relapse prevention and in-vivo exposure with response prevention. Some research is emerging on the use of Dialectical Behaviour Therapy (DBT) for problem gambling, and Christensen et al. (2013) refer to three studies in this respect with a newly-developed Brief DBT treatment package.

13.5.2   Brief Interventions

A variety of brief interventions (ranging from five minutes to four sessions) are referred to in the literature, including Motivational Enhancement Therapy, Motivational Interviewing and brief cognitive-behavioural therapy interventions employed via the telephone, mailed self-help workbooks, internet-based and brief face-to-face sessions, and combinations of these (Rickwood et al., 2010; Hodgins et al., 2011).

13.5.3   Fellowship and Self-Help

Gamblers Anonymous (GA) was started in Los Angeles in 1957 and uses the 12 Step tradition of Alcoholics Anonymous. The nature and structure of GA make it difficult to conduct effective outcome research, but some studies indicate that engagement with GA has better outcomes for problem gamblers than for those who do not (Hodgins et al., 2011).

13.5.4   Family Therapy and Concerned Significant Others

Reference has been made to the Community Reinforcement and Family Therapy (CRAFT) model, a CBT intervention that aims at working with the concerned significant others (CSO) of those with alcohol problems, which has been adapted for gambling. Some limited outcomes have been reported from this, as well as some recent development in the use of congruence couple therapy for problem gambling (Hodgins et al., 2011).

13.5.5   Pharmacological Interventions

A wide range of psychopharmacological agents have been evaluated in the literature in terms of possible treatments for problem gambling, including antidepressants, mood stabilizers and opioid antagonists, but to date no single agent has appeared as a convincing and effective treatment for the disorder (Rickwood et al., 2010). Part of this might be due to the heterogeneity of the symptoms of problem gambling, as well as the high co-morbidity with other disorders, including anxiety, depression and mood disorders (Hodgins et al., 2011; Lorains, Cowlishaw & Thomas, 2011).

13.6   PERSONAL COMMENT AND REFLECTIONS

The chapter up until now has been a review of the leading literature and research relating to problem gambling, and we would like to bring this together with some personal reflections from our own clinical experiences.

Much of this personal experience relating to the treatment of problem gambling comes from work at the National Problem Gambling Clinic in London. To our knowledge, this is the first and only National Health Service (NHS) clinic for problem gambling in the United Kingdom. It treats up to 600 problem gamblers a year, using a predominantly CBT-based group psychological treatment programme modelled on a combination of Petry's (2005) and Blaszczynski's (1995) approaches, with additional motivation interviewing and family therapy components to support this. Most patients are referred into the eight-week group CBT programme, more ambivalent patients receive four sessions of individual motivational interviewing as a prelude to this, families and concerned significant others (CSO) are offered family therapy alongside the eight-week group programme, and complex patients with dual-diagnosis and co-morbid problems are offered individual treatment that incorporates the eight-week CBT programme. In addition to adhering to the more evidence-based approaches as its basic form of treatment, some other approaches, including psychodynamic, social behaviour and network therapy (Copello, Orford, Hodgson & Tober, 2009) and behavioural couples therapy (O'Farrell & Fals-Stewart, 2011) have been trialled at the clinic.

13.7   CONCLUSION

This chapter has attempted to illustrate the nature of problem gambling from a psychological perspective. We have incorporated aetiological, epidemiological and other demographic aspects to place this behaviour in a broader context, but essentially this remains a new and emerging field.

One of the biggest challenges highlighted in this chapter is the wide variety of terms used to describe problem gambling. As part of the basic recommendation that further research continues is the recommendation that a single, more precise definition be established, and that a single (suite of) screening instruments be agreed upon to complement this.

In addition, the growing awareness of this as a public health concern is likely to make the public more aware of the problem and thus to draw more on treatment services, with those treatments possibly becoming more integrated, much as they are with other addiction problems. As problem gambling increasingly becomes part of the addiction literature, so might our view of addictions change to see more the addictive behaviour as playing a key role in the understanding of all addictions, rather than the substance itself.

SUGGESTIONS FOR FURTHER READING

Ellenbogen, S., Gupta, R., & Derevensky, J. L. (2007). A cross-cultural study of gambling behaviour among adolescents. *Journal of Gambling Studies, 23*, 25–39. doi:10.1007/s10899-006-9044-2

Goudriaan, A., Oosterlaan, J., de Beurs, E., & Van den Brink, W. (2004). Pathological gambling: A comprehensive review of biobehavioral findings. *Neuroscience and Biobehavioral Reviews, 28*, 123–141. doi:10.1016/j.neubiorev.2004.03.001

McCormick, R. A., Russo, A. M., Ramirez, L. F., & Taber, J. I. (1984). Affective disorders among pathological gamblers seeking treatment. *American Journal of Psychiatry, 141*, 215–218.

Mishra, S., Lalumière, M. L., & Williams, R. J. (2010). Gambling as a form of risk-taking: Individual differences in personality, risk-accepting attitudes, and behavioral preferences for risk. *Personality & Individual Differences, 49*, 616–621. doi:10.1016/j.paid.2010.05.032

Richard, D. C. S., Blaszczynski, A., & Nower, L. (Eds.). (2013). *The Wiley-Blackwell handbook of disordered gambling.* New York: John Wiley and Sons, Inc.

REFERENCES

Abbott, M., McKenna, B. G., & Giles L. C. (2000). *Gambling and problem gambling among recently sentenced males in four New Zealand prisons.* Wellington, NZ: Department of Internal Affairs.

Abbott, M. W., & Volberg, R. A. (1996). The New Zealand National Survey of Problem and Pathological Gambling. *Journal of Gambling Studies, 12*, 143–160. doi:10.1007/BF01539171

American Psychiatric Association. (1980). *Diagnostic and statistical manual of mental disorders* (3rd ed.). Arlington, VA: American Psychiatric Publishing.

American Psychiatric Association. (2000). *Diagnostic and statistical manual of mental disorders* (4th ed., text rev.). Arlington, VA: American Psychiatric Publishing.

American Psychiatric Association. (2013). *Diagnostic and statistical manual of mental disorders* (5th ed.). Arlington, VA: American Psychiatric Publishing.

Ashley, L. L., & Boehlke, K. K. (2012). Pathological gambling: A general overview. *Journal of Psychoactive Drugs, 44*, 27–37. doi:10.1080/02791072.2012.662078

Blaszczynski, A. P. (1995). The assessment and treatment of pathological gambling. Workshop at the Australian and New Zealand Association of Psychiatry, Psychology and the Law Conference, Melbourne, May.

Blaszczynski, A., & Nower, L. (2002). A pathways model of problem and pathological gambling. *Addiction, 97*, 487–499. doi:10.1046/j.1360-0443.2002.00015.x

Bondolfi, G., Osiek, C., & Ferrero, F. (2000). Prevalence estimates of pathological gambling in Switzerland. *Acta Psychiatrica Scandinavica, 101*, 473–475. doi:10.1034/j.1600-0447.2000.101006473.x

Burge, A. N., Pietrzak, R. H., & Petry, N. M. (2006). Pre/early adolescent onset of gambling and psychosocial problems in treatment-seeking pathological gamblers. *Journal of Gambling Studies, 22,* 263–274. doi:10.1007/s10899-006-9015-7

Carbonneau, R., Vitaro, F., Wanner, B., & Tremblay, R. E. (2011). P01-14 - Gambling frequency and problems: A study across 3 generations. *European Psychiatry, 26,* 14. doi:doi:10.1016/S0924-9338(11)71725-410.1016/S0924-9338(11)71725-4

Chalmers, H., & Willoughby, T. (2006). Do predictors of gambling involvement differ across male and female adolescents? *Journal of Gambling Studies, 22,* 373–392. doi:10.1007/s10899-006-9024-6

Christensen, D. R., Dowling, N. A., Jackson, A. C., Brown, M., Russo, J., Francis, K., & Umemoto, A. (2013). A pilot of an abridged Dialectical Behavior Therapy program as a treatment for problem gambling. *Behaviour Change, 20,* 117–137.

Clarke, D., Abbott, M., Tse, S., Townsend, S., Kingi, P., & Manaia, W. (2006). Gender, age, ethnic and occupational associations with pathological gambling in a New Zealand urban sample. *New Zealand Journal of Psychology, 35,* 84–91.

Clarke, D., & Clarkson, J. (2009). A preliminary investigation into motivational factors associated with older adults' problem gambling. *International Journal of Mental Health & Addiction, 7,* 12–28. doi:10.1007/s11469-007-9079-3

Coman, G. J., Burrows, G. D., & Evans, B. J. (1997). Stress and anxiety as factors in the onset of problem gambling: Implications for treatment. *Stress Medicine, 13,* 235–244. doi:10.1002/(SICI)1099-1700

Copello, A., Orford, J., Hodgson, R., & Tober, G. (2009). *Social behaviour and network therapy for alcohol problems.* Hove: Routledge.

Craig, R., & Mindell, J. (2012). *Health survey for England.* London: The Health and Social Care Information Centre.

Cronce, J. M., Corbin, W. R., Steinberg, M. A., & Potenza, M. N. (2007). Self-perception of gambling problems among adolescents identified as at-risk or problem gamblers. *Journal of Gambling Studies, 23,* 363–375. doi:10.1007/s10899-006-9053-1

Currie, S. R., Miller, N., Hodgins, D. C., & Wang, J. (2009). Defining a threshold of harm from gambling for population health surveillance research. *International Gambling Studies, 9,* 19–38. doi:10.1080/14459790802652209

Delfabbro, P., Lahn, J., & Grabosky, P. (2006). Psychosocial correlates of problem gambling in Australian students. *Australian and New Zealand Journal of Psychiatry, 40,* 587–595. doi:10.1111/j.1440-1614.2006.01843.x

Desai, R. A., Maciejewski, P. K., Dausey, D. J., Caldarone, B. J., & Potenza, M. N. (2004). Health correlates of gambling in older adults. *American Journal of Psychiatry, 161,* 1672–1679. doi:10.1176/appi.ajp.161.9.1672

Dussault, F., Brendgen, M., Vitaro, F., Wanner, B., & Tremblay, R. E. (2011). Longitudinal links between impulsivity, gambling problems and depressive symptoms: A transactional model from adolescence to early adulthood. *Journal of Child Psychology & Psychiatry, 52,* 130–138. doi:10.1111/j.1469-7610.2010.02313.x

Feigelman, W., Kleinman, P., Lesieur, H., Millman, R., & Lesser, M. (1995). Pathological gambling among methadone patients. *Drug and Alcohol Dependence, 39,* 75–81. doi:10.1016/0376-8716(95)01141-K

Frost, R., Meagher, B., & Riskind, J. (2001). Obsessive compulsive features in pathological lottery and scratch-ticket gamblers. *Journal of Gambling Studies, 17,* 519. doi:10.1023/A:1016636214258

Gainsbury, S. M., Russell, A., Hing, N., Wood, R., Lubman, D., & Blaszczynski, A. (2013). How the internet is changing gambling: Findings from an Australian Prevalence Survey. *Journal of Gambling Studies, 31,* 1–15. doi:10.1007/s10899-013-9404-7

Gerdner, A., & Svensson, K. (2003). Predictors of gambling problems among male adolescents. *International Journal of Social Welfare, 12,* 182–192. doi:10.1111/1468-2397.t01-1-00006

Getty, H., Watson, J., & Frisch, G. (2000). A comparison of depression and styles of coping in male and female GA members and controls. *Journal of Gambling Studies, 16*, 377–391. doi:10.1023/A:1009480106531

Govoni, R., Rupcich, N., & Frisch, G. (1996). Gambling behaviour of adolescent gamblers. *Journal of Gambling Studies, 12*, 305–317. doi:10.1007/BF01539325

Grall-Bronnec, M., Wainstein, L., Augy, J., Bouju, G. L., Feuillet, F., Vénisse, J.-L., et al. (2011). Attention Deficit Hyperactivity Disorder among pathological and at-risk gamblers seeking treatment: A hidden disorder. *European Addiction Research, 17*, 231–240. doi:10.1159/000328628

Hall, G., Carriero, N., Takushi, R., Montoya, I., Preston, K., & Gorelick, D. (2000). Pathological gambling among cocaine-dependent outpatients. *American Journal of Psychiatry, 157*, 1127–1133. doi:10.1176/appi.ajp.157.7.1127

Harris, C. R., Jenkins, M., & Glaser, D. (2006). Gender differences in risk assessment: Why do women take fewer risks than men? *Judgment and Decision Making, 1*, 48–63.

Hodgins, D. C., Stea, J. N. & Grant, J. E. (2011). Gambling disorder. *The Lancet, 378*, 1874–1884. doi:10.1016/S0140-6736(10)62185-X

Hodgins, S., Tiihonen, J., & Ross, D. (2005). The consequences of conduct disorder for males who develop schizophrenia: Associations with criminality, aggressive behaviour, substance use, and psychiatric services. *Schizophrenia Research, 78*, 323–335. doi:http://dx.doi.org/10.1016/j.schres.2005.05.021

Holden, C. (2001). *Behavioral addictions: Do they exist? Science, 294*, 980–982. doi:10.1126/science.294.5544.980

Ibáñez, A., Blanco, C., Donahue, E., Lesieur, H., Pérez de Castro, L., Fernández-Piqueras, J., et al. (2001). Psychiatric comorbidity in pathological gamblers seeking treatment. *American Journal of Psychiatry, 158*, 1733–1735. doi:10.1176/ajp.158.10.1733

Jackson, A. C., Dowling, N., Thomas, S. A., Bond, L., & Patton, G. (2008). Adolescent gambling behaviour and attitudes: A prevalence study and correlates in an Australian population. *International Journal of Mental Health & Addiction, 6*, 325–352. doi:10.1007/s11469-008-9149-1

Johansson, A., Grant, J. E., Kim, S. W., Odlaug, B. L., & Gunnar Götestam, K. (2009). Risk factors for problematic gambling: A critical literature review. *Journal of Gambling Studies, 25*, 67–92. doi:10.1007/s10899-008-9088-6

Kalyoncu, Ö., Pektaş, Ö., & Mirsal, H. (2003). Pathological gambling: Biopsychosocial approach. *Journal of Dependence, 4*, 76–80.

Kausch, O., Rugle, L., & Rowland, D. Y. (2006). Lifetime histories of trauma among pathological gamblers. *American Journal on Addictions, 15*, 35–43. doi:10.1080/10550490500419045

Ladouceur, R., Boudreault, N., Jacques, C., & Vitaro, F. (1999). Pathological gambling and related problems among adolescents. *Journal of Child and Adolescent Substance Abuse, 8*, 55–68. doi:10.1300/J029v08n04_04

Ledgerwood, D. M., & Petry, N. M. (2006). Posttraumatic stress disorder symptoms in treatment-seeking pathological gamblers. *Journal of Traumatic Stress, 19*, 411–416. doi: 10.1002/jts.20123

Lorains, F. K., Cowlishaw, S., & Thomas, S. A. (2011). Prevalence of comorbid disorders in problem and pathological gambling: Systematic review and meta-analysis of population surveys. *Addiction, 106*, 490–498. doi:10.1111/j.1360-0443.2010.03300.x

Martínez-Pina A., Guirao de Parga, J. L., Vallverdu, R. F., Planas, X. S., Mateo, M. M., & Aguado, V. M. (1991). The Catalonia Survey: Personality and intelligence structure in a sample of compulsive gamblers. *Journal of Gambling Studies, 4*, 275–299. doi:10.1007/BF01023747

McConaghy, N. (1980). Behaviour completion mechanisms rather than primary drives maintain behavioural patterns. *Activitas Nervosa Superior (Praha), 22*, 138–151.

McLellan, A. T., Luborsky, L., O'Brien, C. P., & Woody, G. E. (1980). An improved diagnostic instrument for substance abuse patients: The Addiction Severity Index. *Journal of Nervous & Mental Diseases, 168*, 26–33.

Moreyra, P., Ibáñez, A., Saiz-Ruiz, J., Nissenson, K., & Blanco, C. (2000). Review of the phenome-nology, etiology and treatment of pathological gambling. *German Journal of Psychiatry, 3*, 37–52.

Morgan Research. (2000). Seventh survey of community gambling patterns and perceptions. Project report. Prepared for Victorian Casino and Gaming Authority. http://vcgr.vic.gov.au/CA256F800017E8D4/Statistics

Najavits, L. M., Meyer, T., Johnson, K. M., & Korn, D. (2011). Pathological gambling and posttrau-matic stress disorder: A study of the co-morbidity versus each alone. *Journal of Gambling Studies, 4*, 663–683. doi:10.1007/s10899-010-9230-0

Nower, L. (2003). Pathological gamblers in the workplace: A primer for employers. *Employee Assis-tance Quarterly, 18*, 55–72. doi:10.1300/J022v18n04_03

O'Farrell, T. J., & Fals-Stewart, W. (2011). *Behavioural couples therapy for alcoholism and drug abuse.* New York: Guilford Press.

Petry, N. M. (2005). *Pathological gambling: Etiology, comorbidity and treatment.* Washington, DC: American Psychological Association.

Petry, N. M., Weinstock, J., Ledgerwood, D. M., & Morasco, B. (2005). A randomized trial of brief interventions for problem and pathological gamblers. *Journal of Consulting and Clinical Psychol-ogy, 76*, 318–328. doi:10.1037/0022-006X.76.2.318

Productivity Commission. (1999). *Australia's gambling industries.* Canberra: Productivity Commis-sion.

Rickwood, D., Blaszczynski, A., Delfabbro, P., Dowling, N., & Heading, K. (2010). *Special report: The psychology of gambling.* Melbourne: Australian Psychological Society. http://www.psychol-ogy.org.au/publications/inpsych/2010/december/gambling

Rönnberg, S., Volberg, R., Abbott, M., Moore, L., Andrén, A., Munck, I., et al. (1999). *Gambling and pathological gambling in Sweden: Report no. 1–3 in NIPH series on problem gambling.* Stockholm, Folkhälsoinstitutet [National Institute of Public Health, NIPH].

Scherrer, J. F., Xian, H., Kapp, J. M., Waterman, B., Shah, K. R., Volberg, R., et al. (2007). Associ-ation between exposure to childhood and lifetime traumatic events and lifetime pathological gambling in a twin cohort. *Journal of Nervous and Mental Disease, 195*, 72–78. doi:10.1097/01.nmd.0000252384.20382.e9

Shaffer, H. J., & Korn, D. A. (2002). Gambling and related mental disorders: A public health analysis. *Annual Review of Public Health, 23*, 171–212. doi:10.1146/annurev.publhealth.23.100901.140532

Shah, K. R., Potenza, M. N., & Eisen, S. A. (2004). Biological basis for pathological gambling. In J. E. Grant, & M. N. Potenza (Eds.), *Pathological gambling: A clinical guide to treatment.* Washing-ton, DC: American Psychiatric Publishing.

Shead, N. W., Derevensky, J. L., & Gupta, R. (2010). Risk and protective factors associated with youth problem gambling. *International Journal of Adolescent Medicine & Health, 22*, 39–58.

Shenassa, E. D., Paradis, A. D., Dolan, S. L., Wilhelm, C. S., & Buka, S. L. (2012). Childhood impul-sive behavior and problem gambling by adulthood: A 30-year prospective community based study. *Addiction, 107*, 160–168. doi:10.1111/j.1360-0443.2011.03571.x

Slutske, W., Eisen, S., Xian, H., True, W., Lyons, M., Goldberg, J., et al. (2001). A twin study of the association between pathological gambling and antisocial personality disorder. *Journal of Abnor-mal Psychology, 110*, 297–308. doi:http://dx.doi.org/10.1037/0021-843X.110.2.297

Smith, N., Kitchenham, N., & Bowden-Jones, H. (2011). Pathological gambling and the treat-ment of psychosis with aripiprazole: Case reports. *British Journal of Psychiatry, 199*, 158–159. doi:10.1192/bjp.bp.110.084996

Taber, J. I., McCormick, R. A., & Ramirez, L. F. (1987). The prevalence and impact of major life stressors among pathological gamblers. *International Journal of the Addictions, 22*, 71–79. doi:10.3109/10826088709027414

Toneatto, T., & Ladouceur, R. (2003). The treatment of pathological gambling: A critical review of the literature. *Psychology of Addictive Behaviors, 17*, 284–292. doi:10.1037/0893-164X.17.4.284

Van Holst, R. J., van Holstein, M., van den Brink, W., Veltman, D. J., & Goudriaan, A. E. (2012). Response inhibition during cue reactivity in problem gamblers: An fMRI study. *PLoS ONE*, 7, 1–10. doi:10.1371/journal.pone.0030909

Vitaro, F., Arsenault, L., & Tremblay, R. (1997). Dispositional predictors of problem gambling in male adolescents. *American Journal of Psychiatry*, *154*, 1769–1770. doi:10.1176/ajp.154.12.1769

Volberg, R. A., Abbott, M. W., Rönnberg, S., & Munck, I. M. E. (2001). Prevalence and risks of pathological gambling in Sweden. *Acta Psychiatrica Scandinavica*, *104*, 250–256. doi:10.1111/j.1600-0447.2001.00336.x

Wardle, H., Moody, A., Spence, S., Orford, J., Volberg, R., Jotangia, D., et al. (2010). *British Gambling Prevalence Survey 2010*. London: National Centre for Social Research.

Wardle, H., Sproston, K., Orford, J., Erens, B., Griffiths, M., Constantine, R., & Pigott, S. (2007). *British Gambling Prevalence Survey 2007*. London: National Centre for Social Research.

Welte, J. W., Barnes, G. M., Wieczorek, W. F., Tidwell, M.-C. O., & Parker, J. C. (2004). Risk factors for pathological gambling. *Addictive Behaviors*, *29*, 323–335.

Welte, J. W., Wieczorek, W. F., Barnes, G. M., & Tidwell, M.-C. O. (2006). Multiple risk factors for frequent and problem gambling: Individual, social, and ecological. *Journal of Applied Social Psychology*, *36*, 1548–1568. doi:10.1111/j.0021-9029.2006.00071.x

Wheeler, B. W., Rigby, J. E., & Huriwai, T. (2006). Pokies and poverty: Problem gambling risk factor geography in New Zealand. *Health & Place*, *12*, 86–96. doi:10.1016/j.healthplace.2004.10.011

Wilber, M. K., & Potenza, M. N. (2006). Adolescent gambling: Research and clinical implications. *Psychiatry (Edgmont)*, *3*, 40–48.

Winters, K. C., Bengston, P., Door, D., & Stinchfield, R. (1998). Prevalence and risk factors of problem gambling among college students. *Psychology of Addictive Behaviors*, *12*, 127–135.

Winters, K. C., Stinchfield, R. D., Botzet, A., & Anderson, N. (2002). A prospective study of youth gambling behaviors. *Psychology of Addictive Behaviors*, *16*, 3–9. doi:10.1037/0893-164X.16.1.3

World Health Organization. (2010). *International statistical classification of diseases and related health problems*. 10th revision. Malta: World Health Organization.

Yip, S. W., Desai, R. A., Steinberg, M. A., Rugle, L., Cavallo, D. A., Krishnan-Sarin, S., et al. (2011). Health/functioning characteristics, gambling behaviors, and gambling-related motivations in adolescents stratified by gambling problem severity: Findings from a high school survey. *American Journal on Addictions*, *20*, 495–508. doi:10.1111/j.1521-0391.2011.00180.x

14 Alcoholics Anonymous and 12 Step Therapy: A Psychologist's View

MARTIN WEEGMANN

NHS and Independent Practice, London, UK

CHAPTER OUTLINE

14.1 INTRODUCTION: PERSONAL CONTEXT

When I entered the field of substance misuse in 1990, it was to work on what was then an NHS in-patient group therapy programme for those in recovery from alcohol and drug dependence.[1] With virtually no experience with the client group, having minimal training on the area from my clinical psychology course, and armed, no doubt, with several (denied!) prejudices ('addicts are all the same', 'they don't really change', treatment pessimism, and so on), I found the experience profoundly humanizing of those I was (supposedly) helping. What most impressed me was how quickly individuals with serious histories of substance misuse and who were recently ill (many were in hospital detoxification prior to the programme), normalized (in the sense of established abstinence), co-operated, expressed themselves and responded to the community ethos of 'living and learning' together. This is not an idealization – protest, resistance and primitive emotional states were also in evidence, but when met by empathy and group challenge, between fellows, hopefully, more often than from staff, could be contained. While staff delivered the professional group therapy during the day hours, I was curious about the quiet and persistent presence of members of Alcoholics Anonymous (hereafter AA) who came from the outside to the ward in the evenings. There were no obvious lines of communication between the day groups and evening meetings, each 'doing their own thing' as it were; neither did clients share much of their learning from these different sources of help, at least not explicitly. Impressive progress was made in the relative safety of the residential programme, although the real challenge was how to sustain that progress once clients departed to re-experience real-world circumstances, social networks and underlying feelings; in the memorable words of one client, 'if only I could take the ward with me'.

With the closure of the programme in 1993, and my relocation within community alcohol and drug services, I continued to develop my skills in a range of psychological approaches. My professional heroes were pioneering American psychologists, such as Alan Marlatt and Bill Miller, whose research and clinical models offered persuasive frameworks of intervention and, in the United Kingdom, psychologists like Jim Orford, whose work on 'excessive appetites' and social and family contexts offered what struck me as sound 'common sense'. Over time, my own professional contribution was to develop a contemporary psychodynamic understanding of addiction, addressing what are often missing dimensions in our work dealing with powerful affective states, unconscious mental life and self-defeating, contradictory motivations in addicts (see Weegman & Khantzian, Chapter 5 in this volume, for more on this). I saw many clients in individual and group psychotherapy who were also attending AA (or NA, or AlAnon) and increasingly wondered, what it was that they found and received from the world of fellowship groups, to which I was not privy? Somewhere along the way, I felt I lacked a deeper understanding of how AA worked, with all its containing and transformative potential. Nervously (I am not an alcoholic and nor have I lived with anyone with addiction), I attended my first 'open meetings' (i.e. open to anyone, including non-alcoholics) of AA around 2002. I went regularly, over several years to this meeting and three other meeting venues in central London. It was a positive step – I guess I had the equivalent for a non-alcoholic of what Bill W. called 'good exposure' on first contact, being impressed by the solidarity of their meetings and the ways in which people disempowered by addictions could listen, learn and find a voice and reconstruct their lives. I witnessed the sustained recovery that I had heard of but not encountered back in the clinic. Not only did I learn professionally, including publishing several papers, but I also found myself personally helped by their traditions and accumulated cultural capital, so that I too could 'keep it simple' and 'in the day', that I too could value my assets, acknowledge my limitations and address my 'spiritual' needs (I prefer words like 'values' and 'meanings' to spirituality, however, I don't quibble over words). After all, when faced in our clinical work with addictive suffering, of the individual and their loved ones, psychologists need resources that help us to persist and sustain realistic hope. In short, as a result of attending open meetings I was confirmed in believing what I had always sensed, that there need be no competition between AA and professional therapy, and indeed that there is much common ground, albeit expressed in different languages; more importantly, that each could help to 'deepen' the other.

The other strands of my relationship, as it were, to AA, were: (1) starting to deploy formal 12 Step Facilitation Therapy with some clients (of which, more later); (2) providing one-day training workshops to staff on AA and 12 Step Therapy, and, finally, (3) becoming a 'non-alcoholic trustee' of the General Services Board of AA, Great Britain.[2] The latter is a privilege and further confirmation of the ways in which those in long-term recovery do indeed turn their lives around. In particular, being a trustee has given me insights into the service structure of AA and the many ways in which recovering people 'give back'. My plea in writing this chapter is simply that psychologists be open and willing to learn from traditions with which they are less, or completely, unfamiliar, and to appreciate the resources clients use (with or without AA) to achieve change, outside the confines of the clinic and the therapeutic hour.

14.2   HISTORY

Like any good idea, its origins were ordinary. AA effectively began in 1930s' Akron, Ohio, when two struggling drinkers – a medic ('Dr. Bob') and stockbroker ('Bill W') – turned to each other, sharing accounts of their struggles with alcohol. Something transformational happened insofar as from these early efforts at self-honesty or testimony, they were enabled (as indeed eventually were others) to rebuild shattered lives and to redefine themselves as 'recovering alcoholics'. The embryo of what was to become AA, one alcoholic helping another, was present in these simple acts of meeting, sharing and acceptance. As alcoholism affects and disempowers others, the wives of those early pioneers (who were mostly men, in that era) began to wonder, 'what is in this for us?' In fact, the involvement of family and use of home as meeting place have been regular features of AA since its inception. From their informal gatherings, Lois W. (wife of Bill W.), together with Anne S. (wife of Dr Bob), and others, thought that the spouses might benefit from formal meetings to share their experiences in living with alcoholic partners, so the various family groups that had sprung up were unified and Al-Anon was born in 1951. Each organization grew dramatically. Although stigma and marginalization of alcoholics and their loved ones were widespread, some have argued that, post-Prohibition, America was ripe for a 'new paradigm' of care (Levine, 1978).

The history of NA is less well documented and needs to be understood within the context of 1950s' America, which, like that of AA 20 years earlier, grew in what White (1998) calls 'inhospitable soil'. Although there had been sporadic attempts by addicts to form fellowships – 'Addicts Anonymous' in Lexington is one example – NA, as we know it today, is chiefly attributed to the efforts of Jimmy K. and his circle, in California. In a reflection on the times, some NA meetings were held secretly ('rabbit meetings') in order to evade police interference. In 1953, NA adopted the 12 Steps and 12 Traditions, identical to those of AA, with the exception of one word ('addiction' rather than 'alcohol') in Step 1: 'We admitted that we were powerless over our addiction and that our lives had become unmanageable.' This chapter concentrates predominantly on AA, the parent fellowship, as it were, from which the formulation of the 12 Steps and 12 Traditions derive. For more on the history and cultural contextualization of AA, see McCrady and Miller (1995), White (1998), Humphreys (2004), and O'Halloran (2008).

14.3   PHILOSOPHY

There were many social, cultural and philosophical influences on AA, in a curious mix of incident, chance and charisma. In reaching out to occluded populations, AA challenged a problematic social legacy, including a lack of humane services and medical recognition of the realities of alcoholism, indeed, often sheer discrimination against alcoholics. AA helped to forge discourses of sickness, replacing those of sinfulness, so that alcoholism could be rescued from moral condemnation and its historical associations with degeneration, weak will and so on; its 'trouble' could be thought about in new ways.

AA is a lay tradition of psychosocial support. Although AA has no creed on the 'true nature of alcoholism' and its members do not sign up to any particular 'theory' of it, the alcoholic is generally seen as suffering from an illness of body, mind and soul, an illness with a progressive course. AA actually blends biomedical, psychosocial and spiritual ideas together (Miller & Kurtz, 1994). There is a form of pragmatism at work, insofar as AA enables problem drinkers to change and in so doing to revise the story of themselves, as 'alcoholics in recovery'. Once drinkers stop drinking, they can begin to transcend previous disorder, lack of self-regulation and postures of blame, self-sufficiency, etc. It takes considerable courage to face the consequences of past behaviour and to conceive of a different kind of future, with putting down the bottle only a beginning. AA invites rigorous examination of behaviour and self, addressing well-practised ('over-learned') lifestyles and defences of denial, disavowal, defiance, and so on. The idea of facing a serious crisis or 'hitting bottom' is emphasized as being a condition of change. In psychodynamic terms, one could translate the emphasis on admitting 'powerlessness' in Step One as a breaking down of omnipotence, or in the words of the earliest, non-alcoholic friend of AA, psychiatrist Henry Tiebout (1944), a process of 'ego reduction'. That the cultivation of humility is so central to AA oral and written wisdom testifies to the importance placed on overcoming such defences, by 'humanizing' oneself.

There is a spiritual, as distinct from religious, dimension to AA recovery. Changing one's patterns means changing one's attitudes and acknowledging the serious imbalances created by drinking, expressed metaphorically as the 'dis-ease' of alcoholism. Carl Jung, who corresponded with Bill W. (1961), first encapsulated an idea of alcoholism as (among other things) 'sickness of the soul', when he pointed out *spiritus contra spiritum* ('spirits drive out spirituality'). In this view, recovery demands thorough-going character change, facing difficult truths and consequences and a willingness to examine previous or ongoing patterns of abusive, 'using' or neglectful relationships, including to self. Without this deeper level of change, it is implied, evasion occurs and real progress is stultified; the distinction in AA between being 'dry' and being 'sober', with its attendant greater 'peace of mind', reflects this. It is relevant to note that interest in 'spiritual dimensions' of change has increased among research psychologists, partly promoted by Bill Miller's (1990) plea. This having been said, there are many dimensions ('ingredients') to change in AA, with each member person fashioning their own recovery; in the words of a participant in a qualitative study of successful AA recovery, 'AA is like a loose-fitting garment … I find myself, somehow, within it, find what is useful for me …' (Weegmann & Piwowoz-Hjort, 2009, p. 291).

AA invites a way of living one's life rather than being a 'treatment' and thus exceeds 'relapse prevention'. It is intimately concerned with care of self, through connection with others in similar situations, and the Steps are metaphors of becoming, inviting an identity shift from the 'user' of the past. Alcoholics can come in from isolation and learn from sober others, moving beyond, in the words of one AA saying, 'the committee of one'. In different words, AA fosters new knowledge of 'oneself as another' (to use a phrase of philosopher Paul Ricoeur, 1990) and is premised on the importance of attending to mutual vulnerabilities and strengths (so-called character defects and assets). From anecdotal observations, I see in AA meetings a mixture of reassuring, impersonal fellowship (structures, democratic traditions, practices that transcend the individual, as in the Greek *koinonia,* communion, to 'have a share in something') and deeply personal programmes of recovery. Kurtz and Ketcham's (1992) notion of *kenosis* is a good illustration of how addiction strips human beings of their capacities, sensitivities and potential. Simply put, *kenosis* denotes an 'emptying out' of the person, as their existence is flattened and tied to the addictive cycle. This links to the idea of 'surrender' in AA, a word that does not usually sit comfortably with psychologists, and which is easily misunderstood as implying passivity or abandonment of personal responsibility. It involves, in practice, the opposite. Recently, UK psychologist Kemp (2013) has looked at the existential aspect of the AA concept of 'hitting rock bottom', closely allied to that of *kenosis.* The 'rock bottom' experience represents a crisis and also an invitation to change, of not going on in the same manner. Whatever one's philosophical take on addiction, surely Humphreys (2011, p. 3) is right to observe that, 'Every important part of the human drama is there in addiction.'

There is much more that could be said, but those interested in reading more about such philosophical aspects of AA, should consult Thune (1977), Kurtz (1982), Kurtz and Ketcham (1992).

AA has influenced many treatment and rehabilitation approaches over the years, such as the Minnesota model, although the influence is somewhat indirect, with the exception of the 12 Step rehabs. However, AA Traditions state that the fellowship be solely concerned with recovery and reaching out to the 'still suffering' alcoholic, thus avoiding involvement with any outside enterprises or controversies. Formal 12 Step Facilitation Therapy arose during the 1990s, when it was used clinically and as a research protocol in Project MATCH (Nowinski & Baker, 1992). Their manual is a user-friendly guide offering a range of self-directed assessments and interventions for those in early recovery compatible with the Steps of AA. It is a professionally delivered therapy which seeks to encourage clients to engage with AA meetings and to progressively deepen their involvement therein. With more ambivalent clients, the manual can be used to test out fears and preconceptions, for example, and as an adjunct to individual and family therapy.

14.4   HOW DOES IT WORK?

I will not formally review the research, but instead venture reflections on four domains. This relates to the hypothesis that there are many dimensions of change in AA, which one distinguished researcher has called 'active ingredients' (Moos, 2008). In his analysis, Moos (2008, p. 387) links these to several theories:

> Social control theory specifies active ingredients such as bonding, goal direction and structure; social learning theory specifies the importance of norms and role models, behavioral economics and behavioral choice theory emphasizes involvement in rewarding activities other than substance use, and stress and coping theory highlights building self-efficacy and effective coping skills.

There is some overlap in my analysis, although the theoretical sources on which I draw are different, if, hopefully, complementary.

14.4.1   AA: Group Therapy

All groups, from the psycho-educational to the analytic, from the structured and time-limited to the unstructured and 'slow-open', have their own norms of interaction, leadership (or its absence) and what can be called 'speech-acts', i.e. discursive norms (forms of speech) as to what constitutes a contribution and act of sharing. AA meetings are no exception to this. In fact, there are rather particular discursive norms and structures in a standard AA meeting (clearly analysed by O'Halloran, 2008), beginning with a reading of the AA preamble (which begins, 'AA is a fellowship of men and women who share their experience, strength and hope with each other ...', and ends, 'Our primary purpose is to stay sober and help other alcoholics to achieve sobriety'). Following a 'main share' by a nominated speaker (agreed in advance), for up to 15 minutes, the meeting is opened up by the chair (all posts rotate in AA) for others to share 'experience, strength and hope', as indicated by hand-raising. Sharing in AA means identification with the main share and revelation about one's struggles, achievements, week's progress, life events, and so on. There is no debate or 'cross-talk', with each person addressing their situation only. There may be other conventions, such as an invitation to 'shy sharers' to talk if they wish, with the 12 Steps and 12 Traditions, and sometimes other AA sayings, displayed on wall posters. The 'serenity' saying ends the meeting.

At first sight, all very different from the professional group; in fact, it might be called 'group therapy without the group therapist' (Weegmann, 2004a). But of course there are group therapeutic factors in all groups (as an aside, nineteenth-century Temperance and fraternal societies were a stunning and popular example of this), such as identification, modelling ('social learning' in the theory used by Moos, 2008), inspiration, instillation of hope, and others. Indeed, sometimes the content of groups is secondary to the process. In the group analytic language with which I am familiar, there is a process of resonance, exchange and reciprocity, richly expressed in AA's emphasis on 'look for similarities not differences' and in the process of identification; the particular speech act, 'Hello, my name is … and I'm alcoholic' is a ritualized expression of this. One could think about such identifications in terms of a process of 'twinship', hence relating to what one has in common with one's 'fellows' (Flores, 1988). In attending open meetings, I observed an ordered rhythm, which, in following a set practice, allows the individual to find a unique voice, an interesting example of a predictable (i.e. structured) unpredictable (i.e. the shares) dynamic (Weegmann, 2004b). There is a great deal of 'self-soothing' in this innovative familiarity, tapping into, as it does, human needs for affiliation and acceptance (see Robinson, 1996, for a similar 'self-psychology' perspective). There are many other aspects to group process in AA meetings and it is important to acknowledge the wider milieu in which meetings take place, including their regularity, association with other meetings, the 'pre-meeting' welcome and in-gathering and 'post-meeting' socialization, coffees, and so on. The discursive exchanges between members, in formal and non-formal time, help create a sense of solidarity which, when internalized, can sustain individuals through the many challenges which they face. Learning toleration of self (inner toleration, toleration of affect, etc.) and others (listening, connecting with, learning) is a vital constituent of developing the art of 'sober dialogue' (Weegmann & English, 2009).

14.4.2   AA: Psychosocial Change

One disadvantage with the contemporary language of 'psychosocial interventions' is that it suggests neat, sealed procedures, whereas, in reality, practice is more likely to be mixed; it also brackets out the importance of the place of the 'therapeutic alliance' common to all therapies. 12 Step Facilitation Therapy is another 'psychosocial intervention', with its manifest attention focused on supporting those in early recovery to understand how the Steps can apply to them (to put them to 'work', as it is said) and to the meetings which they are encouraged to attend. But it, like any other therapy, rests on its efficacy on the qualities of the therapist, their sensitivity, experience, and so on; I have argued elsewhere, with Tim Leighton (Weegmann & Leighton, 2004), that the best spirit in which to apply 12 Step Facilitation Therapy, particularly for new-comers and the unsure ('ambivalent') is that of motivational enhancement.

Although distinct in its culture and governed by a host of lay traditions and practice, many have recognized that change in AA involves the kinds of change addressed by other approaches, including behavioural change, cognitive reconstruction, building alternatives to the drinking lifestyle and self-efficacy. Three examples are; (1) Steigerwald and Stone's (1999) analysis of the process of cognitive restructuring in AA; (2) DiClementi's (1995) consideration of AA in terms of his general 'structure of change' theory; and (3) Wilson, Hayes and Byrd's (2000) comparison of AA and Acceptance and Commitment Therapy ('ACT'), which sees much common ground and advocates the overcoming of polarities.

There are many sayings in fellowship oral and written tradition, sayings which offer useful footholds and reminders to those forging a path away from addiction. They form what could, in the language of Russian (Vygotskian) psychology, be termed 'scaffolding' (McLeod, 2010), suggestions that support developmental change while identifying risk. Consider some instances. 'Recovery is a journey … not a destination' is a reminder of recovery as an ongoing process rather than an event, encouraging continuing work on the self while avoiding complacency, among other things. The NA saying, 'Time to change your playmates, playgrounds and playthings' directly addresses ingrained habits, lifestyles and high-risk situations, as does AA encouragement, 'To avoid slipping, avoid slippery people, slippery places, and slippery things.' Such therapeutic reminders can be thought of as attempts to guide memories, and as practical relapse prevention. Swora's (2001) innovative paper suggests that just as alcoholism damages memory and social relations, the AA programme, including sayings, creates a positive 'community of memory' (a kind of 'non-forgetting', without being chained by the past). A member of Al-Anon, who was a long-term member of a therapy group for family and friends, found comfort in their '3 c's', saying, 'We did not cause it, we can't control it and we cannot cure it.' The saying helped her to cultivate an attitude of loving detachment and to it, the therapy group added a fourth 'c', that of 'care for self'. Finally, from AA, 'I have found that the process of discovering who I really am begins with knowing who I really don't want to be.' This is an evocative and subtle message, showing the importance of forging a 'non-using' identity and consolidating a line/decision/transition, of dis-identification (as distinct from denial) with the active drinker and person of the past associated with it. This is not to simplify the AA programme of change, which consists of more than attending meetings and the use of sayings, although, as is suggested, the latter help the person to recognize common dilemmas and learn from a wider cultural capital. Most who commit and actively involve themselves find a real sense of community and belonging in such fellowships.

14.4.3   AA: Narrative Change

The saying quoted above concerning the dialectic between 'who I am' from 'who I really don't want to be' leads into consideration of the role of narrative identity and change in AA. Narrative psychology (for more on this, see Weegmann, Chapter 9 in this volume) starts from the assumption that we are 'story-creating animals' who continually make sense of our actions and reorient ourselves throughout life within narrative-like structures (Sarbin, 1986; Bruner, 1987). People who face serious adversity, such as alcoholism, develop a means of accounting for their condition and reappraise themselves when they embark upon major change, such as committing to abstinence, often seeing themselves as being different kinds of people as a result (e.g., as 'alcoholic in recovery'). The 'shadow' of any chronic disorder is long, and recovery requires a remarkable readaptation and revision of personal identity. After all, alcoholism or addiction evolves without the suffering individual intending or planning it ('no one sets out to become an alcoholic/addict, but it happens', was a saying which I packaged together over the years) including major biographical disruptions and reductions in dignity. Harré (1997, p. 177) argues that it is through narratives that are expressed "'[the] sort of person one is, what one's strengths and weaknesses are and what one's life has been", and moreover, given that the self-concept is linked to the "stories we tell about ourselves", the actions one performs as oneself'.

It is fair to claim that AA was one of the first mutual help groups to explicitly value the importance of story (telling, sharing and hearing), recognizing that the story can indeed help set one free (Cain, 1991). And acts of telling are not singular events, but require retelling, revision and remembering. All this is achieved, however, not on the basis of a theory, but a valuation in practice of the ordinary word and act of sharing; with characteristic flourish, Bill W. (1949), addressing an audience of American psychiatrists, stated, 'Being laymen we have naught but a story to tell.'

If AA is seen more as a community than a treatment, then it can be argued that AA provides a collective store of tradition and accumulated wisdom, including 'story forms', as it were (Cain, 1991, Valverde & White-Mair, 1999). These story forms help individuals to structure their accounts, although not the detail, which remains unique. One example is the suggestion in AA that when individuals talk, they address, 'what it was like, what happened, and what it is like now'. This is, of course, general, but offers the canvas through which a particular voice is found; like others, Humphreys (2000, p. 504) underlines the message that in AA, 'community narratives and personal stories interact'.

Over time, with abstinence, a sense of becoming, of oneself *now*, is consolidated, hence the formation of a new identity as a person in recovery. These transformations in narrative identity – how people speak and figure themselves, become more unified – are absent, or less emphasized, in other approaches, but are critical to the recovery of a more coherent, ordered sense of self, of auto-biography (Hänninen & Koski-Jännes, 2004). This is consistent with our (Weegmann & Piwowoz-Hjort, 2009) study of long-term recovery, in which participants articulated their journeys from active substance users to 'alcoholics in recovery', and how AA had, over the years, enabled personal transformation and reconnection. Connecting the sense of narrative with the healing potential of the group, Khantzian (1995, p. 164) wisely observes:

> storytelling, sharing and bearing witness to each other's distress, and the traditions of openness and honesty act as sources of comfort and support for people who otherwise would go on in their lives with their distress unnoticed, unspoken and unacknowledged.

What has impressed me about AA is the sheer breadth of its collective, collected narrative resources ('capital' to use a sociologist's term), which are extended in a small way for its members each time an AA meeting occurs. These constitute the tools, scaffolding and therapeutic guides that enable better governance of self, an area to which we now turn.

14.4.4   AA: Structure of Care and Regulation

There are formal and informal aspects of care in AA, from greetings to meetings, 'personal programmes of recovery', networks, sponsors, ways of committing to service, and, of course, plain friendship. We have seen in the section on philosophy that acceptance of mutual vulnerabilities, strengths and talents help individuals to overcome the isolation and dead ends to which addiction has led. This recognition is part and parcel of what could be called a wider 'structure of care' and mutuality in AA.

If addiction is seen a disorder of self-regulation (see McGrath & O'Ryan, Chapter 6 in this volume), then recovery requires, by definition, new ways of consolidating and regulating the self. And just as addiction characteristically isolates individuals, recovery invites reconnection and reintegration within new or previously damaged relationships – a journey from omnipotence (or impotence) to mutuality (Weegmann, 2009). Mack (1981) develops a useful notion of 'self-governance', which he defines as a group of functions concerned with choosing, evaluating, planning and responsibility, broadly speaking, and how problems in these areas ('unmanageability') are addressed by AA. Rightly, he underlines that 'self-regulation' (for all of us) is dependent on the presence of helpful *others*, at least some of the time, of what he calls a 'self-other context'. In a later publication (Khantzian & Mack, 1989), he returns to the subject and considers how AA addresses characterological needs and problems in self-regulation/self-governance. Those in recovery grow in confidence as they retake ownership and management of their lives.

While space does not permit much further elaboration, the varied resources of the AA matrix, as it were, provide many ways in which better self-care is built; the sponsor-sponsee relationship is one obvious example of this. The importance of simple resocialization cannot be under-estimated, such as the adoption of roles within a meeting (e.g. making refreshments, or greeting). Time-limited, varied roles, allow people new experiences and consolidations. The social structures of AA and fellowship values allow graded experiences and responsibilities which run counter to previous substance-using lifestyles and degraded forms of relationship.

14.5   WHAT CAN PSYCHOLOGISTS AND HELPING PROFESSIONALS DO?

We can do many things to help, of which the following are a few suggestions:

- Read about AA, so as to be more familiar with their traditions and practices.
- Ask clients to talk about their experience of learning about themselves from AA meetings.

- Encourage clients to attend AA, regarding it as a form of therapeutic experimentation.
- Attend some 'open meetings'.
- Raise awareness of AA and other fellowships, in teams and within the culture of the services.

For those who wish to deepen their knowledge and experience, the following might be considered:

- Commit yourself for a longer, regular time to 'open meetings'.
- Become acquainted with 12 Step Facilitation Therapy.
- Establish local links to AA and other fellowships, hosting introductions to AA within the service, to which staff and clients alike can be invited.
- Read research relevant to AA and 12 Step Facilitation, including other literature, from sociological and narrative traditions.

14.6   CRITICISMS OF AA

AA, indeed, sometimes even the mention of their name, can arouse strong emotions, either of a positive or negative kind. There are also myths about AA, and in my experience psychologists and therapists are hardly immune from sharing some of these. Certainly some find the language of AA hard to relate to (e.g., use of the 'We' word, 'surrender', even 'alcoholic', which is not a term used in modern diagnostic classifications). Some find the sayings of AA too formulaic. But the notion of a 'Higher Power' is often cited as an obstacle; as a humanist, I can relate to this criticism and prefer the notion of a 'wider wisdom'. Certainly the 'God' word of the Steps, and other AA literature, however much it is qualified ('as we understand Him'), can raise strong, adverse reactions. If it does, I simply reframe the notion as one of 'what gives you hope, or trust, that things can improve and be different?' The important point is to help clients to envisage a resource beyond the self alone, as a source of inspiration and sustenance. I suspect that members of AA relate rather differently to its many dimensions and have certainly come across some successfully sober individuals who have a rather pragmatic stance and who do not emphasize the spiritual side to the programme. On the other hand, many find the spiritual orientation and values absolutely central to their recoveries (here one could reverse Jung's famous saying, 'spirituality drives out spirits'!), which those of us trained in 'secular' therapies can find hard to relate to.

In short, I think as helping professionals it is optimal to cultivate an attitude of interested, encouraging (and sometimes challenging) neutrality with respect to any of the resources that a client encounters or chooses to use. We need to hear criticisms of AA, as we might of any other approach (including our own preferred models) with empathy and reflection, always asking questions within ourselves such as, 'how does the client see it?', 'how come they have that reaction?', 'what is this telling me about their concerns or defences?', 'how ready, willing and able are they to …? and 'is there something that I am missing?'

14.7   POSTSCRIPT

Instead of a conclusion, I end openly in the manner in which I began, on a personal note. With approximately 20 years of clinical, training and publishing experience in substance misuse, I console myself with the paradox that, on the one hand, I know a great deal more than when I started, and salute the efforts of countless research and practising psychologists throughout the world who have helped me to navigate the territory that I came into; on the other hand, I now appreciate how much I do not know, and gladly accept the presence of mysteries and puzzles concerning just how people manage to get so 'sick' (or disordered, or any other word one prefers) and equally how impressive and unpredictable the process of recovery can be. Indeed, one of the further paradoxes in addiction/recovery, is how it is that patterns that seem so compelling and compulsive can give way in the *voluntary* 'act' (the word 'act' is not meant to imply a singular decision or moment in time) of recovery. AA offers us a language with which to capture this paradox, that of 'powerlessness' on the one hand, over substances and the governance (management) of one's life, which, given a process of 'giving up' control (and not just physically), releases a different sort of personal power and choice (see Brown's, 1985 analysis); acceptance is a condition of change. In this connection, I am pleased to notice Jim Orford's (2013) illuminating perspective (rediscovery?) of the themes of power and powerlessness in addicted individuals and in the families affected by them.

I owe a considerable debt of gratitude to AA and the way it has taught me new understandings. AA has also convinced me of the importance of qualitative narrative inquiry alongside other forms of research; AA members might have 'naught but stories' to tell, but stories are a considerable component of human subjectivity and of who we are in the world.

I would like to end with a brief story about Dr Max Glatt, who knew appalling, unimaginable trauma at first hand (his parents were slaughtered in the Holocaust; he and his sister narrowly escaped). He told his medical successor (Dr David Margo; pers. comm.) that in his earlier days, in the 1950s, he complained that his patients did not seem to do very well when they spoke to him, but were much better after speaking to each other! As alcoholism and addiction are traumatizing disorders, in their stripping of human control, health and dignity, AA was born with the discovery that one alcoholic can indeed help another.

NOTES

1)   The North West Thames Regional Drug and Alcohol Dependence Unit was set up by Dr Max Glatt, pioneer in the treatment and rehabilitation of addicted

individuals, in the late 1950s. The ward which housed the programme was renamed the Max Glatt Unit in the early 1990s. Glatt helped bring about important attitudinal shifts within services, from that of seeing alcoholics as unwelcome nuisances to patients requiring treatment (Benaim, 2002). I am unsure from where he derived the therapeutic community principles that underpinned the programme and which so caught my interest as a young psychologist. By the time I joined, although not a 12 Step programme (if greatly influenced by the Minnesota model), it was friendly to, and much encouraging of, AA attendance. When the programme closed in 1993, as a result of changes in commissioning, many former patients and staff mourned its loss.

2) AA recognized the contribution of its 'non-alcoholic friends' from the start, be they doctors, nurses or others. Dr Harry Tibeout, whose work I refer to, was a prominent psychiatrist, who became a staunch supporter of AA and who paved the way for Bill W. to address various medical societies. Non-alcoholics served alongside alcoholics as trustees to the Fellowship from the first board, established in 1938 in America, although the balance shifted from them being in the majority in the early phase to a minority, alongside alcoholics in recovery.

SUGGESTIONS FOR FURTHER READING

Flores, P. (1988). *Group psychotherapy with addicted populations*. New York: The Haworth Press.
Hänninen, V., & Koski-Jännes, A. (2004). Stories of attempts to recover from addiction. In P. Rosenqvist, A. Koski-Jännes, & L. Ojesjo (Eds.), *Addiction and the life course* (pp. 231–246). Helsinki: NAD.
Nowinski, J., & Baker, S. (1992). *The Twelve-Step facilitation handbook: A systematic approach to early recovery from alcoholism and addiction*. San Francisco: Jossey-Bass.

REFERENCES

Benaim, S. (2002). Max Glatt, pioneer in the treatment of alcohol and drug addicts. *Guardian*, 25 May.
Bill W. (1949). The Society of Alcoholics Anonymous. *American Journal of Psychiatry, 106/5*, 370–375.
Bill W. (1961). Letter from Carl Jung. In Bill W. (1967). *As Bill Sees It*. New York: AA World Services Inc.
Brown, S. (1985). *Treating the alcoholic: Adevelopmental model of recovery*. Chichester: John Wiley & Sons, Ltd.
Bruner, J. (1987). Life as narrative. *Social Research, 54*, 11–32.
Cain, C. (1991). Personal stories: Identity acquisition and self-understanding in Alcoholics Anonymous. *Ethos, 19*, 201–253.
DiClementi, C. (1995). Alcoholics Anonymous and the structure of change. In B. McCrady, & W. Miller (Eds.), *Research on Alcoholics Anonymous: Opportunities and alternatives*. New Brunswick, NJ: Rutgers Center for Alcohol Studies.

Flores, P. (1988). *Group psychotherapy with addicted populations*. New York: The Haworth Press.

Hänninen, V., & Koski-Jännes, A. (2004). Stories of attempts to recover from addiction. In P. Rosenqvist, A. Koski-Jännes, & L. Ojesjo (Eds.), *Addiction and the life course* (pp. 231–246). Helsinki: NAD.

Harré, R. (1997). Pathological autobiographies. *Philosophy, Psychiatry and Psychology, 4*, 99–109.

Humphreys, K. (2000). Community narratives and personal stories in Alcoholics Anonymous. *Journal of Community Psychology, 28*, 495–506.

Humphreys, K. (2004). *Circles of recovery: Self-help organisations for addictions*. Cambridge: Cambridge University Press.

Humphreys, K. (2011). *Circles of recovery: An interview with Keith Humphreys by William White*. www.williamwhitepapers.com

Kemp, R. (2013). Rock-bottom as an event of truth. *Existential Analysis, 24*, 106–116.

Khantzian, E. (1995). Alcoholics Anonymous – cult or corrective? *Journal of Substance Abuse Treatment, 12*, 157–165.

Khantzian, E., & Mack, J. (1989). Alcoholics Anonymous and contemporary psychodynamic theory. In M. Galanter (Ed.), *Alcoholism* (vol. 7). New York: Plenum Press.

Kurtz, E. (1982). Why AA works: The intellectual significance of Alcoholics Anonymous. *Journal of Studies in Alcohol, 43*, 38–80.

Kurtz, E., & Ketcham, K. (1992). *The spirituality of imperfection: Storytelling and the search for meaning*. New York: *Bantham Books*.

Levine, H. (1978). The discovery of addiction: Changing conceptions of habitual drunkenness in America. *Journal of Studies on Alcohol, 39*, 143–173.

Mack, J. (1981). Alcoholism, AA and governance of self. In M. Bean, & N. Zinberg (Eds.), *Dynamic approaches to understanding and treatment of alcoholism*. New York: Free Press.

McCrady, B., & Miller, W. (Eds.). (1995). *Research on Alcoholics Anonymous: Opportunities and alternatives*. New Brunswick, NJ: Rutgers Center for Alcohol Studies.

McLeod, S. (2010). Zone of Proximal Development – scaffolding – simply psychology. http://www.simplypsychology.org/Zone-of-Proximal-Development.html

Miller, W. (1990). Spirituality: The silent dimension in addiction research. *Drug and Alcohol Review, 9*, 259–266. doi:10.1080/09595239000185341

Miller, W., & Kurtz, E. (1994). Models of alcoholism used in treatment contrasting AA and other perspectives from which it is often confused. *Journal of Studies of Alcohol, 55*, 159–166. doi:http://dx.doi.org/10.15288/jsa.1994.55.159

Moos, R. (2008). Active ingredients of substance use-focused self-help groups. *Addiction, 103*, 387–396. doi:10.1111/j.1360-0443.2007.02111.x

Nowinski, J., & Baker, S. (1992). *The Twelve-Step Facilitation Handbook: A systematic approach to early recovery from alcoholism and addiction*. San Francisco: Jossey-Bass.

O'Halloran, S. (2008). *Talking oneself sober: The discourses of Alcoholics Anonymous*. Amherst, NY: Cambria Press.

Orford, J. (2013). *Power and powerlessness in addiction*. Cambridge: Cambridge University Press.

Ricoeur, P. (1990). *Oneself as another*. Trans. K. Blamey. Chicago: University of Chicago Press.

Robinson, C. M. (1996). Alcoholics Anonymous as seen from the perspective of self-psychology. *Smith College Studies in Social Work, 66*, 129–145. doi:10.1080/00377319709517484

Sarbin, T. (Ed.). (1986). *Narrative psychology: The storied nature of human conduct*. New York: Praeger.

Steigerwald, F., & Stone, D. (1999). Cognitive restructuring and the 12 Step programme of Alcoholics Anonymous. *Journal of Substance Abuse Treatment, 16*, 321–327.

Swora, M. (2001). Commemoration and the healing of memories in Alcoholics Anonymous. *Ethos, 29*, 58–77.

Thune, C. (1977). Alcoholism and the archetypal past: A phenomenological perspective on Alcoholics Anonymous. *Journal of Studies on Alcohol and Drugs, 38*, 75–88.

Tiebout, H. (1944). Therapeutic mechanisms of Alcoholics Anonymous. *American Journal of Psychiatry, 100,* 488–473.

Valverde, M., & White-Mair, K. (1999). 'One day at a time' and other slogans for everyday life: The ethical practices of Alcoholics Anonymous. *Sociology, 33,* 393–410.

Weegmann, M. (2004a). Alcoholics Anonymous: Group therapy without the group therapist. In B. Reading, & M. Weegmann. (Eds), *Group psychotherapy and addiction* (pp. 27–41). Chichester: John Wiley & Sons, Ltd.

Weegmann, M. (2004b). Alcoholics Anonymous: A group-analytic view of fellowship organisations. *Group Analysis, 37,* 243–258. doi:10.1177/0533316404041276

Weegmann M. (2009). Is Alcoholics Anonymous a therapeutic community? *Therapeutic Communities, 30,* 95–109.

Weegmann, M., & English, C. (2009). Beyond the shadow of drugs: Groups with substance misusers. *Group Analysis, 43,* 3–21. doi:10.1177/0533316409357131

Weegmann, M., & Leighton, T. (2004). Psychosocial approaches to addiction number 4: As easy as one, two, three: twelve-step facilitation therapy. *Drugs and Alcohol Today, 4,* 34–39. doi:http://dx.doi.org/10.1108/17459265200400046

Weegmann, M., & Piwowoz-Hjort, E. (2009). 'Naught but a story': Narratives of successful AA recovery. *Health Sociology Review, 18,* 273–283.

White, W. (1998). *Slaying the dragon: The history of addiction treatment and recovery in America.* Bloomington, IN: Chestnut Health Systems.

Wilson, K., Hayes, S., & Byrd, M. (2000). Exploring compatibilities between ACT and 12 Step treatment for substance abuse. *Journal of Rational Emotive and Cognitive-Behavioural Therapy, 18,* 209–234. doi:10.1023/A:1007835106007

15 Relapse Prevention: Underlying Assumptions and Current Thinking

ROBERT HILL AND JENNIFER HARRIS

*Addictions Clinical and Academic Group, South,
London and Maudsley NHS Foundation Trust, London, UK*

CHAPTER OUTLINE

15.1   INTRODUCTION

Relapse prevention (RP) appears deceptively straightforward to understand. An individual implements a change in relation to a specified piece of behaviour. It is taught as a component of this change strategy in order to minimize the risk that the individual does not revert to the previous behaviour. The components of relapse prevention include behavioural, cognitive, emotional and social factors. In this chapter we aim to provide an up-to-date overview of RP as well as highlighting some of the more interesting conundrums and difficulties associated with it.

15.2   WHAT IS RELAPSE PREVENTION?

There are many definitions of RP:

> Relapse Prevention (RP) is a self-control programme designed to teach individuals who are trying to change their behaviour how to anticipate and cope with the problem of relapse. In a very general sense, relapse refers to a breakdown or failure in a person's attempt to change or modify any target behaviour. (Marlatt & George, 1984)

> Relapse prevention can be conceptualized as essentially a problem-solving process and a reorientation of life attitudes and values. (Giannetti, 1993, p. 159)

> Relapse prevention is a generic term that refers to a wide range of cognitive and behavioural strategies designed to prevent relapse in the area of addictive behaviours and that focus on the crucial issues of helping people who are changing their behaviour to maintain the gains that they have made during the course of treatment of self-change. (Donovan, 2005, p. 5)

> Relapse prevention may be seen as a self-management programme designed to enhance the maintenance stage of the process of change. (Gossop, 1996, p. 163).

These definitions capture the main focus to be found in most relapse prevention programmes, namely the maintenance of positive change. As part of this, RP is also focused on the avoidance of negative states and difficult situations. RP can thus be thought of as 'doing something in order not to do something else'. As these definitions make clear, RP can be something that is taught to people, as well as a self-management strategy. RP is often referred to in three different ways: (1) as a theoretical model (Marlatt & Gordon, 1980); (2) as a strategy; and (3) as an intervention. RP programmes can thus be any, or all, of these things. What is clear is that the term 'relapse prevention' has become a dominant part of addictions discourse with many skills-based CBT treatments considered under the umbrella of RP (Hendershot, Witkiewitz, George & Marlatt, 2011).

Theory → Strategy → Components

The distinction between these three ways of viewing RP is important. If it is a theoretical model, then there are good reasons for ensuring that both health workers and clients have a good working understanding of the model. If it is a strategy, then it is probably sufficient to know the main thrust of the approach. If it is an intervention, then it may be sufficient to focus on particular components of the intervention only. It is our experience that staff tend to be taught RP as a theoretical model, but then communicate this to clients more as a strategy, and then finally focus down on specific components of the model either in one-to-one or in group settings (Hill & Harris, 2011). There are some advantages to this approach. At one level it could be argued that it is the job of health care professionals to translate complex ideas and models into readily accessible and understandable material. Thus, health care workers act as translators of theory so that clients can become agents of change. There are some potential disadvantages to this approach, namely the potential for the RP model to get diluted over time, that new workers to the profession may only be taught about the strategy without the theory, or there may be increased selectivity or bias about which components of RP are taught. Thus, although the Rule Violation Effect is an important aspect of Marlatt's model, it is one that is rarely focused on in RP programmes, and therefore an important component of understanding how lapses can turn into relapses is ignored. Instead, the overall message that one should do one's best to ensure that a lapse does not turn into a relapse is focused on by staff. In essence, this chapter attempts to acquaint or reacquaint the reader with three of the more well-known RP models so that informed translation of both their theory and strategic components can take place. Before we do this, it is important to say something about the assumptions underlying RP.

15.2.1   Relapse Prevention Is the Sufficient Effect

For some individuals, building RP into their change programme will be sufficient for them to prevent further lapses or relapses through the operation of learnt strategies. The individual may have made some overall changes to their lifestyle, or implemented strategies to prevent lapses and relapse. This is the gold standard of treatment: the delivery of an intervention resulting in long-term behavioural change. However, in addiction services, it is a minority of individuals who will experience successful change immediately without either lapsing or relapsing. For the majority, there will be difficulties sustaining change. In such situations, RP is once again offered, and it is here that one is confronted with the conundrum of behaviour change.

15.2.2   Reoccurrence of the Original Behaviour: A Philosophical Conundrum

Assuming that an individual has some experience of successful behavioural change and there is a reoccurrence of the original behaviour, relapse prevention has to deal with the fact that at a certain point in time the individual did something that resulted in successful behaviour change and at a later point in time they reverted to their old behaviour. To give a concrete example, a client successfully stops drinking alcohol after an inpatient admission for alcohol detoxification. Three months later, the client takes an alcoholic drink, something which, strictly speaking, is a lapse and then resumes drinking alcohol regularly, the more typical relapse. Usually relapse refers to a return to the same substance. However, we could envisage the case whereby an individual gives up alcohol and then three months later starts using crack cocaine, and although this is not a relapse to the same substance, it is reasonable to say that it is a relapse into an addictive pattern of behaviour.

There are a number of ways of thinking about the above scenario. At a basic level one could simply say that the individual has changed their mind about what they were doing, and that their return to the previous behaviour is merely an exercise in free choice. Thus, one can imagine a situation where an individual undertakes an existential re-evaluation of what was important in their life, so that although sobriety was a meaningful state or goal while an inpatient, it became less and less relevant when back at home. This reassessment of values, of what is important in life, again implies a rational component and insight into what matters in life. There is a degree of merit to this argument if one accepts that ultimately we all have free will in relation to acts that are freely chosen and where there is no external coercion. Obviously one has to ask whether in the case of addiction, such acts relating to the object of addiction are ever truly freely chosen, and also whether coercion can be as internal as external. The brain that requires pleasurable reinforcement may be as coercive as one's best friend propping up the bar urging you to have just one drink for old time's sake.

Clearly, the stance one takes in relation to this question is important, if it is a rational choice, then more relapse prevention is uncalled for, however, if relapse is defined in terms of the absence of rational choice (precisely because it is an addiction), then more relapse prevention would seem to be a good thing. Fellowship groups at first sight tend to take a clear-cut stance on this question, namely, that addiction is a disease and that the individual is powerless in relation to the disease. However, even here, the situation is by no means clear-cut, for if an individual can behave rationally in respect to how they deal with the disease, for example, by following the 12 Steps, then presumably there is no absence or reduction of rationality if they choose not to follow such a recommendation. RP would, however, tend to suggest that at certain times of high emotional intensity, rational self-control tends to be disrupted, short-term consequences come to the fore and deferred gratification is minimized.

Another way to account for a relapse is to focus on the possibility that what worked was relevant only at a certain point in time or for a certain time, so that the skills and motivation to retain the required behaviour change only worked in certain circumstances, and that when those circumstances changed, then the buffer against relapse was removed. Sobriety when in residential treatment is the norm (and also the criterion for remaining there), yet relapse rates remain high after leaving. This may be explained by a change in motivation or reassessment of values, but it is also possible that the skills learnt failed the generalizability tests to everyday life and had poor ecological validity.

RP also needs to deal with the fact that addiction is for many clients as much an undesirable state of affairs as a desirable one. The reality of ambivalence is a powerful reminder that substances function both to attract and repel, often in asynchronous time. When these experiences occur together, it becomes the well-known experience of craving – where one both wants and doesn't want at the same time. Of course the wanting and the not wanting in all probability refer to different components of the addiction experience – I want to be enveloped and warmed by heroin, but I don't want to then feel guilty. Strictly speaking, such thoughts do not occur at the same time, but the subjective experience is such that the thoughts can seem to come one on top of each other.

It is all too easy to assume non-rational reasons for relapse, as if failure can be located entirely within the individual's wavering motivation or lack of skills. If one accepts that rationality does not magically disappear when someone becomes addicted, then in each individual lapse situation, the question of the exercise of free choice versus irrational compulsion needs to be addressed.

Historically the situation was a lot easier. Prior to cognitive-behavioural approaches to relapse prevention, addiction treatment approaches were dominated by moral, disease and spiritual models (see, e.g., Ogden, 2012). From the moral perspective, addiction and relapse were seen as either a lack of will or lack of moral character; from a disease model, addiction is considered in terms of physiology and heredity, and relapse is viewed as a disease being reactivated. The spiritual model views addiction as a loss of contact with a higher power. What all of these models tended to share was a focus on the individual being in denial about what they needed in order to become well, and, thus, if they did not manage to change their behaviour, or sustain such change over time, then they were said to be in denial. The remedy was also quite clear. Manipulation, cajoling, intimidation and indoctrination were all quite acceptable ways of breaking through the wall of denial. It is a bit akin to the shaking of a child in order to get them to see sense regarding a misdeed they have committed, or dangerous situation that they had put themselves in. The goal was to verbally inform and berate, and if a health message was not getting through, then one ordered a larger megaphone or more people to deliver the message. The following description of synanon peer-led meetings by Yablonksy in the United States highlights this approach quite nicely:

> A key point of the sessions is an emphasis on extreme, uncompromising candour about one another. "No holds or statements are barred from the group effort at truth-seeking about problem situations, feelings, and emotions of each and all members of the group." The synanon is, in some respects, an emotional battlefield. Here an individual's delusions, distorted self-images, and negative behavior are attacked again and again. The verbal-attack method involves exaggerated statements, riddicule and analogy. The "attack," paradoxically, is an expression of love. (Yablonsky, 1965, pp. 137–138)

We have moved a long way from such approaches today, partly because health education campaigns and motivational interviewing (Miller & Rollnick, 2013) have taught us that they tend not to work, at least for the majority of people. However, it would be naïve to think that what we do now is without its biases and subjective components, for to talk about addiction is also to talk about language, cultural artefacts, research, social pressures and educational hegemony. What one learns to do is generally what one ends up doing, so that our current state of thinking about RP will determine how RP is practised.

15.3   MODELS OF RELAPSE PREVENTION

Addiction is still essentially characterized as a chronic, relapsing condition with periods of remission and relapse. Some consider relapse to be the rule rather than the exception (De Leon, 1993), with relapse being the most often cited obstacle to successful treatment outcomes (Witkiewitz & Marlatt, 2007).

Findings from both old and recent studies suggest that lapse is most common during the first two or three months after treatment and that while the risk is not linear over time, the risk slows down as the length of abstinence increases (Sutton, 1979). Analysis of survival curves found that an average of 65% of a sample drank alcohol, smoked or used heroin within the first three months of treatment (Hunt, Barnett & Branch, 1971). More recent work by Witkiewitz and Masyn (2008) looking at 563 clients, after a community alcohol detoxification, found the highest risk of lapse within the first two months, followed by three to seven months after, with decreasing risk over eight to twelve months. While 30% of clients continuously abstained, 70% had at least one lapse. Those who lapsed showed three drinking trajectories: (1) heavy, frequent drinking (6%); (2) 'prolapsing' – frequent drinking after lapse, but return to less frequent (12%); and (3) infrequent, moderate drinking (82%). The strongest predictors of heavy, frequent drinking were alcohol dependence and coping behaviour.

15.3.1   The Original Model of Relapse Prevention (Marlatt & Gordon, 1985)

On the whole, when people talk about relapse prevention, they are talking about the original model of relapse developed by Marlatt and Gordon and published in their 1985 book. This original model captured an important conceptual shift from moral, disease and spiritual models of addiction, to a cognitive behavioural one. Marlatt and Gordon's model opened up a more flexible, optimistic view of behaviour change and lapse to that which had been previously held. Thus, a lapse was not viewed as a failure, but rather as part of a process, a temporary setback on the road to change, and providing opportunities for learning, self-understanding and intervention. The model offered a framework to understand the process of lapse/relapse and, importantly, offered a set of cognitive and behavioural strategies, both specific and global, in order to prevent or limit relapse episodes. The model suggested that high-risk situations (HRS) can trigger craving/urges to use/drink. Where individuals have prepared a positive coping response, they reduce their likelihood of relapse and increase their self-efficacy. However, failure to cope with a HRS is likely to reduce their self-efficacy, and through cognitive processes, such as positive outcome expectancies and rule violation effect, increases the chances of a lapse leading into a relapse.

Thus, RP strategies aims to teach individuals to anticipate, recognize and cope with the possibility of relapse through identifying and coping with HRS, enhancing self-efficacy, lapse management and cognitive restructuring. Drink/drug diaries, the Inventory of Drinking Situations (Annis, Graham & Davis, 1987), the Inventory of Drug-Taking Situations (Annis, Martin & Graham, 1992) and the Situational Confidence Questionnaire (Annis & Graham, 1988) all offer useful tools for identifying such high-risk situations.

More global interventions focus on supporting longer-term change through identifying and coping with covert determinants of relapse such as lifestyle imbalance, craving, and cognitive and behavioural processes that set up lapse by a series of decisions over time (e.g. seeking immediate gratification, denial, justification and seemingly irrelevant decisions (SIDs)). RP focuses on promoting lifestyle balance so that the 'shoulds' of life do not outweigh the 'wants' and result in a desire for indulgence. Hence RP also entails working on balanced lifestyle, stimulus control, urge management, and individualized relapse road maps. Clients' longer-term maintenance is likely to be maximized by timely access to additional resources that support lifestyle balance and learning skills to promote well-being, meaningful relationships and life purpose. Interested readers can find an excellent description of the original model by Larimer, Palmer and Marlatt (1999) along with relatively recent client and therapist workbooks (Daley & Marlatt, 2006a, 2006b).

A number of research studies have investigated the reliability of the RP model (e.g. Carroll, 1996; Irving, Bowers, Dunn & Wang, 1999; Agboola, McNeill, Coleman & Leonardi Bee, 2010). The Relapse Prevention and Extension Project (PREP) supported the overall model of relapse process, for example, finding that relapse was predicted by coping and not simply by exposure to high-risk situations (Lowman, Allen & Stout & the Relapse Research Group, 1996). The study supported other findings that many relapse episodes involve situations with negative emotional states, and the role of the rule violation effect in precipitating a relapse, specifically in those who had a greater belief in the disease model and higher commitment to abstinence (Larimer et al., 1999).

While RP does not seem to be associated with higher long-term abstinence rates than other active treatments, the studies do support the effectiveness of RP interventions in reducing the frequency and severity of relapses, and also in positively impacting on mental health (Carroll, 1996; Irving et al., 1999). Carroll (1996) suggests that there is a delayed emergence effect, with better longer-term outcomes in the maintenance phase, i.e. one-year follow-up, as clients come to learn and establish skills. Irving et al.'s (1999) meta-analysis found that RP is equally efficacious across inpatient and outpatient settings, as well as in individual and group delivery. There is some evidence that while RP offers benefit for all substances (Carroll, 1996), Irving et al. (1999) found it most effective for reducing alcohol and poly-substance use, and least effective for tobacco and cocaine use. This would point to the need to tailor RP approaches for tobacco and cocaine treatments. Review studies indicated the value of combining RP with pharmacotherapy for alcohol treatment (Irving et al., 1999) and smoking programmes (Agboola et al., 2010).

15.3.2 The Dynamic Model of Relapse (Witkiewitz & Marlatt, 2004)

Although the original model of relapse offered a useful framework and set of techniques, it did face criticisms for considering the relapse process as linear and continuous, and also underplaying the importance of negative emotional states and cravings. On the basis of research tracking drinking trajectories and clinical observations of sudden changes in drinking behaviours, Marlatt and his collaborator Witkiewitz (2004), building on the work of others, subsequently put forward their dynamic model of relapse. This model is based on dynamic systems theory and catastrophe modelling to capture how a sudden discontinuous change in behaviour can result from slight continuous changes in system parameters. Specifically, it focuses on how a small shift in one physiological, psychological or social factor can tip the balance from abstinence to lapse or even sudden, abrupt return to relapse ('fall off the wagon'), or vice versa (Witkiewitz & Marlatt, 2007).

Witkiewitz and Marlatt (2007) give a useful summary of the theoretical thinking behind this model and how they applied the cusp catastrophe model to relapse through detection of 'catastrophe flags' (Gilmore, 1981) and stochastic catastrophe modelling of alcohol treatment outcome data.

The dynamic model views lapse as a complex system of multiple elements that interact dynamically within the context of a high-risk situation to promote effective coping or tip the balance towards lapse. It conceptualizes a temporal relationship between predisposing vulnerability factors (tonic or 'distal relapse risks') and phasic processes (or 'proximal relapse risks') that interact within the context of an immediate HRS; the phasic response represents the turning point that can tip the balance and result in sudden changes in substance use. Tonic processes confer chronic vulnerability to lapse / substance use; these include background factors such as degree of dependence, psychiatric conditions and cognitive impairment. Phasic processes reflect responses to the immediate HRS and these include cognitive processes, self-efficacy, physical withdrawal, craving, coping behaviours, affective state and shift in social support.

From a clinical perspective, the dynamic model encourages clinicians to develop detailed formulations for each client to best understand the complex interplay of salient distal and proximal risk factors for each individual. Mitcheson et al. (2010) draw on a range of cognitive-behavioural models to offer practical approaches to formulating an individual's needs.

The dynamic model emphasizes negative affect as a significant predictor of relapse, and specifically identifies craving as the mediating factor between negative affect and relapse. This is supported in the COMBINE study (Anton et al., 2006) which used a multi-method approach to evaluate latent class models of a sample of 1,383 participants over 68 weeks post alcohol treatment. Their findings supported a relationship between small changes in mood and large changes in drinking behaviour. This highlights the importance of targeting craving, negative affect and stress during treatment, particularly among individuals with dual diagnosis, and also the importance of targeting craving and negative affect post treatment. They recommended using relapse road maps and warning clients about the HRS of negative emotions. This would also highlight the value of appropriate mental health screening and support as part of overall treatment.

Hufford, Witkiewitz, Shields, Kodya and Caruso (2003) concluded that a higher distal risk at intake increased a client's susceptibility to responding to small changes in proximal risks with drastic changes in drinking following treatment. They recommend discussing risk with the client and offering interventions to target the proximal risks. A client with lower distal risk at intake may be less susceptible to sudden, drastic changes in drinking, with their risk proportional to the increases in proximal risks, suggesting value in monitoring proximal risks.

15.3.3   Mindfulness-Based Relapse Prevention (MBRP; Marlatt, Bowen, Chawla & Witkiewitz, 2008)

Dr Alan Marlatt's personal discovery of the benefits of transcendental meditation in the 1970s influenced his professional practice. In the early days of RP, Marlatt included the Buddhist practice of Vipassana ('seeing things as they really are') to develop lifestyle balance among high-risk drinkers (Marlatt & Marques, 1977). This ultimately laid the foundation for Mindfulness-based Relapse Prevention (MBRP; Marlatt, Bowen, Chawla & Witkiewitz, 2008). It is patterned after/on mindfulness-based stress reduction (MBSR; Kabat-Zinn, 1990), mindfulness-based cognitive therapy (MBCT; Segal, Williams & Teasdale, 2002), and Daley and Marlatt's (2006b) relapse prevention protocol. (This is also discussed in McGrath and O'Ryan, Chapter 6 in this volume.)

MBRP is an eight-week outpatient programme of two-hour sessions and daily home practice. It incorporates components such as formal mindfulness practice (body scan, mindful movement, sitting meditation, loving kindness, mountain meditation and walking meditation), informal practice (mindfulness of daily activities, urge surfing and SOBER breathing space), and coping strategies. RP skills are presented and practised in a way that is consistent with a mindfulness approach. The process of the group models inquiry of the immediate experience in the present moment rather than narration, evaluation and interpretation. The principle of present moment focus is extended to encourage participants to differentiate between direct experience and reactions to experiences that often proliferate into further secondary responses, then to recognize when they are caught up in stories and reactivity, realize their choice to pause and return to the present experience. Participants are invited to explore how this process might be familiar and related to craving, and to develop compassion and non-judgement through understanding this is a universal experience and how all our minds are. A sense of compassion and curiosity about the struggles of daily practice normalizes these challenges and encourages gentle open-ended questions about the potential benefit of regular practice.

Craving and the desire to avoid negative affect are primary triggers to substance use. MBRP directly addresses these key relapse risks through encouraging individuals to move step-by-step away from automatic pilot and destructive behaviour, towards moment-by-moment awareness, acceptance and choice. It encourages individuals to deepen their awareness and acceptance of uncomfortable states, see thoughts as thoughts, thereby encouraging a thoughtful choice rather than an automatic/habitual/conditioned response. This has particular salience for coping with negative affect, craving and pain, all of which are commonly reported triggers to lapse.

Marlatt emphasizes the importance of facilitators' personal practice of mindfulness so that they can respond with understanding, sensitivity and compassion from their own lived experience of the struggles of consistent practice. Regular attendance by participants is vital, especially of the first session. Those with trauma histories are invited to have their eyes open and experiment with posture to feel safe during, for example, the body scan. There is some suggestion that between-session practice and therapeutic alliance promote increases in initial mindfulness (Bowen & Kurz, 2012), although the authors speculate that other factors might better support longer-term mindfulness.

There have been exciting results from studies evaluating the benefit of MBRP. It has been shown to be associated with reduced drug/alcohol use and improved abstinence rates (Carroll, 1996; Irving et al., 1999; Kadden, 2001). MBRP also outperformed a 'treatment-as-usual' group receiving standard outpatient aftercare using a 12-step process-oriented format bringing significantly lower rates of substance use. The authors found that craving was mediated by acceptance, awareness and non-judgement (Witkiewitz, Bowen, Douglas & Hsu, 2013). Brewer et al. (2009) found that cocaine and alcohol users randomly assigned to the MBRP group showed lower psychological and physiological responses to stress in comparison to those assigned to the CBT treatment group. MBRP further shows particular benefit for individuals with dual diagnosis (Hoppes, 2006; Witkiewitz & Bowen, 2010). As well as showing positive outcomes, participants appear to find this treatment acceptable (Bowen et al., 2009) although Skanavi, Laquelle and Aubin (2011) write that MBRP requires intensive participation and is best suited to highly motivated clients.

Neuroimaging has allowed us to examine how brain areas associated with craving and negative affect are positively affected by mindfulness training (Brewer et al.,2009; Witkiewitz, Lustyk & Bowen, 2012) and overall it seems that mindfulness meditation may affect neural responses to negative affect, and may reverse, repair or compensate for neuro-adaptive changes associated with addiction (Witkiewitz, Lustyk & Bowen, 2012).

15.4   ADDRESSING CO-EXISTING MENTAL HEALTH

It is well known that many clients who struggle with addiction also contend with a co-morbid mental health problem (Axis I) or personality disorder (Axis II) (see Huxley, Chapter 10 in this volume, for a more detailed discussion). Recovery for each difficulty may not be at the same stage, and each presents a relapse risk in the other (Groce & Ryglewicz, 1998). It is clearly important that services can accurately assess co-occurring mental health difficulties, regularly monitor mood and offer appropriate psychiatric medication and psychosocial interventions alongside any RP work. It is thought that the repeated disruptions in neurotransmitters (such as serotonin, dopamine and corticotropin-releasing factors) associated with long-term substance use, increase an individual's vulnerability to relapse when craving. Similarly, over repeated use, depressed/distressed states or thoughts come to be associated with relapse-related thoughts and cravings. Mindfulness increases awareness of these learned patterns and encourages individuals to learn new responses. Indeed, there is promising evidence for the benefit of MBRP for those who face dual recovery (Hoppes, 2006; Witkiewitz & Bowen, 2010). Brewer, Bowen, Smith, Marlatt and Potenza (2010) offer a discussion of the pathways that might be involved in depression and substance use to better understand how mindfulness positively affects each.

15.5   NEUROPSYCHOLOGICAL AND ASSOCIATED DIFFICULTIES WHEN UNDERTAKING RP

There is considerable evidence for neuropsychological deficits in alcohol dependence (Knight & Longmore, 1993; Walker, Staton & Leukefeld, 2001; and see Morrison and Svanberg, Chapter 7 in this volume). The role of thiamine deficiency in Wernike's disease is also well established (Kopelman, 1995). Around half of all clients entering treatment for alcohol dependence have some cognitive impairment (Wang et al., 1993; Morgenstern & Bates, 1999).

While RP recognizes that an individual's motivational state can change over time, it tends to assume a level playing field with regard to their abilities. In some respects, it is an empty vessel model in which the client needs to be filled up with RP information and strategies. It also assumes that individuals are essentially equal in being able to access the strategies they need when they need them. While this is an ideal situation, it does neglect the issue of differential capabilities and the damage caused by substance use to self-regulating capacities and memory systems. This is a complex area that requires a great deal of work to deal with adequately. Aside from the fact that some individuals may have specific learning or sensory difficulties, which always needs to be taken into account when teaching, there are four main components that we would like to draw the readers attention to, and which need to be taken into consideration when delivering RP: (1) current cognitive functioning – IQ; (2) attentional ability; (3) memory; and (4) executive functioning.

People obviously differ in their level of overall intelligence, the distinction between average IQ and slightly above and slightly below average probably do not manifest themselves in everyday situations particularly strongly. Extremes at both ends probably do, and it is important to adapt any RP strategy for these extremes. Poor literacy should not be conflated with low IQ, and disrupted schooling may be a far more salient factor when thinking about RP than low IQ.

Attention is very much the building block of any learning strategy, and if an individual has poor attention, then any subsequent failure of RP may be more to do with this than anything else. Attention is, of course, not a unitary construct. Thus, we can measure sustained attention (keeping on task for a long period of time), focused attention (attending to the specific relevant information and excluding that which is extraneous), and divided attention (attending to more than one thing at a time). Difficulties in any of these areas will require an adaptation of the RP approach.

If attention is the ability to attend to information in the first place, memory is the ability to register that information into some form of short- or long-term storage and then being able to access such information when needed. There are many different forms of memory, but arguably one of the most important is prospective memory – the ability to remember to do something in the future. RP essentially is also about remembering to do x instead of y in the future and to recall what that entails. Disruption to this often means that someone fails to sustain change, not because their strategies fail, but because they do not remember to use such strategies. Individuals also differ in the extent to which they can freely recall information and their ability to recognize information, given a suitable cue. Recognition memory tends to be better for most people than free recall and this should therefore be built into the way RP is taught.

Finally, one needs to consider executive functioning (EF). This is:

> [a] multifaceted neuropsychological construct that can be defined as (1) forming, (2) maintaining, and (3) shifting mental sets, corresponding to the abilities to (1) reason and generate goals and plans, (2) maintain focus and motivation to follow through with goals and plans, and (3) flexibly alter goals and plans in response to changing contingencies. (Suchy, 2009, p. 106)

Given the importance for recovery of forming and sustaining goals and plans, maintaining motivation and altering plans and goals in response to new information, any deficit in these areas would, it could be argued, have a huge effect on the ability to pursue treatment goals and remain abstinent. To give some examples: (1) it could be argued that high levels of relapse in alcohol dependence are related to specific difficulties with inhibition in relation to cravings or alcohol exposure; (2) that alterations in motivational states belong to the EF category rather than something more nebulous like 'will power'; (3) that long-term rewards, or deferred gratification, can be compromised by inefficient goal planning; (4) that clients who engage in 'seemingly irrelevant decisions' are actually displaying a deficit in planning, rule-following and decision-making; and (5) that high-risk situations require a form of rule switching so that the individual needs to suddenly change their response set. In other words, because EF effects many higher-order reasoning processes, one could anticipate any test deficits to be translated into real-world functioning.

In terms of assessing everyday functioning, there appear to be three problems: (1) that while the more ecologically valid tests of EF may display some degree of verisimilitude, they tend to lack veridicality; (2) that dysfunction of the pre-frontal cortex (PFC) may not translate into behavioural dysfunction at all; and (3) that one of the most important components of EF, namely, the ability to function in a socially appropriate way by exercising good judgement and appropriateness in social contexts is rarely touched on in tests of EF. This social or affective dimension of EF certainly makes sense clinically, and a distinction has been drawn between so-called 'cool' and 'hot' EF (Zelazo & Cunningham, 2007). Cool EF is conceptualized as being activated in abstract situations and requiring cool reasoning abilities. Hot EF is activated in emotional or motivational-type situations. Zelazo and Cunningham (2007) suggest that cool EF processes are governed by the dorsolateral pre-frontal cortex, while hot EF is governed by the ventromedial pre-frontal cortex. In addition, hot EF is thought to be governed by the right PFC and cool EF by the left. While this simple binary division is of relatively recent origin, there does seem to be some neuroanatomical support for such a distinction, and theoretically it may come to explain some of the discrepancies that can be found between relatively intact EF test performance and seemingly impaired EF functioning in real-world contexts, and vice versa.

Interestingly, Zelazo and Cunningham (2007) note:

> the link between EF and emotional regulation (ER) is most closely seen when the problem to be solved *just is* that of modulating emotion, as in ER. In fact, in such cases, EF just is ER – the two constructs are isomorphic.

Uekermann and Daum (2008) have shown how people with alcohol dependence have difficulties in accurate emotional processing of facial expressions, i.e. taking longer to decode facial expressions and over-estimating intensity of emotions.

If the hot/cool hypothesis turns out to be true, and research such as Uekermann and Daum's (2008) begins to explore this, it would have enormous implications for our understanding of addictive behaviours and EF. As things currently stand, however, one would have to say that deficits in EF obviously matter in so far as these indicate change in an individual's ability to perform well in abstract or cool tests of EF, but in terms of how these translate into everyday emotional life, we currently just do not know. The challenge will obviously be how one can begin to go about testing such emotional intensity in an ethical and accurate manner.

It is also important to also acknowledge the role that other factors such as mental states, psychotropic medication and physical health can have on both motivation and cognitive capacity. To assume that an individual with low mood, long-term health problems and on current psychotropic medication is going to have the same resources to attend to, understand and implement RP strategies as someone without such difficulties would be an extreme leap of faith. This, then, if for no other reason, is a good rationale for the employment of psychologists in the establishment, review and supervision of RP programmes.

15.6 CONCLUSION

It has been our intention in this chapter to highlight some of the more interesting questions concerning relapse prevention, as well as outlining three of the influential RP models. To conclude we want to briefly say something about RP where a client's goal is not total abstinence. An obvious example in the United Kingdom is the increasing number of people, particularly younger sections of the population, who are engaged in periodic but regular binge drinking. Here the goal may not be abstinence, but harm reduction or drinking in moderation. Does RP have anything particular to offer with regard to such groups? Generally, where people are still using drugs or alcohol and they are seeking behavioural change, they are either looking to minimize, reduce or control their use of the target substance, or they are looking to deal with some form of causal outcome from such use, for example, reducing cocaine use after excessive drinking, or trying to reduce their anger after drinking. RP can have a role to play in such scenarios, provided that the model is adapted slightly, particularly that the wording of strategies is made relevant to a goal of moderation, and also that the target behaviour to be changed is clearly specified. Such goals might focus on drinking days, quantities consumed or on other social consequences such as absences from work. Developing strategies to manage such changes, promoting self-efficacy and drawing on global interventions to address covert antecedents are areas where RP can play a significant role.

Although we have not dealt with mutual aid and support groups in this chapter, we would like to highlight its importance in promoting and sustaining recovery as self-help groups can be a highly effective support in promoting behaviour change. Professionals facilitating client's access to mutual aid or self-help groups, such as AA, are extremely important and should be suggested as a matter of course at the beginning of any treatment journey, or as part of routine information-giving for individuals with substance misuse problems (see Weegmann, Chapter 14, in this volume, for a more detailed discussion). One of the main reasons people report finding self-help groups useful is that everyone has gone, or is going, through the same thing and can therefore provide understanding and support, based upon personal experience. Public Health England (2013) recommends a three-stage process for facilitating access to mutual aid:

1) Introducing mutual aid.
2) Encouraging the client to engage with a mutual aid group.
3) Taking an interest in the client's experience of mutual aid groups.

Many self-help groups are increasingly focusing on what is known as 'recovery capital' which refers to the sum of resources necessary to initiate and sustain recovery from substance misuse. As such, it conveys an extremely positive message regarding the reason for changing addictive patterns of behaviour and becomes in many ways a more positive way of conveying to clients the reasons for ensuring a robust relapse prevention strategy.

SUGGESTIONS FOR FURTHER READING

Daley, D., & Marlatt, G. A. (2006a). *Overcoming your drug or alcohol problem: Effective recovery strategies workbook.* New York: Oxford University Press.

Daley, D., & Marlatt, G. A. (2006b). *Overcoming your drug or alcohol problem: Effective recovery strategies therapists guide.* New York: Oxford University Press.

Larimer, M. E., Palmer, R. S., & Marlatt, G. A. (1999). Relapse prevention: An overview of Marlatt's cognitive-behavioural model. *Alcohol Research and Health, 23*, 151–160.

REFERENCES

Agboola, S., McNeill, A., Coleman, T., & Leonardi Bee, J. (2010). A systematic review of the effectiveness of smoking relapse prevention interventions for abstinent smokers. *Addiction*, *105*, 1362–1380. doi:10.1111/j.1360-0443.2010.02996.x

Annis, H. M., & Graham, J. M. (1988). *Situational Confidence Questionnaire (SCQ)*. Toronto, ON: Addiction Research Foundation.

Annis, H. M., Graham, J. M., & Davis, C. S. (1987). *Inventory of Drinking Situations (IDS) user's guide*. Toronto, ON: Addiction Research Foundation.

Annis, H. M., Martin, G., & Graham, J. M. (1992). *Inventory of Drug-Taking situations (IDTS) user's guide*. Toronto, ON: Addiction Research Foundation.

Anton, R. F., O'Malley, S. S., Ciraulo, D., Cisler, R. A., Couper, D., Donovan, D. M., … Zweben, A. (2006). Combined pharmacotherapies and behavioral interventions for alcohol dependence. The COMBINE study: a randomized controlled trial. *The Journal of the American Medical Association*, *295*, 2003–2017. doi:10.1001/jama.294.17.2003

Bowen, S., Chawla, N., Collins, S., Witkiewitz, K., Hsu, S., Grow, J., et al. (2009). Mindfulness-based relapse prevention for substance use disorders: A pilot efficacy trial. *Substance Abuse*, *30*, 205–305. doi:10.1080/08897070903250084

Bowen, S., & Kurz, A. S. (2012). Between-session practice and therapeutic alliance as predictors of mindfulness after mindfulness-based relapse prevention. *Journal of Clinical Psychology*, *68*, 236–245. doi:10.1002/jclp.20855

Brewer, J. A., Bowen, S., Smith, J. T., Marlatt, G. A., & Potenza, M. N. (2010). Mindfulness-based treatments for co-occurring depression and substance use disorders: What can we learn from the brain? *Addiction*, *105*, 1698–1706. doi:10.1111/j.1360-0443.2009.02890.x

Brewer, J., Sinha, R., Chen, J. A., Michalsen, R. N., Babuscio, T. A., Nich, C., et al. (2009). Mindfulness training and stress reactivity in substance abuse: Results from a randomised, controlled stage I pilot study. *Substance Abuse*, *30*, 306–317. doi:10.1080/08897070903250241

Carroll, K. M. (1996). Relapse prevention as a psychosocial treatment: A review of controlled clinical trials. *Experimental and Clinical Psychopharmacology*, *4*, 46–54. link.springer.com/chapter/10.1007/0-306-48581-8_92.

Daley, D., & Marlatt, G. A. (2006a). *Overcoming your drug or alcohol problem: Effective recovery strategies workbook*. New York: Oxford University Press.

Daley, D., & Marlatt, G. A. (2006b). *Overcoming your drug or alcohol problem: Effective recovery strategies therapists guide*. New York: Oxford University Press.

De Leon, G. (1993). What psychologists can learn from addiction treatment research. *Psychology of Addictive Behaviors*, *7*, 103–109. doi.apa.org/journals/adb/7/2/103

Donovan, D. M. (2005). Assessment of addictive behaviors for relapse prevention. In D. M. Donovan, & A. G. Marlatt (Eds.), *Assessment of addictive behaviours*. New York: Guilford Press.

Giannetti, V. J. (1993). Brief relapse prevention with substance abusers. In R. A. Wells, & V. J. Giannetti (Eds.), *Casebook of brief psychotherapies: Applied clinical psychology* (pp 159–178). New York: Plenum Press.

Gilmore, R. (1981). *Catastrophe theory for scientists and engineers*. New York: Wiley.

Gossop, M. (1996). Cognitive and behavioural treatment for substance misuse. In G. Edwards, & D. Dare (Eds.), *Psychotherapy, psychological treatments and the addictions*. C ambridge: Cambridge University Press.

Groce, R. G. & Ryglewicz, H. (1998). *Dual diagnosis, relapse prevention monograph: A report on the training Initiative 1997–1998*. Portland, ME: Co-occurring collaborative of southern Maine. http://ccsme.org/userfiles/files/relapse20mono.pdf

Hendershot, C. S., Witkiewitz, K. A., George, W. H., & Marlatt, G. A. (2011). Relapse prevention for addictive behaviors. *Substance Abuse Treatment, Prevention & Policy*, *6*, 17–33. doi:10.1186/1747-597X-6-17

Hill, R. G., & Harris, J. (2011). *Principles and practice of group work in addictions.* London: Routledge.

Hoppes, K. (2006). The application of mindfulness-based cognitive interventions in the treatment of co-occurring addictive and mood disorders. *CNS Spectrums, 11,* 829–851. doi:http://dx.doi.org/10.1017/S1092852900014991

Hufford, M. H., Witkiewitz, K., Shields, A. L., Kodya, S., & Caruso, J. C. (2003). Applying nonlinear dynamics to the prediction of alcohol use disorder treatment outcomes. *Journal of Abnormal Psychology, 112,* 219–227. doi:http://dx.doi.org/10.3109/10550499508997419

Hunt, W. A., Barnett, L. W., & Branch, L. G. (1971). Relapse rates in addiction programs. *Journal of Clinical Psychology, 27,* 455–456. doi:10.1002/1097-4679(197110)27:4<455::AID-JCLP2270270412>3.0.CO;2-R

Irving, J. E., Bowers, C. A., Dunn, M. E., & Wang, M. C. (1999). Efficacy of relapse prevention: A meta-analytic review. *Journal of Consulting & Clinical Psychology, 67,* 563–570. doi:10.1037/0022-006X.67.4.563

Kabat-Zinn, J. (1990). *Full catastrophe living: Using the wisdom of your body and mind to face stress, pain, and illness.* London: Piatikus Books.

Kadden, R. M. (2001). *Cognitive-behaviour therapy for substance dependence: Coping skills training.* Connecticut: University of Connecticut Press.

Knight, R. G., & Longmore, B. E. (1993). *Clinical neuropsychology of alcoholism.* Hove: Lawrence Erlbaum Associates.

Kopelman, M. D. (1995). The Korsakoff syndrome. *British Journal of Psychiatry, 166,* 67–85. doi:10.1192/bjp.166.2.154

Larimer, M. E., Palmer, R. S., & Marlatt, G. A. (1999). Relapse prevention: An overview of Marlatt's cognitive-behavioural model. *Alcohol Research and Health, 23,* 151–160.

Lowman, C., Allen, J., & Stout, R. L. & the Relapse Research Group. (1996). Replication and extension of Marlatt's taxonomy of relapse precipitants: Overview of procedures and results. *Addiction, 91,* 51–71. doi:10.1046/j.1360-0443.91.12s1.16.x

Marlatt, G. A., Bowen, S., Chawla, N., & Witkiewitz, K. (2008). Mindfulness-Based Relapse Prevention for substance abusers: Therapist training and therapeutic relationships. In S. Hick, & T. Bien (Eds.), *Mindfulness and the therapeutic relationship.* New York: Guilford Press.

Marlatt, G. A., & George, W. H. (1984). Relapse prevention: Introduction and overview of the model. *British Journal of Addiction, 79,* 261–273. doi:10.1111/j.1360-0443.1984.tb00274.x/full

Marlatt, G. A., & Gordon, J. R. (1980). Determinants of relapse: Implications for the maintenance of behaviour change. In P. O. Davidson, & S. M. Davidson (Eds.), *Behavioural medicine: Changing health lifestyles.* New York: Brunner/Mazel.

Marlatt, G. A., & Gordon, J. R. (1985). *Relapse prevention: Maintenance strategies in the treatment of addictive behaviors.* New York: Guilford Press.

Marlatt, G. A., & Marques, J. K. (1977). *Meditation, behavioural self-management: strategies, techniques and outcomes.* New York: Brunner/Mazel.

Miller, W. R., & Rollnick, S. (2013). *Motivational interviewing: Helping people change.* New York: Guilford Press.

Mitcheson, L., Maslin, J., Meynon, T., Morrison, T., Hill, R., & Wanigaratne, S. (2010). *Applied cognitive and behavioural approaches to the treatment of addiction: A practical treatment guide.* Chichester: Wiley-Blackwell.

Morgenstern, J., & Bates, M. E. (1999). Effects of executive function impairment on change processes and substance use outcomes in 12-step treatment. *Journal of Studies on Alcohol and Drugs, 60,* 846–855. doi: http://dx.doi.org/10.15288/jsa.1999.60.846

Ogden, J. (2012). *Health psychology: A text book.* Buckingham: Open University Press.

Public Health England (PHE). (2013). *Facilitating access to mutual aid: Three essential stages for helping clients access appropriate mutual aid support.* London: Public Health England.

Segal, Z. V., Williams, J. M. G., & Teasdale, J. D. (2002). *Mindfulness-based cognitive therapy for depression.* New York: Guilford Press.

Skanavi, S., Laquelle, X., & Aubin, H. (2011). Mindfulness based interventions for addictive disorders: A review. *Encephale, 37,* 379–387. 55. doi:10.1016/j.encep.2010.08.010

Suchy, Y. (2009). Executive functioning: Overview, assessment, and research issues for non-neuropsychologists. *Annals of Behavioural Medicine, 37,* 106–116. doi:10.1004/s12160-009-9097-4

Sutton, S. R. (1979). Interpreting relapse curves. *Journal of Consulting and Clinical Psychology, 47,* 96–98. doi:http://dx.doi.org/10.1037/0022-006X.47.1.96

Uekermann, J., & Daum, I. (2008). Social cognition in alcoholism: A link to prefrontal cortex dysfunction. *Addiction, 103,* 726–735. doi:10.1111/j.1360-0443.2008.02157.x

Walker, R., Staton, M., & Leukefeld, C. G. (2001). History of head injury among substance users: Preliminary findings. *Substance Use and Misuse, 36,* 757–770. doi:10.1081/JA 100104089

Wang, G. J., Volkow, N. D., Roque, C. T., Cestaro, V. L, Hitzemann, R. J., Cantos, E. L., tee al. (1993). Functional importance of ventricular enlargement and cortical atrophy in healthy subjects and alcoholics as assessed with PET, MR imaging and neuropsychological testing. *Radiology, 186,* 59–65. doi:10.1148/radiology.186.1.8416587

Witkiewitz, K., & Bowen, S. (2010). Depression, craving and substance use following a randomized trial of Mindfulness-Based Relapse Prevention. *Journal of Consulting and Clinical Psychology, 78,* 362–374. doi:http://dx.doi.org/10.1037/a0019172

Witkiewitz, K., Bowen, S., Douglas, H., & Hsu, S. H. (2013). Mindfulness-Based Relapse Prevention for substance craving. *Addictive Behaviors, 38,* 1563–1571. doi:10.1016/j.addbeh.2012.04.001

Witkiewitz, K., Lustyk, M. K., & Bowen, S. (2012). Re-training the addicted brain: A review of hypothesized neurobiological mechanisms of Mindfulness-Based Relapse Prevention. *Psychology of Addictive Behaviours, 27,* 351–365. doi: 10.1037/a0029258

Witkiewitz, K., & Marlatt, M. (2004). Relapse prevention for alcohol and drug problems: That was Zen, this is Tao. *American Psychologist, 59,* 224–235.

Witkiewitz, K., & Marlatt, A. (2007). Modelling the complexity of post-treatment drinking: It's a rocky road to relapse. *Clinical Psychology Review, 27,* 724–738. doi:10.1016/j.cpr.2007.01.002

Witkiewitz, K., & Masyn, K. E. (2008). Drinking trajectories following an initial lapse. *Psychology of Addiction Behaviours, 22,* 157–167. doi:10.1037/0893-164X.22.2.157

Yablonsky, L. (1965). *The tunnel back: Synanon.* New York: Macmillan.

Zelazo, P., & Cunningham, W. (2007). Executive function: Mechanisms underlying emotion regulation. In J. Gross (Ed.), *Handbook of emotion regulation* (pp. 135–158). New York: Guilford Press.

16 Working with Ambivalence about Change: Motivational Interviewing

LISA DUTHEIL AND ALINA GALIS

Camden and Islington NHS Foundation Trust, London, UK

CHAPTER OUTLINE

16.1   INTRODUCTION

Over the last few decades since Motivational Interviewing (MI) was first formulated by American psychologist William Miller (1983), it has evolved to become an integral part of routine care in drug services in the United Kingdom (Pilling, Hesketh & Mitcheson, 2010). MI started as a counselling style in the treatment of alcohol misuse and has rapidly expanded across the whole gamut of addictive behaviours, chronic health conditions, educational and correctional services. There is an extensive body of research that points to its efficacy (Morton et al., 2015; Lundahl et al., 2013; Martins & McNeil, 2009) which will be discussed in more detail later in this chapter.

16.2   DEFINITION

The definition of MI has evolved over the years to reflect new clinical observations, applications and research. Miller and Rollnick provide a technical definition of MI as

> a collaborative, goal-oriented style of communication with particular attention to the language of change. It is designed to strengthen personal motivation for and commitment to a specific goal by eliciting and exploring the person's own reasons for change within an atmosphere of acceptance and compassion. (2013, p. 29)

Miller and Rollnick conceptualized MI as a framework with two main components: (1) a relational component that encompasses the spirit of MI; and (2) a technical component that encompasses the guidelines for an intentionally directive counselling style. Central to this concept is the exploration of ambivalence (Miller & Rollnick, 2009; but see Miller & Rose, 2015, for clarification of when not to explore ambivalence – essentially when the decision to change has already been made).

Ambivalence is an internal mental state of having conflicting thoughts and feelings towards something. Clients with substance misuse issues are normally fully aware of the risks. They often present with wanting to stop and, at the same time, wanting to continue to drink, or use. MI posits that motivational fluctuations are a normal part of ambivalence, rather than representing non-compliance or resistance (Miller & Rollnick, 2013). Intentionally exploring this ambivalence is a key component of the natural change process (Rockville, 1999). MI is designed to enhance motivation by resolving ambivalence in the direction of change (Arkowitz & Miller, 2008). 'The skill is to discern a ray of change talk within the sustain talk, like spotting a lighthouse in a storm. It is not necessary to eliminate the storm, just follow the signal' (Teresa Moyers, quoted in Miller & Rollnick, 2013, p. 178).

16.3   HISTORICAL PERSPECTIVE

MI emerged in the early 1980s as an alternative approach to prevailing substance misuse treatments (White & Miller, 2007). In community settings, substance misuse intervention (particularly in the United States) was dominated by the 12 Step Fellowship Programmes, for example, Alcoholic Anonymous (AA) and Narcotics Anonymous (NA) (discussed in more detail by Weegmann, Chapter 14 in this volume). Both have strong spiritual and moralistic dimensions within a mutual aid format, and a goal of lifelong abstinence. Clinical settings at that time generally emphasized the negative physical, psychological and social consequences of substance misuse, reflecting an assumption that clients needed to be educated about the dangerous consequences of their substance misuse in order to overcome their denial, resistance and irrational thoughts (Miller & Rose, 2009). The style of such interventions was often judgmental and confrontational, leading Miller to reflect:

> It is no coincidence that MI emerged in the context of addiction treatment. I was puzzled that the writings and opinions of practitioners in this field were so disparaging of people with substance use disorders, characterizing them as being pathological liars with formidable immature personality defences, in denial and out of touch with reality. I knew very little about alcoholism. I relied heavily on listening to clients on the ward, learning from them and trying to understand their dilemma. (Miller & Rollnick, 2013, p. 8)

It was against this background that Miller started to develop a different therapeutic approach. During the preparation for a clinical trial, Miller (1983) and his team found that irrespective of the type of intervention used in the treatment for alcohol misuse, the best outcomes were linked to the clinicians who responded with empathy to the ambivalence expressed by the client. 'Pushing or arguing against resistance seemed particularly counterproductive, in that it evoked further defence of the status quo. A guiding principle of MI was to have the client, rather than the counsellor, voice the arguments for change' (Miller & Rose, 2009, p. 2).

Miller first formalized his clinical observations in 'Motivational Interviewing with Problem Drinkers; (1983). In a departure from the confrontational models that blamed the lack of progress on clients' resistance, Miller argued that motivation is part of an interpersonal process that can be facilitated by Rogerian-style counselling, and that it is the individual who bears the responsibility for change. In 1989, Miller met Dr Stephen Rollnick and their collaboration led to their first MI book, *Motivational Interviewing: Preparing People for Change*. In 2002, they published a second edition that extended the application of MI across different clinical settings. In the most recent third edition, published in 2013, they have incorporated the knowledge gained from over 25,000 MI-related articles and 200 randomized clinical trials (Miller & Rollnick, 2002; 2013).

16.4   THEORETICAL INFLUENCES

MI was initially developed from clinical practice rather than being derived from theory. The conceptual approach Miller and Rollnick developed has been fitted with behaviour change theories, interpersonal processes and linguistic models.

The strongest influences come from the person-centred, humanistic tradition. The therapist is seen as a facilitator displaying the Rogerian core conditions of unconditional positive regard, congruence and empathy (Rogers, 1959). The central hypothesis is that each individual has vast intrinsic resources and a natural tendency toward self-actualization that can be brought to light within a non-judgemental environment (Rogers, 1961).

However, MI significantly differs from person-centred therapy in that it is explicitly goal-oriented towards behavioural change. The MI clinician intentionally directs the client towards change by deliberately eliciting and reflecting back statements that indicate the possibility of change ('change talk'), while consciously omitting utterances that point to the preservation of the status quo ('sustain talk') (Miller & Rollick, 2013).

The focus of MI on discrepancy and ambivalence within a process of change has links to Festinger's (1957) cognitive dissonance theory. Festinger posits that dissonance between certain behaviours and cognitions leads to discomfort, which in turn would motivate the individual to strive towards consistency and balance. Autonomy, a core value in MI, builds on some aspects of Brehm's reactance theory (Brehm, 1966). Brehm explains that individuals react with opposition and hostility when they perceive that their freedom of choice is limited by external influences.

MI is compatible with, and has been closely associated with the transtheoretical model of change (TTM; Prochaska & DiClemente, 1984; DiClemente & Velasquez, 2002). Both share an underlying assumption that substance misuse clients do not necessarily start treatment with a commitment to change. The TTM model proposes that when making behavioural changes people move, not necessarily sequentially, through five stages: (1) pre-contemplation; (2) contemplation; (3) preparation; (4) action; and (5) maintenance. This staged process can be a useful guide in tailoring interventions to the client's readiness to change (see Miller & Rose, 2015).

MI has a strong emphasis on language as a key predictor of change (Hettema, Steele & Miller, 2005). It is further informed by linguistic theories, such as Self-Perception Theory (Bem, 1972), which suggests that self-generated arguments for change lead to behaviour change; and Speech Act Theory (Austin, 1962; Searle, 1969), which examines linguistic statements expressing commitment (Moyers et al., 2007). These concepts form an integral part of MI, where the relationship between change talk and behavioural change is similarly mediated by the client's commitment language.

MI has also been linked to chaos theory as an attempt to understand how a brief intervention can trigger change from a highly persistent behaviour. Change is not always a gradual, linear process and may occur as 'sudden insight', or as 'mini-epiphanies' (Miller, 2004). The increasing emphasis in MI on acceptance, compassion and values also has clear theoretical links with Acceptance and Commitment

Therapy and other mindfulness-based approaches (Wagner, Ingersoll & Rollnick, 2012; see also McGrath & O'Ryan, Chapter 6 in this volume).

16.5   THE SPIRIT OF MI

Miller and Rollnick have placed increasing emphasis on the spirit of MI alongside the specific techniques used within it, with both being seen as necessary to its effectiveness. At its core, the spirit of MI refers to a way of being with a person, not a way of doing something to them (Miller & Rollnick, 2002). Metaphorically, MI is like a 'ballroom waltz', led skilfully 'one moves with rather than against the person' (Miller & Rollnick, 2013, p. 15). Adherence to the spirit of MI has been shown to predict treatment outcome (Miller & Mount, 2001; Madson & Campbell, 2006; Gaume, Gmel & Daeppen, 2008).

There are four core interrelated elements in the spirit of MI: (1) partnership; (2) acceptance; (3) compassion; and (4) evocation (Miller & Rollnick, 2013). MI is done in the context of a profoundly respectful partnership between equals, whereby the practitioner facilitates the client's intrinsic resources for change. Acceptance of the client means honouring their absolute worth and autonomy, namely, their individual freedom of choice and capacity for self-direction. Affirmation means highlighting the client's strengths and efforts (Miller & Rollnick, 2013). Compassion is seen as the active promotion of the client's welfare and needs rather than sympathy and identification. Finally, evocation departs from the deficit model that focuses on problem areas needing expert correction and instead empowers the client to use their intrinsic resources and further supports their capacity to make autonomous choices.

Practising within the spirit of MI means that clinicians should avoid falling into various traps that may hinder the client's successful engagement. Clinicians need to refrain from assuming an expert position (expert trap), advising the client on what they need to do (righting reflex), or labelling the client as having a problem (labelling trap) (Beutler & Harwood, 2002; Miller & Rollnick, 2013).

In this way, the overall style of MI is essentially a guiding style, whereby the clinician guides the client towards aligning their behaviour to their behavioural ideas and core values (Miller & Rollnick, 2013). This guiding style enables the clinician to steer a course between the potential pitfalls of directing the client in what to do (risking reinforcing the status quo), and following where the client leads the conversation (risking getting stuck in ambivalence) (Miller & Rollnick, 2013).

16.6   CHANGE TALK, SUSTAIN TALK AND DISCORD

Miller and Rollnick (2002; 2013) use the term 'change talk' to refer to any client speech that promotes the possibility of change. In conjunction with psycholinguist, Paul Amrhein, they identified different types of change talk (acronym DARN CAT; see Table 16.1).

Table 16.1 *Types of change talk*

	Statements signifying change	*Stage of change talk*
Desire	Change is wanted	
Ability	Change seems possible	
Reasons	There are specific reasons for change	Preparatory
Need	Change is imperative	
Commitment	Contracting to change	
Activation	Being ready and prepared to change	Mobilizing
Taking Steps	Actively moving towards change	

Source: Adapted from Miller and Rollnick 2013.

As Miller and Rollnick (2013) explain, clients' self-expressed talk of desiring change, feeling able to change, having reasons to change, and needing to change are all indications that the person is preparing for change. Crucially, this type of talk does not specify that change is actually going to happen. It usually precedes change talk where the client is mobilizing towards change, for example, where he/she commits to change in some way, or in taking steps to move towards change (e.g. setting a date for a community detox). Nonetheless, it is important not to jump ahead of the client and push for mobilizing change talk before the client is ready to give it (Miller & Rollnick, 2013).

Another useful categorization of preparatory change talk is between the importance of change (desire, reasons and need) and confidence to change (ability). Clients usually need to have some confidence that change is possible before they feel ready to implement change, therefore MI specifically aims to elicit confidence talk to increase self-efficacy as well as importance talk (Miller & Rollnick, 2013).'The smallest glimmer of change talk may be a coal that, if given some air, will start to glow, becoming the fuel of change' (Miller & Rollnick, 2013, p. 103).

The same categories of change talk can also be applied to 'sustain talk', the type of talk that expresses a tendency to preserve the status quo. In earlier editions of Miller and Rollnick's *Motivational Interviewing* books (1992; 2002), sustain talk was conceptualized as part of resistance along with disturbances in the therapeutic alliance, for example, defensiveness, antagonism and interrupting. However, Miller and Rollnick (2013) now view the concept of sustain talk as more consistent with their overall model, to distinguish it from these other difficulties which are now called discord. Sustain talk merely reflects ambivalence, which, in MI, is a normal part of the change process. In a similar vein to the principle of previous formulations of MI theory to 'roll with resistance' (e.g. Miller & Rollnick, 1992; 2002), and in the spirit of MI, there is a need to respond to sustain talk collaboratively, with acceptance, and through honouring the client's autonomy.

16.7   THE FOUR MI PROCESSES

MI is comprised of four overlapping processes: (1) engaging; (2) focusing; (3) evoking; and (4) planning, which Miller and Rollnick (2013) conceptualize as stair steps that the clinician and client move up to reach change. The steps start from status quo, stepping up to 'engaging' (shall we travel together?), followed by 'focusing' (where to?), moving up to 'evoking' (whether and why?), before finally stepping up to 'planning' (how and when?).

16.7.1   *Engaging*

Engaging refers to 'the process of establishing a mutually trusting and respectful helping relationship' (Miller & Rollnick, 2013, p. 39), and is the step upon which all later progress is founded. Discord is particularly likely to arise during engaging where negative expectations of treatment or an atmosphere of non-mutuality communicated through various therapist traps arise (e.g. question and answer trap, labelling trap, expert trap). Practising the spirit of MI is integral to successful engaging, since involving the client fully as the active agent of change is less likely to promote passivity or defensiveness, and consequent discord.

16.7.2   *Focusing*

Focusing involves collaboratively deciding on a direction through mutually agreeing one or more specific goals. The client may present with a myriad of different hopes and expectations for change, this is in contrast to the clinician, who, depending on the service context, may have a clear focus of change in mind. Successful focusing thus exemplifies the guiding style of MI, whereby the clinician helps the client make sense of, and prioritize, their different concerns in order for a specific direction of change to emerge.

16.7.3   *Evoking*

Evoking can be seen as the core process of MI (see Miller & Rose, 2015), eliciting from the client language that favours change in order to resolve ambivalence. Once change talk increases and sustain talk correspondingly decreases, momentum increases as clients literally 'talk themselves into change' (Miller & Rollnick, 2013, p. 28).

16.7.4   *Planning*

Planning, as the final process, is a transition from general intention to change (the outcome of the evoking process) toward a specific implementation plan, which is collaboratively agreed.

Miller and Rollnick (2013) emphasize that progress through the processes depends solely on where the client starts their change journey. Misjudging where the client begins in either direction can hinder change. Lingering too long in a process when the client is ready to move on can also erode the client's momentum for change (Stotts, Schmitz, Rhoades & Grabowski, 2001). Thus, with a client who presents clear motivations to change, it may be better to move straight to planning once engagement is established (Miller & Rollnick, 2013; Miller & Rose, 2015). Moving ahead of the client, for example, moving ahead to planning change before the client has decided to change (premature focus trap) can lead to the client defending the status quo, or result in discord and possible disengagement.

16.8   CORE MI SKILLS

There are numerous MI skills that convey the spirit of MI and help the clinician move with the client through the different processes. Before outlining some process-specific MI strategies, we will outline the core skills that cut across all processes more or less equally. These consist of four communication skills: (1) Open-ended questions; (2) Affirmations; (3) Reflections; and (4) Summaries (acronym OARS), which have been a key part of MI since its inception, and Providing Information and Advice, which Miller and Rollnick (2013) also cite as a core skill. We also include here another area which has increased in importance as the MI model has developed: Exploring Goals and Values, since we have found this to be an invaluable tool throughout all the processes.

16.8.1   OARS: Open-Ended Questioning

Open-ended questions invite the client to reflect before responding, and allow a wide range of possible replies, whereas closed questions usually yield a short answer and thus generally restrict the response.

Open-ended questions can be used in all four processes, but have a particularly important role during the evoking process (evocative questions), where they are used to elicit change talk. An example is, 'What might be the good things about change?' which can then be followed by further open questions aimed at eliciting elaboration (Miller & Rollnick, 2013).

16.8.2   OARS: Affirming

Affirmations are statements that reflect the underlying belief of MI. As Wagner and Ingersoll (2013) explain, the focus of affirming is firmly on the client, unlike agreeing or approving, which are more practitioner-centred. Affirmations can be either general statements valuing the client (e.g. commenting that it is good to see him/her), or specific, for example, noticing positive qualities such as strengths or efforts. Specific affirmations, in particular, can then evoke self-affirmations, which can directly facilitate change (Miller & Rollnick, 2013).

Affirmations need to be based on accurate empathy for the client and also to be couched in a way that the client is able to accept. We have found that with many clients, levels of self-criticism and mistrust are so high at the start of therapy that any affirmation is hard to accept, and that a gradual, generally affirming style initially works best, with an increase in the frequency and specificity of affirmations as engagement develops.

16.8.3   OARS: Reflections

Reflections can be statements that make a guess (for the client to confirm or not) about the person's meaning, which facilitate further exploration of the client's perspective, and thus, in MI, form a substantial proportion of the clinician's responses (Miller & Rollnick, 2013).

Simple reflections, which repeat or just slightly rephrase the client's content, are important, especially in engaging, where they can be used to convey acceptance quickly. Complex reflections, which add meaning or emphasis, are tools in later MI processes where they selectively reflect change talk and help accelerate change (Miller & Rollnick, 2013).

As Miller and Rollnick (2013) further state, such complex reflections may make a guess at the unspoken meaning, for example, the client's feelings, or what will come next in the dialogue. They can also change the emphasis of what the person has said. Understating the meaning slightly (e.g. using irritated for angry) can facilitate a process whereby the person is continuing to explore the original meaning, whereas overstating or amplifying the meaning (e.g. using furious for angry) can lead to the client minimizing it. This type of amplified reflection is an effective reaction to sustain talk because the client is more likely to respond from the other side of ambivalence.

Similarly, double-sided reflections are also effective in evoking change talk. The format of double-sided reflections, as suggested by Miller and Rollnick (2013), is to link both sides of ambivalence, usually by acknowledging the sustain talk and then following it with previously expressed change talk, for example, 'On the one hand, you think that drinking relaxes you and, on the other hand, you feel really irritable when you have a hangover the next day.'

16.8.4   OARS: Summarizing

Summarizing essentially integrates multiple reflections, which can reinforce what the client has said and enables the information to be processed in a new way (Miller & Rollnick, 2013). Summaries can be used to gather together items as they accumulate (collecting summary), connect reflections from different time points (linking summary), or wrap up a topic or session by pulling the main points together (transitional summary). An especially important type of transitional summary is a recapitulation, which gathers all the change talk voiced so far and presents it back to the client. This recapitulation is then followed by a key question (e.g. 'Where does this leave you?') to facilitate the client in deciding the next step (Miller & Rollnick, 2013). 'Summaries weave together all of the different strands into a single piece, containing all the colours, that is easy to see' (Miller & Rollnick, 2013, p. 69).

16.8.5   *Providing Advice and Information with Permission*

Providing advice and information can form a key part of facilitating change, providing it is done in an MI-consistent way. Under the 'elicit-provide-elicit sequence' (Miller & Rollnick, 2013), the clinician first elicits permission to provide information as well as the client's own knowledge around the topic, then provides clear information specifically tailored to the client, emphasizing their freedom to disregard it, before finally eliciting the client's own interpretation of the information's meaning and relevance. Where information has a 'do' element, i.e. advice, Miller and Rollnick (2013) recommend providing a menu of options from which the client can choose.

16.8.6   *Exploring Values and Goals*

Exploring values and goals can help understand what ultimately motivates a person. It can be a powerful tool during early MI processes in highlighting the client's priorities and determine a focus of work. During later processes, values exploration can highlight discrepancies between core values and current behaviour, which can be a powerful motivator for change (Miller & Rollnick, 2013).

A values interview uses open-ended questions to identify core values and how they are expressed in a client's life. Miller and Rollnick (2013, p. 80) have devised a Values Card Sort, with 100 values (e.g. caring, challenge, fitness, family, novelty) printed onto separate cards. The client initially sorts them into different piles based on their perceived importance, and then narrows the choices down to five or ten core values which can be explored further using the values interview.

16.9   MI STRATEGIES MORE SPECIFIC TO PARTICULAR PROCESSES

There are many additional strategies which can be used at different points to facilitate change. We have selected some of these strategies that we have found useful in our clinical work and presented them in Table 16.2.

Table 16.2   *Summary of additional MI strategies*

MI Process	Strategy	Brief description
Engaging	MI Assessment Sandwich (Martino et al., 2006)	Preceding and ending standardized assessments with open-ended exploration of client's concerns using OARS
Focusing	Agenda mapping (Miller & Rollnick, 2013)	A meta-conversation summarizing possible options for focusing so that a clear direction can be collaboratively agreed

(Continued)

Table 16.2   *(Continued)*

MI Process	Strategy	Brief description
Evoking	Importance and confidence rulers (Butler et al., 1999)	Scaling client's views of the importance and confidence of making change to elicit change talk
	Envisioning (Miller & Rollnick, 2013).	Imagining in detail a changed future without the target behaviour. This can include writing a letter from the future self who has changed to offer encouragement to the client in the present
	Evoking strengths (Miller & Rollnick, 2013)	Identifying client's perceived strengths that can be used for change through exploration using OARS, selecting characteristics from a list (e.g., characteristics of successful changers, Miller & Rollnick, 2013), or reviewing past successes and eliciting the strengths involved
	Reframing (Miller & Rollnick, 2013).	Offering a different perspective to sustain talk e.g. reframing 'nagging' as 'concern' or 'lapse' as 'temporary'. Agreeing with a twist can also be used to reframe discord
	Decisional balance (e.g. Martino et al., 2006)	Exploring pros and cons of change. To be consistent with the aim of MI to promote change (see Miller & Rose, 2015), it needs to be conducted in a way that acknowledges and respects sustain talk but emphasizes change talk (e.g., by ending on it), and used primarily with people who already show a commitment to change
Planning	Brainstorming (e.g. Miller & Rollnick, 2013)	As with a CBT problem-solving approach (e.g. Williams, 2001), formulating a clear plan can be assisted by brainstorming with a list of all possible options and then weighing each in turn in order to select a preferred option.

Source: Adapted from Miller and Rollnick 2013.

16.10   EVIDENCE FOR THE EFFICACY OF MI

Research on MI has grown substantially over the past three decades. Most studies have looked into the effects of MI with individual clients, either using 'pure' MI or its adaptation, Motivational Enhancement Therapy (MET; Miller, Zweben, DiClemente & Rychtarik, 1992), a manual-based approach combining three to four sessions of MI with personalized feedback. In this section we highlight several large-scale studies on the efficacy of MI for substance misuse, which we consider representative of the wider evidence base.

Large-scale studies of MI have included two multi-site trials of psychological treatments for alcohol misuse (Allen et al., 1997; UKATT Research Team, 2005) which compared MET to other psychological therapies. Several meta-analyses have examined the effects of MI, MET or MI combined with CBT on alcohol misuse (e.g. Vasilaki, Hosier & Cox, 2006; Carey, Scott-Sheldon, Carey & DeMartini, 2007), alcohol and drug misuse (e.g. Smedslund et al., 2011) and substance misuse and other problem health behaviours (e.g. Burke, Arkowitz & Machola, 2003; Hettema et al., 2005; Lundahl, Kunz, Brownell, Tollefson & Burke, 2010).

The NICE Guidelines for harmful and dependent alcohol use (NICE, 2011) provide a review of the effectiveness of using MI, MET or combined interventions for alcohol misuse, with expert recommendations on how to apply this best in practice. It recommends that motivational interventions are added to any psychosocial intervention for alcohol misuse.

In evaluating the efficacy of MI, there are three main findings that emerge consistently throughout the studies cited above:

1) MI is superior to no intervention, minimal intervention or assessment / feedback only.

2) MI is equally as effective as other psychological interventions or treatment-as-usual in substance use. This was despite MI interventions typically being delivered in much smaller doses than the comparison treatments.

3) The effects of MI appear to be strongest initially and tend to diminish at the first year of follow-up.

Despite this pattern of findings, many authors have commented on the substantial variability in effect sizes, even when focused on the same problem behaviour (e.g. Hettema et al., 2005; Miller & Rollnick, 2013). Part of the difficulty is that few studies control for the fidelity with which MI is practised. Miller and Rollnick (2013) comment that inadvertent use of MI is not measured in control conditions, which could be significant given the universality of its use within the substance misuse field.

The vast majority of studies focus on alcohol misuse, and the strongest findings of MI efficacy relate to this domain. The evidence in relation to drug misuse is more mixed. Pilling and colleagues (2010) cite support for its use as a pre-treatment for cannabis, stimulant and opiates misuse. The lack of clear evidence with clients in structured substance misuse treatment may be confounded by poor intervention matching; where clients are already motivated, MI may have a counterproductive effect (Allen et al., 1997; Stotts et al., 2001; Miller & Rose, 2015). This relates to another limitation of all manual-based MI studies, and may explain the typically lower effect-sizes for these, since manualized approaches may not be sensitive to the client's state of readiness of change (Hettema et al., 2005). While variability in effects exist, understanding of the exact mechanisms of change in MI remains limited, although reviews examining the impact of particular MI processes on outcome are emerging, for example, Apodaca and Longabough (2009).

The consistent pattern of broad findings across numerous studies of different design and population suggest that MI is an effective intervention with substance misuse. Miller and Rollnick (2013) make several recommendations for improving the quality of outcome research, which address many of the methodological issues raised above and, if followed, may add further weight to the evidence base in favour of MI. These range from ensuring and documenting the level of proficiency therapists have in MI, frequently monitoring MI fidelity through examining client and therapist outcomes, and measuring (unintentional) use of MI in control interventions. They also caution against rigidly adhering to a treatment manual, since effective MI needs to respond flexibly to whatever the client is offering.

16.11   INTEGRATING MI WITH OTHER APPROACHES

The spirit and technical components of MI can be more generally applied in clinical practice to facilitate engagement, focus and motivation and to respond to any challenges that arise. The evidence base on such approaches is developing, but there are indications that they may enhance retention and adherence (Arkowitz, Miller, Westra & Rollnick, 2008). CBT appears to have been most successfully combined with MI to date (e.g. Rosenblum et al., 2005; Westra, 2012), and this section will focus on its application to psychological disorders other than substance misuse.

There are two broad ways in which MI can be combined with other therapies. First, in what Miller and Moyers (2006) call an alternation model, where the clinician uses MI in order to focus on the client's motivation for change and then switches back to another model when this task is completed. In this way, MI has been commonly combined with other therapeutic approaches as a pre-treatment intervention. Westra and Dozois (2006) employed a three-session MI pre-treatment group to enhance the effects of subsequent group CBT for anxiety disorders (panic disorder, social phobia and GAD), and reported increased confidence for change and greater participation and response to CBT. MI as a pre-treatment has also been successfully used to enhance subsequent engagement in therapy for obsessive compulsive disorder (Tolin & Maltby, 2008) and post-traumatic stress disorder (Murphy, 2008).

The other main approach is to treat MI as a clinical style which infuses all treatment tasks throughout an alternative therapy. Miller and Rollnick (2013) describe the underlying spirit of MI as being capable of acting as a firm foundation to many clinical approaches. Kouimtsidis, Reynolds, Drummond, Davis and Tarrier (2007) describe MI combined with a CBT programme for relapse prevention with opiate drug users. Arkowitz and Burke (2008) report successfully integrating MI throughout the course of CBT for depression, as have Treasure and Schmidt (2008) in their cognitive-interpersonal approach to eating disorders. Integrating MI into psychological interventions for clients with dual diagnosis has been shown to improve engagement and medication adherence (Graeber, Moyers, Griffith, Guajardo & Tonigan, 2003; Steinberg, Zeidonis, Krejei & Brandon, 2004; Martino & Moyers, 2008).

Treatment fidelity with each component is a special issue with any combined interventions (Haddock et al., 2012). Arkowitz and colleagues (2008) argue that both the spirit of MI and specific MI strategies need to be present in order to achieve an integrated MI/CBT approach. Wagner and Ingersoll (2013) also comment that in some respects CBT and MI are very different, particularly in terms of the level of didactic learning inherent in most CBT models, suggesting it can be hard to ensure that both components are adequately represented in a combined model.

16.12   USING MI IN GROUPS

Despite the appeal of harnessing the mutual support of a group of people, as well as the potential cost-effectiveness (Sobell, Sobell & Agrawal, 2009), the transfer from individual MI to group MI is a complex one. While 'Group interactions [can act] as the match that sparks change' (Wagner & Ingersoll, 2013, p. 71), particular issues (e.g. see Miller & Rollnick, 2013; Wagner & Ingersoll, 2013) are how to give each group member the time to generate and explore their change talk, as well as how to avoid group members reinforcing each other's sustain talk. Due to these factors, Miller and Rollnick (2013) recommend clinicians hone their skills in individual MI before attempting to conduct group MI. We would add that deliverers of group MI should also be experienced group facilitators.

The existing evidence base for MI groups is promising but remains limited at this time (Wagner & Ingersoll, 2013). MI groups have been either 'pure' MI (e.g. Brown et al., 2006; La Chance, Feldstein Ewing, Bryan & Hutchison, 2009), or combined with other therapeutic approaches such as CBT (e.g. Bailey, Baker, Webster & Lewin, 2004) and studies include several randomized controlled trials (e.g. Bailey et al., 2004; LaBrie, Thompson, Huchting, Lac & Buckley, 2007; La Chance et al., 2009). A very similar pattern of findings emerges to that of the overall MI evidence base (see above). This clearly indicates that, despite variability in effects across studies, both pure and combined group MI can be effective in reducing alcohol and drug use. There are further suggestions that when group sustain talk and discord are specifically addressed, as in Santa Ana, Wolfert and Nietert (2007), group process effects (e.g. universality, cohesion, increased self-efficacy) may be additive to those of MI (Wagner & Ingersoll, 2013).

16.12.1   *Clinical Example of an MI Group*

In our service, we use a three-session Moving Forward MI workshop (see Table 16.3) in order to help clients explore their readiness for change, increase confidence in their ability to change, and plan the next steps on their recovery journeys. The first two sessions are each two hours long and take place a week apart, with the third session a month later (this latter session was added following client feedback).

Table 16.3   *A brief summary of the Moving Forward MI workshops*

WORKSHOP 1

Setting the scene

- Introductions
- Generating group rules
- Collaborative agenda setting (integrating participants' hopes bubbles with facilitators' agenda bubbles)

What recovery can look like

- Peer facilitator shares their recovery journey with a focus on positive changes

Envisioning exercise

- Group brainstorm of different areas of one's life that might be affected by changing substance use at a self-determined point in the future
- Group exploration on what changes they would like to make to their current situation to move closer to the envisioned future

Readiness for change

- Group ranks vignettes containing examples of individuals at various levels of 'readiness for change' from 'most likely to change' to 'least likely to change'
- Group discussion of the effects and strength of change talk
- Individuals invited to identify a specific, achievable 'step towards change' they are prepared to try out over the next week.

Check-out

- Summary (highlighting change talk and goals for next week)
- Participants' feedback on experience of group
- Collaborative agenda-setting for next session

WORKSHOP 2

- Review of agenda and group rules

Review of 'step towards change'

- Group discussion of home practice, affirming all efforts as progress

Internal resources for change

- Discussion of previous difficult changes and reflection on participants' skills and personal strengths which enabled these

External resources for change

- Group brainstorm of possible professional and personal support networks
- Facilitators seek permission to briefly share local recovery menu and invite clients to explore further in session or key-working

Moving Forward Plan

- Group members fill in the workshop to recap Change Talk, Positive Strengths and Next Steps to change

Check-out

- Feedback
- Importance and confidence rulers

WORKSHOP 3

- Review discussion of progress, and group generates ways to help each progress further
- Feedback and importance and confidence rulers

The workshops are facilitated by two staff members (typically a clinical psychologist and a trainee, or assistant psychologist) and a recovery peer volunteer. We have found the role of the recovery peer to be invaluable through the affirmation, encouragement and instillation of hope they typically provide to clients throughout the sessions.

Groups have been relatively small (maximum six people), enabling ample opportunity to elicit change talk from each client. Pre-session activation tasks such as clients writing down 'hopes' for each workshop promote a sense of partnership. Similarly, collaboratively formulating the group rules involves group members as active participants in setting up safe conditions for the workshops, and we have found that this is sufficient to avoid the potential negative group processes highlighted in the literature above.

The main challenge experienced has been working with clients presenting with different readiness for change, ranging from contemplating initial change to looking for support with commitment to changes that have already been made. This has resulted in facilitators being flexible with group content to reflect the different change perspectives and to avoid the demotivating effects of either premature focus, or holding clients up in previous processes.

Although formal evaluation of the workshops is at an early stage, initial analysis of scores on importance and confidence rulers measured pre-workshop 1, post-workshop 2 and post-workshop 3, have suggested that completion of the workshops positively increased the importance of change and particularly confidence for change. The numbers attending Workshop 1 have been relatively small, but retention of clients across Workshops 2 and 3 has been very high. Qualitative feedback from participants and their keyworkers has also been positive.

16.13   LEARNING MI

MI when done well can appear easy, but it requires careful training and practice over time. Miller and Moyers (2006) describe a progression of eight steps to develop skills as an MI practitioner. The first step emphasizes the importance of developing the ability to embody the spirit of MI. They suggest that clinicians first need a willingness and openness to MI's underlying philosophy to allow for other core skills to develop over time. Linked to this, the second step focuses on learning interpersonal skills of person-centred counselling with an emphasis on accurate empathy and use of OARS.

The next three steps focus on developing skills in working with ambivalence, sustain talk and discord. First, clinicians need to develop skills in recognizing different types of change talk (as shown in Table 16.1). Then, in step 4, they can develop directive skills of eliciting, and responding, to client's change talk to actively enhance a client's commitment to change. Step five focuses on using reflections skilfully to avoid triggering resistance. Steps six and seven focus on the skills necessary to guide behaviour change with a client. Miller and Moyers (2006) emphasize the skill of appropriate timing 'knowing when to move on to a change plan', alongside the importance of change plans being developed by the client without over-guidance by the clinician.

Step seven returns to the skills learnt in step four, with a focus on eliciting and consolidating commitment talk.

The eighth and final step involves developing the skill of flexibly moving between MI and other evidence-based interventions, alongside the ability to identify which clients would benefit from an MI approach or another form of therapy (Miller & Moyers, 2006).

In the United Kingdom, two- or three-day BPS-approved MI training workshops are available and are a good introduction to the foundations of MI. However, workshops can only act as a starting point to developing into a skilled practitioner. In our clinical teams, it is common for colleagues to say they 'do' MI when in fact they do not, and we too have found it easy to fall into habits of more prescriptive or confrontation styles in an attempt to motivate our clients. Training research has shown that attending workshops alone does not significantly impact client changes or observed proficiency in MI skills, despite clinicians' self-rating competence in MI (Miller & Mount, 2001; Miller, Yahne, Moyers, Martinez & Pirritano, 2004). Ongoing supervision with attention to feedback on actual practice and coaching and guidance on improving performance is recommended (Miller et al., 2004; Arkowitz & Miller, 2008). The eight steps can provide a useful framework to assess development in MI skills and to focus ongoing training and supervision (Miller & Moyers, 2006). We also recommend using standardized measures of MI integrity such as the MITI (Moyers et al., 2010) as part of clinical supervision.

16.14 CONCLUSION

This chapter sought to provide an overview of the main components of MI along with its current application. MI is a well-established, effective treatment for different substance use disorders, with a particularly strong research base in alcohol misuse. Increasingly, research is emerging that MI is not only effective in individual therapy but also in group treatments (e.g. Brown et al., 2006; LaChance et al., 2009), where if skilfully facilitated, group processes may have additive effects to MI (Wagner & Ingersoll, 2013). Of course, as with MI as a whole, understanding the underlying mechanisms of change remains relatively primitive. Nonetheless, how group processes can provide further momentum for change clearly warrants further investigation.

In addition to working directly with substance use, most substance misuse psychologists also work with other co-morbid psychological disorders (see Huxley, Chapter 10 in this volume). Therefore, developing evidence on the effectiveness of MI for treatment of psychological disorders has important practice implications. Research to date indicates that combining MI with CBT either as a pre-treatment or a fully integrative therapy may be effective for a range of psychological disorders (e.g. Arkowitz & Burke, 2008; Westra & Dozois, 2008). Therapy invites clients to engage in change, sometimes of massive dimensions, therefore it is useful to have tools which explicitly acknowledge and address ambivalence. We have found that the MI spirit of partnership, acceptance, compassion and evocation, combined with its specific focus on change, have the potential to blend with all elements of our practice.

Further research is needed to clarify who might benefit most from MI in this context, for whom MI might be contra-indicated, and how MI can be combined most effectively with CBT while adhering to the principles of each. A future area of development is the integration of MI with other therapeutic approaches. In particular, as highlighted above, there are increasing parallels between elements of MI, ACT and mindfulness-based approaches, and given the emerging evidence of the effectiveness of contextual behavioural approaches for substance use disorders (McGrath & O'Ryan, Chapter 6 in this volume; Bowen, Witkiewitz & Chawla, 2012; Wilson, Schnetzer, Flynn & Soloman Kurz, 2012), we would welcome further exploration of how a more formal partnership between MI and these therapies might work.

Finally, although only forming a small section of this chapter, we feel that the importance of regular training and supervision cannot be emphasized enough. Commitment to progressive skills development is vital to ensure the integrity of MI and to embed it as widely as possible into substance misuse service provision.

SUGGESTIONS FOR FURTHER READING

Arkowitz, H., Westra, H. A., Miller, W. R., & Rollnick, S. (Eds.). (2008). *Motivational interviewing in the treatment of psychological problems*. New York: Guilford Press.

Miller, W. R., & Rollnick, S. (2002). *Motivational interviewing: Preparing people for change* (2nd ed.). New York: Guilford Press.

Miller, W. R., & Rollnick, S. (2013). *Motivational interviewing: Helping people change* (3rd ed.). New York: Guilford Press.

REFERENCES

Allen, J. P., Mattson, M. E., Miller, W. R., Tonigan, J. S., Connors, G. J., Rychtarik, R. G., et al. (1997). Matching alcoholism treatments to client heterogeneity: Project MATCH posttreatment drinking outcomes. *Journal of Studies on Alcohol, 58*, 7–29. doi:10.15288/jsa.1997.58.7

Apodaca, T. R., & Longabough, R. (2009). Mechanisms of change in motivational interviewing: A review and preliminary evaluation of the evidence. *Addiction, 104*, 705–715. doi:10.1111/j.1360-0443.2009.02527.x

Arkowitz, H., & Burke, B.L. (2008). Motivational interviewing as an integrative framework for the treatment of depression. In H. Arkowitz, H. A. Westra, W. R. Miller, & S.Rollnick (Eds.), *Motivational interviewing in the treatment of psychological problems* (pp. 145–172). New York: Guilford Press.

Arkowitz, H., & Miller, W. R. (2008). Learning, applying and extending motivational interviewing. In H. Arkowitz, H. A. Westra, W. R. Miller, & S. Rollnick (Eds.), *Motivational interviewing in the treatment of psychological problems*. New York: Guilford Press.

Arkowitz, H., Miller, W. R., Westra, H. A., & Rollnick, S. (2008). Motivational interviewing in the treatment of psychological problems: Conclusions and future directions. In H. Arkowitz, H. A. Westra, W. R. Miller, & S. Rollnick. (Eds.), *Motivational interviewing in the treatment of psychological problems* (pp. 324–342). New York: Guilford Press.

Austin, J. L. (1962). *How to do things with words*. Oxford: Oxford University Press.

Bailey, K. A., Baker, A. L., Webster, R. A., & Lewin, T. J. (2004). Pilot randomized control trial of a brief alcohol intervention group for adolescents. *Drug and Alcohol Review*, *23*, 157–166. doi:10.1080/09595230410001704136

Bem, D. J. (1972). Self-perception theory. In L.Berkowitz (Ed.), *Advances in experimental social psychology* (vol. 6, pp. 1–62). New York: Academic Press.

Beutler, L. E., & Harwood, T. M. (2002). What is and can be attributed to the therapeutic relationship? *Journal of Contemporary Psychotherapy*, *32*, 25–33. doi:10.1023/A:1015579111666

Bowen, S., Witkiewitz, K., & Chawla, N. (2012). Mindfulness based relapse prevention: Integrating meditation into the treatment of problematic substance misuse. In S. C. Hayes, & M. E. Levin (Eds.), *Mindfulness & acceptance for addictive behaviours* Oakland, CA: New Harbinger Publications.

Brehm, J. W. (1966). *A theory of psychological reactance*. Cambridge, MA: Academic Press Inc.

Brown, T. G., Dongier, M., Latimer, E., Legault, T., Seraganian, P., Kokim, M., et al. (2006). Group-delivered brief interventions versus standard care for mixed alcohol/ other drug problems: a preliminary study. *Alcoholism Treatment Quarterly*, *24*, 23–40. doi:10.1300/J020v24n04_03

Burke, B. L., Arkowitz, H., & Machola, M. (2003). The efficacy of motivational interviewing: A meta-analysis of controlled clinical trials. *Journal of Consulting and Clinical Psychology*, *71*, 843–861. doi:10.1037/0022-006X.71.5.843

Butler, C., Rollnick, S., Cohen, D., Russell, I., Bachmann, M., & Stott, N. (1999). Motivational consulting versus brief advice for smokers in general practice: A randomized trial. *British Journal of General Practice*, *49*, 611–616.

Carey, K. B, Scott-Sheldon, L. A., Carey, M. P., & DeMartini, K. S. (2007). Individual-level interventions to reduce college student drinking: A meta-analytic review. *Addictive Behaviors*, *32*, 2469–2494. doi:10.1016/j.addbeh.2007.05.004

DiClemente, C. C., & Velasquez, M. M. (2002). Motivational interviewing and the stages of change. In W. R. Miller, & S. Rollnick (Eds.), *Motivational interviewing: Preparing people for change* (2nd ed., pp. 201–216). New York: Guilford Press.

Festinger, L. (1957). *A theory of cognitive dissonance*. Stanford, CA: Stanford University Press.

Gaume, J., Gmel, G., & Daeppen, J. B. (2008). Brief alcohol interventions: Do counsellors' and patients' communication characteristics predict change? *Alcohol & Alcoholism*, *43*, 62–69. doi:10.1093/alcalc/agm141

Graeber, D. A., Moyers, T. B., Griffith, G., Guajardo, E., & Tonigan, S. (2003). A pilot study comparing motivational interviewing and an educational intervention in patients with schizophrenia and alcohol use disorders. *Community Mental Health Journal*, *39*, 189–202. doi:10.1023/A:1023371705506

Haddock, G., Beardmore, R., Earnshaw, P., Fitzsimmons, M., Nothard, S., Butler, R., et al. (2012). Assessing fidelity to integrated motivational interviewing and CBT therapy for psychosis and substance use: The MI-CBT fidelity scale (MI-CTS). *Journal of Mental Health*, *21*, 38–48. doi:10.3109/09638237.2011.621470

Hettema, J., Steele, J., & Miller, W. R. (2005). Motivational interviewing. *Annual Review of Clinical Psychology*, *1*, 91–111. doi:10.1146/annurev.clinpsy.1.102803.143833

Kouimtsidis, C., Reynolds, M., Drummond, C., Davis, P., & Tarrier, N. (2007) *Cognitive-behavioural therapy in the treatment of addiction: A treatment planner for clinicians*. Chichester: John Wiley & Sons, Ltd.

LaBrie, J. W., Thompson, A. D., Huchting, K., Lac, A., & Buckley, K. (2007). A group motivational interviewing intervention reduces drinking and alcohol-related negative consequences in adjudicated college women. *Addictive Behaviors*, *32*, 2549–2562. doi:10.1016/j.addbeh.2007.05.014

La Chance, H., Feldstein Ewing, S. W., Bryan, A. D., & Hutchison, K. E. (2009). What makes group MET work? A randomized controlled trial of college student drinkers in mandated alcohol diversion. *Psychology of Addictive Behaviours*, *23*, 598–612. doi:10.1037/a0016633

Lundahl, B. W., Kunz, C., Brownell, C., Tollefson, D., & Burke, B.L. (2010). A meta-analysis of motivational interviewing: Twenty-five years of empirical studies. *Research on Social Work Practice, 20,* 137–160. doi:10.1177/1049731509347850

Lundahl, B. W., Moleni, T., Burke, B. L., Butters, R., Tollefson, D., Butler, C., & Rollnick, S. (2013). Motivational interviewing in medical care settings: A systematic review and meta-analysis of randomized controlled trails. *Patient Education & Counselling, 93,* 157–168. doi:http://dx.doi.org/10.1016/j.pec.2013.07.012

Madson, M. B., & Campbell, T. C. (2006). Measures of fidelity in motivational enhancement: A systematic review of instrumentation. *Journal of Substance Abuse Treatment, 31,* 67–73. doi:10.1016/j.jsat.2006.03.010

Martino, S., Ball, S. A., Gallon, S. L., Hall, D., Garcia, M., Ceperich, S., et al. (2006) *Motivational interviewing assessment: Supervisory tools for enhancing proficiency.* Salem, OR: Northwest Frontier Addiction Technology Transfer Center, Oregon Health and Science University.

Martino, S., & Moyers, T. B. (2008). Motivational interviewing with dually diagnosed patients. In H. Arkowitz, H. A. Westra, W. R. Miller, & S. Rollnick. (Eds.), *Motivational interviewing in the treatment of psychological problems* (pp. 277–303). New York: Guilford Press.

Martins, R. K., & McNeil, D. W. (2009) Review of Motivational interviewing in promoting health behaviors. *Clinical Psychology Review, 29,* 283–293.

Miller, W. R. (1983). Motivational interviewing with problem drinkers. *Behavioural Psychotherapy, 11,* 147–172. doi:10.1017/S0141347300006583

Miller W. R. (2004). The phenomenon of quantum change. *Journal of Clinical Psychology, 60,* 453–460. doi:10.1002/jclp.20000

Miller, W. R., & Mount, K. A. (2001). A small study of training in motivational interviewing: Does one workshop change clinician and client behaviour? *Behavioural and Cognitive Psychotherapy, 29,* 457–471. doi:10.1017/S1352465801004064

Miller, W. R., & Moyers, T. B. (2006). Eight stages in learning motivational interviewing. *Journal of Teaching in the Addictions, 5,* 3–17. doi:10.1300/J188v05n01_02

Miller, W. R., & Rollnick, S. (1992). *Motivational interviewing: Preparing people for change.* New York: Guilford Press.

Miller, W. R., & Rollnick, S. (2002). *Motivational interviewing: Preparing people for change* (2nd ed.). New York: Guilford Press.

Miller, W. R., & Rollnick, S. (2009). Ten things that motivational interviewing is not. *Behavioural and Cognitive Psychotherapy, 37,* 129–140. doi:10.1017/S1352465809005128

Miller, W. R., & Rollnick, S. (2013). *Motivational interviewing: Helping people change* (3rd ed.). New York: Guilford Press.

Miller, W. R., & Rose, G. S. (2009). Toward a theory of motivational interviewing. *American Psychologist, 64,* 527–537. doi:10.1037/a0016830

Miller, W. R., & Rose, G. S. (2015). Motivational interviewing and decisional balance: contrasting responses to client ambivalence. *Behavioural and Cognitive Psychotherapy, 43,* 129–141. doi:10.1017/S1352465813000878

Miller, W. R., Yahne, C. E., Moyers, T. B., Martinez, J., & Pirritano, M. (2004). A randomized trial of methods to help clinicians learn motivational interviewing. *Journal of Consulting and Clinical Psychology, 72,* 1050–1062. doi:10.1037/0022-006X.72.6.1050

Miller, W. R., Zweben, A., DiClemente, C. C., & Rychtarik, R. C. (1992). *Motivational enhancement therapy manual: A clinical research guide for therapists treating individuals with alcohol abuse and dependence* (vol. 2. Project MATCH Monograph Series). Rockville, MD: National Institute on Alcohol Abuse and Alcoholism.

Morton, K., Beauchamp, M., Prothero, A., Joyce, L., Saunders, L., Spencer-Bowdage, S., et al. (2015). The effectiveness of motivational interviewing for health behaviour change in primary care settings: a systematic review. *Health Psychology Review, 9*, 205–223. doi:10.1080/17437199. 2014.882006

Moyers, T. B., Martin, T., Christopher, P. J., Houk, J. M., Tonigan, J. S., & Amrhein, P. C. (2007). Client language as a mediator of Motivational Interviewing efficacy: Where is the evidence? *Alcoholism: Experimental & Clinical Research, 31*, 40s–47s. doi:10.1111/j.1530-0277.2007.00492.x

Moyers, T. B., Martin, T. J., Manuel, J. K., Miller, W. R., & Ernst, D. (2010). *revised global scales: Motivational interviewing treatment integrity: 3.1.1.* New Mexico: University of New Mexico Center on Alcoholism, Substance Abuse and Addictions (CASAA).

Murphy, R. T. (2008). Enhancing combat veterans' motivation to change Posttraumatic Stress Disorder symptoms and other problem behaviours. In H. Arkowitz, H. A. Westra, W. R. Miller, & S.Rollnick. (Eds.), *Motivational interviewing in the treatment of psychological problems* (pp. 57–84). New York: Guilford Press.

NICE (National Institute for Health and Clinical Excellence) (2011). *Alcohol-use disorders: diagnosis, assessment and management of harmful drinking and alcohol dependence.* London: National Institute for Health and Clinical Excellence.

Pilling, S., Hesketh, K., & Mitcheson, L. (2010). *Routes to recovery: Psychosocial interventions for drug misuse.* London: National Treatment Agency for Substance Misuse.

Prochaska, J. O., & DiClemente, C. C. (1984). *The transtheoretical approach: Towards a systematic eclectic framework.* New York: Dow Jones Irwin.

Rockville, M. D. (1999). *Brief interventions and brief therapies for substance abuse.* Rockville, MD: US Substance Abuse and Mental Health Services Administration: Center for Substance Abuse Treatment.

Rogers, C. (1959). A theory of therapy, personality and interpersonal relationships as developed in the client-centered framework. In S. Koch (Ed.), *Psychology: A study of a science* (vol. 3) *Formulations of the person and the social context.* New York: McGraw-Hill.

Rogers, C. (1961). *On becoming a person: A therapist's view of psychotherapy.* London: Constable.

Rosenblum, A., Foote, J., Cleland, C., Maguira, S., Mahmood, D., & Kosanke, N. (2005). Moderators of effects of motivational enhancements to cognitive behavioural therapy. *American Journal of Alcohol Abuse, 31*, 35–58. doi:10.1081/ADA-37562

Santa Ana, E. J., Wolfert, E., & Nietert, P. J. (2007). Efficacy of group motivational interviewing (GMI) for psychiatric inpatients with chemical dependence. *Journal of Consulting and Clinical Psychology, 75*, 816–822. doi:10.1037/0022-006X.75.5.816

Searle, J. R. (1969). *Speech acts.* Cambridge: Cambridge University Press.

Smedslund, G., Berg, R. C., Hammerstrom, K. T., Steiro, A., Leiknes, K. A., Dahl, H. M., et al. (2011). *Motivational interviewing for substance abuse.* Cochrane Database of Systematic Reviews (5). doi:10.1002/14651858.CD008063.pub2.

Sobell, L. C., Sobell, M. B., & Agrawal, S. (2009). Randomized controlled trial of a cognitive behavioural motivational intervention in a group versus individual format for substance use disorders. *Psychology of Addictive Behaviors, 23*, 672–683. doi:10.1037/a0016636

Steinberg, M. L., Zeidonis, D. M., Krejei, J. A., & Brandon, T. H. (2004). Motivational interviewing with personalized feedback: A brief intervention for motivating smokers with schizophrenia to seek treatment for tobacco dependence. *Journal of Consulting and Clinical Psychology, 72*, 723–728. doi:10.1037/0022-006X.72.4.723

Stotts, A. L., Schmitz, J. M., Rhoades, H. M., & Grabowski, J. (2001). Motivational interviewing with cocaine-dependent patients: A pilot study. *Journal of Consulting and Clinical Psychology, 69*, 858–862. doi:10.1037/0022-006X.69.5.858

Tolin, D. E., & Maltby, N. (2008). Motivating treatment refusing patients with obsessive compulsive disorder. In H. Arkowitz, H. A. Westra, W. R. Miller, & S. Rollnick. (Eds.), *Motivational interviewing in the treatment of psychological problems* (pp. 85–108). New York: Guilford Press.

Treasure, J., & Schmidt, U. (2008). Motivational interviewing in the management of eating disorders. In H. Arkowitz, H. A. Westra, W. R. Miller, & S. Rollnick. (Eds.), *Motivational interviewing in the treatment of psychological problems* (pp. 194–224). New York: Guilford Press.

UKATT Research Team. (2005). Effectiveness of treatment for alcohol problems: Findings of the randomized UK alcohol treatment trial (UKATT). *British Medical Journal, 331*, 541–544. doi:10.1136/bmj.331.7516.541

Vasilaki, E. I., Hosier, S. G., & Cox, W. M. (2006). The efficacy of motivational interviewing as a brief intervention for excessive drinking: A meta-analytic review. *Alcohol and Alcoholism, 41*, 328–335. doi:10.1093/alcalc/agl016

Wagner, C. C., & Ingersoll, K. S. (2013). *Motivational interviewing in groups*. London: Guilford Press.

Wagner, C. C., Ingersoll, K. S., & Rollnick, S. (2012). Motivational interviewing: A cousin to contextual cognitive behavioural therapies. In S. C. Hayes, & M. E. Levin (Eds.), *Mindfulness & acceptance for addictive behaviours* (Chapter 5). Oakland, CA: New Harbinger Publications.

Westra, H. A. (2012) *Motivational interviewing in the treatment of anxiety*. New York: Guilford Press.

Westra, H. A., & Dozois, D. J. A. (2008). Integrating motivational interviewing into the treatment of anxiety. In H. Arkowitz, H. A. Westra, W. R. Miller, & S. Rollnick. (Eds.), *Motivational interviewing in the treatment of psychological problems* (pp. 25–56). New York: Guilford Press.

Westra, H. A., & Dozois, D. J. A. (2006). Preparing clients for cognitive behavioural therapy: A randomized pilot study of motivational interviewing for anxiety. *Cognitive Therapy and Research, 30*, 481–498. doi:10.1007/s10608-006-9016-y

White, W. L., & Miller, W. R. (2007). The use of confrontation in addiction treatment: History, science, and time for change. *Counsellor, 8*, 12–30.

Wilson, K., Schnetzer, L. W., Flynn, M. K., & Soloman Kurz, A. (2012). Acceptance and Commitment Therapy for addiction. In S. C. Hayes, & M. E. Levin (Eds.), *Mindfulness & acceptance for addictive behaviours* (Chapter 1). Oakland, CA: New Harbinger Publications.

Williams, C. (2001). *Overcoming depression: A five areas approach*. New York: Oxford University Press.

17 'Beyond Workshops': Turning Evidence for Psychosocial Interventions into Embedded Practice

LUKE MITCHESON[1], CHRISTOPHER WHITELEY[2], AND ROBERT HILL[3]

[1]Addictions Services, South London and Maudsley NHS Foundation Trust, London, UK; and Alcohol, Drugs & Tobacco Division, Public Health England, London, UK
[2]Psychology Department, South London and Maudsley NHS Foundation Trust, London, UK
[3]Addictions Clinical and Academic Group, South London and Maudsley NHS Foundation Trust, London, UK

CHAPTER OUTLINE

17.1   INTRODUCTION

The evidence base for psychological interventions is by now well established (Roth, Fonagy, Parry, Target & Woods, 2006); psychosocial interventions represent the sole treatment for many addiction problems and a cornerstone for all (BPS, 2012). Furthermore, programmes of evidence-based psychological interventions are a marker of quality service provision and are deployed to achieve and maintain positive recovery-related outcomes. However, adoption of these interventions into routine clinical practice is limited, as is an understanding of the best ways to achieve successful implementation (BPS, 2012). Lack of understanding of the complexities of implementation may lead to the erroneous conclusion that the intervention is in itself ineffective. This is an important issue for policy-makers and clinicians as it is estimated it can take as long as 25 years from the time evidence for an intervention is established for it to be widely adopted in the treatment field (Gotham, 2004). This challenge to understand systems and the complexities of organizational and individual practitioner behaviour change is an opportunity for psychologists to use their knowledge and formulation skills.

17.2   WHAT IS IMPLEMENTATION?

Dissemination of an idea through formal or informal academic, clinical or organizational networks is not the same as implementation. Yet dissemination is often the best way to describe implementation efforts. Dissemination may sow the seeds for change, but germinating these seeds requires something different (SAMHSA, 2009). A workshop, or training event, is a typical example of a dissemination intervention commissioned with the aim of changing clinical practice. Managers are generally appreciative of workshops as they are relatively easy to arrange and are a tangible indicator of action to develop their workforce. It is our experience that clinicians are also usually appreciative of workshop events; it is time away from clinical duties to reflect and think about their work. These may be worthy outcomes, but we should not harbour the illusion that the workshop alone will achieve the outcome of adoption of the intervention into routine clinical practice.

Fixsen, Naoom, Blase, Friedman and Wallace (2005) developed the notion of an 'implementation headset' to emphasize the different thinking required around implementation, and note that the implementation component is generally not well articulated in change strategies and consequently is often under-resourced. This problem of lack of resources extends into research concerning how to successfully carry out implementation. Gotham (2004) makes the distinction between technology development, technology dissemination and technology implementation. Technology development refers to developing the evidence base that interventions are efficacious and effective. Technology dissemination covers the spread of information regarding these to target audiences; technology implementation refers to the use and application of these interventions in a way that maintains their effectiveness and quality. Of the three, Gotham argues that implementation is the least researched component of the process by which research makes its way into practice. Gotham's definitions provide some clarity, although the terms dissemination and implementation are often used synonymously in the literature. Gotham argues that dissemination ends with the decision to adopt and this is largely a mental exercise. Implementation picks up after this decision has been made and refers to the actual change in practice which requires action. The focus of this chapter is on implementation as defined by Gotham, but we recognize that dissemination is a necessary part of this broad process; clinicians need to know about an intervention if they are to be able to use it.

Implementation refers to the set of processes in a context by which a plan is executed to achieve a specific outcome. This draws out two key elements in addition to the implementation target intervention itself: (1) implementation as a process, and (2) implementation in a context.

17.2.1   Implementation as a Process

It is perhaps obvious to point out that implementation is a process. However, understanding implementation in this way highlights first, that it is not a 'one-off' event, and, second, that it requires ongoing effort and resource. In reality, implementation will involve a number of simultaneous actions and processes. There are well-articulated process models which specify the necessary organizational steps to plan and execute a change programme (Capobianco, Svensson, Wiland, Fricker & Ruffolo, 2007). There are also a variety of psychologically-informed models that seek to explain how these processes lead to organizational change, such as the Diffusion of Innovation Theory (Rodgers, 2003).

17.2.2   Implementation in a Context

The second key point to emphasize is that implementation efforts always occur in a social/structural context. Context is the stuff that sits around and between 'the good idea' and the execution of the plan. Context by definition implies a set of unique influences. It follows that a successful implementation programme in one area will not necessarily translate to another. What will work in one team may not work in another. Context refers to the influences within the immediate implementation setting and also the wider political and policy environment. Within these contexts there are multiple participants with competing, and sometimes conflicting, agendas. Most managers and staff will have had some experience of the promise of a new initiative not being realized, and will have noted the initial enthusiasm dissipate over time. Invariably the 'old way of doing things' re-emerges and things settle down until the next directive requires a response. Teams at the forefront of implementation efforts are obviously central, and their interests, which may never be fully articulated, may still be highly influential in maintaining the status quo. Senior management may be the source of these directives, but they are generally responding to wider organizational initiatives or commissioning concerns. Commissioners' interests are in turn shaped by central government policy which is shaped by political interests. The English drug treatment system, for example, has seen a number of shifts in policy direction over the past 15 years, with the current political interest focusing on service users leaving treatment drug-free, including prescribed opiate substitution medications.

Accounting for, and understanding, these contextual factors in a programme of implementation will be integral to its success.

17.3 IMPLEMENTATION SCIENCE

The recognition that implementation is worthy of study in its own right has led to the development of a body of work which can be broadly labelled as implementation science (see, e.g. Damschroder et al., 2009). It is multi-disciplinary and draws on a broad range of schools within sociology and psychology.

Implementation science identifies barriers to implementation strategies and develops explanatory theories with which to understand and guide the process. Rodger's (2003) Diffusion of Innovation theory is one example of a model that can be used to identify potential barriers and facilitators of change to form theory-based hypotheses about how change will occur.

17.4 CONSOLIDATED FRAMEWORK FOR IMPLEMENTATION RESEARCH (CFIR; DAMSCHRODER ET AL., 2009)

More recent efforts have been focused on synthesizing some of the key elements of these theories to provide an overarching model with which to study implementation. Damschroder et al. (2009) developed the Consolidated Framework for Implementation Research (CFIR) as a comprehensive set of constructs from 19 conceptual models that have an evidence base for their influence on organizational effectiveness and implementation. Their aim is to help researchers organize the complex array of influences on implementation. The CFIR draws on existing theories from across disciplines, but consolidates the key constructs into a single model. It is worth stating at this point, that while this is a model with which to develop implementation research, we believe it also provides direction for implementation efforts by highlighting the key elements to consider. The CFIR consists of five domains outlined below:

1) the intervention characteristics
2) the outer setting
3) the inner setting
4) the individuals involved
5) the implementation process.

17.4.1   Intervention Characteristics

It should be expected that the more complex the intervention to be implemented, the more of a challenge the implementation will be. Other factors to consider are: the relative advantage of the new intervention to existing practice, compatibility with existing practice, the strength of evidence supporting the intervention, the acceptability to service users, and the costs associated with implementation. Damschroder and Hagedorn (2011) highlight a further important characteristic: the relative adaptability of the intervention to the specific needs of staff and context. Rodgers (2003) terms this 'reinvention'. The extent to which an evidence-based intervention can be adapted while still maintaining its integrity is difficult to specify, but the point remains that the ability to adapt an intervention can enable staff acceptance and ownership and is therefore an important aspect to consider.

17.4.2   Outer Setting

The outer setting refers to the context in which the organization undertaking the implementation programme resides. Important influences on the treatment system in England that could be considered in terms of outer setting are the Home Office Drug Strategy (2010) and the Medications in Recovery report (Public Health England, 2012). Wales, Scotland and Northern Ireland will have a similar set of documents that will shape the implementation context.

Ideally the commissioning environment would support implementation efforts, but there may be a number of conflicting demands and expectations to contend with which draw on staff and management resources. This is particularly pertinent in a time of reduced state funding and, in England, seismic changes in commissioning structures. There is also the issue of change fatigue to consider. Drug treatment is one of the most heavily politicized areas of health policy, leading to a high level of scrutiny and pressure to adapt to the requirements of changing political administrations. These may even run counter to the evidence base, and can only have a detrimental effect on organizational focus and energy.

Schmidt et al. (2012) state that there is a lack of systematic understanding of how state and local government should promote clinical innovation, although there is some emerging understanding of how they can impede it. This includes lack of funding and failure to support training. In their study of attempts to overcome barriers to implementing evidence-based treatments in drug and alcohol treatment settings, they found that a co-operative division of labour between policy-maker-provider partnerships was related to successful systems change. They found that a co-ordinated combination of 'from above' (from government and commissioners) and 'from below' (treatment centres) achieved the greatest success.

17.4.3   Inner Setting

The inner setting is influenced by the outer setting but refers to the characteristics of the organization in which the implementation occurs. There are a host of issues to consider here which may fall under the heading of organizational culture, which itself is a somewhat abstract concept. These would include: the organizational readiness to change, the extent to which learning is encouraged and resourced, the identified need for change, and relative priority in the context of other initiatives. The Organisational Readiness to Change (ORC) tool (Lehman, Greener & Simpson, 2002) can be deployed to highlight a number of these issues. The thinking behind the development of the ORC is that institutional readiness to change will effect adoption of an intervention. An important part of the organizational characteristics are leadership engagement and, in the case of psychological interventions, the existence of suitably qualified staff able to provide the clinical leadership to these programmes. The British Psychological Society has published a document on the roles and responsibilities of clinical psychologists, and makes a strong case for their role in leading the implementation of psychological treatment programmes (BPS, 2012). This is not to limit the leadership to this small profession, but, to make the point, that there needs to be expertise in organizations to hold the overarching governance and integrity of programme development. Other crucial elements of the inner setting are the extent to which the organization has a culture that supports supervision and sanctions this to focus on clinical work rather than just performance and risk.

A further factor to consider here is whether treatment providers may be ideologically committed to a particular approach (Manuel, Hagedorn & Finney, 2011). This may be more of an issue in the United States, but the point is relevant globally. If there is a potential for a clash between the existing ideology and the change in practice, the process needs to account for this with a stronger emphasis on more collaborative bottom-up approaches that emphasize the commonalities of the approaches. In England, the shift from a harm reduction to a broad recovery focus is a good example of this potential ideological conflict. Some staff fear that a recovery focus undermines the harm reduction gains and evidence base of existing treatment options. This is still being played out, but the authors' experience is that listening to staff and developing a shared consensus of recovery that builds on a pragmatic harm reduction base enables shifts in practice to occur.

As well as having appropriately competent staff to lead the change programme and staff to deliver the intervention, the inner setting includes the wider institutional resources. These may include more prosaic issues such as access to counselling rooms and the internet, manuals and specific materials to support client work.

17.4.4   *Individuals Involved*

This focuses on the characteristics of the individuals within the organization, particularly their knowledge, skills and experience, and professional identity, as well as their personal qualities. Rodgers (2003) noted that those willing to adopt new innovations tended to have higher levels of education with more favourable attitudes to change and science. The CFIR highlights that individuals have agency; meaning while they are influenced by organizational culture, they also influence and shape it. Much of this can be understood in terms of staff engagement, which has become a particular concern in the NHS following the Francis Report (Francis, 2013). Staff engagement is considered crucial for the delivery of compassionate care and arguably will impact on implementation efforts (Point of Care Foundation, 2014). Engagement will determine whether staff believe change is worthwhile and whether management and clinical leaders are worth listening to. Engagement will be influenced by the extent to which staff are listened to and their level of responsibility. Issues such as supervision and meaningful appraisal and professional development opportunities will be important in determining the extent of staff engagement, highlighting the interrelationship between inner setting and the organization.

Michie et al. (2013) have developed a consensus on 12 key domains relevant for understanding how staff change their behaviour. These are drawn from psychological theories of human behaviour and, as with the CFIR, are intended to guide research efforts and form better theories to support implementation. The domains include: knowledge, skills, motivation, etc. and are a useful reference point to inform implementation efforts.

Staff characteristics such as low job satisfaction, or a poor sense of being valued and supported, can be serious barriers to implementation. The National Centre for Education and Training on Addiction in Australia has developed a workforce development resource kit (Skinner, Roche, O'Connor, Pollard & Todd, 2005) that identifies key points for workforce development including managing performance, well-being and support. The argument is, that by focusing on staff engagement, this will establish the appropriate context for developing professional practice. However, for some staff, it may simply be the case that the change requirements are beyond their immediate resources however much the organization nurtures them. Their ongoing presence may present a serious implementation barrier, so in these instances it may be better if human resources can assist staff to find a more suitable working environment. Finally, an integral part of implementation should be the clients themselves (Gotham, 2004), and service user involvement from the outset, and in development of the change plan, is recommended.

17.4.5   The Implementation Process

The fifth element of the CFIR is the implementation process itself. As stated previously implementation is not a one-off event, but a series of processes within which specific actions will need to be undertaken. It follows that having a plan is an essential element of implementation. This will always involve a planning stage, or a diagnostic analysis (NHS Centre for Reviews and Dissemination, 1999). This should determine the characteristics outlined in the other elements of the CFIR model, and inform the actual change strategy itself. There are numerous process models to draw on, but some key elements are common to all. In addition to the planning stage, there needs to be an engagement plan and identification of the key people to support the implementation process. People may need to be employed with the specific responsibility for leading the implementation project. Formal project management processes may well assist the execution of the plan, and a final essential element is the evaluation of progress and collecting outcomes. Setting up structures that can capture this data, and involving staff in formal briefings about progress would be considered good practice and part of assisting staff engagement.

Two useful resources for unpacking the process of implementation are the Substance Abuse and Mental Health Services Administration Technical Assistance Publication *Implementing Change in Substance Abuse Treatment Programs* (SAMHSA, 2009), and the *Integrating Multiple Evidence-Based Practices in a Public Mental Health Organization Implementation Field Guide for Project Managers and Clinical Supervisors* (Capobianco et al., 2007).

Capobianco et al., (2007) set out a four phase process: (1) preparing for action; (2) developing the work plans; (3) implementing the evidence-based practices; and (4) sustaining these practices. Within each of these phases are a series of logical steps which would address a number of the issues identified in the inner setting and individuals domains. The SAMHSA document sets out a similar process, but also makes some useful points which caution against elevating an adherence to process above common-sense adjustments to emerging issues. The authors argue that change is not a linear process and preconceptions about how change should occur will be counterproductive. An essential part of the process is vigilance to unanticipated implementation barriers and corrections to the process in consultation with the stakeholders. This suggests the need for a project management group who hold sufficient interest and authority to enable adjustments and changes. Ongoing evaluation through the implementation process will be required to inform these adjustments. The SAMHSA document also makes the point that change is not a discrete event; it is ongoing and part of a process of continual quality improvement. Rather like the need for after-care post detoxification, they argue for follow-up processes to bed in the organization's new accomplishments.

Schmidt et al. (2012) identified the dynamic process between policy development and implementation efforts and found that partnerships 'felt their way towards a bundle of strategies that fit the contours of their environments'. Consequently they write that 'a certain degree of chaos' should be expected, although the ultimate concern should be patient outcome and long-term sustainability and not the 'elegance of the process by which it came about'.

To what extent has the thinking around the CFIR contributed to developments in the substance misuse field? This is very much a work in progress. Damschroder and Hagedorn (2011) introduce the CFIR in the context of a special issue of *Psychology of Addictive Behaviors*. They suggest that the CFIR fulfils a need in organizing implementation research and developing an evidence base where there is currently little. In the same journal issue Manuel and colleagues reported a review of 21 studies to ascertain factors related to successful implementation of psychosocial interventions (Manuel et al., 2011). The CFIR is a useful reference point for their analysis, which indicates that most studies have focused on the individual level; investigating issues, such as the impact of training on clinicians' practice, rather than factors manifest at an organizational level. They also note that the absence of conceptual models to inform implementation strategies makes it difficult to identify what may help, or hinder, the process. Importantly, they raise the issue that what providers say they do, and what they actually do, may not match, and changes in practice are rarely explored in relation to client outcomes, which, they argue, should be central to implementation efforts. In terms of what works, they argue that implementation is more likely when the whole organization is the focus, rather than specific teams, or individuals, and that the implementation efforts should be consistent with external expectations (such as those of commissioners). Manuel et al. (2011) also highlight the need for system and service user needs assessment as part of the process, and staff involvement in the actual process, with opportunities for discussion of implementation barriers and objective evaluation of change.

The CFIR defines five points of focus but they all simultaneously influence the implementation process and each other. A study by Becan, Knight and Flynn (2012) demonstrates this complex synergy. Their focus was on staff adoption of an intervention and how leaders foster this personal commitment. They found that trying new practices was accounted for through a combination of an innovative organization, engaged leaders and staff who had attributes that fostered change. Staff with attributes such as efficacy and a belief in professional growth facilitated the impact that leadership had on innovation adoption. Staff with more positive perceptions of leadership also more frequently reported adoption and more characteristics orientated towards embracing change. One of the key findings from this study is that perceptions of opportunities for professional growth were most strongly related to innovation adoption. This study highlights the complex links between leadership, staff characteristics and innovation adoption, and the mutually reinforcing links between them. The picture the CFIR describes of complex interaction at different levels within systems is also apparent within the recent NICE Public Health Guidance on (Health) Behaviour Change recommendations for implementing effective interventions (NICE, 2014). These include: taking an organization-level rather than an individual-level approach, a congruence with local and individual needs, assessing practitioners, and providing feedback.

As a tool for organizing implementation research, the predictive potential of the CFIR has not yet been explored. However, as a framework for developing a plan within a specific context, it directs the attention to the key areas and develops an understanding of the complexities involved.

17.5 IMPLEMENT WHAT? EVIDENCE-BASED INTERVENTIONS VERSUS EVIDENCE-BASED PRACTICES

The National Institute for Clinical Health and Excellence (NICE) have produced guidelines which recommend a number of psychosocial interventions for the treatment of drug and alcohol problems (NICE, 2007; 2011). The development of NICE guidance begins with a search and review of the highest quality research evidence. Randomized controlled trials are generally seen as the gold standard, with further consideration given to the extent to which extraneous factors are ruled out. Large multi-site trials are particularly favoured. These trials apply considerable resources to ensure adherence to manuals and competent delivery. As 'jobbing' clinicians will know, this well-resourced and focused attention is a far cry from the reality of implementation in day-to-day treatment settings.

In the previous section, the CFIR domains highlighted the 'noise' that the development of evidence-based interventions seek to tune out. This includes clients with complex needs, often screened out of efficacy trials. It follows that, even if feasible, it may not be desirable, or even ethical, to implement as per the research trials. One solution is more effectiveness trials but, again, the level of scientific rigour required creates a set of artificial circumstances from which we may not learn much about implementation. Orford (2008) has articulated a critique of addiction research which is useful in moving the question of, 'what to implement?' forward. He writes that research assumes a technological model of treatment which is far-removed from the complexities of changing addictive behaviour and unnecessarily elevates the significance of professionally dominated treatment. Central to this is what he terms the 'dodo bird effect' or the 'outcome equivalence paradox'. In research, most treatments show an effect and where there are differences these can generally be explained in terms of therapist allegiance to the model. One conclusion to draw from this critique is to focus on change processes and elements common to evidence-based treatments rather than focusing on a specific treatment approach. Using the Motivational Interviewing literature as an example, it is possible to identify key elements which many other approaches would have in common, these include:

- building self-esteem;
- developing client competence / self-efficacy;
- raising concern about a problem;
- developing knowledge of strategies to change;
- having clear goals.

Moos (2007) argues a similar point, and suggests that instead of focusing on specific treatment approaches, training should focus on common treatment processes such as: promoting social support, focusing on goals and structure in life, as well as encouraging clients to take up new, rewarding activities and build their self-efficacy and coping skills. These can be broadly defined as 'evidence-based practices' which Manuel et al. (2011) define as 'more discrete, flexible therapeutic techniques that may include components of evidence based treatments'. They argue that these may be easier to implement than evidence-based treatments and cite the example of 'rolling with resistance' – a term developed in the Motivational Interviewing literature. This also seems to reflect the thinking in the latest NICE Guidance on Health Behaviour Change (2014) which suggests a focus on adopting broad evidence-based practices.

The dodo bird paradox and the other worldly nature of treatments found to be effective in randomized controlled trials suggest a focus on common processes which we have sought to link to the term evidence-based practices. These may make the focus of implementation more manageable and draw staff with different theoretical orientations to a common purpose.

17.6   CASE STUDIES IN MOTIVATIONAL INTERVIEWING AND TREATMENT EFFECTIVENESS (MAPPING)

17.6.1   *Motivational Interviewing*

Motivational Interviewing (MI) is a counselling approach used to promote behaviour change (Miller & Rollnick, 2013; discussed in more detail by Dutheil and Galis, Chapter 16 in this volume). It is an evidence-based intervention that has informed the development and practice of brief interventions and structured advice-giving. There are unlikely to be practitioners in the field who have not heard of it, or not had some training in the approach. The utility of MI, and the ubiquity of knowledge about it, make it an interesting case study to think about implementation issues.

The authors of this chapter have all delivered MI workshops with the assumption this would in some way lead to a change in the practice of the attendees. We now know that the evidence suggests this will not happen unless there are post-training enhancements. For example, Miller, Yahne, Moyers, Martinez and Pirritano (2004) found that, in addition to a two-day workshop, written feedback on taped clinical material, or telephone coaching using role play, was required for skills to improve, compared to a group that received no training. This is a good illustration of the difference between dissemination (the workshop) and implementation (workshop plus post-training enhancements). Clearly, the provision of these post-workshop enhancements also requires a more systems-level change and an understanding that learning MI is a process, not a one-off event.

These findings on training outcomes have been incorporated into the third edition of the *Motivational Interviewing* textbook (Miller & Rollnick, 2013). The authors make a strong case for thinking beyond the simple training model to a more contextualized plan that is relevant to clinical and organizational needs. As an example they cite an issue of client attrition early in treatment. The focus of an organizational response could be to have MI-competent practitioners able to work at the front end of the treatment pathway. Training would flow from this service and attention could focus on structures that would sustain and develop these practitioners' competencies in MI within this element of the pathway redesign.

Miller and Rollnick (2013) do not quite dismiss the value of workshops altogether; workshops may orientate an organization to the approach, and they can be used to identify individuals with an interest and an ability to receive further training with the necessary investment in post-training supervision. This is consistent with one of the authors' own research, where it was found that training led to a shift towards a more general orientation to MI, described as the "spirit of motivational interviewing" but led to no discernible change in MI skill competence (Mitcheson, Bhavsar & McCambridge, 2009).

Miller and Rollnick say workshops should be explicit about these less ambitious aims: learn about MI, decide whether to proceed with learning how to do it, and learn how that might be done. Recruiting MI-orientated practitioners from these workshops could be useful to an ongoing implementation plan as they can become 'opinion leaders' and used to develop capacity in the longer term.

It is interesting to note Miller and Rollnick's evolving thinking about MI at a more organizational level with attention to the setting elements (staff resources, time, etc.) to support the process. They cite an example of a request they received to train all the staff in a large organization. They were able to shape this instead into a programme that focused on sustained capacity building for MI. They made the case for developing in-house experts who would understand the implementation context, provide training for new staff as they join the organization, and be able to provide the governance and leadership for bedding in the approach. Key to this was training people able to facilitate MI in peer supervision groups, within which practice can be observed and discussed. The authors also make points about the risks of imposing training from above and delivered by outsiders. In an MI formulation – why wouldn't one expect resistance from the staff team, or at least some defence of the status quo? The implication here is a focus on context and, wherever possible, grounding the intervention in the issues staff have identified, perhaps themselves recognizing MI as one possible solution. Miller and Rollnick (2013) present MI practice, and the values required to adopt this, as a possible candidate for facilitating wider organizational change. They make the point that parallel processes are often operating within organizations, including the clinical consultation. How staff talk to clients may well reflect how their managers talk to them, and this can reflect the culture of the whole organization. This links to the points made about staff engagement earlier in this chapter and the finding that better engaged staff achieve better client outcomes. If we want our staff to be empathic to clients, convey understanding, and guide them to their own solutions, then perhaps this is how managers should approach staff too.

17.6.2   *Beyond Workshops*

The case for ongoing supervision to learn and develop MI skills is clear. The need for organizational buy-in to resource this is therefore essential. One element of this is having supervisors able to deliver the kind of supervision relevant to developing MI skills and it seems logical to assume that the supervisors themselves should be confident and competent in their MI practice. However, these staff also need to be competent in delivering supervision. One resource the authors have found useful has been developed in order to assist in the implementation of the NICE psychosocial guidelines for drug misuse (Pilling, Hesketh & Mitcheson, 2010). This 'toolkit' describes a set of competencies for MI (and other NICE-recommended interventions) using a generic framework relevant to all psychotherapies. The competencies are described at four levels: generic, basic, specific, and meta-competencies. 'Generic are common to all psychological interventions and describe the ability to relate to people; 'basic' competencies are those most commonly used by the modality; and 'specific' covers the more technical and advanced techniques. 'Meta-competencies' refer to the abilities to adapt the intervention and understand when, and when not, to deploy it. We think this framework is one way to focus supervision. The framework allows individuals to assess themselves and be assessed by others with clear targets for setting goals in clinical practice. The toolkit also includes a competency framework for supervisory practice. We think competency frameworks can be contrasted with an approach that focuses on manualized delivery of an intervention. One can imagine a scenario where a worker adheres closely to a manual but the delivery lacks the necessary competency to make it useful for the client. Again, the MI literature provides an example of how limited the use of manuals as an implementation tool might be without the necessary attention to competency. A study by Amrhein, Miller, Yahne, Palmer and Fulcher (2003), investigating client commitment to change and subsequent behaviour change, required counsellors to adhere strictly to a protocol for delivery of MI. At a certain point in the consultation, the therapist was required to introduce and agree a change plan. Some of the clients responded to this with a big drop-off in commitment to change language. This was a consequence of the trial protocol, but if extended to think about everyday practice, this could be usefully understood in terms of meta-competency. A meta-competent MI practitioner would pick up that the client was not ready for a change plan and adjust their counselling accordingly, taking a more guiding stance.

MI is also a useful case to think about the difference between evidence-based practices as distinct from evidence-based interventions. The example of 'rolling with resistance' has already been cited, and the authors have experience of working with teams to develop mapping tools to support this type of guiding conversation. Specific practices associated with MI lend themselves very well to visual articulation of the conversation (Day, 2013). The benefits of mapping generally are described in the next section, but the collaborative process that use of maps can entail is specifically congruent with the values and process of delivering MI.

In summary, the MI literature is notable for the attention to developing an evidence base for training methods in the approach. There is a lot to learn here regarding psychological approaches generally and the need for post-training supervision is essential. Recognition of the need to engage the key individuals in the issues pertinent to them, and effecting change at the level of the wider organizational culture, are also more widely relevant. Extracting evidence-based practices from the approach, and developing implementation tools, such as maps of these conversations, may be useful.

17.6.3   *International Treatment Effectiveness (Mapping)*

The International Treatment Effectiveness Project (ITEP) was a collaborative project between the Institute of Behavioral Research (IBR) in Texas, the National Treatment Agency for Substance Misuse (NTA) in England, and a number of English drug and alcohol service providers. The aim was to improve the effectiveness of drug treatment by implementing the increased use of effective psychosocial interventions in keyworking. ITEP, and its later development BTEI (Birmingham Treatment Effectiveness Initiative), are adaptations of the work of the IBR aimed at enhancing the quality of drug treatment interventions. ITEP centres around the use of 'mapping' tools in keyworking, where the maps visually convey key elements for a structured conversation derived from evidence-based psychosocial interventions. ITEP is not in itself a psychosocial treatment, but rather a vehicle for using elements of established interventions. The evaluation of the initial project was reported by the NTA (Campbell, Finch, Brotchie & Davis, 2007). The experience of the ITEP project and subsequent developments have numerous elements illustrative of implementation processes.

The collaborative nature of the initial project brought together academics, policy-makers, commissioners, service providers and service users. This reflects the complex synergy across individuals involved in implementation, advocated as essential for successful systems change by Schmidt et al. (2012). This also defines a broad context for the project at a time when the NTA was focusing the treatment system on improvements to effectiveness. Service providers taking part expressed an interest to do so, and staff identified from the services were involved with the academics at IBR and staff at NTA in developing the manual and materials. This 'buy-in' and the cohesive relationships that this process fostered are considered to be key to the success of the project (Campbell et al., 2007). It may also be important to note that services volunteering to take part in a project of this nature may say something about the existing nature of those organizations as fertile for successful implementation. This may indicate enthusiasm and commitment to change within the culture and in individuals in those organizations, along with other important factors of the CFIR domain 'inner setting'. It may also signal that the ITEP approach was already in line with the existing philosophies of the services.

Notably, ITEP placed significance on a whole-organization approach to implementation. Within each service there was engagement from key senior staff and high-level senior management, facilitating a wider service commitment, including clinical staff and service users. The project included the use of the Organisational Readiness to Change (ORC; Lehman et al., 2002) and Client Evaluation of Self in Treatment (CEST; Institute of Behavioral Research, 2007) measures. Taken together, the ORC, assessing staff views of the service, and CEST service users' appraisals of their treatment experiences, provided an assessment of the organizational climate before the planned implementation started and at the end of the project. These measures give information on areas where services are functioning well and where there needs to be improvement. Use of the CEST also fulfils Gotham's (2004) criteria for the involvement of service users in the processes of implementation. The use of the ORC and the CEST is also in line with Manuel et al.'s (2011) principles of system and service users' need assessment as the basis of successful implementation. In a much wider use of the ORC and CEST in the United Kingdom, Simpson et al. (2009) found that service users had better treatment engagement where services were able to foster communication, participation and trust among staff, and where services had both a clear mission and were open to new ideas and practices.

ITEP does not rely on keyworkers having high-level knowledge or training in psychosocial interventions. Through the maps, staff are equipped with the basics to systematically deliver an intervention. Therefore, the formal training element of implementing ITEP was relatively brief. The project employed a 'train the trainer' model, with some staff from each organization receiving training in how to use ITEP from

IBR, and in turn, these staff taking these approaches back to their services and teams The formal training component was only a small part of staff competence development and maintenance. Ongoing supervision for staff was provided by a psychologist supporting their confidence and competence to deliver the interventions, demonstrating the iterative process of implementation.

Aspects of the intervention itself may also be significant in the implementation process. ITEP and mapping tools generally are often positively received by keyworkers and service users as relatively simple, but useful, and with a strong face validity. Other advantageous characteristics of the intervention include its adaptability and flexibility, factors stated as important by Damschroder and Hagedorn (2011). By not drawing only on one psychosocial intervention or approach, it can have wide recognition and appeal for staff with various existing skills and model preferences. It is the experience of the authors that busy keyworkers often appreciate guidance and reminders of specific psychosocial interventions that the maps bring. ITEP is often appreciated by managers as a tangible indication of structured interventions being delivered in keyworking sessions. Within the ITEP project, service users fed back that the maps provided a focus for keywork sessions. In addition, mapping tools already had a strong evidence base for increasing the effectiveness of drug treatment in a number of relevant domains: reduced drug use (Joe, Dansereau, Pitre & Simpson, 1997), improved service user attendance at keywork sessions (Joe, Dansereau & Simpson, 1994), and less injecting and crime (Pitre, Dees, Dansereau & Simpson, 1997).

By inserting key elements of proven psychosocial interventions into bite-sized keywork session exercises, ITEP also makes use of evidence-based practices, as described by Manuel et al. (2011), rather than more complex systematic evidence-based treatments.

The ITEP project was regarded as having demonstrated the acceptability and use of mapping tools in drug treatment services. Psychosocial interventions were received positively by staff and service users, there was evidence of constructive changes in practice and some improved service user outcomes. In terms of successful implementation, organizational backing has been seen as key, along with support and congruence with external context. The pragmatic and adaptable nature of the intervention, along with the effective involvement of staff and service users, was also significant. Only a relatively small part of the implementation process involved formal training, instead, staff competence was supported through supervisors with wide-ranging expertise in both psychosocial interventions and supervision.

17.7   CONCLUSION

To conclude, it is worth exploring some of the common pitfalls of implementation strategies as well as highlighting those factors that we know are clearly likely to enhance the likelihood of success.

At the beginning of this chapter we highlighted the fact that implementation is the result of a process of dissemination, and of agreed adoption, usually within some service, or organizational context.[1] It is important to note that if something goes wrong at either of these stages, then the possibility of successful implementation is greatly reduced. For instance, dissemination in and of itself does not mean that there is agreement as to the merits of a particular course of action. Even where there is a high degree of evidence for an intervention, some practitioners will still rate clinical judgement and historical clinical practice more highly. In such cases, open discussion about the merits and concerns of any new innovation is key to dealing with unexplored and subtle means of resistance. Knowing that staff have concerns does not preclude adoption of a new intervention and, arguably, helps both staff and more senior management to understand what any potential roadblocks could be.

A second major issue with dissemination relates to the organizational assumptions made concerning the flow of information. It is well known that the simple provision of information neither guarantees that it will have been attended to (read, listened to, and so forth) nor, perhaps more importantly, that it will have been understood. Any therapist who asks a client who appears to have clearly attended during a session will be all too familiar with the small amount of material that they are able to recall when asked to summarize what they have taken from a session.

Third, special care needs to be taken where what one is disseminating is an idea or a conceptual model of good practice, something that is particularly salient post-Francis. In this example, the translation of an important principle such as compassion will have a high degree of face validity and result in almost universal nods and agreement. However, such concepts require a solid working up into coherent behavioural and attitudinal outcomes, something that the British Psychological Society is keenly pursuing.

When there is a decision to adopt, there needs to be clarity about whose decision this is and what scope there is to influence the decision. What also needs to be clearly specified are the time-scales, scope (full implementation, partial, pilot study, and so forth), and what the potential governance structures are. In other words, there needs to be a clear plan of action about what is going to be implemented prior to any implementation efforts themselves. The decision as to what is being adopted (and as importantly what is not), needs to be circulated to all parties. This highlights the fact that dissemination, to be effective, should be an ongoing communicative process.

Leadership and ownership of the decision to adopt are important, not only in terms of accountability, but also in terms of product champion/expertise. While it is not universally the case that those who make final decisions know the most about the particular area, they usually know who does and what is involved in the process. Clearly, while consensual agreement is arguably the gold standard when it comes to organizational change, one needs to be on guard against the seductiveness of group think where fundamental assumptions remain unchallenged.

Difficulties associated with implementation are myriad, but in relation to psychosocial interventions, a few deserve particular attention. First, there is the issue of adherence to treatment methodologies and possible dilution over time. This can be monitored and ideally rectified through regular and effective supervision structures. Second, there is the question of whether organizational support, including effective management and resource management structures, exists and is in place to ensure that the infrastructure is optimally[2] designed for the interventions to be implemented successfully. Third, are there structures in place so that new staff, whether full-time, part-time, or locum, are recruited specifically to fulfil the requirements of the post?

It would be easy to say that those factors that are likely to enhance implementation are simply the opposite of those difficulties highlighted above. While this is to some extent true, the avoidance of bad practice, as every therapist knows, does not necessarily lead to the adoption of good practice.

There are at least five key components to the successful implementation of good practice. The first is having knowledge of best practice; second, is being able to value this; third, is having the skills to implement what one knows; fourth, is to have support of the system in which one is working to use such knowledge and skills. Finally there needs to be a governance structure involving feedback and reinforcement of good practice. With such components in place, the likelihood of success surely increases, and with it both staff satisfaction and user outcomes.

NOTES

1) Even though sole practitioners may seem to be operating outside of a service context, they will still be operating within some organizational context and be bound by various forms of governance and/or agreed models of good practice.

2) Optimal structures may be viewed as ideal types, adequate may be a more realistic baseline as to what is provided.

SUGGESTIONS FOR FURTHER READING

BPS (British Psychological Society). (2012). *The contribution of clinical psychologists to recovery-oriented drug and alcohol treatment systems.* Leicester: British Psychological Society.

Damschroder, L. J., & Hagedorn, H. J. (2011). A guiding framework and approach for implementation research in substance use disorders treatment. *Psychology of Addictive Behaviors*, 25, 194–205. doi:http://dx.doi.org/10.1037/a0022284

Day, E. (2013). *Routes to recovery via the community.* London: Public Health England.

REFERENCES

Amrhein, P. C., Miller, W. R., Yahne, C. E., Palmer, M., & Fulcher, L. (2003). Client commitment language during motivational interviewing predicts drug use outcomes. *Journal of Consulting and Clinical Psychology*, 71, 862–878. doi:http://dx.doi.org/10.1037/0022-006X.71.5.862

Becan, J. E., Knight, D. K., & Flynn, P. M. (2012). Innovation adoption as facilitated by a change-oreinted workplace. *Journal of Substance Abuse Treatment*, 42(2), 179–190. doi:10.1016/j.jsat.2011.10.014

BPS (British Psychological Society). (2012). *The contribution of clinical psychologists to recovery-oriented drug and alcohol treatment systems.* Leicester: British Psychological Society.

Campbell, A., Finch, E., Brotchie, J., & Davis, P. (2007). *The international treatment effectiveness project: Implementing psychosocial interventions for adult drug misusers*. London: National Treatment Agency for Substance Abuse (NTA).

Capobianco, J. A., Svensson, J. S. M., Wiland, S. R., Fricker, S. B., & Ruffolo, M. C. (2007). *Integrating multiple evidence-based practices in a public mental health organization: An implementation field guide for project managers and clinical supervisors*. Ann Arbor, MI: University of Michigan Press.

Damschroder, L. J., Aron, D., Keith, R., Kirsh, S., Alexander, J., & Lowery, J. (2009). Fostering implementation of health services research findings into practice: A consolidated framework for advancing implementation science. *Implementation Science, 4*(1), 50. doi:10.1186/1748-5908-4-50

Damschroder, L. J., & Hagedorn, H. J. (2011). A guiding framework and approach for implementation research in substance use disorders treatment. *Psychology of Addictive Behaviors, 25*, 194–205. doi:http://dx.doi.org/10.1037/a0022284

Day, E. (2013). *Routes to recovery via the community*. London: Public Health England.

Fixsen, D., Naoom, S. F., Blase, K. A., Friedman, R. M., & Wallace, F. (2005). *Implementation research: A synthesis of the literature*. Florida: University of South Florida.

Francis, R. (2013). *Report of the Mid-Staffordshire NHS Foundation Trust Public Inquiry. HC 947*. London: The Stationery Office. www.official-documents.gov.uk ID 2535334 01/13

Gotham, H. J. (2004). Diffusion of mental health and substance abuse treatments: Development, dissemination, and implementation. *Clinical Psychology, 11*, 160–176. doi:10.1093/clipsy.bph067

Home Office. (2010). *Drug Strategy 2010: Reducing demand, restricting supply, building recovery: Supporting people to live a drug-free life*. London: HM Government. https://www.gov.uk/government/publications/drug-strategy-2010–2

Institute of Behavioral Research. (2007). *Client Evaluation of Self and Treatment (CEST)*. Fort Worth, TX: Texas Christian University, Institute of Behavioral Research. http://ibr.tcu.edu/

Joe, G., Dansereau, D., Pitre, U., & Simpson, D. (1997). Effectiveness of node-link mapping-enhanced counselling for opiate addicts: A 12 month post treatment follow-up. *Journal of Nervous and Mental Diseases, 185*, 306–313. doi:http://dx.doi.org/10.1097/00005053-199705000-00004

Joe, G., Dansereau, D., & Simpson, D. (1994). Node-link mapping for counselling cocaine users in methadone treatment. *Journal of Substance Abuse, 6*, 393–406. doi:http://dx.doi.org/10.1037/0893-164X.9.3.195

Lehman, W. E. K., Greener, J. M., & Simpson, D. D. (2002). Assessing organizational readiness for change. *Journal of Substance Abuse Treatment, 22*, 197–210.

Manuel, J. K., Hagedorn, H., & Finney, J. (2011). Implementing psychosocial interventions for substance use disorders. *Psychology of Addictive Behaviors, 25*, 225–237. doi:10.1037/a0022398

Michie, S., Richardson, M., Johnston, M., Abraham, C., Francis, J., Hardeman, W., et al. (2013). The behaviour change technique taxonomy (v1) of 93 hierarchically clustered techniques: Building an international consensus for the reporting of behaviour change interventions. *Annals of Behavioural Medicine, 46*, 81–95. doi:10.1007/s12160-013-9486-6

Miller, W. R., & Rollnick, S. (2013). *Motivational interviewing: Helping people change* (3rd ed.). New York: Guilford Press.

Miller, W. R., Yahne, C. E., Moyers, T. B., Martinez, J., & Pirritano, M. (2004). A randomized trial of methods to help clinicians learn motivational interviewing. *Journal of Consulting and Clinical Psychology, 72*, 1050–1062. doi:10.1037/a0022238

Mitcheson, L., Bhavsar, K., & McCambridge, J. (2009). Randomized trial of training and supervision in motivational interviewing with adolescent drug treatment practitioners. *Journal of Substance Abuse Treatment, 37*, 73–78. doi:http://dx.doi.org/10.1016/j.jsat.2008.11.001

Moos, R. H. (2007). Theory-based active ingredients of effective treatments for substance use disorders. *Drug and Alcohol Dependence, 88*, 109–121. doi:10.1016/j.drugalcdep.2006.10.010

NHS Centre for Reviews and Dissemination (University of York). (1999). Getting evidence into practice. *Effective Health Care Bulletin, 5*, 1–16.

NICE (National Institute for Health and Clinical Excellence). (2007). *Drug misuse: Psychosocial interventions.* NICE Clinical Guideline 51. London: National Institute for Health and Clinical Excellence.

NICE (National Institute for Health and Clinical Excellence). (2011). *Alcohol-use disorders: Diagnosis, assessment and management of harmful drinking and alcohol dependence.* NICE Clinical Guideline 115. London: National Institute for Health and Clinical Excellence.

NICE (National Institute for Health and Clinical Excellence). (2014). *Behaviour change: Individual approaches.* NICE Public Health Guidance 49. London: National Institute for Health and Clinical Excellence.

Orford, J. (2008). Asking the right questions in the right way: The need for a shift in research on psychological treatments for addiction. *Addiction, 103,* 875–885. doi:10.1111/j.1360-0443.2007.02092.x

Pilling, S., Hesketh, K., & Mitcheson, L. (2010). *Routes to recovery: Psychosocial interventions for drug misuse: A framework and toolkit for implementing NICE-recommended treatment interventions.* London: BPS & NTA.

Pitre, U., Dees, S. M., Dansereau, D. F., & Simpson, D. D. (1997). Mapping techniques to improve substance abuse treatment in criminal justice settings. *Journal of Drug Issues, 27,* 431–444. doi:10.1177/002204269702700215

Point of Care Foundation. (2014). *Staff care: How to engage staff in the NHS and why it matters.* London: Point of Care Foundation. http://www.pointofcarefoundation.org.uk/Downloads/Staff-Report-2014.pdf

Public Health England (PHE). (2012). *Medications in recovery.* London: NTA & NHS.

Rodgers, E. M. (2003). *Diffusions of innovations* (4th ed.). New York: Free Press.

Roth, A., Fonagy, P., Parry, G., Target, M., & Woods, R. (2006). *What works for whom? A critical review of psychotherapy research* (2nd ed.). London: Guilford Press.

SAMHSA, Center for Substance Abuse Treatment. (2009). *Implementing change in substance abuse treatment programs.* Technical Assistance Publication Series 31. HHS Publication No. (SMA) 09-4377. Rockville, MD: Substance Abuse and Mental Health Services Administration.

Schmidt, L. A., Rieckmann, T., Abraham, A., Molfenter, T., Capoccia, P. R., Gustafson, D. H., et al. (2012). Advancing recovery: Implementing evidence-based treatment for substance use disorders at the systems level. *Journal of Studies on Alcohol & Drugs, 73,* 413–422. doi:http://dx.doi.org/10.15288/jsad.2012.73.413

Simpson, D. D., Rowan-Szal, G. A., Joe, G. W., Best, D., Day, E., & Campbell, A. (2009). Relating counselor attributes to client engagement in England. *Journal of Substance Abuse Treatment, 36,* 313–320. doi:10.1016/j.jsat.2008.07.003

Skinner, N., Roche, A. M., O'Connor, L., Pollard, Y., & Todd, C. (Eds.). (2005). *Workforce development TIPS (Theory Into Practice Strategies): A resource kit for the alcohol and other drugs field. Flinders University, Adelaide,* Australia: National Centre for Education and Training on Addiction (NCETA).

Index